Domesticating

—

Democracy

SUSAN HELEN ELLISON

Domesticating

Democracy The Politics of Conflict Resolution in Bolivia

Duke University Press   Durham and London   2018

Printed in the United States of America on acid-free paper ∞
Text designed by Courtney Leigh Baker
Cover designed by Matthew Tauch
Typeset in Minion Pro and Trade Gothic Bold Condensed #18 by
Westchester Publishing Services

Library of Congress Cataloging-in-Publication Data
Names: Ellison, Susan (Susan Helen), author.
Title: Domesticating democracy : the politics of conflict resolution in
    Bolivia / Susan Helen Ellison.
Description: Durham : Duke University Press, 2018. | Includes
    bibliographical references and index.
Identifiers: LCCN 2017049284 (print)
LCCN 2017056249 (ebook)
ISBN 9780822371786 (ebook)
ISBN 9780822370932 (hardcover : alk. paper)
ISBN 9780822371083 (pbk. : alk. paper)
Subjects: LCSH: Conflict management—Bolivia—El Alto. | Social
    conflict—Bolivia—El Alto. | Dispute resolution (Law)—
    Bolivia. | Mediation—Bolivia—El Alto. | Conciliation (Civil
    procedure)—Bolivia. | Non-governmental organizations—
    Political activity—Bolivia—El Alto.
Classification: LCC HN280.E38 (ebook) | LCC HN280.E38 E45 2018
    (print) | DDC 303.6/90984—dc23
LC record available at https://lccn.loc.gov/2017049284

Cover art: Design and illustration by Matthew Tauch. A sewing
machine stitches the rainbow-checkered wiphala flag utilized
by indigenous movements in Bolivia and adopted as an official
national symbol under Evo Morales.

For my parents, HELEN STANLEY MCCLOY,
LINDA RAYMOND ELLISON, and WILLIAM L. ELLISON JR.

And for my *comadres, compadres, ahijadas y ahijados.*

Les agradezco por hacerme parte de sus familias,
este gran tejido de amistad, cariño, y compromiso

This book was made possible thanks to the many people who sat down to talk with me about their experiences participating in conflict-resolution programs, working within the Bolivian justice system, or laboring in non-governmental organizations in El Alto and La Paz, Bolivia. Many of you described your lives as driven by a commitment to improving access to justice and achieving substantive democracy in Bolivia, and you were extremely generous in sharing your experiences as you wrestled with how best to accomplish those goals. I owe a special debt of gratitude to people connected to the integrated justice centers—staff, interns, and former volunteers—and the Bolivian Ministry of Justice, for allowing me to work closely with them. So too I am indebted to the clients of the centers and others I met along the way—whether in conference rooms, in classrooms, in courtrooms, or on the streets—who were willing to share their stories with me, both the painful and the happy. Some of you appear here under pseudonyms. Others of you do not appear in the text but are very much present, nonetheless. You shaped this project and my thinking. And you are always on my mind as I try to get it right, try to show the commitments and conflicting agendas, frustrations, and triumphs, of the many people whose *proyectos de vida* are entangled with the country's *proceso de cambio*—including those who critique it. Thank you for your openness, insights, time, and thoughtfulness in the many conversations we have shared over the years.

I am deeply grateful to the people who nurtured this project from its beginnings at Brown University: Kay B. Warren, Daniel J. Smith, Jessaca Leinaweaver, and Keith Brown. Each of you played a critical but distinct role in helping me grow as a scholar. Kay, you may not remember offering me—a stranger at the time—advice in your Harvard office back in 2000. I was fresh out of college and considering graduate school, and you urged me not to apply until I had a clear vision of the project I wanted to undertake. So I didn't apply to graduate school that year. Instead, I got a job that led me to Bolivia for four years. Six years and a master's degree later, I applied to PhD programs, and at the last minute discovered you had moved to Brown. And I applied. You, like everyone on my PhD committee, encouraged my ideas, pushed my thinking, and helped me wrestle with the inevitable dilemmas. Thank you. James Doyle, Sohini Kar, Colin Porter, Stacey Vanderhurst, Láura Vares, and Caitlin Walker, you also have been there since the beginning. You are brilliant interlocutors, but more importantly, you are wonderful people and dear friends, and I could not have gotten through this process without you. Thank you for laughing with me, crying with me, writing with me, and taking the requisite dance breaks in Giddings—located, ever so fittingly, at the corner of Power and Hope (streets).

Many friends and colleagues generously read applications, papers, and, ultimately, draft chapters as this project unfolded (including those named above). You have made me a better writer and thinker, and I am grateful for your critical eyes and listening ears: Paja Faudree, Andrea Flores, Kathleen Millar, Katie Rhine, Jessica Cooper, Carmen Soliz, Abou Farman, Inna Leykin, Katharine Marsh, Bianca Dahl, Erin Raffety, Rose Wellman, Naomi Murakawa, Hillel Soifer, Jennifer Ashley, Jorge Derpic, Amy Kenmore, Magnus Pharao Hansen, Bhawani Buswala, Yana Stainova, Hunter Farrell, Catia Confortini, Audrey Pieper, Rachel Douglas-Jones, and the participants in the Wenner-Gren–sponsored "Hope and Insufficiency" workshop and the "Oikos" seminar at Princeton. While I worked at Princeton University, Carol Greenhouse and João Biehl offered vital guidance, while Carol Zanca, Mo Lin Yee, Gabriela Drinovan, and Alan Mann kept my head on straight. Celeste Alexander, Pablo Landa, Peter Locke, Sebastián Ramírez, Joel Rozen, Megan Steffen, Serena Stein, and Shreya Subramani were convivial conversation partners. At Wellesley College, a wonderful team of colleagues has encouraged and advised me through the final stages of this book, including Adam Van Arsdale, Anastasia Karakasidou, Deborah Matzner, Peggy Levitt, Kelly Rutherford, Smitha Radhakrishnan, Liza Oliver, Julie Walsh, Petra Rivera-Rideau, Justin Armstrong, Elizabeth Minor, Sara Lewis, Sara Wasserman, Ryan Quintana, Octavio González, Ed Silver, Spencer Hey, Igor Logvinenko, and Adriana Mihal.

I am grateful to my editor at Duke, Gisela Fosado, for her guidance and encouragement. Special thanks go to Lydia Rose Rappoport-Hankins for steering me through the book's production. Two anonymous reviewers offered fine-grained readings of the manuscript and clarifying suggestions, and I enormously appreciate their generative feedback.

As I was formulating this project and later grappling with what I found, I relied on the scholarship, critical perspectives, and advice of Silvia Rivera Cusicanqui, Pamela Calla, Germán Guaygua, Juan Arbona, and Helene Risør. Nancy Postero has been a generous mentor all along the way, talking through ideas, reading drafts, encouraging persistence, and generally offering her limitless wisdom in all things. I am especially grateful to the Universidad de la Cordillera for the academic affiliation as I conducted research, as well as to the Bolivian Vice Ministry of Justice and Fundamental Rights, and Vice Minister Nelson Cox Mayorga, for the formal affiliation with the ministry as I worked in the integrated justice centers. I offer a special thank-you to Bolivia's former chief justice and president, Dr. Eduardo Rodríguez Veltzé, for his assessment of judicial reform and foreign aid in Bolivia.

My fieldwork experience was enriched by a wonderful crew of *bolivianistas*, who debated policy, assembled in Bolivia's National Museum of Ethnography and Folklore conference room, shivered in late-night Federation of Neighborhood Associations gatherings, trekked to Sucre, and crowded into each other's homes for thoughtful and rowdy conversations about politics, our research, and our own proyectos de vida: Yvonne Goodson, Nancy Egan, Lesli Hoey, Gabriel Hetland, Raúl Rodriguez Arancibia, Sarah Hines, Karl Swinehart, Chuck Sturtevant, Sara Shahriari, Magalí Rabasa, Nate Freiburger, Marcelo Bohrt Seeghers, Kevin Young, Nicole Pacino, Rubén Chambi Mayta, Santos Tola, Claudia Terrazas Sosa, Sarah Henken, Chenoa Stock, and Carmen Rosa Mamani Espinal.

A vibrant intellectual community has influenced this project—and me—in different ways, including Richard Snyder, Ieva Jusionyte, Cathy Lutz, Matt Guttmann, Jim Green, Sherine Hamdy, Angelica Duran Martinez, Harris Solomon, Christine Reiser, Kendra Fehrer, Rebecca Galemba, Yağmur Nuhrat, Kristin Skrabut, Bryan Moorefield, Kim Lewis, Chelsea Cormier McSwiggin, Alyce de Carteret, Ana Catarina Teixeira, Sinem Adar, Erin Beck, Jennifer Costanza, Noelle Brigden, Andrea Maldonado, Elizabeth Bennett, Ann Barham, and Alissa Wilson—who invigorated everyone and everything she touched for the better. Kathy Grimaldi was my anchor during much of the research phase of this project, and I thank her, Matilde Andrade, and Margie Sugrue, as well as Susan Hirsch and José Torrealba for their support throughout. Ajantha Subramanian and Michael D. Jackson led me back to anthropology while I was at Harvard Divinity School. Richard G. Fox, Lisa Baldez, John Herzfeld, and Melissa Derrick Martin helped set me on this path so many years ago. And Mandy Rice has listened to my stories and encouraged me along the way.

Indeed, this book project has deep roots. It dates back to 2000, when I first traveled to Bolivia with the Washington University in St. Louis Catholic Student Center. We were slated to volunteer with an organization serving Cochabamba's street kids. Instead, thanks to a chance encounter with Amanda Martin, I would end up using that summer to investigate U.S. drug policy while interviewing women incarcerated in the San Sebastian women's prison in Cochabamba (along with Kate McCoy). I later returned to the country in 2001 to begin a four-year stint working with a national network of Bolivian organizations pursuing social and economic justice. There are many people who played an enormously consequential role in this long journey, and two of those most dear to my heart are Kate McCoy and Rob Young, my kindred spirits. GeorgeAnn Potter and Melissa Draper were some of the first people who interpreted political events in Bolivia to me. From 2001 to 2005, my committed colleagues and conversation partners spanned hemispheres: Maria Arroyo, Rebecca Barnes, Samuel Condori, Peter Davies, Sister Anitawa Fearday, Maggie Fogarty, Jason and Felicia Gehrig, Father Mike Gillgannon, Melanie Hardison, Brad Hestir, Enriqueta Huanto, Lourdes Huayhua, Alejandrina Ibáñez, Clotilde Loza, Lynn McClintock, Dan Moriarty, Sister Joan Mury, Jean Norris, Del Olsen, Julieta Paredes, Luis Pérez, Tim Provencal, Joanna and Erwin Ramos-Romero, Cecilia Requena, Sara Weinstein, and Rina Yanapa. Andrea and Andy Baker, Hunter and Ruth Farrell, Lionel Derenoncourt, and Cati Williams were my core community of accountability and care, each exemplifying different ways to struggle for justice and find joy along the way.

Mary Fred Coy and Stuart McCloy lovingly supported my mother, Helen, (and me) during the long stretches when I was away, as did the entire McCloy-Coy family. Thank you for all you did for her. Zoraida, Irma, Samuel, Braulio, y Basílica, *gracias por hacerme parte de sus familias.* Elizabeth López, *no hay palabras suficientes para expresar mi gratitud por ser mi hermana en la lucha, por el amparo que me brindas y el empuje que me das.*

My fieldwork was made possible thanks to the generous support of the Jacob K. Javits Fellowship, a Social Science Research Council SSRC-ACLS International Dissertation Research Fellowship, a Wenner-Gren Foundation International Dissertation Research Fellowship, a National Science Foundation dissertation research fellowship (jointly funded by the Cultural Anthropology and Law and Social Sciences programs), the Tinker Field Research Grant through Brown's Center for Latin American and Caribbean Studies, and Brown University's Graduate Program in Development summer research grant. An earlier version of chapter 6 was published as "You Have to Comply with Paper: Debt, Documents, and Legal Consciousness in Bolivia," *Journal of the Royal Anthropological Institute* 23(3). Material from chapter 2 appears in "Corrective Capacities: From Unruly Politics to Democratic *Capacitación*," *Cambridge Journal of Anthropology* 35(1).

Finally, I want to thank my parents for shaping how I relate to the world and write about it. My father and stepmother, Bill Ellison and Linda Raymond Ellison, sat down at the dinner table every night, where we would talk through the major controversies of the day, including the multiple and conflicting perspectives that accompanied them. Their journalistic ethos has profoundly influenced the ways I approach fieldwork and tell stories—even if my grammar leaves much to be desired. My father, Bill, is my most enthusiastic cheerleader and approaches everyone he meets as worlds unto themselves, each one worth knowing and from whom much can be learned. My stepmother, Linda, encourages me to think of the world as bigger than my own experience or troubles. She read to me every night as a child, taking me to Narnia and to a *Little House in the Big Woods*, and taught me to listen to the rhythm of language. My mother, Helen McCloy, instilled in me a love of poetry and an eye for composition that inflects my writing to this day. She was invested in the lives, victories, and struggles of my friends in Bolivia, asking after them by name. All three of my parents encouraged me to take risks, to pursue social justice, to find my voice, and to *really* listen to the voices of others. I am grateful for their love, patience, and support throughout.

All of these people—and many more whom I have not been able to name here—have influenced this book for the better. Any omissions, errors, or failings are mine alone.

Given a choice between a boiling, violent and a freezing, apathetic society as reaction to massive needs-deprivation, topdogs tend to prefer the latter. They prefer "governability" to "trouble, anarchy." They love "stability." Indeed, a major form of cultural violence indulged in by ruling elites is to blame the victim of structural violence who throws the first stone, not in a glasshouse but to get out of the iron cage, stamping him as "aggressor." —JOHAN GALTUNG, *Peace by Peaceful Means*

Luz v. Jhonny

Luz and her companion crouch in the front seat of the car, scanning the yogurt factory doorway for a familiar figure. They are watching for Luz's estranged husband, Jhonny, who is coming off the night shift. We have been sitting like this, our breath barely visible in the inky darkness, since about 5:30 A.M. We are here to "serve" Jhonny with an invitation to conciliation—a form of voluntary, third-party mediation. In Bolivia, alternative dispute resolution (ADR) programs aim to transform the ways people like Jhonny and Luz handle their conflicts. But ADR programs also aim to transform Bolivians as citizens and, indeed, to transform Bolivian democracy.

Right now, however, we are focused on spotting Jhonny.

Trucks bearing the company logo are lined up awaiting entry. Minibuses periodically deliver workers for the early-morning shift. The sky turns rosy as a slow trickle of workers exits the factory, nodding to the security guards, shivering against the piercing cold.

We are not much warmer in the car Luz borrowed from her *compadre de matrimonio*—the godfather of her marriage to Jhonny. A male friend has accompanied her. I learn he works with Jhonny and supplied the information about Jhonny's shift hours so that Luz could catch him as he left work. I never learn if he is Luz's friend, a relative, a lover, or merely a coworker of Jhonny's who is sympathetic to her plight.

We wait. And wait. On edge. As we continue to monitor the exit, Luz turns to me, eyes apprehensive, and pleads: "I'm too nervous! Can you do it? I don't want him to see me. Can you just do it?"

I waver, but agree to hand Jhonny the letter and explain conciliation to him when he emerges.

After several close calls, a lean, hunched man appears in the doorway. "It's him!" Luz and her friend yelp in unison.

I'm out the door, calling his name, walking briskly.

No response.

I call again, "Jhonny!" He turns his head slightly in my direction but continues walking down the block. "Jhonny!" I insist, trotting across the dusty, cobbled street. Jhonny stops, alarmed, and turns toward me. "*¡No te asustes, no te asustes!*" Do not be afraid, I try to reassure him.

I tell him, "My name is Susan and I am from an integrated justice center. Your wife came to the center asking for help inviting you to conciliation. Conciliation is not a court process. Conciliation is about trying to find a solution to our conflicts. The idea is to have the help of a conciliator, a mediator, create a space where the two of you can talk through your problems and arrive at a mutually beneficial agreement," I say, repeating my oft-rehearsed script.

As I speak, I run my finger along the lines in the letter that explains conciliation to invitees. I am parroting the short speeches I have heard center interns and staff deliver to potential clients when they inquire about legal aid and conciliation services.

Jhonny nods, hesitantly, his arms still outstretched as if anticipating a punch. He says, "You know my wife came here claiming I had abandoned her with five kids—making a scandal at work."[1]

I respond, "Whatever your problems, with conciliation you can talk about the issues and try to reach an agreement that is satisfying to you both. Conciliation isn't reconciliation. Some people do decide to work things out, to give each other a second chance, but others want to separate definitively. Those are things you two can discuss and put in an accord, a written agreement."

Jhonny nods again. "I understand."

"You should really think about coming," I say, adding the little push I have learned from my colleagues: "It's a good way to avoid the courts."

I know that "the courts" will conjure many things for Jhonny, all of them negative. As many have insisted to me over the years, in Bolivia "there is no justice." Invoking "the courts" is code for tortuous administrative formalities, costly lawyers, and state agents more often associated with bribes and insults than fairness and succor. "Justice" is something that is mocked, or something that is manipulated, many Bolivians lament.

And that's the point of the extrajudicial conciliation services offered at the integrated justice center (IJC): it's the easier, faster, more economical option, meant to appeal to Bolivians fed up with state bureaucracies and skeptical of the state legal system's ability to deliver justice.

I do not mention the fact that Luz may simultaneously pursue a criminal case against him for domestic violence. After months at the center, I know many women like her will not.

"Yes, yes, I understand," Jhonny repeats. "I will come [to the center]."

And he does.

This little stakeout was unusual. Most clients at Bolivia's IJCs were expected to deliver their invitations to conciliation on their own. It is, after all, an *invitation* for a voluntary process, not a court summons. Conciliation is meant to be a friendly means to resolve disputes.

But Luz was afraid.[2]

I had met Luz the previous day, when she approached the desk I was sharing with Angelica, the newest intern at the IJC in District 6 of El Alto, Bolivia. Luz had come to the center to ask for advice on a problem she had with her husband who, she claimed, was violent and had been hiding out at his sister's house, trying to escape her requests for financial support. Luz explained to Angelica that some years earlier, Jhonny had shoved her down a deep ravine, shattering her leg. She was hoping to bring him to the center so that he would promise to use his medical insurance to pay for the removal of several screws that were causing her discomfort.

But Luz's more pressing concern, she explained, was a debt she owed. She was due to make a quota payment on a loan from BancoSol that she took out at Jhonny's request, and she needed her husband to help her cover the quota payment.

Angelica discussed with Luz her options for initiating a domestic violence case against her estranged husband, and she drafted letters of referral to the forensic medical examiner and a nongovernmental organization (NGO) offering psychological services where she could obtain the documentation she would need as evidence. But Luz still insisted that she wanted to bring her husband to the center sooner, to try conciliation first. She suggested, however, that she was afraid to go alone, so she begged me to accompany her. "If I go to his sister's house, she'll just refuse to open the door," Luz explained. "I want to catch him at work so that he can't escape." I happened to live close to the factory where Jhonny worked, and I agreed to go with her.

As I wrote up my field notes the following day, I could hear Luz sobbing through the conciliator's glass window. She sat next to Jhonny, who had—despite my doubts—shown up for the session. Luz gasped for breath and the conciliator held an X-ray up to the light. The metal screws in her leg were visible even to my untrained eye. Whether the injury occurred as Luz described it, I cannot verify, but Jhonny sat next to her looking sullen. I did not enter the conciliation session since I delivered the invitation letter and did not want to create any feelings of partiality (a recurring preoccupation among conciliation practitioners).

An hour later, the couple emerged. Jhonny ran across the street to make copies of the conciliation accord, which outlined the agreement they had apparently reached. Surprised and impressed that things had seemingly worked out, I wished Luz good luck.

Later that evening, however, I received a call from a very upset Luz. "Doctorita," she moaned, "he falsified his signature!"[3]

"On the accord?" I asked.

"Yes," Luz responded mournfully. "He used a fake signature."

HOW DID LUZ end up crouching outside a yogurt factory at 5:30 A.M.? Why turn to ADR rather than take her abusive husband to court for domestic violence? Understanding how she got there—and the choices she made—requires knowing a bit more about Luz's case and the ways it reflects broader patterns of economic insecurity linked to violence and debt. But it also requires a deeper historical and political analysis of programs like those operating out of Bolivia's IJCs and how they reflect broader foreign-funded efforts to transform conflict and, indeed, politics in Bolivia. Knowing that history, we might also ask, how could a conflict-resolution program aiming to help women like Luz become swept up in a larger debate over Bolivian democracy?

ADR programs like the one where I met Luz have become a commonsense platform for judicial reformers, democracy promoters, and good governance advocates worldwide.[4] In the United States, ADR is now taken for granted as the first resort for many civil and domestic disputes, including divorce proceedings. In addition to court-annexed conciliation—which is directly affiliated with courts and aimed at facilitating settlements between disputing parties—ADR encompasses a broader range of platforms. These include *extrajudicial* community mediation (often facilitated by volunteers) and commercial arbitration for business disputes.

Beyond these institutional mechanisms for resolving conflict, the language of ADR is likely familiar to readers. How many of us have learned to reframe our feelings in "I" statements (rather than accusatory ones beginning with "you"), to practice "active listening" techniques, and to identify the best alternative to a negotiated agreement (BATNA) of our counterpart in a business negotiation?[5] ADR is the stuff of corporate meetings, handbooks, and international symposia on better negotiation tactics. Recognizing the gendered dimensions of employment negotiations, female academics are encouraged to adopt negotiation techniques to improve their salary offers and to resist the socially ingrained tendency to *not* negotiate better packages. These are skills, toolkits, and methods often celebrated for improving communication and facilitating cooperation with outcomes that are beneficial to all parties.

But throughout the world, the micropractices of negotiating a better salary offer or child support in the wake of divorce cannot be uncoupled from the macro-politics of ADR as a tool of democracy promotion and good governance platforms. These methods have spawned interdisciplinary fields of study concerned with peacemaking, academic journals, and NGOs specializing in transitional justice.[6] International NGOs and the United Nations deploy conflict-resolution programs in the wake of genocide and civil unrest. Canadian donors have encouraged indigenous communities downstream from multinational mining operations to utilize ADR to settle complaints over ecological degradation and its remediation with company officials. German-funded projects have deployed ADR-trained analysts to rural communities beset by conflicts over territory ripe for agricultural production and export. Thus ADR encompasses a multiscalar set of theories about conflict and its resolution, as well as techniques that travel from bedrooms to boardrooms, and from court-annexed conciliation services to commissions on truth and reconciliation.

In Bolivia, a network of IJCs enables women like Luz to access pro bono legal aid and conciliation services in order to resolve disputes with domestic partners and neighbors. Originally funded by the United States Agency for International Development (USAID), these ADR programs encourage the urban poor to circumvent the courts and avoid overburdened state institutions, thereby assuming personal responsibility for the resolution of their problems rather than relying on frustrating legal bureaucracies. Broader conflict-resolution programs also have targeted the more combative, confrontational organizing tactics of the city's "militant" labor/trade unions and neighborhood associations. These "conflictual" movements, critics argue, threaten to destabilize Bolivian democracy and inhibit economic growth through unrelenting street protests.

Donors have advanced ADR as both a substitute to backlogged courts and as a means to instill Alteños—residents of El Alto—with more deliberative democratic temperaments.[7] In so doing, this constellation of programs yokes intimate conflict to political upheaval, and overburdened courts to stunted economic development. Bolivian ADR programs profess to improve access to justice, deepen democracy, improve governance, and create the conditions under which private enterprise might flourish.

Yet ADR and allied democracy-promotion programs have become entangled in a much larger national debate over who sets the terms of democracy and what justice should look like in a plurinational Bolivia (that is, a multicultural society with a large indigenous majority). Foreign-funded judicial reform and democracy-assistance programs date back to the 1990s, when legal experts introduced ADR alongside larger modernization and economic reform projects. But conflict-resolution programs took on new resonance in October 2003 following massive protests that rocked the city of El Alto and surrounding hamlets (see the "Uprising" interlude in this book). The government of Gonzalo Sánchez de Lozada responded with military force. As Bolivia grappled with the aftermath, foreign donors renewed their efforts to reform Bolivian democracy and to deescalate simmering tensions through conflict-resolution programs.

In 2008, the Morales administration put USAID under the microscope, accusing the American mission of funding his right-wing opposition and seeking to undermine his leftist government. Morales, Bolivia's first indigenous president, rallied his base of support—the coca growers' unions in the Chapare and Yungas regions—and accused USAID of political meddling (injerencia), later severing diplomatic relations with the United States. The accusations sent existing programs into a period of prolonged uncertainty about whether their projects would continue or face imminent closure. The United States eventually suspended its democracy-assistance programs, and in 2013, the Morales administration expelled USAID from the country. USAID had already transferred full control of its ADR programs to the Bolivian Ministry of

Justice, while other European-funded conflict-resolution projects continued to operate through the work of Bolivian NGOs and through bilateral aid to the government.[8]

Regardless of who is executing them, however, conflict resolution, development, and related democracy-assistance programs continue to spark debate over the aims and strategic interests behind foreign aid—the ubiquitous *cooperación internacional.*[9] Critics argue that Bolivia has become a kind of "project-protectorate" (Rodríguez-Carmona 2009), colonized by NGOs and good intentions. Or, in Steven Sampson's terms (2002), one of many "project societies," in which aid structures simply reproduce themselves as local elites and NGOs struggle over scarce resources.

This book examines how foreign aid ideologies, about legitimate democratic personhood, participation, and justice, chafe against local meanings of social relations, political engagement, and conflict in the city of El Alto. In particular, I follow donor efforts to promote ADR through workshops, public forums, and especially through the creation of a national program of IJCS meant to pull Bolivians out of the formal/state legal system. I show how the unfolding (geo)politics of foreign-funded conflict-resolution programs have become entangled with Andean kinship practices, local political tactics, and postcolonial governance projects. In the process, these ostensibly apolitical technocratic aid programs have been *hyper*politicized in Bolivia—as they have in other countries targeted by U.S. democracy assistance, such as Egypt and Russia.[10]

The stated aim of El Alto's IJCS—like the one where I met Luz—has been to help Bolivians find relief for their everyday disputes outside the state legal system. Yet ADR experts sometimes blanched when I described cases like hers because they seemed to undercut the very reasons that advocates celebrate conciliation: informality, mutuality, voluntariness, and a more satisfying alternative than the courts. ADR advocates praise these qualities as particularly valuable in countries like Bolivia, where the justice system is notoriously despised. But this book is less about how ADR *should* be enacted than what actually happens when foreign aid programs hit the ground—in conciliation appointments, in the streets, outside yogurt factories, and in people's homes. The following chapters link intimate experience of violence and economic insecurity to globally circulating aid programs that seek to transform democratic institutions and influence political behavior.

Alteños' use of ADR offers insights into broader questions of conflict, violence, and economic precariousness in a booming Latin American city. It also reveals how intimate violence and economic vulnerability are entangled with larger efforts to transform democratic institutions and practices. In contrast to conciliation's small-scale, technocratic, and therapeutic intervention, Alteños clamor for a broader conceptualization of justice—and a democratic system capable of redressing structural forms of violence and economic insecurity—even as they utilize these stopgap measures to make do in the meantime.

ADR in an Era of Plurinationalism

Anthropologists have long studied dispute-resolution mechanisms in the communities where they work.[11] Legal scholars once characterized the kinds of third-party mediation that anthropologists studied in "traditional" communities as "primitive" and premodern forms of law.[12] Those practices have since been recast as thoroughly modern and even more "civilized" than formal courts; indeed, many "Western"-style ADR programs initially took their inspiration from indigenous and popular justice practices from South African Tswana to rural Mexican villages—and from the writings of anthropologists working there.[13] ADR first gained widespread recognition during the 1970s and 1980s during the American community mediation movement, with its most famous program being the Community Boards of San Francisco.[14] Professional mediation is now widely used at the level of international relations and between private corporations.[15] In the Bolivian context, ADR gained traction during the 1990s, as donors promoted commercial arbitration, a history I explore further in chapter 1. The *appeal* of informal dispute-resolution mechanisms in Bolivia, however, owes much to two major factors.

The first was—and continues to be—the widespread distrust many Bolivians feel toward the state legal system, as well as other state bureaucracies.[16] As the anthropologist Daniel Goldstein has argued, many Bolivians living in marginalized neighborhoods experience the law *not* as "a force for ordering things and making them knowable and predictable . . . but [rather] something that in local perspective is barely distinguishable from illegality" (2012: 7). Bolivians endure endless *trámites* (paperwork) and accompanying *coima* (small bribes) as they navigate labyrinthine bureaucracies; poor and especially indigenous Bolivians report subtle disregard and outright humiliation at the hands of European-descendent and *mestizo* bureaucrats. Goldstein has characterized the arbitrary application of Bolivian laws and regulations as a process of "disregulation," a "manufacture of organized disorder that is fundamental to contemporary urban governance" (2016: 237). Disregulation is not just a matter of state institutions lacking the technical skills or resources to more systematically apply existing laws or to ensure that their agents are informed about proper protocol. Municipal authorities *benefit* from keeping poor Bolivians in a state of permanent "suspended animation," extracting fines and fees from poor itinerant vendors who circulate without proper registration (237). By allowing the urban poor to continue to operate outside formal regulation, government authorities never have to resolve the root causes of their precarious livelihoods—or offer real alternatives.

Horror stories about Bolivian bureaucracy are so notorious and widespread that while I conducted fieldwork in 2011 the *government* sponsored a competition for "el peor trámite de mi vida," or "the worst bureaucratic paperwork experience of my life."[17] Among Bolivia's many bureaucracies, it is the legal system and its accomplices—police, lawyers, and related institutions— that elicit the most anger and fear. The Morales administration made "decolonizing public administration" part of its political platform: simplifying bureaucratic formalities, prosecuting public officials for corruption, ensuring services are available in Aymara, Quechua, and Guarani. Nevertheless, many Bolivians remain deeply skeptical of the state legal system's ability to secure justice or treat them with fairness and respect. This is especially true for Bolivians whose vulnerability to bureaucratic mistreatment is amplified by scarce financial resources, darker complexions, or other markers betraying their lower-class status. It is in this context that informal conflict resolution and pro bono legal services hold such appeal.

The second factor contributing to ADR's appeal is the historical confluence of donor platforms and social movement demands. The push for legal pluralism in Bolivia intensified in the 1990s as social movements and public intellectuals agitated for the recognition of cultural difference and indigenous autonomy.[18] To stake their claims, activists built on the intellectual work of the Katarista movement, and drew on globally circulating rights language rooted in international treaties such as the International Labour Organization's Indigenous and Tribal Peoples Convention (169), adopted in 1989.[19] During this same period, Bolivia embarked on a series of reforms aiming to decentralize state administration and budgeting practices (see chapter 1).[20] Critics such as Silvia Rivera Cusicanqui (2012) have argued that state reforms adopted a superficial, folkloric/ornamental, and essentialist mode of multiculturalism that masked continued social, political, and economic inequalities and softened the effects of stringent economic reforms. Nevertheless, these policies formally embraced the co-existence of multiple legal orders and created new avenues for political mobilization.[21]

In 2009, Bolivia's Constituent Assembly redrafted the political constitution of the state, launching the Plurinational State of Bolivia: one country, many nations contained within. Often glossed as *usos y costumbres* (customary law), indigenous, aboriginal, and peasant justice is now codified, alongside indigenous autonomy.[22] In the years since its adoption, however, social movements, anthropologists, and government ministries have wrestled with how to meaningfully enact the constitution's promise of indigenous sovereignty: where are those borders? Are there limits to indigenous jurisdiction for crimes like rape and murder? What does decolonization mean for the many millions of Aymara, Quechua, and Guarani Bolivians who make their primary residence in urban centers, and who are embedded within multiple social networks and associations—ranging from urban trade unions to rural *cabildos* (indigenous councils)?[23]

When I first began researching foreign-funded ADR and affiliated "access to justice" programs, a number of people suggested I should be studying indigenous conflict-resolution mechanisms if I wanted to see authentic forms of popular justice and understand Bolivia's effort to put that much-promised legal pluralism into practice. They pointed to the flexibility of community justice. These oral, dynamic, and nonrigid practices, they argued, resist stable definitions and institutionalization, raising questions about the effects of codifying such practices. Scholars and activists I met were busy cataloguing the variety of conflict-resolution practices in rural hamlets. Such projects paralleled efforts to promote "Western-style" ADR in cities like El Alto, Santa Cruz, and La Paz.[24]

Advocates have dubbed these twin efforts MORCS (metodos *originarios*, or *aboriginal/indigenous* methods) and MARCS ("metodos *alternativos*," or *alternative* dispute resolution methods), presenting them as parallel—if distinctive—frameworks. Both approaches aim to decenter the state legal system from people's lives. As I show in the second half of the book, popular understandings of legal pluralism enacted through autonomous regions may reproduce a billiard-ball image of legal processes, where "Western" and "indigenous" practices are seen as disconnected systems allowed to coexist. By contrast, I demonstrate how these legal systems and practices are in fact deeply interpenetrated.[25] Nevertheless, the appeal of informal dispute resolution—in institutional settings like the IJCs or movements for indigenous sovereignty—owes much to this larger historical context.

After several years working with Bolivian activists and social movements (see "Uprising"), and in conversation with Bolivian scholars such as Rivera Cusicanqui and Pamela Calla, I decided not to focus my attention on movements for indigenous autonomy and legal pluralism. Instead, I turned my analytic lens to programs that have supported those movements—and sometimes aimed to change them, or, that have provoked their ire. I turned to the donor-backed projects targeting the city of El Alto—and Bolivian democracy more generally—through the promotion of ADR.

Debates over the aims and effects of ADR are not unique to Bolivia. Much of the vast practitioner literature describes ADR techniques and theorizes best practices for achieving good outcomes.[26] By contrast, early critical analyses of ADR centered on whether informalism extended the reach of state power into the lives of citizens via nonstate forms, while others pointed to the ways that practitioners and community mediation programs resisted that state-expansionist project.[27] A number of ADR's early critics argued that it merely serves to control and channel other possible (and perhaps more radical) expressions of community organization and political dissent while producing a hegemonic "ideology of mediator neutrality" or "harmony ideology."[28]

Indeed, early critics of informalism maintained that neighborhood justice centers like those operating in El Alto or San Francisco were not innocent of political aims. Richard Hofrichter (1982), for example, suggested that private dispute resolution served to "dampen class conflict" by redirecting people away from class-based organizing and collective action. Rather than seeing themselves as aggrieved groups demanding redress as a collective, people come to see themselves as private consumers pursuing the satisfaction of their individual complaints (1982: 240). What ADR advocates celebrated as a decentralized, participatory approach to resolving conflict, detractors saw as a managerial scheme that obscured broader patterns—erasing politics entirely. As Christine Harrington concurred, "The origins of these problems are depoliticized or ignored, and the resolutions are internalized by the individualized form of participation. Conflict in this setting is absorbed into a rehabilitative model of minor dispute resolution" (1982: 62). Ugo Mattei and Laura Nader (2008) have pushed the critiques further. They argue that the entire "rule of law" paradigm—including the international export of ADR—enables elite actors to *plunder* poor nations.[29] It does so by encouraging poor countries to "harmonize" commercial laws with international standards and enact privatization schemes that serve the interests of foreign investors and national elites, while undercutting more antagonistic forms of seeking justice, such as street protest.

These assessments point to the multiple meanings of key terms in conflict analysis and resolution. How something is defined—as a means of resistance or a mechanism of control—is deeply political and historically contingent, revealing the diversity of approaches taken by people and organizations appealing to informalism. Yet donor platforms advocating ADR often obscure those contingencies by presenting ADR as a natural outgrowth of native traditions and more humanistic approaches to achieving justice. These debates and accusations are particularly pertinent to the Bolivian context, where recurring political upheaval is coupled with distrust of legal bureaucracies—as well as skepticism over foreign-funded projects aiming to displace them with substitutes such as ADR.

The legal scholar Amy Cohen (2006) has criticized the debate over ADR in the United States for its emphasis on abstract aims—focusing on what ADR is *meant* to do, whether it is a tool of liberation and empowerment or purely one of social control. By contrast, Cohen argues for focusing primarily on ADR *in practice* around the world. In many ways this project responds to Cohen's call. I would argue, however, that separating the two questions— abstract aims versus local applications—fails to account for the full picture of how these concepts and practices travel as development models. It also misses the ways that abstract donor aims come to circumscribe the terms of the debate by determining which kinds of work get funded.

Failing to attend to the intentionality behind these programs and the ways local practices sometimes converge with donor agendas can err on the side of celebrating complexity at the expense of recognizing hegemony. How has informal dispute resolution become, to borrow a concept from Kay Warren and David Leheny (2010), an "inescapable solution"? How did such conflict-resolution programs emerge as a component of democracy-assistance programs more broadly—in Bolivia and other "conflict-prone" parts of the world? What impact have they had on political struggles and the lives of the people they touch? What do they reveal about efforts to shape democracy in Bolivia? I propose we approach these questions through the lens of what it means to "domesticate democracy."

Domesticating Democracy

Democracy means a lot of different things to different people, be they electoral observers in Venezuela or neighborhood activists in Detroit. As a system of government, democracy is, at its core, the ability of people to exercise power over the decisions that affect their lives. Accounts of *liberal* democracies frequently stress the countervailing forces of individual freedoms and institutionalized constraints: what puts liberal in liberal democracy is the preoccupation with protecting liberty—and the grounding of that liberty in rights-bearing individuals. But these commitments, liberals argue, must be accompanied by mechanisms for protecting minority groups from the potential abuses of majority rule. Although democracies are frequently assumed to extend universal suffrage to all citizens, voting rights have been a hard-won battle for many groups in formal democratic states. In Bolivia, questions of *substantive* democracy have pivoted around the exclusion and later managed—or what Rivera Cusicanqui calls a "conditional"—inclusion of the country's indigenous majority; historically, political and economic power has been consolidated in the hands of ruling Euro-descendent and mestizo elites.

In describing liberal democracy, many people cite a litany of characteristics, ranging from free and fair elections, to mechanisms that prevent the consolidation of power in any one governing branch ("checks and balances"), to particular values such as tolerance and pluralism as reflective of a democratic ethos. Democracy also is associated with a whole host of rights, including freedom of the press and of association; freedom of information, speech, and movement; private property ownership; and religious freedom.

Rather than taking categories like "democracy" or typologies of democratic governance for granted, anthropologists frequently emphasize that political forms and practices are not so easily segregated into democratic or *not democratic*. We learn more, perhaps, by understanding how and under what conditions people who are "differently situated in relations of power" characterize something as democratic or not (Paley 2002: 471). As I found while conducting research in El Alto, the same political tactics some activists described to me as undeniably and even radically democratic, others characterized as grossly antidemocratic, authoritarian, and a violation of individual rights (Ellison 2015). Similarly, Matthew Gutmann reflects, "Democracy's very multivalence is a key reason for the zeal with which so many people have employed the term to dramatically different ends in recent history."[30] Paying attention to the micropolitics through which these meanings are consolidated, negotiated, or disputed provides insight into what democracy means to people in practice.[31] Timothy Mitchell has taken the argument about democracy's multiple meanings further, stating that

> it can refer to ways of making effective claims for a more just and egalitarian world. Or, it can refer to a mode of governing populations

that employs popular consent as a means of limiting claims for greater equality and justice by dividing up the common world. Such limits are formed by acknowledging certain areas as matters of public concern subject to popular decision while establishing other fields to be administered under alternative methods of control . . . (2011: 9)

As component parts of larger democracy-assistance programs, the practices of judicial reform, good governance projects, training workshops targeting civil society, and ADR programs are enmeshed in these struggles.[32]

Research on U.S. democracy assistance has tended to focus on (1) the intellectual and institutional history of democracy promotion as a form of U.S. foreign policy and aid intervention;[33] (2) both the declared and the strategic (that is, undeclared) *intent* behind individual American administrations and particular democracy-promotion paradigms;[34] (3) lessons learned or "best practices" in the field of democracy-assistance implementation;[35] and (4) the challenges of *quantifying and measuring* the impact of democracy-promotion interventions.[36] Many of these projects reflect a normative commitment to liberal democracy as a project worthy of refinement and dissemination.

By contrast, critics of U.S. democracy assistance in Bolivia have tended to analyze it almost exclusively as a tool of imperial expansion. They see the United States as a puppeteer that uses covert mechanisms to direct local NGOs and government ministries toward ends that are amenable to U.S. strategic interests—in collaboration with national elites.[37] Such analyses criticize the liberal ideologies and strategic objectives expressed in declassified (or WikiLeaked) cables between the American mission and the U.S. State Department, but they offer little sense of how democracy-promotion programs operate on the ground or what effect, if any, they produce. Instead, they frequently remain at the level of intentionality and ideology. Doing so, however, flattens the complicated history and political terrain of NGO work and development-assistance programs in Bolivia—as in other parts of the world.[38]

Democracy promotion, judicial reform, and ADR are not the sole property of the United States or USAID. Conflict-resolution programs share a number of assumptions that crosscut other kinds of development aid (i.e., women's empowerment projects or participatory budgeting), whether they are run by USAID or funded by other donors on friendlier terms with the Morales administration. Further, it would be a mistake to conflate participation in these programs with being right-wing or anti-Morales, given Bolivia's long-standing reliance on foreign aid and NGOs. As a consequence, many Bolivians across the political spectrum have found work with foreign-funded development projects, whether they were program designers, water engineers, or drivers of jeeps that transported German aid workers to remote outposts.[39]

Focusing exclusively on U.S. strategic interests, while understandable given the pattern of interventionism spanning from the Monroe Doctrine to the Cold War and beyond, may miss the subtle ways these programs operate as techniques of governance. It also tends to narrow our focus to aid directed to groups that Morales identifies as his opposition (even if that is a shifting category). It further narrows our analysis of informalism to U.S. foreign aid, rather than reckoning with the larger constellation of donor institutions that share similar approaches and assumptions about the social, economic, and political good produced through ADR. Much like debates over informalism in the United States, the challenge remains the linking of critical analyses of operating ideologies with the lived effects of these projects. I suggest we might think about ADR as one technique of domesticating democracy. *Domestication* helps us get at the stated and strategic aid objectives of democracy-assistance programs, the suspicions they generate, and the effects they produce in people's lives.

Domesticate is a politically charged verb. It suggests an effort to control, tame, break, or train. For political activists wary of co-optation, it suggests an attempt to neutralize opposition. Within the Morales administration, it's about subterranean efforts to subjugate Bolivians to imperialist projects. Indeed, donors and local contractors sometimes articulated their objectives to me through the equally charged language of pacification (*apaciguar*, or to calm, appease, pacify, or mollify an angry population). Ironically, critics have accused the Morales administration of operating with a similar disciplinary attitude toward its internal critics.

I use the term because it captures something of the operating logic behind democracy-assistance programs, but also the ways critics *perceive* them—on several registers. Both donors and ADR advocates characterized their efforts as cultivating not *docile* populations (that is, subjugated to external control), but rather more *constructive* ones (agentive, autonomous citizens who make their/the nation's future). They insist they don't want tame Bolivians, but rather Bolivians capable of negotiating their demands through established democratic channels and toward productive ends, promoting the common good rather than divisive sectorial interests. But that is the point of my argument about domestication's many valences. ADR programs fit within a larger assemblage of institutions and reformers seeking to mold *particular* kinds of citizens out of "conflictual" Bolivians.

The question is not whether democracy-assistance programs encourage Bolivians to *have a say*, it's what *kind* of voice they should use to articulate those claims. Donor representatives with whom I spoke lamented not Bolivian apathy before politics—frequently the object of political empowerment projects—but rather *overly bellicose* modes of political participation.[40] That is, a recurring concern among democracy-assistance programs is not about a lack of political engagement, but rather about a tendency to engage in forms of political action that critics deem destabilizing, illiberal, or authoritarian.

Those critiques sometimes conflate street protest and property destruction with physical violence, characterizing all three as threats to a functioning, stable democracy. Yet ADR advocates point to the very real physical violence that erupts during both political disputes and intimate ones. Domestication, therefore, refers to the processes through which conflict-resolution programs seek to discipline disruptive political tactics in the service of democratic governability, as well as to deescalate and displace physical violence as a means of resolving disputes.

Thinking about what it means to domesticate democracy further invokes ideals of national sovereignty: the domestic as dominion over one's own country. To what extent do Bolivian political leaders and citizens choose their own path, and to what extent have multilateral donors, foreign governments, and corporations shaped domestic policies? These questions have haunted development aid in Bolivia since the 1950s, when tensions arose, for example, over the "inherent asymmetry" of U.S.-Bolivia cooperation in the healthcare sector (Pacino 2016: 30). As the historian Nicole Pacino argues, during the Cold War era, the Bolivian "Health Ministry's reliance on U.S. financial and technical assistance for developing a national health program was a source of wounded Bolivian pride and internal organizational friction" even as both governments benefited from the relationship (2016: 30).

Under the Morales administration, Bolivia has confronted the role that various international donors and multilateral agencies have played in shaping (some would say dictating) its national policies: remaking Bolivia's economy, funding basic infrastructure and social services—often in the wake of those same economic reforms—and prosecuting the drug war. Whether through plans to export lithium reserves to China, talk of nuclear power plants with Russia, or close diplomatic relations with Venezuela's Hugo Chávez (before his death), Morales has sought to displace U.S. sway. Yet these new political alignments do not release Bolivia from foreign economic investments and political influence, but rather reconfigure how these international relations shape national development projects and political debates.[41]

Domestication can also refer to how liberal democracy is "translated," "vernacularized," "hybridized," or "refracted" in particular contexts.[42] Maxwell Owusu (1997), for example, characterizes the process of domesticating democracy as the ongoing work required to transplant democracy into a new cultural-political context; democracy is domesticated, Owusu argues, as it is adapted to a new national or cultural "soil." By contrast to botanical metaphors, Shoko Yamada (2014) emphasizes how shifting conceptualizations of citizenship and democracy reflect the interests of political elites at particular junctures, and how such elites inscribe those politically useful definitions into textbooks and other civic education materials.[43] For Yamada, domestic or national elites frame democracy in terms amenable to their continued rule.

Thinking domestically also draws attention to ADR's entanglements with *other* domestics, that is, *domestic* policy debates *internal* to the United States and other foreign donors. Declassified documents convey the anxieties that leftist leaders like Evo Morales provoke in Washington—as internal reports characterize Morales as a *cuadillo* and narco-terrorist/guerrilla. However, as Winifred Tate (2015) has shown in her ethnography of Plan Colombia and U.S. policymaking, those strategic interests are often as much about turf battles between Republicans and Democrats at "home" in the United States as they are about a perceived communist (or terrorist) threat. As Tate argues, the moniker "narco-guerrilla" emerged as a particularly useful category to justify continued institutional funding in the post–Cold War era, as military agencies fretted over shrinking budgets.[44]

Further, in her study of Finnish humanitarian efforts, the anthropologist Liisa Malkki explores the "domestic arts" of volunteers knitting trauma teddies distributed to children in war zones—projects often undertaken to deal with the volunteer's own loneliness. Rather than dismiss these arts as inconsequential, Malkki insists they are revelatory of how "the practices of aiding 'distant others' . . . are as domestic as they are foreign—as much about 'the home' . . . as they are about any foreign elsewheres" (2015: 10). Thus multiple, embedded "domestics" inhere in any analysis of postconflict or democracy-assistance programs. These include the operating ideologies and the power struggles that occur, for example, on the floor of U.S. Congress or in political think tanks *prior* to becoming entangled with questions of national sovereignty in places like Bolivia. But they also include the ways lonely knitters find solace in the moral figure of distant suffering children.

Finally, we might also think about domestic relations as a target for democracy-assistance programs. Feminist scholars have long argued that "the separation of domestic (kinship) and public (political and economic) relations should not be presupposed but rather should be a matter of historical and ethnographic inquiry" (McKinnon and Cannell 2013: 13).[45] Here, I want to underscore how aid programs imagine this relationship, as the so-called private realm becomes an object of intervention seeking to remake citizens and their relationship to state institutions—and to each other. And this is where much of my own focus centers, particularly in the second half of the book. That is, how have intimate, household relations, like the conflict between Luz and Jhonny, become the stuff of democracy-assistance programs and related entrepreneurial citizenship projects, and with what effects? How are political economic relations erased in the process? These are multiscalar moves—by me, but also by democracy-assistance programs themselves.

For many ADR advocates, the grinding experiences of conflict and violence that characterize intimate relations in El Alto are matched only by the routine abuses of state bureaucracies. Alteños find themselves enduring interminable lines and bureaucratic red tape in order to obtain basic public services for their homes and to exercise their citizenship rights.[46] By contrast, ADR advocates argue that informal dispute resolution can spare the urban poor from the recurring indignities, frustrations, and abuses of legal bureaucracies as they cope with domestic tensions. ADR allows clients to repair intimate relations, but it also indirectly aims to repair relations between states and their citizens—who have been estranged by bureaucratic mistreatment.

Domestication also draws our attention to ongoing efforts to redirect the solutions that people seek for their problems further inward, toward the intimate, interpersonal realm—with the expectation that friendlier techniques of conflict resolution might transform Bolivian citizens in addition to liberating them from abusive and neglectful state institutions. Thus *domestic*-ate gestures toward the ways that democracy-promotion efforts strive to rehabilitate "conflictual" Bolivians as political actors *and* as husbands, wives, neighbors, parents, and in-laws. By learning how to listen to one another, how to negotiate, how to work through problems via better communication techniques, advocates hope ADR will relieve tensions both in the home and in the country as a whole. This approach reflects a postulation about how conflict *and its resolution* scale up between intimate disputes and larger political ones. Taken together, these interventions reflect an ongoing effort to foster modes of citizenship I characterize as "entrepreneurial" and "counterinsurgent" in the service of democratic governance and economic development.

Entrepreneurial and Counterinsurgent Citizens

Definitions of citizenship frequently center on legal status—tied to particular states, premised on certain requirements, and endowed with particular rights and duties. Much as they do with "democracy," however, anthropological approaches to citizenship move beyond legal categories to instead consider a broader array of emotions, practices, ethics, and claims making.[47] Citizenship might be understood, as James Holston (2009) suggests, as a method of distributing *inequalities* rather than rights. Among the Mohawk of Kahnawà:ke, Audra Simpson speaks of *feeling* citizenship; under conditions of settler colonialism, *feeling* citizenship "may not be institutionally recognized, but [is] socially and politically recognized in the everyday life of the community" (2014: 175). These are emotionally charged and shared frames of reference for particular communities, "and people get called out on them" on street corners and in tribal council meetings all the time (175). These more expansive understandings of citizenship include the ways people declare their belonging to a variety of sociopolitical bodies, assert rights, stake claims to entitlements, and fashion themselves as political actors, whether or not they are officially recognized as the legal members of a particular polity. These approaches also provide avenues for analyzing how people articulate what belonging or inclusion mean to them—in contradistinction to "top-down" efforts to produce particular kinds of citizen-subjects.[48]

My approach here pivots around analyzing the *kind* of citizen that democracy-assistance programs envision—explicitly, but more often implicitly—and how ADR is implicated. When articulated through the vocabulary of citizenship, those framings often center on the unresponsiveness of state agents to citizen demands, the need to cultivate healthy expressions of political dissent, and debates over whether people's rights are respected. However, I argue that ADR is enmeshed in larger development paradigms and political-economic reforms that link self-fashioning, economically mobile, and financially "empowered" subjects with the rights, obligations, and proper conduct of good citizens. These broader citizenship projects connect the actions of protesters to those of ambulant market vendors, and the behavior of women blockading traffic during national strikes to those starting small businesses.

What I want to emphasize here are the ways that individual liberty, political participation, and entrepreneurship get lashed up together under the umbrella of democracy-assistance programs and allied development projects. I describe these framings—and the standards of behavior they entail—as the hallmarks of entrepreneurial and counterinsurgent citizenship.

Democracy-promotion programs have roots in liberal preoccupations with protecting individual liberty, as well as cultivating and unleashing active citizens, "transforming the apathetic into the politically active, the indolent into the productive, and the dependent into the independent" (Cruikshank 1999: 25).[49] Many democracy-assistance programs couple this concern for safeguarding individual liberty (i.e., in weighing and exercising one's conscience in political matters) with ideals of entrepreneurial autonomy. Over the last three decades an assemblage of institutions, including foreign donors, has encouraged Bolivians to adopt market solutions to social welfare and as an expression of individual freedom. In many parts of the world, Bolivia included, this orientation toward the entwining of political and economic liberalism is often associated with "neoliberal" economic reforms. Neoliberalism, as the political geographer David Harvey succinctly explains, is "a theory of political economic practices that proposes that human well-being can best be advanced by liberating individual entrepreneurial freedoms and skills within an institutional framework characterized by strong private property rights, free markets and free trade. The role of the state is to create and preserve an institutional framework appropriate to such practices" (2005: 2). Beyond specific policy measures, however, scholars such as the political philosopher Wendy Brown argue that neoliberalism "imposes a market rationale for decision making on all spheres" of life (2005: 42).[50] People "who are 'entrepreneurs of themselves,'" the anthropologist Elizabeth Dunn explains, "flexibly alter their bundles of skills and manage their careers, but they also become the bearers of risk, thus shifting the burden of risk from the state to the individual" (2004: 22).[51]

One of the most ubiquitous expressions of entrepreneurial citizenship has been the effort to extend "financial inclusion" through small loans to the poor. Microfinance is a diverse and shifting sector; broadly, it entails "the sale of standardized financial services in small quantities at high volumes. The basic product is credit, running on cycles that are usually shorter than one year, offered on a cost-covering-to-profitable basis, normally with successively larger loans being issued in each cycle" (Mader 2016: 8).[52] Much like the enormous variety of actors involved in democracy-assistance programs, actors composing the microfinance sector include multilateral aid agencies, NGOs, for-profit financial institutions, think tanks, and private donors—from Bill Gates to your aunt who made a loan to a woman she saw listed on the Kiva website. The microfinance industry now cites numbers ranging from 91.4 to 195 million borrowers to $100.7 billion distributed in loans worldwide

(Mader 2016: 10). The enormity of these numbers has been matched only by the impacts they have claimed to make.

Microfinance programs have frequently targeted women through the language of empowerment, promoting *national* development through individual women's increased autonomy over their bodies, livelihoods, and life choices.[53] Lending programs include loans to small groups, as well as individual loan recipients, and accompanying budgeting and business-plan training sessions. But they also have encompassed often-mandated workshops aimed at encouraging particular bodily orientations toward self-care, reproductive health, and hygiene.[54] Financial inclusion through access to credit is thus attached to other projects aiming to promote women's empowerment through education, birth control, and courses on political leadership.

As Sian Lazar argues, in the Bolivia context the question was not *whether* residents have a "credit culture" but rather *what kind* and the extent to which it is linked up with formal financial institutions (2004: 305). In El Alto, widespread practices of interpersonal lending once served as a primary source for credit—whether through moneylenders, friends, or kin. Many of the stories explored in this book follow center clients who are enmeshed in complex webs of debt owed to intimate social relations *and* banking institutions. Women like Luz. What microfinance has done is connect more people to financial institutions and to encourage particular kinds of behavior associated with being creditworthy and achieving "more efficient self-help through credit" (Mader 2016: 2).[55] Subsequent studies of microfinance have been far less enthusiastic, finding little evidence to support optimistic proclamations, or finding the impact it has made downright insidious.[56] Nevertheless, those doubts have not slowed the expansion of the field. Indeed, Mader argues that the microfinance sector has largely come unmoored from the antipoverty, women's empowerment goals that once motivated it; instead, "the process of expanding microfinance becomes the end in itself," a process Mader characterizes as the "financialization of poverty," a mechanism for expanding the frontier of finance and extracting surplus from the poor (2016: 19).

"Entrepreneurial citizenship" is thus promoted through microfinance agencies encouraging women to pursue credit as a means for personal and family uplift. It is promoted through donor institutions like the International Republican Institute, inviting small business owners to Washington, D.C., as "model citizens," explicitly linking economic liberalism and the individual entrepreneurship of small business owners to a performance of virtuous citizenship. To borrow from Hannah Appel, entrepreneurial citizenship expresses a "neoliberal imagination of democracy-as-market-efficiency-and-access" (2014: 620). As I show in this book, it is further operationalized when Bolivians adopt tools of negotiation to privately manage conflicts tied to indebtedness, allowing them to repay their institutional bank loans according to schedule.

In this context, programs promoting citizen-entrepreneurs act within nodes of what the philosopher Michel Foucault (1995 [1979]) called "governmentality": state agencies and NGOs entice people to adopt new techniques of self-reliance and self-discipline. One of the most concrete ways to think about neoliberal governmentality is through the everyday ways we internalize norms of behavior measured through performance indicators, quality assurance monitoring systems, evaluation reports, and other bench-marks of success.[57] These appear to be neutral mechanisms aimed at ensuring we get things we value: transparency, accountability, and quality assurance. Yet critics have been particularly attuned to the ways that these audit tech-niques have encouraged people to "identify with the goals of . . . increased market fitness through efficiency, empowerment, and self-improvement" *to the exclusion* of other possible life projects or values (Vannier 2010: 284). And this is the crux of the tensions I explore in the chapters that follow.

Alongside these efforts to promote an empowered, entrepreneurial citi-zenry, donors, NGOs, and government agencies alike have also sought to shape a mode of political engagement that I characterize as "*counter*insurgent." Holston (2009) coined the term "insurgent citizenship" to describe the ways marginalized Brazilians make incursions on urban space as a means of claiming citizenship rights they had been denied. By contrast to the formal inclusion expected for citizens, historically what many Brazilians have ex-perienced instead is "differentiated." Differentiated citizenship refers to the gradations in rights that people are actually able to enjoy in practice, given the persistence of exclusions based on race, class, gender, and other markers of social difference. These are gradations familiar to many Bolivians, par-ticularly the country's indigenous majority.[58] Yet Holston argues that urban squatters on São Paulo's peripheries make claims to their "right to the city" through the very legal frameworks that were used to marginalize them, de-ploying rights discourses, bureaucratic strategies, and the occupation of urban space to build their homes.

Alteños frequently celebrate the 2003 uprising as a reflection of their rebellious and *insurgent* character: a willingness to put their bodies on the line for justice. Anthropologists and historians too have pointed to Bolivia's "culture of rebellion and political turmoil" (McNeish 2008: 92; Lazar 2008). This form of insurgency includes the ways indigenous Bolivians have made incursions into urban space marked "white" through legal and discursive tactics similar to those described by Holston, but also through embodied, transgressive spectacles of dance and protest that make claims on political power beyond institutional frames.[59] From social movements to the election of Evo Morales, Alteños and other indigenous Bolivians have indeed made inroads on the exercise of power, within the city and on the national stage. By contrast, I put the *counter* in counterinsurgent to characterize ongoing, top-down efforts to transform political tactics deemed too conflictual amid these battles.

Counterinsurgent citizens turn inward for the resolution of their problems rather than toward confrontation, and toward the negotiation table rather than street protest. In some ways, these approaches parallel Holston's Paulistas, who creatively deploy land titles, liberal rights discourses, and proper bureaucratic channels to achieve substantive rights. Holston himself takes issue with the persistent "incivilities" that haunt Brazilian sociopolitical life, including graffiti and other signs of urban disorder and hostility. In the Bolivian context, reform projects often distinguish between good citizenship practices and bad sectarianism, trying to steer people toward the former. The latter includes those political tactics utilized by many social organizations— often criticized as authoritarian and illiberal threats to individual liberty and democratic stability.[60]

My aim here is to analyze how these programs *construe* citizenship beyond legal definitions of membership, obligations, and rights to include appropriate modes of political participation, moderated communication, as well as economic self-sufficiency. Many democracy-assistance programs explicitly understand their work as remaking Bolivians from the inside out, transforming first their dispositions toward conflict, their interpersonal relationships, and, finally, broader patterns of social conflict in the country.

An entrepreneurial and counterinsurgent citizen demonstrates her enterprising spirit as she pursues credit and achieves economic independence. She also demonstrates her responsibility as a citizen and a person in the ways she manages her interpersonal disputes. She doesn't wait on the state to intervene, and when she does need to air her grievance on political matters, she channels her frustrations through designated institutional mechanisms and not street protests. She is a fully active and mature citizen not only in the realm of political participation (in elections, in neighborhood associations) but also in her livelihood strategies and the way she manages home economics. It is at the intersection of these twin efforts to promote an entrepreneurial and counterinsurgent citizenry that I locate my analysis of ADR. ADR operates as one "technology of citizenship" among many others (Cruikshank 1999). This technology of citizenship links notions of active participation in democratic processes and institutions with self-governance, entrepreneurial modes of uplift, and peaceful means of conflict resolution.

Yet neoliberal logics of individual "responsibilization" always exist alongside other competing ideas about what it means to be a moral person, and how moral personhood relates to social responsibility (Trnka and Trundle 2014) and economic justice (Lazar 2012). So too competing ideas about what kinds of political action are legitimate, including more confrontational tactics (Ellison 2015). What happens, then, when these modes of entrepreneurial and counterinsurgent citizenship bump up against other meanings of belonging and justice?

The people who came to the ijcs rarely talked about "citizenship" in the ways that ADR advocates, donors, political scientists, and anthropologists did. Instead, they invoked dilemmas and disappointments couched in the language of justice and responsibility. The intersection of these two concepts might be better captured by the English word *accountability*. Their invocation of responsibility—applied to kin and state agents alike—hails these modes of entrepreneurial and counterinsurgent citizenship, finding them deficient.

In the ijcs, Alteños spent a lot of time talking about debts. As they sought to hold each other to account during conciliation sessions, the tabulations they made were frequently quite explicit. They entailed debts owed, both moral and material, to neighbors, kin, and banking institutions. Clients often contrasted themselves with "irresponsible" kin, or commended others for being *responsable* in the face of economic duress, fulfilling their social and economic commitments to others.

In a context of widespread neoliberalization, it would be easy to interpret Alteños' appeals to responsibility through a similar frame of "responsibilization"—an indication that people have internalized this orientation.[61] Yet as I show in the latter half of the book, ijc clients hitched notions of responsibility to a broader understanding of social obligation that entails a sustained relationship—even if it is one that has fallen into asymmetrical disrepair.

The value expressed through the language of responsibility was not about greater market efficiency but rather the ways people's entrepreneurial aspirations had warped and strained their ability to meet their obligations *to others*. These debts, calculated on the backs of smudged envelopes or counted off on their fingers, were less about the rational management of financial resources (though that too was a concern) than an expression of disillusionment and growing distrust. Local idioms of responsibility also point to the ways that intimate relations can become grindingly burdensome when they are subject to prolonged economic vulnerability. As friends and kin struggle to cope with precarious incomes and physical insecurity behind the walls of their *domicilios*—the multigenerational compounds that shelter extended families—they grapple with the fallout produced by their participation in entrepreneurial modes of citizenship.

Mitchell has argued that, increasingly, "democratic struggles become a battle over the distribution of issues, attempting to establish as matters of public concern questions that others claim as private" (2011: 9). Following Mitchell, what happens in ADR sessions is revelatory of how simple technical interventions aiming to improve access to (extra)legal services can redistribute public concerns as private ones. But ADR projects also draw our attention to another dimension of this "battle over the distribution of issues": ADR frames the the acceptable communicative parameters for how people might thrust those concerns back across the imagined private/public divide.

ADR in Action

This book seeks to connect the geopolitical to the intimate and national struggles over justice to the everyday experiences of people targeted by aid programs, as well as those responsible for implementing them. I do so by moving from the design of donor-funded projects to the practices of people hired in Bolivia to administer them, to the people whose lives are impacted by ADR programs in El Alto.[62] For fifteen months (2010–2011), I worked in foreign-funded legal aid centers and conflict-resolution programs, and I visited the criminal courts in El Alto and La Paz.[63] As I did so, I tracked two broadly defined categories of aid interventions targeting social and interpersonal conflict in Bolivia. The first includes ADR programs intended to help the general public, particularly social movements, to adopt negotiation strategies and communication tools for deescalating social and political conflict. The second includes the specific work of the IJCS, which offer pro bono legal aid services, but promote extrajudicial mediation as an alternative to the state legal system.[64] Both approaches endow ADR with the power to facilitate personal and social transformation.

Many ADR programs promote conflict-resolution methods through training workshops, public forums, model debates (*conversatorios*), radio programs, and national ad campaigns. Their audiences included everyone from schoolchildren to union leaders and state officials. I attended many such events, as well as book launches, the National Summit on Alternative and Indigenous Dispute Resolution, and, most recently, the 2016 Justice Summit (Cumbre de Justicia). I interviewed jurists and policymakers, donor representatives and aid recipients, NGO staff and workshop participants, and Bolivian officials at the Ministry of Justice. I also enrolled in a two-month-long diploma course to understand (and receive) the training that was shaping a new generation of conflict-resolution experts (*conflictologos*) in Bolivia.

Among participants, I witnessed passionate debates about the usefulness or inappropriateness of ADR models that have traveled from Harvard University's Program on Negotiation, foreign law schools, and international donors. Those conversations further revealed the ways local aid "translators" or development "brokers" are putting ADR programs and resources in conversation with Bolivian debates about legal pluralism and indigenous modes of conflict resolution.[65] I also spent four months attending one of the criminal courts in La Paz—with the aim of better understanding the challenges facing the formal legal system and motivating appeals to informalism.

The bulk of my time, however, was spent working in one of El Alto's six IJCs. I served in an official capacity as an intern with formal affiliation with the Vice Ministry of Justice and Fundamental Rights. I worked alongside public servants, student interns, and the few volunteers who continued to return to the center even after the volunteer program had been officially phased out. Alongside interns like Angelica, who was attending to Luz's case, I registered detailed histories of domestic violence, interpersonal conflicts, and various other problems that brought residents to the center—from formalizing land titles to fights over inheritance. Our day-to-day tasks included orienting clients about their legal and nonlegal options, setting up conciliation appointments, and drafting transfer letters to other agencies (e.g., the forensic medical examiner, child protective services).

I observed the work of center staff and sat in on conciliation sessions. Attending conciliation sessions allowed me to observe the ways staff utilized ADR, how clients responded to those methods, and to catch the turns of phrase and complaints that were written out of the succinct, bullet-pointed final accords. With the permission of all parties, I conducted in-depth follow-up interviews with clients about domestic violence, debt conflicts, and corruption in the justice system, among other recurring themes. Through those interviews, I could further situate conciliation sessions within a broader array of conflict-management strategies people in El Alto employ *outside* such institutions, including the use of kin, neighborhood associations, and rural indigenous community leaders (*Mallkus*).

Because I was working as an intern at the center, the position posed unique ethical challenges for how to best approach people whose stories and experiences I wanted to follow more closely through follow-up interviews. People often approached the intern desk where I sat with difficult issues on their minds—and I never wanted anyone to feel that they had to assent to participating in my study before getting access to center resources or other help. As a consequence, I would approach people after their intake sessions were over, after they had their conciliation invitations and other necessary documents arranged, and sometimes weeks after we had first met, to ask whether I might interview them further about their experiences.

Nearly everyone I asked said yes, as long as I could work around their busy lives rearing children, selling produce in the market, or traveling long distances hauling merchandise for other vendors. I interviewed women butchers outside their corner shops and *prestamistas* (moneylenders) as they leafed through bits of collateral in their homes. I spent many hours sharing tea and flaky empanadas as women mapped out their debts and detailed histories of violence in their lives. I flipped through cosmetic magazines as Mary Kay vendors tabulated sales and recounted struggles to obtain child support from estranged husbands. I listened in as brothers and sisters quietly debated how best to care for a disabled sibling after their elderly parents died.

These men and women were incredibly generous in allowing me to ask questions about difficult and sometimes embarrassing topics, and they offered their own theories of and insights into the challenges they were facing. I hope that chapters 4, 5, and 6 in particular help put some flesh, sweat, and tears into an otherwise abstract debate about ADR, foreign aid, and crumbling U.S.-Bolivia relations.

In addition to the clients of ADR, however, I also spent a great deal of time speaking with its practitioners. ADR is, for its advocates, an ethical field, a concrete means to contribute to the social good, a practice that enables intimate partnerships and large social movements to transform violence into constructive solutions, and a valuable mechanism to rescue potential victims from abusive legal bureaucracies. The people I met working as conciliators, running conversatorios on peaceful conflict resolution, and training NGO workers and public servants in negotiation tactics were a varied bunch, politically and socioeconomically. They came to their work in ADR along different paths. Some were *militantes* of the Movement Towards Socialism (MAS) party and others were university students eager to gain experience for their résumés. Some were lawyers, and others were housewives eager to cultivate dimensions of themselves beyond childrearing. But they almost all articulated *proyectos de vida* (life projects) rooted in "making a living, while doing some good" (see chapter 3).

Take, for example, Dr. Paloma Gil and the law intern Azucena, whose story opens chapter 1. The enormous respect that Paloma inspired in neighborhood residents, leaders, former volunteers, and center staff was palpable. Paloma began working with the IJCS as a volunteer while they were under the auspices of USAID. She was later hired as a center director, and I met her as a public servant of the Morales administration. Paloma was driven by a fierce commitment to stopping the endless cycle of bureaucratic inertia that left residents of El Alto fumbling their ways between legal and administrative offices with no relief in sight. She wanted to be that relief.

Like Dr. Paloma, the staff and interns at the center where I spent my days were often empathetic with their clients, outraged at the institutional deficiencies and discrimination they faced, and troubled by the grim family situations they encountered. They also were service providers who made mistakes, grew weary with difficult clients (and prodding anthropologists), and engaged in routine office politics and gossip. Some reproduced racialized ideologies about "conflictual" Indians, while others were active leaders in the effort to implement indigenous legal sovereignty in places like Jesús de Machaca. Many of them were facing struggles not unlike those of their clients: they grappled with family conflicts and debt burdens and sought professional opportunities for career advancement.

They also generously shared with me the ambivalence they felt toward donor objectives. They struggled with uncertainty regarding their real contributions to their clients' lives. And they reflected on their aspirations for the justice system, the country, and their own families. For all that and more, I am enormously grateful. It is my hope that in turn, my critical analysis of the workings of ADR is recognizable to the people who are featured here. They may disagree with my conclusions—or find that the issues I choose to highlight are irrelevant to their own purposes.[66] But it is my hope that they feel I have represented them as multidimensional people wrestling with multidimensional dilemmas.

A note on my use of pseudonyms: all the names of center clientele have been changed, as have those of bureaucratic staff, interns, and volunteers. The same goes for the names of most NGOs appearing in the book, although they will likely be recognizable to a Bolivian audience familiar with their well-known work on these themes. The names of public intellectuals and prominent activists speaking at public events, as well as government officials and foreign aid representatives speaking in their institutional capacities, remain unchanged.

Organization of the Book

The book that follows is divided into two parts. In the first, I focus on the history, politics, and practices of foreign aid programs, and I follow the experiences of the people tasked with implementing them: aid workers, development professionals, and volunteers responsible for the spread of ADR in Bolivia. I open the second half of the book with a short "Recess," in which I describe life in the Alto Lima neighborhood and point to the ways the IJC operating there exemplifies struggles over legal pluralism in Bolivia. Following this brief, scene-setting interlude, the second half of the book focuses on the everyday work of one center; the efforts of volunteers, professional staff, and interns; and, especially, the experiences of its clientele. While my research was primarily located in District 6, I conducted interviews with the directors, staff, and interns working at both El Alto's and La Paz's centers, and I draw on their perspectives for comparative purposes.

Their stories illuminate a significant tension between the causal relationship that ADR advocates ascribe to interpersonal and social conflict in El Alto and the ways Alteños themselves experience that causal relationship. As I show in these final three chapters, many ADR advocates I spoke with saw conflict as "scaling up" from the interpersonal to the social—that is, social conflict was generated by people's failure to find redress for everyday experiences of interpersonal conflict. In this conceptualization of conflict, if we fix the micro dimensions of conflict (e.g., by teaching people interpersonal conflict-resolution skills), we can fix the macro (widespread protests, blockades, and other disruptive approaches to demanding redress).

ADR programs have accompanied ongoing waves of aid intervention that have sought to produce what I characterize as entrepreneurial and counterinsurgent citizens in Bolivia, as in many other parts of the world. These broader development platforms do so by conflating market access and efficiency with democracy, and good citizenship with orderly political participation and entrepreneurship.[67] Against this narrowing of political-economic imaginations, social movements have occupied streets and redrawn constitutions, to varying degrees of "success."[68] And yet, in the meantime, people like Luz and Justa, Manuela, and Lourdes—whom you will meet—frequently turn to these very same donor projects to deal with the fallout produced by their participation in development projects' entrepreneurial invitations.

Indeed, conciliation programs allow Alteños like Luz to manage the intimate conflicts and economic uncertainty that neoliberalism has wrought in their lives, to find some redress for their grievances. But their use of ADR does not blind them to the political-economic roots of their woes. Instead, residents of El Alto regularly point to the macro political-economic dimensions of those conflicts, repoliticizing intimate disputes—even as they seek immediate relief through the resources that ADR offers in the meantime.

It's October 2003, and residents of the city of El Alto have laid siege to Bolivia's adjacent seat of government, La Paz. Although the flashpoint of the uprising was the export of Bolivia's natural gas supplies, the popular protests express a deeper dissatisfaction with neoliberal economic-development policies and the state of democratic institutions in the country.[1] Protests in El Alto escalated rapidly after the military opened fire on residents in the rural Altiplano town of Warisata, killing several people, including a child. People are still reeling from news that the military descended on the town in helicopters in order to break up a blockade there and to "liberate" tourists trapped in the nearby vacation destination, Sorata. The intervention, however, only succeeded in enflaming widespread anger about the government's use of violence to suppress protests. It proved to be a crucial turning point in helping to galvanize the disparate protests taking place in El Alto and surrounding rural hamlets. Now, those protests rally around a common battle cry: gas for Bolivia and the resignation of Bolivia's president, Gonzalo Sánchez de Lozada (or "Goni" as he is commonly known). As the government's repression increases, the demand for President Sánchez de Lozada's resignation intensifies.

I have been working as the facilitator for a national network of Bolivian grassroots groups, NGOs, and faith-based organizations that have joined together to look at the structural causes of poverty in Bolivia. In February, I had watched curling smoke plumes rise from neighborhoods in downtown La Paz as protesters burned government buildings and political party headquarters. Stopped by my neighbor from venturing out, I instead watched from my apartment, located high on one of La Paz's steep *laderas* (hillsides) facing El Alto, Villa Copacabana. The February violence was provoked by a new tax system pushed by the IMF. Angered by the new policies, Bolivia's police force abandoned their posts and took to Plaza Murillo (home to the Presidential Palace and Congress) to protest. There, they were joined by young students from a nearby school. The protests turned deadly. The military fired on the crowd of rock-throwing students, and police shot back at the military using their own service weapons. For several days afterward, the wafting traces of burning buildings and paperwork filled the crater of La Paz.

Now, in October, I watch once again as tear-gas plumes and smoke hover around the city. This time, they rise from blockades that burn where the cities of La Paz and El Alto meet.[2] Street traffic vanishes as the stranglehold grows tighter. Airlines stop running. Food shortages strip the markets bare. Friends concerned about me, a young foreign woman living alone, walk several miles to bring me a wilted head of lettuce they managed to stockpile before foodstuffs grew scarce. A neighbor's family secretly makes bread in their bakery's large brick oven, dispensing it to their closest relatives. One brings me a gift of still-warm, crusty *marraqueta*. I offer her a few eggs in return. For those of us living in La Paz, we can only imagine what is happening in El Alto by listening to radio reports and talking anxiously with friends there.

As news of more deaths and injuries comes in, people call radio stations pleading with neighbors to let ambulances through the blockades. One DJ begs, "If any health center is listening to this broadcast, please send help to . . ." But emergency vehicles can't respond. They have no gasoline. The wounded and dead must be wheelbarrowed to makeshift hospitals or morgues. Several stations continue to offer live updates even as they receive threats of military intervention. Neighbors gather to protect them. Listeners call in sobbing, terrified by what is happening, pleading with the government not to kill more people. Others speak with hushed voices, expressing their pain and shock. One caller identifies himself as a *conscripto*, a young soldier fulfilling his mandatory military service—probably a kid just out of high school. In a defiant yet shaking voice he tells listeners, "I am here with others in the ***** Battalion. We are ready to support our people. We are ready to disobey orders. We call on others to join us." For a moment I can't

MAP 1 (RIGHT) The conjoined cities of El Alto and La Paz, with El Alto occupying a high plain that surrounds Bolivia's seat of government, La Paz, located in the deep basin below. Their geographic proximity has been critical to the power of El Alto residents, who use street protest and blockades to make demands on political elites living and working in neighboring La Paz.

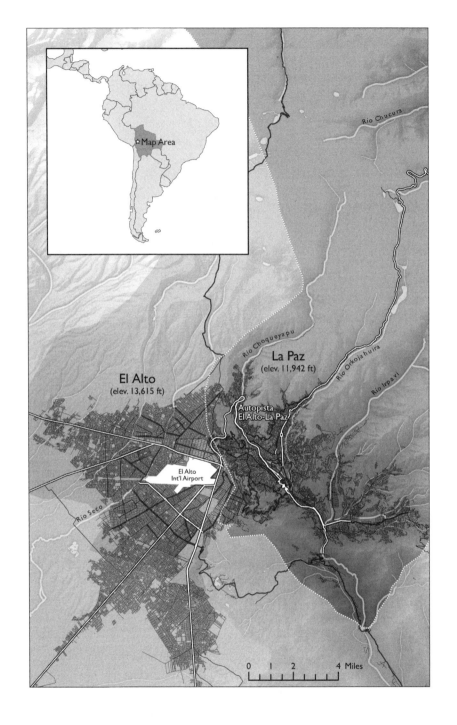

Rio Chucura

Rio Choqueyapu

La Paz
(elev. 11,942 ft)

Rio Orkojahuira

Rio Irpavi

El Alto
(elev. 13,615 ft)

Autopista
El Alto-La Paz

El Alto
Int'l Airport

Rio Seco

Map Area

0   1   2   4 Miles

believe he has just identified himself publicly. Other rumors spread of the military executing young conscripts for refusing orders, for refusing to fire on the civilian population of El Alto. Those stories circulate as evidence of the brutality of the government, which is asking the nation's children to fire on their parents, grandparents, and siblings.

In the Villa Adela neighborhood, where I would later live with my *compadres* (the co-parents of my goddaughter), a man calls the radio station to say that people there are forming a mob to seek out the families of the local police in order to take revenge. The DJ tries to calm him down, pleading with him and others not to confront the military or attack police families. The caller responds, "Mr. Journalist, you have to understand. Our people are dying. We cannot let it continue. We must take a stand. We are ready to die confronting the military if necessary." Calls pour in from other El Alto residents saying this is the wrong approach. That Alteños must stop attacking Alteños. The poor can't keep hurting the poor.

I receive a call from a friend, Enriqueta, who lives in the El Alto neighborhood of Rio Seco. She breathes heavily into the phone as we speak. She is running. I can hear hollow popping noises in the background and what sounds like the loud whir. I think, *Helicopter?* "Where are you running?" I shout into the phone, alarmed. "I'm here in my neighborhood. We're trying to help the wounded," she pants. I beg her to be safe, to stay home. "I have to help," she insists and keeps jogging toward the injured.

Another friend, Rina, who lives on the precipitous La Paz ladera opposite me, calls to check in. "Imagine the mothers. Imagine the widows!" Rina wails. "So much suffering. They should feel anguish—killing their brothers and sisters. But they feel nothing. Shooting from the helicopters, the snipers, oh!" Rina's voice shakes with rage: "They don't see us as human. They're just killing us."

As the deaths continue to mount, people's tone changes. Neighbors sit around sharing what we can learn from friends and relatives in other neighborhoods, on the radio or television. An older woman in my building, who has never shown any sympathy for *campesino* (peasant) or indigenous movements, holds a hand to her mouth and winces as her daughter tells us of yet another report of deaths. But rather than blame the protesters (as she once did), she now blames the president and his repressive tactics.

President Gonzalo Sánchez de Lozada declares that he will not give in to the growing pressure to step down. The American diplomatic mission issues statements saying that the United States will stand behind Goni and his bid to remain in power—to preserve Bolivian democracy. Critics scoff at the notion that democracy can be preserved through violent repression. Amid increasingly violent reprisals, support for Goni quickly erodes.

As the violence and uncertainty intensify, I ask my friend and colleague Rina—an indigenous Aymara agronomist who people often assume is my *empleada* (maid) because of her ethnicity—what she thinks will happen. She responds, "[Goni] will eventually have to resign. He just will. That's how it's always happened. [Indigenous] people didn't know how to read, how to write. They had to struggle. The people have always had to struggle. You weren't allowed to study, but the people fought for their rights. The indigenous were slaves to the masters—that's all. But now the people are many. They've studied, and now they are aware."

"And one day," Rina concludes, "they will govern. They are preparing themselves."

Rina is right.

Two years later, Evo Morales Ayma is elected Bolivia's first indigenous president.

IN MANY WAYS this project dates back to the initial grief, uncertainty, and recovery that followed what became known as "Black October." The uprising worried political analysts, catalyzed a series of donor interventions, and rearranged national political platforms. The U.S. Mission contracted its Office of Transition Initiatives (OTI) to begin a short-term, intensive intervention with the stated aim of deescalating conflict at the invitation of then-president Carlos Mesa.[3] Other donors also reconfigured their work to tackle issues related to the October unrest. At the time neither my colleagues nor I knew much about OTI. What we did know was that a funding surge had hit El Alto, and many NGOs were scrambling to apply for those resources. Members of our network hotly debated whether to submit a project proposal—and whose interests such funding ultimately served.[4]

When I left Bolivia in 2005, heading back to the United States to pursue graduate studies, several organizations I knew were mobilizing to gain access to U.S. democracy-assistance funding in El Alto. When I returned three years later, the tide had shifted. The United States Agency for International Development (USAID) was in the middle of a political firestorm, and its beneficiaries were suspect. What I had thought was merely an intense internal debate among NGOs and activists over the stated and strategic aims of American funding—and whether an organization could accept such funding and remain relatively independent of donor objectives and interests—was now a hot-button political issue on a national stage. And, indeed, when I began working on this project, representatives of both the Morales administration and the U.S. government would reflect back to me what they thought my research might reveal: American imperialism at work, or productive insights into how to make U.S. aid more palatable to a skeptical audience.

The 2003 uprising and its continued effects have deeply shaped the ways both Bolivians and foreign researchers like myself think about struggles over Bolivian democracy. Media and scholarly coverage of the 2003 uprising—and the political events that followed—tend to focus on the spectacle: spectacle in protest and violent repression, spectacle in charismatic leadership and symbolic political actions, spectacle in public lynchings of suspected criminals and effigies hung in warning, spectacle in dance parades that overrun capital streets and neighborhood plazas and that enact forms of sociality that bind people together and enable collective action. Indeed, there is a lot of spectacle in Bolivia, and those studies offer enormous insights into the eventful forms of protest, sociality, and violence that shape life and politics in the country.[5] The collapse of U.S.-Bolivia relations also has proven to be rather theatrical.

And yet, this focus on the "event"—on that moment in 2003 when El Alto laid siege to La Paz—may erase the longer history of indigenous mobilizations leading up to the October unrest. Those movements have been building since the 1970s and grew more powerful in the 1990s, but they frequently invoke their precursors: indigenous uprisings during the colonial era.[6] Moreover, it narrows our focus to overt expressions of political dissatisfaction: mass street protests, strikes, blockades, and revolutionary discourses in public forums. The political conflagration that erupted over USAID's post-2003 democracy-assistance funding also obscures a longer history of aid interventions and liberal reforms. Those interventions include earlier efforts to remake Bolivia's political institutions and economic policies—advocated by a variety of financial institutions and bilateral donors. It is to this deeper history of aid, the responses it has provoked, and the effects it has produced that I now turn.

Fix the State or Fix the People?

Azucena's Dilemma

Azucena is growing restless. The shared printer is down. With the integrated justice center (IJC) director away for a meeting at the Ministry of Justice, the interns are at a loss about how to do our work—which relies heavily on printing letters of referral to the forensic medical examiner, invitations to conciliation sessions, and *memoriales* (legal briefs) for those clients pursuing domestic violence cases in the formal legal system. Luckily it is a slow day, and we are approaching lunch, when clients rush home to prepare meals and claim their children from school. Azucena wanders around the emptying room as if lost, declaring herself useless.

On this chilly morning I want to take advantage of the center's emptiness to get Azucena's opinion. I had spent several days a week visiting one of the criminal tribunals in La Paz, trying to understand the kinds of problems that prompted foreign aid programs to focus their funding so heavily on judicial reform during the 1990s. Throughout Bolivia, the law and its accompanying institutional apparatus are widely perceived to be *antithetical* to justice, whether in their absence or their arbitrary and abusive presence.[1] Azucena— who spent six years working as an intern in Bolivia's court system—knows I've been seeing her old stomping ground firsthand.

FIGURE 1.1 One of El Alto's integrated justice centers. Photo by author.

"You worked in one of the tribunals before," I say. "What do *you* think should be done to improve the administration of justice?"

Azucena folds her legs and gray scarf at the same time, tilting her head pensively. She rattles off a list of problems, ascribing blame: lawyers who don't orient their clients well because they care more about making money than poor people's needs; insensitive interns who constantly force people to correct their documents and come back later—so they can delay cases and thus lighten judges' workloads.

"I also hear a lot of complaints about *notificaciones* [process serving]," I offer. Azucena nods, consternation spreading across her face.

"Well, *that* I have seen with my own eyes," she groans. "Once, when I was working in the [main El Alto courthouse], one of the interns was attending to the accused in a contraband case. The [accused] said, 'Look, you aren't going to serve me the notification.' This is the way people delay justice," Azucena tells me, going on to explain a variety of "payment" options for securing the delay through bribes. "Afterward I asked [the intern], 'Why are you doing that?' And he responded, 'Everyone does this. It's normal.' These guys [who were paying off the intern] were functionaries of the deputy mayor of [a highland town]. They do everything they can to delay justice."

It is a familiar refrain for me: accusations of people slipping money to interns and state functionaries to avoid being served, delaying their court cases indefinitely. I had witnessed many such cases be "suspended" due to failed notifications while observing the La Paz tribunal. "Yes," I nod along. "I hear complaints about the Central de Notificaciones [notification headquarters]."

"The Central is a different issue," Azucena clarifies. "The Central has to notify jurors. Let's say you have to do a lottery of twenty-five people. And you have three cases. That's seventy-five people a day you have to notify. And then you maybe have other notifications. You just don't have enough time. I remember coming home at night when I was working for the Central in El Alto and I would just be pissed-off [*renegando*]. I would sit down at the kitchen table and invent things."

Azucena explains that she would return home, physically unable to meet her case allotment. Sometimes, she concocted the details: "I'd write, 'the house had a green garage,' because they *all* have green garages, right? 'It was located in front of a yellow house.' I felt bad about it, but I just didn't have enough time! Some days I also would have to go to the FELC-C [a special unit in the fight against crime], San Pedro [men's prison], Obrajes [women's prison] too. The first time I went to San Pedro—you won't believe it—I showed up and the officer asked for my credential and sent me in. It's a zoo. And I got robbed! Someone stole my cellphone. As I was leaving another officer said, 'Why did you go in? Just leave the notification at the front desk.' But I didn't know any better! So each day I would maybe manage to notify five people. *Five people*!" She moans, eyes wide.

"Five people out of seventy-five?" I gasp.

"Yes, five. Maybe it was supposed to be more than seventy-five. Let's see. How many jurors are notified? Twelve, right? And maybe I would have five cases. So you do the math."

Azucena's point was not about exact numbers. It was about larger patterns in the administration of justice in Bolivia and what it was like to be one person reproducing those patterns as she wandered El Alto's largely unmarked streets looking for juror residences, navigated the city's perpetual traffic snare, and descended into adjacent La Paz to visit the men's and women's prisons.

Azucena often expressed remorse about her participation in the very practices many Bolivians cite when they complain about the justice system. We talked about the practice of charging unofficial fees for paperwork (*coima*, a word for small bribes greasing the wheels of bureaucracy), as well as the pressures she received from both interns and even judges to do so. Azucena's recollections mirrored the angry testimonies I heard from people who had the misfortune of passing through the state legal system—whether as plaintiff or the accused. But other state bureaucrats also voiced dismay. Over several months I watched as one incensed functionary serving in a La Paz courtroom set out to extirpate her tribunal of the ordinary acts of corruption that occurred on a daily basis, openly calling out the other functionaries for accepting bribes. In a court system staffed largely by unpaid, university-age interns, several young people on her staff defended the practice of coima as reasonable; how else would they pay for their bus fares?

During her work at the IJC, I watched Azucena dutifully strive to embody the ideals of the alternative dispute resolution (ADR) programs: refusing to accept money when it was offered, treating clients with enormous respect and patience—even though she would shake her fists and vent frustration once certain "aggressive" clients were out of earshot. She was now a law student and often pondered what role she would play as a professional in the Bolivian justice system. Could she be different?

When I first met Azucena, she recommended conciliation to clients out of obligation—and insisted that it was the only reason she would do so; over many months, however, she developed the sense that it might, in fact, be a better option than the courts. After so much time encouraging center clients to pursue conciliation, *por la vía buena, hablando* (taking the good path, talking), she wondered if she should train to be a conciliator herself.

But there is another story concealed in Azucena's shifting views on conciliation. It's a story about foreign aid. It's a story about how multiple donor institutions came to promote conciliation as the solution to an unreliable and overburdened justice system, for foreign companies and ordinary Bolivians alike. It's a story about how ADR traveled from corporate boardrooms, World Bank policy conferences, the U.S. State Department, the Harvard Program on Negotiation, and even the notebooks of legal anthropologists, to the dusty neighborhoods of El Alto.

Azucena's professional trajectory has been profoundly marked by Bolivia's entanglement with a broad range of judicial reform agendas funded by foreign donors and guided by international legal experts. Those efforts include creating Bolivia's human rights ombudsman and reforms to Bolivia's criminal code that replaced the inquisitorial model—where judges ruled with little need to publicly defend their verdicts—with an adversarial system and juries. They also include Bolivia's counternarcotics laws (Law 1008) and training programs aimed at attorneys and judges—just to name a few.

How, then, did ADR become part of that reform agenda and travel to Bolivia, to El Alto, into Azucena's life trajectory and into the everyday encounters she had with center clientele? What was the analysis that drove such interventions, and what roles did particular policies and donor institutions play in promoting a shift from aid centered on institutional reforms to the formal legal system to the promotion of *informal* mechanisms for resolving disputes?

This chapter offers a bird's-eye view of larger shifts in donor-backed governance strategies concerned with democratization, judicial reform, and governability. I argue that the IJCS and allied programs targeting Bolivian civil society reflect a larger shift in donor governance strategies and democratization priorities. It is a shift from a primary focus on *institutional* capacity building to capacitación, or skill-set training, centered on individual citizens and the ways they are embedded in "conflictual" interpersonal, social, and political spaces.

I could translate capacitación as capacity building or simply "training." The open-ended term suggests practical instruction that targets individuals and groups for information sharing, guidance, and strengthening abilities, whether institutional or personal.[2] But here I use *capacitación* (rather than the English *capacity building*) to mark a shift in donor priorities. I do not mean to suggest that something called capacitación was not an integral part of previous waves of aid intervention. Indeed, during the 1990s many donor platforms encompassed training programs seeking to equip judges, legislators, and bureaucrats with knowledge and technical skills that, donors believed, would enable them to enact the kinds of institutional reform that many good governance and democracy-assistance programs sought to promote. Additionally, Bolivia's Law of Popular Participation (LPP) spawned many NGO projects and workshops *capacitando* (training) people in how to make claims on state resources through new institutional channels. However, in utilizing the term capacitación analytically, what I want to underscore is the ever-greater emphasis on the *person* and the *interpersonal* as the locus of political transformation rather than the agents or institutions of the state—whether national, regional, or municipal.

The anthropologist Nancy Postero (2007) has noted that Bolivia's process of neoliberal restructuring included remaking, expanding, and strengthening democratic institutions—not simply the contraction of the state, as critics often characterize neoliberalism.[3] As Carol Greenhouse explains, "Neoliberalism endorses the expansion of the private sector as the basis for governance, but neoliberal reform as a process requires extensive state action" (2009: 5). My argument here is that the emphasis on capacitación represents a sharper turn in neoliberal rationalities and reform priorities, away from remaking institutions toward rehabilitating interpersonal behavior. Advocates envisioned ADR as a mechanism for deescalating conflict by actually responding to people's pressing needs (giving them a more satisfying experience with a statelike entity) *while also* transforming the way they relate to such bureaucratic institutions: If you can't fix a broken system, keep people out of it. Take away their desire for it in the first place; replace it with a sense of being empowered to care for oneself.

Critical development scholars and anthropologists studying policymaking have suggested that Latour's concept of the "assemblage" reflects the "real-world heterogeneity of the things that actually go into the making of public policy" (Greenhalgh 2008: 12).[4] Tania Li speaks of the "multiple authorities devising improvements," a vast "assemblage" that becomes, if only briefly, "stabilized as a discursive formation" that "supplies a complex of knowledge, and practice in terms of which certain kinds of problems and solutions become thinkable whereas others are submerged, at least for a time" (2005: 386). Ethnographic work can illuminate how, "despite fragmentation and dissent, heterogeneous actors in development are constantly engaged in creating order through political acts of composition" through acts of translation (Lewis and Mosse 2006: 14).

The ways that particular policy problems are identified "do not simply reflect a reality that exists in nature," the anthropologist Susan Greenhalgh argues. "Instead they may actively constitute a new reality by shaping *what is thinkable* in the domain of population" or other sites of intervention (2008: 10).[5] Once "embedded in public policy and bureaucratically enacted," Greenhalgh explains, "a powerful problematization can remake the world in which we live" (2008: 10). Such framings of a problem in need of intervention become "sticky" and can be difficult to dislodge.

My aim here is to trace the emergence of a donor policy consensus that promoted ADR in Bolivia. Attending to how donors identified what was "wrong" with Bolivia forces into the light processes that are often "black boxed" or obscured from view (Latour 1999: 70). The residue of those efforts sits in conference documents and project evaluations and in the memories of people who participated in their design.[6] Accordingly, this chapter examines the historical contingencies and policy shifts that went into declaring ADR a promising solution for Latin America's—including Bolivia's—legal woes.

These development and judicial reform projects have influenced the personal and professional trajectories of people like Azucena and her peers. Later chapters will explore the experiences of ADR "translators" or policy "brokers" who have helped expand conciliation's reach, as well as the ways these programs impact the lives of El Alto residents. Or, to quote Tania Li, "what happens when those interventions become entangled with the processes they would regulate and improve" (2007: 27). For now, let me begin with a brief history of Bolivia-U.S. Cold War entanglements.

From the Alliance for Progress to the Washington Consensus

Since the nineteenth century the United States has shown its interest in and a willingness to shape and even strong-arm the political and economic life of its southern neighbors. Early U.S. diplomatic efforts toward Bolivia were driven by an interest in the country's mineral wealth and a concern with stemming the tide of economic nationalism, which threatened those interests.[7] Starting in the 1940s, foreign aid interventions in Bolivia frequently involved technical assistance and technology transfer, infused with a healthy dose of anti-indigenous bias that blamed Bolivia's indigenous cultures for impeding modernization.[8] By the 1950s, anticommunist agendas were the primary force behind American aid programs in Bolivia, as the United States sought to defuse the revolutionary fervor taking root in Latin America.[9]

Bolivia's 1952 revolution intensified American concerns over economic nationalism and leftist influence in the region. Yet rather than rely on overt military intervention that it had elsewhere in the region, the United States employed an economic development strategy. The historian James Siekmeier has argued that the United States chose to support the more conservative-centrist elements within Bolivia's Nationalist Revolutionary Movement (MNR) party in an effort to prevent the rise of a potentially *more* leftist, *less* U.S.-friendly regime (2011: 5–6).[10] Bolivian political elites, for their part, largely embraced this developmentalist orientation; officials welcomed Western aid even as they tried to court both sides of the Cold War scramble to win allegiance among so-called Third World countries. Centrist MNR offi-cials "discovered that they could increase the flow of assistance," Siekmeier explains, "either by claiming outright that more assistance would prevent the nation from falling to communism or by quietly reaching out to the East bloc" (2011: 5). Following a military coup in 1964, Bolivia was wracked by frequent coups and countercoups over the next decade, and each military regime sought to suppress dissent and to crush labor movements with the help of American economic and military aid.

Throughout the 1960s, 1970s, and 1980s, U.S. financial aid was driven largely by concerns over leftist movements in the Americas, as the Kennedy and later Johnson and Reagan administrations funded counterinsurgency efforts in the region.[11] The Kennedy administration's Alliance for Progress aimed to foster U.S.-friendly, stable democracies in Latin America through economic development. The United States intended for economic develop-ment and infrastructure projects to help undercut the appeal of labor unions and other movements for more radical/leftist political regimes, winning hearts and minds to the U.S. cause.[12]

Economic development would continue to serve as a tool of U.S. diplo-macy following Bolivia's transition to democracy. When Hernán Siles Zuazo was elected president in 1982, he took the helm of a country on the verge of economic collapse, reestablishing formal (if fragile) democracy in Bolivia. Unable to guide the economy out of the crisis, he left a legacy of hyperinfla-tion to his successor, Víctor Paz Estenssoro. And Paz Estenssoro, for his part, turned to foreign advisors to cope with the spiraling crisis.

The Bank and Bolivia: Judicial Reform as a Tool of Market Liberalization

On August 29, 1985, Paz Estenssoro issued Supreme Decree No. 21060, abruptly liberalizing Bolivia's economy. No. 21060 served as the blueprint for stringent economic-restructuring measures dubbed "shock therapy." The lib-eralization and stabilization plan was designed by Harvard wunderkind Jef-frey Sachs to rein in the rampant hyperinflation that had gripped the country since Hernán Siles left office.[13] The austerity measures enacted through the New Economic Policy (NEP) accomplished that goal, reducing inflation. But the measures also triggered wide-ranging negative consequences that con-tinue to haunt the country—and galvanize social movements—to this day.[14] Among the immediate effects of No. 21060, 23,000 miners (out of 30,000) were fired from state-owned mines and 120 factories were shuttered.[15] Many of the displaced made their ways to the periphery of Bolivia's administrative capital, La Paz, settling into the windswept plain of El Alto. Others turned toward coca production in the lowland regions of the Chapare and Yungas. Those settlements—both urban El Alto and the more rural coca-producing regions—have since played a decisive role in Bolivian politics.

During this period, often glossed "Latin America's lost decade," Paz Estenssoro's administration relied heavily on the World Bank (WB) and International Monetary Fund (IMF) to cope with the debt crisis. Thus when Bolivians cite *el neoliberalismo*—as *dirigentes* (union leaders), political elites, and ordinary citizens often do—they are not merely throwing around an empty category. Neoliberalism has a very specific, historical meaning in the country, even if political leaders invoke it quite freely to denounce their opposition. Bolivia was the testing ground for many of the first waves of structural adjustment programs (SAPs) that the IMF and WB would later advocate worldwide, and served as a guinea pig for policy platforms that constituted the foundation of the "Washington Consensus."[16] Accompanying these measures was the arrival of microfinance. As Philip Mader notes, "Starting with Bolivia in the 1980s, microcredit featured in structural adjustment plans, concomitantly with policies for reforming national financial sectors and easing international capital flows" (2016: 90). These economic policies accompanied other restructurings, including decentralization and education reform.[17] Judicial reform would follow, rising to prominence during the 1990s under the leadership of the WB, Inter-American Development Bank (IDB), and the American Bar Association, among other influential institutions.

Economists were coming to see the law and good governance as critical to their economic agenda. It was a shift that would reshape policy coalitions and donor platforms in countries like Bolivia for years to come. In 1995, for example, the WB organized a conference that brought together an emergent transnational network of aid institutions, scholars, and Bank employees that were promoting the rule of law as a necessary precondition to effective market expansion.[18] That conference reflected a growing donor policy consensus about the importance of judicial reform and good democratic governance in the service of private-sector interests and economic growth.[19] As Sri-Ram Aiyer, director of the Bank's Technical Department of the Latin America region, argued, judicial reform "must foster an enabling legal and judicial environment that is conducive to trade, financing, and investment" (1995: vii).

This was not the first time donor institutions debated the role of the law in fostering economic growth; in the 1960s, the law and development movement also sought to link the two issues.[20] As Stephen Humphreys has argued, however, "the active mobilization of law across borders for economic and political ends" dates back to the colonial era (2010: 109). What signaled the newness of the 1990s wave of judicial reform was the ways donor institutions braided together concerns over economic liberalization, *democracy* and human rights, and the modernization of the state and its administrative institutions.[21] Reform was a matter of both state contraction and business-friendly intervention, unleashing the potential of private enterprise.[22]

Embedded within these larger agendas, reformers argued that ADR mechanisms like commercial arbitration would provide foreign investors and national entrepreneurs with more trustworthy mechanisms for resolving their disputes *outside* of the state legal apparatus. As the American Bar Association's Bryant Garth argued in a 1995 conference paper, private justice was appealing to multinational corporations that preferred to avoid the "home court" advantage of resolving disputes in host countries or getting ensnared in corrupt and backlogged legal systems.

Bank officials drew connections between their economic agenda and the good governance programs sponsored by donors like the United States Agency for International Development (USAID).[23] Ultimately judicial reform is necessary, bank officials argued, to ensure the "certainty and predictability" that investors crave, and good democratic governance was critical to that project (Shihata 1995: 13).[24] Yet bank representatives were at pains to reiterate that their institutional mandate was a circumscribed one. Reform advocates constructed the rule of law paradigm as a technocratic endeavor that could shed its political trappings; indeed, reformers saw depoliticization as a positive outcome. As Garth insisted, "Legal reform is no longer seen as the key to social change, with the result that there is now the possibility of 'depoliticizing' legal aid. Instead of seeing legal aid as the cutting edge of a political movement, it can now be considered a fundamental right of citizenship under the rule of law" (1995: 90).

The shared and recurring conceptual language and references to each other's work illuminates how donor institutions were exchanging analysis, debating theories, and comparing "best practices" in these regionwide meeting spaces. Through conferences like this one, an emerging assemblage of judicial reform advocates was taking shape in Latin America. Bolivia would put this emerging policy consensus and accompanying intervention strategies to the test.

Reforming Bolivia's Courts and Building Democratic Institutional Capabilities

By the time ADR arrived in Bolivia, it reflected a transnational narrative about how Latin American state institutions hindered private enterprise and stunted development. The same year it hosted the above-mentioned conference (1995), the WB began financing an overhaul of Bolivia's justice system. The project would accompany Bolivia's second wave of structural adjustment and a broader donor preoccupation with modernizing and decentralizing Bolivian state institutions.[25] In 1998, the Spanish Agency for International Development Cooperation (AECID) joined the effort, focusing its attention on training judges and attorneys.

As the WB conference heralded, this shared reform agenda understood market expansion to be the crucial mechanism for reducing Bolivia's poverty levels, which were the highest in South America. As the Bolivian project stated, its primary objective was to "create a judicial system that contributes to economic growth, facilitating the activities of the private sector and social well being, *guaranteeing basic rights to citizens.*"[26] In one brief statement of purpose, Bolivia's Judicial Reform project conjoined—perhaps conflated— the commercial and social aims of donor interventions, linking both to citizenship rights.

While the program incorporated ADR as a mechanism to address the concerns of investors, the WB was not the only donor institution supporting ADR in Bolivia. The IDB worked with Bolivian chambers of commerce in Santa Cruz and Cochabamba and the La Paz Bar Association to institutionalize commercial arbitration and spread information about its use to lawyers, judges, and businesses. Predating those efforts, USAID subcontracted commercial arbitration work to the Inter-American Bar Foundation (IABF) in 1990,[27] initiating its own Administration of Justice project in 1992. Bolivia adopted Law 1770 in 1997, institutionalizing commercial arbitration and conciliation. Following its adoption, USAID supported several pilot projects with law schools and NGOs that extended conciliation services to the broader public in a limited capacity.

During this period, USAID began reconfiguring the country's criminal procedures code. The project was contracted to Management Sciences for Development (MSD), a for-profit development firm specializing in justice-sector intervention. However, USAID's technical assistance team worked closely with their counterparts in the German Technical Cooperation Agency (GTZ).[28] The new Code of Criminal Procedures (CCP) dismantled the inquisitorial system, replacing it with an accusatorial/adversarial model, introducing citizen judges (juries), and making trials oral and public, among other "modernization" reforms.[29] USAID's and GTZ's technical assistance teams labored to create the necessary legal/legislative framework for the reform, trained jurists in the new code and its implications, and targeted the broader public with information campaigns about the new system. In its strategic objective close-out report, USAID celebrated the CCP's impact for reducing the average criminal case trial length from 868 days to 140 and cutting the cost of such a trial from $2,854 to $367.[30]

Many of these efforts aimed to help Bolivian courts fight the drug war—on the judicial battlefield. This strategic priority meant providing the legal and physical infrastructure necessary not only to prosecute offenders for drug-related crimes, but also to increase the presence of state institutions in coca-producing regions like the Chapare and Yungas. USAID reports also emphasized the backlog of cases created by the counternarcotics legislation that U.S. donors had pushed—Bolivia's Law 1008.[31]

Like the WB, USAID characterized these interventions as elements necessary to promote the rule of law, ensure stability, and thus enable economic development.[32] Unlike the WB, which regularly reasserted the purely economic priorities of its mandate, USAID could more freely acknowledge the political dimensions of its portfolio. In project reports, USAID framed its CCP reform as part of a larger effort to improve the accountability of the Bolivian state to its citizens and safeguard the credibility of democratic *institutions*. USAID's judicial reform project was slated to close in 2003, despite complaints from both Bolivian counterparts and donor representatives that many interventions had not achieved their goals. In the wake of those disappointments, however, USAID would renew its emphasis on ADR, reframing conciliation as a resource for transforming Bolivian citizens and helping them to avoid infuriating state bureaucracies.

The Politics of Diagnostics: (Re)making Sites of Intervention

A decade after the first stirrings of judicial reform initiated under the WB and the Spanish Agency for International Development Cooperation (AECID), the Bolivian Ministry of Foreign Affairs published a project evaluation. It was scathing. The evaluation states bluntly that reform interventions were largely "irrelevant" and "impertinent," and that the limited achievements wholly failed to justify the total financial investment of donor institutions.[33]

While the report delivered a more favorable verdict of training programs run by AECID, it described the WB-sponsored project as essentially a flop.

The evaluation blamed a lack of will and even antagonism on the part of its Bolivian counterparts (2002: 22). Why the animosity? Critics argued that the reforms "had their origin in the political realm and did not emerge from the needs of the Judicial Branch. . . . As a consequence, the Judicial Branch saw the reforms as an imposition from political sectors and not a need of their own, causing [the Judiciary] . . . to become an opponent to the transformations" (22). The targets of this particular judicial improvement scheme had rejected the proposed modernization plans, arguing that they were irrelevant to the real needs of the justice sector.

By contrast, the report accused members of the Supreme Court of resisting changes that would erode their power and threaten their "conservative legal culture," as several people would later describe the conflict to me in interviews. The report cites turf battles and overreaching by the new institutions created to help renovate the courts; internal disagreements over institutional roles; and profound uncertainty about what, exactly, the new laws permitted. It offers a bleak account of near-total reform impasse and wasted investment.[34] The Bank's effort to promote ADR occupies only a brief and unfavorable paragraph: the ADR initiative had a "negligible impact" (9).

My point here is that the Judicial Reform project evaluation (2002) did work beyond merely reporting breakdowns in communication or misallocated funds back to the project's funders. It ultimately reproduced many of the assessments that framed aid interventions in the first place. Bolivian bureaucrats and state institutions had proven themselves to be the impediment to modernization and economic growth that donors expected them to be all along. Such documents effectively anticipate potential critiques of their intervention strategies as the predictable response of bureaucrats or institutions that find their personal, political, and economic interests threatened by change. Although these criticisms were directed at Bolivia-specific programs, the assessments reflected a global pattern of reformers diagnosing state institutions and bureaucrats as obstacles to improvement.[35]

This perceived failure of judicial reform and the underlying donor theory of the state set the stage for what I characterize as a renewed emphasis on ADR with an expanded mandate: to transform not the state, but rather how Bolivian citizens relate to it. In 2003, shortly after the Ministry of Foreign Affairs published the unfavorable evaluation, Bolivia was engulfed in a series of conflicts that ultimately brought down President Gonzalo Sánchez de Lozada (Goni). Goni's first term (1993–1997) had ushered in many of the economic reforms and decentralization measures that defined the 1990s and accompanied judicial reform. The October 2003 uprising and the generalized sense that prior institutional reforms had failed helped to build momentum for a renewed emphasis on *informal* institutions, civil society, and Bolivian political culture.

Stated versus Strategic Goals

As USAID closed out a strategic objective grant titled "Increased Citizen Support for the Bolivian Democratic System" (1998–2003), it surveyed the state of "democratic values" and attitudes in Bolivia and expressed alarm. The aim of the programs housed under this strategic objective, the report explained, had been to improve government responsiveness—and thus deescalate potential unrest. USAID hoped that constituency outreach might help "overcome the distrust many citizens harbor toward governing institutions" and "act to reduce the threat that anti-system misinformation campaigns can lead to further political instability."[36] Yet just as this credibility-building programming came to a close, the city of El Alto erupted in massive protests. The government of Gonzalo Sánchez de Lozada quickly lost its moral authority as it deployed military troops to breach blockades and used live ammunition on unarmed protesters. On October 17, 2003, Sánchez de Lozada fled the country for exile in the United States. As Sánchez de Lozada's vice president, Carlos Mesa, assumed the presidency, he swore an oath to respond to the "October Agenda," to take seriously the demands it expressed. As an indication of his commitment, Mesa promised to usher in a special assembly to refashion Bolivia's Constitution and to confront endemic racism against indigenous Bolivians.

USAID's analysts watched these unfolding events and expressed enormous misgivings about the future of Bolivian democracy and efforts to redress Alteños' demands. They reported concerns that the Constituent Assembly would provoke greater political instability, fretting it might "create expectations that it cannot fulfill, or it may embark on debates that unleash deep-seated social, regional, political, economic and ethnic conflicts" (6). Indeed, all of the people I interviewed about the creation of Bolivia's network of IJCs identified a single root of the program: the 2003 uprising. "It grew out of 2003," the program director, Esteban Piñera, told me, "a petition from the Mesa administration asking for help to lower the conflictivity in El Alto."[37] Piñera argued that the demand for the industrialization of gas was a symbolic expression of frustration by people who had no sense of a real or satisfying future for themselves or their children. That prolonged, unaddressed discontent threatened to destroy Bolivian democracy.[38] As Piñera explained, "A society in conflict is continually reproduced, causing these conflicts to magnify to the extent that they produce conflicts on the scale of what we [saw in 2003]. As a consequence, [Bolivian] democracy was at risk." Piñera's assessment mirrored that of USAID reports: the "conflictualness" of El Alto, like that of the country as a whole, was antithetical to a functioning, stable democracy, and by extension, the stable investment environment required by investors and for economic growth.[39]

At the time, the USAID contractor MSD was wrapping up its work as an implementing partner of the "Increased Citizen Support for the Bolivian Democratic System" strategic objective (SO). Piñera said that his American colleagues urged the project team to respond to the recent events. He explained, "All of the contracts [related to the code of criminal procedures] were coming to a close, and this [opportunity] comes to me like an anecdote [at the end of the project]. And then Mesa's new government enters [the presidency]. What can we do? [USAID] said there were justice centers in Central America, I think—in Colombia or Ecuador. So we could reproduce one of those centers to help, shall we say, put the lid on [*tapar*] the spaces of conflictivity that existed in El Alto."

In Piñera's framing the IJCS—inspired by donor and contractor models in other countries—were proposed as a mechanism for "putting a lid" on conflict in El Alto, as a means to deescalate social unrest and help Mesa reestablish governability in the country. Whether donors understood ADR as an exceptionally constructive way to deal with recurring interpersonal and social conflict, or simply a vehicle for institutional presence in El Alto (and other "conflictual" places), was up for debate.

Piñera's colleague, Cecilia Ibáñez, told me that USAID representatives were deeply alarmed by the 2003 uprising. "El Alto, the epicenter of the conflict, was marked as the 'most *conflictive* city on the planet,'" she told me, chuckling a little at the idea that El Alto could epitomize the worst expression of global conflict. Yet that perception, she told me, drove the intervention strategy. According to Ibáñez, the team working with MSD was asked to find a way to help USAID get a toehold in El Alto. Ibáñez explained,

> You'll remember that moment was like an enormous shock; [Goni] leaves and Mesa is left in his place. What was going to happen? The social organizations had been growing stronger in Bolivia, but with that event, well, here's an indicator [of how the donor reacted]: the message

we received was that we needed to find a way to work in El Alto. So after the gas war, the crisis, and Sánchez de Lozada's resignation, well, we were with MSD at the time—in the final year of the project. And they say that they are thinking of shifting the focus toward that objective: We have to find some way to work in El Alto.

Specifically, the team was encouraged to target particular neighborhoods that had been identified as contributing to the conflict. As Ibáñez explained, the project initially targeted District 5 because of its key role in the uprising. "I mean, it wasn't like, 'well, the next step is conciliation.' [Rather] there was a fear about what could happen, and we were asked specifically to work in District 5. District 5 was the epicenter of the gas war." Ironically, the team was never able to get the land necessary to build a center there, or to secure buy-in from the local neighborhood association. With the District 5 project floundering, delegates from other neighborhood associations seized on the opportunity to bring the legal aid *obra* (project) to their zone.[40]

The uprising in El Alto was clearly a galvanizing factor in U.S. democracy assistance. But the project also targeted other "conflictual" regions of the country—namely areas enflamed by ongoing counternarcotics interdiction as well as significant waves of highland migration. Ibáñez added, "Afterward, Plan 3000 came up—and that isn't innocent either, that it was Plan 3000 in Santa Cruz, and it was the Chapare in Cochabamba, the Yungas. I mean, they were strategic areas to enter and to have a presence, to do something." Plan 3000 is a poor neighborhood located on one of Santa Cruz's outer *anillos*, or rings. A prosperous and ever-expanding city, Santa Cruz is designed like a bull's-eye, radiating outward from a core of wealth to working-class, poorer, and more heavily indigenous neighborhoods located on the outermost concentric circles. Plan 3000 is heavily populated by highland migrants—indigenous Aymara and Quechua Bolivians whose presence is a notable source of tension with lowland *mestizo* elites who largely occupy neighborhoods in the city's more central rings.[41]

Just as El Alto's mix of displaced miners and indigenous highland migrants encircle La Paz, so too Plan 3000's concentration of highland *kolla* migrants occupies the periphery of Santa Cruz. The city, known for the wealth of its mestizo and white elites, has been the political hub of the Media Luna (half moon) region, home to some of the Morales administration's most outspoken and organized critics, as well as the scene of a number of spectacularly violent attacks on indigenous Bolivians by white supremacist groups.[42] In contrast to these urban tensions, interventions in the Yungas and Chapare were linked to conflicts generated by the U.S.-backed drug war. That connection frustrated Bolivia's former chief justice (and interim president), Dr. Eduardo Rodríguez Veltzé.[43]

"Have You Come to Resolve Your Problems or Ours?"

When we met in his temporary office in the library of La Paz's Catholic University in 2011, Dr. Rodríguez was still battling treason charges. In 2006, the Morales administration initiated an investigation of Rodríguez for his role in decommissioning aging Chinese missiles at the behest of the U.S. government while he was serving as interim president between June 2005 and January 2006 (following Goni's flight and Mesa's later resignation; see "Uprising"). But Rodríguez's entanglement with the stated and strategic interests of American foreign policy predated his fateful entry into Bolivian politics. As a lawyer and then chief justice of the Bolivian Supreme Court, Rodríguez had long observed donor efforts to reform Bolivia's justice system, and he regarded many of those attempts with deep skepticism.

As the country director for the United Nations' Latin American Institute for the Prevention of Crime and the Treatment of Offenders prior to his election to the Supreme Court, Rodríguez scrutinized USAID's efforts to reform Bolivia's CCP during the mid-1990s. Later, while serving as interim president in 2005, Rodríguez would sign into law the creation of the National Access to Justice Program (Programa Nacional de Acceso a la Justicia) under Decree No. 28586. The decree was a bricolage of earlier reform efforts that, Rodríguez believed, reflected strategic donor interests rather than a sincere concern for redressing the needs of ordinary Bolivians. As a result, he argued, foreign aid interventions in Bolivia were consistently "disorganized," and donors pressured Bolivian officials to implement ill-fitting programs, showing "an unacceptable doctrinal influence" rather than a willingness to listen to the problems that Bolivian jurists prioritized.

Rodríguez insisted that USAID "didn't want to hear anything about" the findings of the court's self-diagnostic on weaknesses in the justice system in years prior. Instead, he argued, they were driven by a predetermined, cookie-cutter aid model and the overriding priorities of the backed drug war. Rodríguez explained, "I realized that USAID's interest was to renovate the criminal justice system, as they were doing throughout the region, with a special interest in . . . narcotics trafficking. They *only* wanted to hear about criminal justice, so we had some really big differences [of opinion] because there was a total imbalance of funding that was dedicated to serving their interest in criminal justice." USAID, he argued, was single-minded in its pursuit of the judicial needs of the drug war. And he extended this analysis to the work of ADR.

Rodríguez situated the U.S.-financed IJCs within a larger aid platform concerned with coca eradication and drug interdiction in the Andean region. "It was tied to the drug war," he insisted. "Where did they want to put the centers? El Alto. The Chapare. The Yungas. That's when I realized exactly what was happening. And I said, 'Have you come here to resolve your problems, or ours?'" Rodríguez insisted that while the Yungas and Chapare had more obvious connections to coca production, donors and government officials fretted that El Alto was playing an increasingly prominent role in drug trafficking. While Ibáñez and Piñera attributed USAID's ADR projects to El Alto's "conflictualness," Rodríguez credited them to anticipatory narcotics interdiction. For Rodríguez, the topography of USAID funding mapped directly onto the geography of both existing and anticipated counternarcotic battles.

Reading USAID project summaries, one gets a similar impression. Those reports speak of decongesting Bolivian courts in the service of improving access to justice for ordinary citizens, but explicitly link those efforts to freeing up Bolivian courts *to prosecute drug offenses*. USAID reports also link the American-backed drug war and the promotion of ADR:

> One of the most serious challenges facing the Government of Bolivia is a lack of public access to the formal justice system. This poses serious threats to the legitimacy of the Bolivian government. USAID supports the use of ADR, especially commercial arbitration and conciliation, as a way to increase public access to justice and reduce the backlog of cases in the Bolivian court system. This alleviates the burden placed on courts *and allows them to focus on anti-narcotics* and broader judicial reform objectives.[44]

Thus donor reports link efforts to reduce the cost and length of criminal trials and to improve citizen confidence in state institutions to the effort to fight the drug war. The connection, however, is a puzzling one, given that the cases addressed by conciliation are primarily *civil* cases, like child support, domestic conflicts, and contract disputes, which do not typically clog the *criminal* courts.

One explanation for the puzzling linkage may be the prevalence of mixed criminal and civil courts in rural and underserved urban areas. ADR programs could, then, help decongest courts responsible for handling drug cases, and in so doing, further an explicit geopolitical interest driving American-financed judicial reform programs concerned with stemming the flow of narcotics across borders and into U.S. homes. However, this is not the only possible explanation for the repeated references to the drug war. Alternatively, the authors of USAID project reports and program summaries may strategically be framing their interventions as essential to the U.S.-backed drug war in an effort to *justify* continued funding to these reports' primary audience: a U.S. Congress that is often more concerned with proving itself tough on crime and drugs to its own constituents than with the pressing justice needs of Bolivians.

As Winifred Tate (2015) documents in her research on Plan Colombia, shrinking post–Cold War budgets led U.S. military officials to reframe their efforts in Latin America as being focused on counternarcotics; the ominous "narco-guerrilla" category built on previous decades' counterinsurgency efforts, and it was enormously effective in justifying continued institutional funding in the region. Similarly, Judith Tendler's (1975) early research on USAID explores the ways *domestic* debates shape USAID's foreign-development frameworks, while Mark Schuller's (2012) ethnographic research on Haitian NGOs reveals the ways that Republican efforts to challenge the Clinton administration had enduring consequences for aid platforms targeting Haiti. Thus the recurrent appeal to ADR's strategic usefulness in fighting the drug war may simply be an artifact of report writers' need to position American democracy assistance as furthering U.S. security interests in an idiom that carries political weight on U.S. soil. In these ways, domestic battles in the United States have implications for both aid platforms and the ways they are represented to various audiences in project design, reports, and interviews with anthropologists.

Although it is difficult to discern (un)stated strategic interests from more opportunistic framings, based on the firsthand experience of people who were asked to design the centers, it appears that one of the primary objectives was to install centers that would increase an institutional presence in so-called brown areas like the Chapare and Yungas.[45] As one project summary reported, the "citizens will have a much greater confidence in their political system and institutions of government. *State presence will have increased, especially in the Chapare and Yungas regions where illicit coca is grown.*"[46] Project summaries tend to emphasize the centers as a mechanism of improving citizen confidence in the Bolivian state's capacity to deliver services—and of expanding the reach of bureaucratic agents into regions where they were once absent. Although the centers would offer *extrajudicial* conciliation, they would nevertheless be linked to the Ministry of Justice. The installation of centers in Plan 3000 would support a similar interpretation.

For donors, El Alto, the Chapare, Yungas, and Plan 3000 raised serious questions about "governability" in Bolivia, as well as what several USAID reports characterize as "antisystem" and authoritarian predispositions that threaten to undermine liberal democratic values and incite political instability. These tendencies, analysts argued, manifest during repeated bouts of social conflict, including the 2003 uprising. Writing shortly after that event, one USAID report observed, "A significant challenge facing Bolivia is its inability to manage political conflict productively and efficiently. Rather than resolving conflict, Bolivia passes inconclusively through regular crises that weaken respect for the state. . . . Although Bolivia has made enormous strides in judicial reform, considerable work is needed to convince the public that the rule of law is a reality."[47]

These critical analyses characterize recurring social and interpersonal conflict as an abiding threat to democracy and symptomatic of the persistent weakness of democratic institutions, as well as underdeveloped democratic sensibilities. Donors did not reject the importance of institutional reform; however, I want to suggest that the promotion of ADR reflects a further shift in intervention priorities from reforming *institutional* capabilities to transforming civil society, democratic habits, and interpersonal conflict management skills held by individuals and groups.

From Institutional Capabilities to *Capacitación*

Members of the centers' design team and the staff of the IJCS often sought to distinguish their personal ethical and political commitments to improving the lives of poor residents of El Alto from the strategic aims motivating the U.S. funders. Staff members were resentful of the ways that they had become embroiled in the Morales administration's accusations against USAID, and I explore those ambivalences further in chapter 3. What I want to highlight in this final section, however, are the ways that the donor concern with "putting a lid" on conflict in El Alto *intersected* with the design team's ideas about how best to resolve people's profound frustrations with state institutions. These two agendas *coincided* as the project shifted its intervention strategy from one preoccupied with institutional reform to an approach that emphasized self-reliance and the acquisition of citizenship skills, among them, conflict-resolution toolkits—an objective I explore in more depth in the following chapter.

In my interviews with design team members, Bolivian contractors frequently told me that the 2003 uprising reflected legitimate frustrations about both state institutions and the unrelenting exclusion of indigenous Bolivians from social, political, and economic life. Alteños, they argued, were profoundly fed up with corruption and backlogs in the courts, everyday injustices, and the failure of the state to satisfy their demands for basic social services. Planning documents they showed me suggested that Bolivia was facing a profound crisis of the state and especially the justice system, and prior institutional reforms had failed to redress these problems. Yet rather than continue to focus primarily on improving state legal services and institutional capacities, American aid programs turned their attention to El Alto's "conflictual" civil society. The stated aim was to respond to Alteños' demands for justice through informalism, while also training people to assume responsibility for resolving their disputes.

The project's emphasis on citizenship rights, Ibáñez explained, grew out of the initial needs survey that their team conducted in El Alto following the uprising (see chapter 3). That survey process led the team members to theorize the relationship between individual, interpersonal, and large-scale social conflict. For example, Ibáñez explained, "What we saw was that many of the problems that people had were not about 'I have a problem in the dividing wall with my neighbor.' It was 'I don't have water, or the mayor's office isn't being responsive' on administrative issues. So what did we say? What was our hypothesis? The thing that is a small conflict today can become an uprising [*revuelta*] tomorrow." For Ibáñez, everyday frustrations with state institutions on an *individual* level scaled up to broader social conflict.

The project coordinator Esteban Piñera and the educator Paola Chacón also saw conflict moving between scales, though in slightly different terms. While Ibáñez highlighted frustrations with municipal offices and political turmoil generated by inadequate infrastructure, Piñera and Chacón made connections between *interpersonal*, intimate disputes and broader social conflict; seemingly private conflicts such as domestic violence, child-support claims, and fights with neighbors and mothers-in-law were linked to the recurring social tensions gripping El Alto. As Piñera explained, "Family conflict produces more conflicts, stronger conflicts." Broader social conflicts, Piñera explained, are exacerbated by unresolved *interpersonal* disputes; high levels of irritability combined with stagnant courts made for a lot of unhappy people. The combination of unhappy citizens and unresponsive state institutions was responsible for unrelenting conflict. For Piñera, widespread social unrest could be understood as a kind of "scaling up" of interpersonal disputes, as unsettled frustrations escalate into unquenched rage. In these narratives, deescalating interpersonal conflict and violence was the key to deescalating public expressions of El Alto's "conflictivity."

In such analyses, the so-called public and private are intimately linked. Members of the contracting team argued that conciliation would help improve people's perceptions of state bureaucracies and democracy more generally by helping them avoid frustrating bureaucratic encounters. But ADR would also serve as a mechanism for helping to "form"—helping to *trans*form—Bolivian citizens. The centers were to provide *formación* (education) or *capacitación* (training, or in my usage, person-centered capacity building) in mediation and conflict resolution on two levels: first, by training a cadre of neighborhood volunteers in conflict-resolution skills, and, second, by providing ADR services to ordinary Alteños, who would seek out mediation for specific complaints—and go home with a new toolkit to manage conflict in other realms of their lives.

Neighborhood volunteers would serve as a critical node for helping residents of El Alto begin to understand their rights and obligations as Bolivian citizens, equipped with knowledge about laws enshrining human rights and empowered to resolve their problems for themselves rather than relying on an ineffectual, unresponsive state. As Ibáñez explained, "For me the centers are an opportunity to begin to educate/form citizens [*formar ciudadanos*], right? That it is not just about these twenty who come to work as volunteers at the center, but rather that permanently you are seeing a change, permanently you are seeing people being educated [*formandose*] so that they don't depend on formal authorities, because formal authorities don't give them any answers." The design team's early education efforts included training neighborhood volunteers about human rights issues and conciliation skills, both of which, they believed, would serve as building blocks of democratic personhood. Volunteers would then be empowered to embody those skills both in their daily work at the centers and in other dimensions of their lives—at home, at the local parent-teacher association, or in their mothers' clubs and labor unions.

The notion that ADR can profoundly transform society is not unique to Bolivia or new to popular justice campaigns.[48] During the World Bank conference described above, an Argentine jurist, Gladys Stella Álvarez, addressed ADR's transformative properties. Álvarez, who helped bring conciliation to Argentina and then export "best practices" to countries like Bolivia, argued that ADR could bring its "essentially democratic nature" to enable a deeper kind of change, beyond institutional reform. ADR held within it, she insisted, "the possibility of it inducing a paradigmatic social change from a culture of encouraging litigation to one of pacification (peacefulness) and cooperation" (Álvarez 1995: 79).[49]

But ADR's transformative agenda has deeper roots.

As Harrington (1982) documented, the antecedents of ADR date back to the American Progressive Era (during the late nineteenth and early twentieth centuries) and the movement to "socialize the law" among poor and working-class immigrant populations in the United States. Advocates promoted an entire therapeutic-judicial apparatus rooted in dealing with delinquent children through the newly created juvenile courts. "The state, represented by probation and patrol officers," Harrington explains, "was cast in the role of 'friend,' helping poor and working class immigrant children to become socialized or 'Americanized.' Both developments rendered the courts more interventionist" (1982: 51). Later reformers justified the informal dispute resolution as a "decentralized management model" in which "minor disputes are channeled into appended tribunals that emphasize therapeutic intervention by trained lay citizens. Individuals, assisted by mediators, seek to reach an agreement on how to restructure their future behavior to avoid or prevent conflict" (1982: 62).

Merry and Milner (1995) have traced the many contexts in which popular justice and community mediation programs have aspired to "reshape society and to give greater power over the handling of their conflicts to relatively powerless people" (9). In particular, American community justice models emphasized "helping individuals achieve full personhood and a stress on the expression of feelings as a way of resolving conflicts" (9).[50] The model of the Community Boards of San Francisco heavily influenced the ideological underpinnings of the broader ADR movement in the United States, as well as later efforts by USAID and the American Bar Association to export popular justice models worldwide. The Community Boards in particular emphasized notions of empowerment, self-reliance, and volunteerism as foundational to the construction of civic-mindedness and democratic practice. In this model, "empowerment suggests an enhanced self-reliance and a greater control over one's life. Through training and the participation of disputants, community mediation claims to empower both mediators and disputants by enhancing their capacity to manage their own conflicts" (16).

Similarly, the team designing Bolivia's IJCs understood their work to be empowering both mediators *and* disputants via new skills in ADR. Trainers would equip Bolivian volunteers and ADR practitioners with the tools they would need to help facilitate forms of communication and self-expression that were amenable to personal, interpersonal, and broader social transformation. Further, the centers would offer a space for El Alto residents to exercise their "rights and obligations," and acquire the aptitudes to do so. As one internal planning document explained, bypassing the bureaucratic tangle to rectify birth certificates would help clients obtain the very documents necessary to exercise their citizenship rights. Program designers such as Piñera characterized self-reliance to be an empowering opportunity not only to gain the tools of formal citizenship (i.e., birth certificates), but also to exercise *substantive* citizenship rights, and they linked both to the behavioral and characterological dimensions of ADR. That increasing self-reliance would further relieve overburdened institutions and relocate citizenship practices. As Ibáñez articulated it, "They don't depend on formal authorities, because formal authorities don't give them any answers."

Ibáñez's statement expresses widespread sentiments about the failures of the Bolivian legal system and people's deep-seated desire to escape its clutches. Indeed, the anthropologist Daniel Goldstein (2012) developed a similar kind of conflict-resolution program in the neighborhood where he works in Cochabamba in response to these familiar frustrations. The turn to extrajudicial conciliation in both cases reflects a convergence of popular anger *and* neoliberal approaches to the state and citizenship. Efforts to expand ADR *beyond* the commercial realm *and in the service of ordinary Bolivians* have accompanied development platforms that encourage citizens to take an entrepreneurial and self-actualizing approach to their own welfare with the effect of reducing demands on the state for redressing their grievances.[51]

One place this confluence is most evident is in the ways extrajudicial conciliation programs sought to incorporate neighborhood volunteers. ADR advocates celebrate the capacity of volunteers to embody citizenship practices and to serve as a node for helping others to cultivate those capabilities. But volunteerism can also be understood as yet another level of outsourcing the labor of development work itself. Volunteerism may extend the neoliberal processes of "off shoring, deskilling, and flexibilization," which "has impacted both aid practitioners and the character of aid work" (Hindman and Fechter 2011). That is, where anthropologists have highlighted the ways that NGOs now provide social service previously supplied by the state, we might say that volunteers are now taking over the labor of professional NGOs.[52] They are state agents twice removed. As such, volunteerism is exemplary of this shift in intervention strategies (from institutional capacity building to capacitación)—one that dovetails with promoting entrepreneurial and private-sector solutions to the problems poor people face. As I explore in the next chapter, it also reflected concerns that donors had about Bolivians themselves—especially the so-called *illiberal* tendencies of Alteños. But the turn to extrajudicial conciliation was not simply an imposed system. Rather, its appeal—to Bolivian contractors and to the very people who would utilize those conciliation centers—owes much to the fact that ADR responds to very real and persistent problems in the Bolivian justice system.

Conclusion

When I first met Azucena, she was a recently appointed intern at the IJC and was highly suspicious of the conciliation component of its legal aid work. She scoffed at the notion that ADR could really be useful for resolving people's problems. "After so many years working in the courts, you just can't convince me in a couple of months that conciliation is better," she initially shrugged. She would encourage clients to try it, she said, because it was her job. During her time at the center, however, I witnessed a significant transformation as Azucena herself began to promote conciliation rather enthusiastically as a more satisfying alternative to the formal legal system. I would catch her eye after listening to her counsel a new center client on the benefits of ADR: "It's free, faster than the courts, it's about both parties being satisfied with the outcome. Isn't it better to work things out by talking?" Azucena would notice my amused look, laugh, and roll her eyes. "I know, I know! I've been indoctrinated," she once hooted in mock exasperation. During the course of her work at the center, Azucena had shifted from being court-centric to someone who was seriously considering the value of ADR for the clients she served. When I asked, she said she wasn't sure if it was because she really believed it, or she had just repeated it enough times that she had been "indoctrinated." Either way, her own professional and personal trajectory mirrored—and was shaped by—shifts in foreign-funded reform programs; when I returned to visit Azucena five years later, she was teaching conciliation in a Bolivian university. She had become an ADR professional.

I have argued that the creation of Bolivia's IJCs reflects a broader shift in the strategies of foreign aid programs that have sought to promote judicial reform, from that of strengthening democratic and legal institutions—that is, institutional capacity building—to capacitación: equipping ordinary Bolivians with skill sets and values that are more amenable to liberal democracy and governance. These programs build on a longer history of donor efforts—

especially U.S. efforts—to promote economic and political liberalization and stabilization.

Although conceptually different, negotiation, mediation, conciliation, and commercial arbitration are components of a broader package of ADR programming introduced into Bolivia by foreign donors and Bolivian advocates as a more satisfying alternative to the state legal system. Bolivia was well on its way to further consolidating and normalizing mechanisms for ADR via commercial arbitration when the 2003 uprising in El Alto created a sense of urgency among many aid programs. That urgency crystallized in the widespread call for the broader dissemination of ADR into marginalized neighborhoods that served as epicenters for the conflict.

For democracy-promotion contractors, the 2003 uprising reflected the failures of prior waves of institutional reform. It also justified a programmatic shift that advocated bypassing state institutions in order to promote more "democratic" attitudes and practices among the general populace. This shift reflects a broad concern among foreign aid institutions and Bolivian technocrats with the "ungovernability" of many of Bolivia's more contentious populations, namely the residents of the city of El Alto and regions facing tumult over counternarcotics policies. Yet while the sites of intervention have shifted, the overarching goals of furthering a particular model of democratic governance combined with ongoing market reform have not.

Bolivia's IJCs emerged in response to events unfolding in Bolivia, but they also transcend the Bolivian context. They sit at the intersection of ongoing modernization and justice-sector reforms throughout Latin America, the U.S.-financed drug war, and a preoccupation with Bolivia's "ungovernability." The push to get Bolivians out of the justice system also reflects existing donor ideologies about the state, as friend or foe, of private enterprise, as well as the influence of social scientific theories about the importance of civil society in consolidating democracy. Early reformers operated out of a shared assumption: what is good for business is good for people. And yet, while ADR flagged in the commercial realm, it has flourished among projects promoting conciliation, mediation, and other ADR skills for the broader public, especially the poor.

USAID was not alone in making this shift. As I show in the next chapter, the European Commission, the United Nations, and German aid agencies (among others) all provided funding for nonviolent conflict resolution and "Culture of Peace" campaigns. As Ibáñez told me, "I could see that many of the [agencies of the] Cooperación saw what was coming and for that reason decided to change the course of their work toward issues that let them work closer with the community." This shift was driven in part by donor anxieties about "ungovernable" groups and protracted conflict in the country. But it also reflected, Ibáñez insisted, a genuine concern for helping redress Alteños' grievances because "the truth is, there was a lot of conflict."

Cultures of Peace, Cultures of Conflict

The Bolivian nonprofit organization JUNTOS ("together" in Spanish) is holding a public *conversatorio*, or model public dialogue, during the annual La Paz book fair.[1] School children race around the booths, laughing and lunging at each other while staff members from JUNTOS instruct others on a puzzle meant to teach cooperation and group problem solving. The event is part of JUNTOS's ongoing "Culture of Peace" campaign, which is financed by European aid agencies. The campaign advocates instilling participants with capacities—skill sets and values—that foster tolerance and peaceful conflict resolution.

Invited speakers sit in an inner circle on an elevated platform, while spectators form an outer ring. Over the din of the book fair, organizers play an opening song about the value of cultural pluralism and openmindedness meant to inspire the discussion. The master of ceremonies (MC) then invites us to observe how participants will be modeling a dialogue on diversity, demonstrating the importance of listening and learning to speak one's opinion respectfully while reflecting on the song's themes.

The MC tells the crowd, "These skills are useful for addressing both fights in your home, and fights in your neighborhood as well." In that brief comment, he summarizes a notion that has guided many recent foreign-funded interventions into conflicts in Bolivia: that training individuals in conflict-resolution skill sets will be transferable to larger-scale social conflict. The underlying—and frequently unstated—assumption is that this transfer also will help promote greater economic and political stability.

Over the next hour, participants take turns around the circle, sharing their thoughts. Most fall back on vague platitudes about the richness of diversity and unity amid difference. They are, almost universally, positive expressions: diversity is good, is beautiful; it makes us stronger. That is, all are positive until we reach Julieta Paredes.[2] Paredes is a well-known Aymara feminist activist, and the only person to explicitly criticize the exercise itself when given her turn to speak. Julieta leans forward, telling the crowd, "Look, it's a nice desire, it's well intentioned. But reality isn't like that. We aren't the same, however much we want to be." She goes on to comment on the hidden economic inequalities that surround everyone observing the model dialogue. "Some [Aymara women] came here with 10 *pesitos* in their pockets to spend on a book," Julieta continues, "while others can buy as many as they like. We are *not* the same," Julieta proclaims. "If we can't deepen the discussion on these issues, we'll just end up singing about pretty, superficial things."

As the session comes to a close, I approach Julieta, who smiles wryly. "How boring was *that*?" she laughs. "A lot of pretty talk?" I offer. Julieta shakes her head. "It's like throwing water on something when really we should just burn it all down."

THIS CHAPTER EXAMINES how discourses and practices of alternative dispute resolution (ADR) have traveled to Bolivia under the banner of promoting a "culture of peace" against Bolivia's—and especially El Alto's—supposed "culture of conflict" and confrontation. Foreign and Bolivian political analysts (and residents themselves) frequently characterize El Alto as a city beleaguered by poverty, social exclusion, disorder, and institutional disrepair. Some political analysts also have blasted what they describe as the "premodern" aspirations of Bolivian social movements, and the radical, self-defeating, and sector-specific demands of Bolivia's labor unions, which frequently utilize more confrontational political tactics such as street protests, blockades, and strikes to make their demands known.[3] More sympathetic critiques focus on the routinization of protest at the expense of other possible tactics, and interrogate the ways patronage (*pega*) shapes political engagement.[4] If Bolivian political tactics are routinely antagonistic, critics warn, El Alto magnifies those patterns.

Against these tendencies, the "culture of peace" concept has become ubiquitous, informing foreign aid programs, NGO projects, and domestic policy agendas alike. The appeal to construct a "culture of peace" is even enshrined in Bolivia's new Political Constitution of the State—adopted under the leadership of President Evo Morales. Article 108 (4) includes among the responsibilities of Bolivian citizens the obligation to "defend, promote, and contribute to the right to peace and to foment a culture of peace."

Much like democracy, "culture of peace" means rather different things to different people and institutions. Many Bolivian NGO representatives I spoke with were quick to caution that they didn't mean the *absence* of conflict. Rather, they sought to eradicate violence and aggressive confrontation as a means for resolving conflicts—which they described as a normal part of all human social life and institutions. Their aim, they insisted, was conflict *transformation*, emphasizing the productive nature of conflict for enabling social change and achieving social justice. Conflict, such advocates explained, becomes *unproductive* when it veers into violence, when it is not thoughtfully channeled toward finding solutions that are reasonably acceptable to all parties.

Many Bolivian proponents of the culture of peace concept (which I explain further below) cite ADR as a useful means to achieve their goals, and vice versa. ADR is a broad category that encapsulates techniques, methods, concepts, and approaches to conflict and its resolution, while "culture of peace" is a widely circulating phrase invoked by people across the political spectrum. For advocates, it's an ethos, an orientation that can be cultivated, and the practical toolkits of ADR help people nourish those sensibilities. Thus ADR is distinct from but related to the appeal to constructing a "culture of peace." Nevertheless, the two are often invoked interchangeably as mutually reinforcing practices and dispositions, including effective communication skills and a willingness to listen, deliberate, and negotiate solutions.

The "neutral, third-party mediator" personifies the stated intentions of ADR: to offer technical and apolitical intercession into conflicts, from the interpersonal to the transnational. Conversatorios—or model dialogues— exemplify the related project of promoting a culture of peace. Conversatorio is a term commonly used in Bolivia to describe public events meant to inform, analyze, and discuss current events, usually with the help of a guest specialist or a panel of experts. Conversatorios as they are used in culture of peace campaigns have an additional instructive aim: to model peaceful negotiation and deliberation in contradistinction to confrontational forms of politics or violent clashes, opening spaces for *rehearsing* a more respectful and measured encounter.

Yet participating audiences regularly raise serious questions about all the talk of peacemaking—equating it with demobilization and pacification—and even question the format of the conversatorio itself. This skepticism is not unique to Bolivia. As Anthony Wanis-St. John and Noah Rosen (2017) have argued, proponents of (nonviolent) direct action and negotiation often find themselves opposing one another (i.e., Sharp 2002), articulating some of the very critiques and oppositional framings expressed by activists and negotiation advocates in this book.[5] Nevertheless, those reactions sometimes surprise and unnerve workshop leaders by challenging them in ways that might better be described as *contestatorios*, or "talkbacks."

The local practice of holding conversatorios is derived from the Spanish verb *conversar*, or to chat/talk.[6] By contrast, I derive contestatorio from the verb *contestar*: to respond, but also mouth off. As one participant quipped when questioning a conversatorio facilitator, "When the Indian is bad, it's because he talks back [*porque es contestón*]." During such contestatorios, participants sometimes disagree over the substance of the debate, but they also raise questions about how they are invited to participate within it. In this chapter, I argue that in so doing, participants *refuse* the conversatorio's format as a *proxy* for the ways they are asked to restrict their expressions of dissent to particular communicative parameters.[7] As I show, conversatorios unmask competing political stakes and expectations of state-citizen relations as skeptical participants revalorize demonized capacities. Those combustive reactions reflect ongoing struggles over the limits of what critics have called "neoliberal multiculturalism."[8]

The anthropologist Charles Hale popularized the term "neoliberal multiculturalism" to account for the ways neoliberal reformers throughout the Americas "pro-actively endorse a substantive, if limited, version of indigenous cultural rights, as a means to resolve their own problems and advance their own political agendas" (2002: 487).[9] Drawing on Silvia Rivera Cusicanqui's term *indio permitido* or the "permitted Indian," Hale and other critics argue that this approach to difference authorizes a domesticated form of indigenous cultural rights by limiting more radical demands to transform power relations. In the context of settler colonialism, the Dené political philosopher Glen Coulthard has argued that First Nations have lost their critical edge by continuing to rely on the settler-colonial governments—such as the United States, Canada, and Australia—for acknowledgment, rights, and the restitution for past wrongs.

By contrast to acquiescence before such forms of cultural recognition, the anthropologist Audra Simpson argues that Kahnawá:ke Mohawk reject the terms of inclusion offered by settler states; rather than claiming American or Canadian citizenship, they assert their membership in a sovereign political order. In so doing, Kahnawá:ke Mohawk show that "there is an alternative to 'recognition,' the much sought-after and presumed 'good' of multicultural politics. The alternative is 'refusal' . . . a political and ethical stance that stands in stark contrast to the desire to have one's distinctiveness as a culture, as a people, recognized" (2014: 11; McGranahan 2016). What, then, are the politics of recognition, or refusal, operating in Bolivia's plurinational state?

Plurinational Bolivia is in many ways quite distinct from the contexts in which Simpson and Coulthard are writing (the settler colonial states of the United States and Canada): Bolivia is home to a large indigenous majority, and the president rose to power on a tide of indigenous mobilizations, some of it coinciding with multicultural reforms that emerged in the 1980s and 1990s. Yet Bolivia continues to reckon with the substantive transformations and limits facing a presidency whose platform celebrated cultural distinctiveness. Evo's administration promised national policies built around indigenous precepts and the rights of Pachamama (a vital force often glossed as Mother Earth).[10] Nevertheless, the Morales administration has been locked in ongoing conflict with lowland Mojeño-Ignaciano, Yuracaré, and Chimán demanding the right to prior consultation on mega projects in their territory—communities with their own complex relationship to extraction-based development.[11]

What contestatorios—as a mode of refusal—reveal are the underlying normative expectations that undergird "culture of peace" and conflict-resolution campaigns as they unfold in Bolivia. Those expectations include what communicative actions are admissible, as well as people's refusal to abide by those terms. They also point to widespread attributions of "conflictivity" to the essence or "culture" of particular groups, as well as reveal the perspectives of those who value Alteños' capacity to interrupt.

I begin by exploring some of the ways conflict has been "culturalized" (and thus racialized) in Bolivia. In doing so, I am drawing on the work of Wendy Brown (2008) and Mahmood Mamdani (2005), who have examined the processes by which commentators attribute *il*liberalism and certain modes of doing (*il*liberal) politics to particular cultures, religions, or ethnic groups. As Mamdani has suggested, this culturalization of politics asserts "that every culture has a tangible essence that defines it and then explains politics as a consequence of that essence" (Mamdani 2005: 17). This critique of cultural-

FIGURE 2.1 Protesters from El Alto march in downtown La Paz. Photo by author.

ization puts anthropologists in the position of writing against static theories of culture—something anthropologists have long abandoned—while still trying to suggest that there are distinctive ways of interpreting and being in the world that deserve our understanding.[12] Talking in cultural terms in Bolivia can veer from blatantly pathologizing to uncritically celebrating—and both are ahistorical. Explaining the origins of conflict in El Alto as an essential cultural product fails to show both the historical dimensions of practices deemed "cultural" as well as how people are thoughtfully analyzing power and making strategic choices. Those concerns surface as culture of peace promoters encounter consternation and barbed responses among the people whose politics they seek to transform.

A Culture of Conflict

Who embodies the ethic or culture of peace? Who is tolerant? Who practices deliberation? By contrast, whose behaviors are marked as particularly conflictual, and why? Which political actions are categorized as illiberal, authoritarian, barbaric, or antidemocratic—and who decides on the litmus test for these qualities? This is the stuff of theoretical debates in the social sciences, particularly political science and political philosophy.[13] In Bolivia, these debates are also reflected in popular explanations for recurring conflicts in the country. As I show, a widespread emphasis on the *cultural* dimensions of conflict reinforces the idea that certain groups are predisposed to authoritarian, antidemocratic, and illiberal forms of political engagement.

The preoccupation with Bolivia's political stability and its contentious populations is not a new phenomenon. Further, advocates have called for building a culture of peace throughout the country. Here, however, I want to interrogate how the specific populations associated with El Alto—especially the city's predominantly indigenous residents—have provoked acute political anxieties. By characterizing Alteños as unruly and even menacing, critics locate conflictualness in the racially marked bodies of particular groups of citizens.

Located four thousand meters above sea level, the city of El Alto envelops Bolivia's government seat, La Paz, which is built into a deep basin in the Andean high plain. Because of La Paz's geographical features, El Alto essentially acts as a gateway between the city and the rest of the country, a quality that has proven enormously consequential when residents of El Alto mobilize and block entry into the capital, as they did in 2003. Although administratively independent since 1988, the social, political, and economic lives of the two cities are deeply intertwined.

Rural migrants first began gathering around the "marginal/segregated" outskirts of La Paz following Bolivia's 1952 Revolution, which constitutionally freed indigenous peoples from bonded labor and re-categorized them as *campesinos*, or peasants.[14] Despite its progressive aims, the 1952 Revolution was not terribly unlike sixteenth-century efforts to move indigenous people along the spectrum of humanity through their incorporation into township *reducciones*.[15] Bolivia's Nationalist Revolutionary Movement (MNR) sought to pull rural Andeans along that spectrum from *Indios* (Indians) to campesinos (peasants) via their incorporation into *sindicatos campesinos*, or peasant unions.[16] These policies reflected the "continued need for political technologies that would include Indians in 'modern' Bolivia but would also ensure their control and continued subordination" (Postero 2007: 39).[17] MNR's solution to the "Indian problem" was a controlled inclusion.

But those revolutionary rural unionization schemes did not remain rural. During the 1980s, El Alto experienced a population explosion when a severe drought struck the already-arid region in 1982–1983. Subsistence-based indigenous farmers moved to El Alto in the tens of thousands. They were quickly joined by droves of tin and silver miners who were displaced when Bolivia adopted stringent structural adjustment policies and closed state-owned mines in 1985 (as described in the previous chapter). Thus the 1952 Revolution's sindicatos campesinos and their organizational tactics would later play a profound role in shaping political life of El Alto—and other cities throughout the country.[18] To this day, many residents of El Alto maintain ties to their natal rural hamlets, traveling home to fulfill social obligations and leadership roles, harvest crops, and host fiestas.

The Revolution's nationalization project, which targeted the country's largest mines, similarly shaped labor union tactics in the country.[19] Following the privatization of state-owned mines in the 1980s, displaced miners brought those strategies to El Alto as thousands were put out of work. The confluence of populations—and the rapidity of their migration to El Alto—had a striking effect upon the social and political organization of the city. As Juan Arbona and Benjamin Kohl explain, "This intense migration has created a political culture that combines aspects of trade unionism with traditional forms of land-based organization within a context of marked economic insecurity and social frustration" (2004: 258). Many of those frustrations have concentrated around the lack of basic social services, including clean water and sanitation systems.

Political organizing in El Alto also was profoundly shaped by the very neoliberal reforms that accompanied the good governance and judicial reform agendas of the 1990s and described in the previous chapter. As the Law of Popular Participation (LPP) created a new system for channeling citizen participation through grassroots territorial organizations (GTOS), it also shifted the scale of political mobilizations.[20] GTOs directed people away from the sindicatos (trade, labor, and peasant unions) that called for massive, national mobilizations and instead equipped Bolivians with "the idioms of modern bureaucratic democracy" and participatory budgeting, keeping their attention tuned to local struggles over scarce resources (Postero 2007: 153). Andrew Orta calls this the "localizing thrust of neoliberalism" (2013: 112; Medeiros 2001). In the process, LPP reforms and subsequent good governance and civil society projects sought to redefine legitimate mechanisms for political participation, as well as expressive modes of doing politics.[21] Thus the LPP drew Bolivians into a new democratic structure for channeling their participation, while simultaneously seeking to undermine the "collectivist" or corporatist politics of *sindicalismo*—the disruptive power of organized labor.

Ironically, the very mobilizations that took root in El Alto in 2003 were enabled by the LPP, which provided residents with political tools, new ways

FIGURE 2.2 Protesters block a major La Paz intersection. Photo by author.

FIGURE 2.3 A prominent billboard reads "El Alto is not a problem for Bolivia; it's a solution." Photo by author.

of imagining themselves as political actors, and novel channels for mobilization. Indeed, Sian Lazar (2008) has called the confluence of the LPP and sindicato organizing forms in El Alto the "organizational bases for revolt." Nevertheless, the LPP proved incapable of delivering on many of its promises, exacerbating poor—and especially indigenous—Bolivians' frustrations with their continued political, economic, and social exclusion. Political analysts, for their part, remained preoccupied with Alteños' persistent recourse to "confrontational" tactics.[22]

Following the October 2003 uprising, the United States Agency for International Development (USAID) commissioned a report, headed by the Bolivian analyst Rafael Indaburu Quintana. Indaburu and his team developed a "rapid assessment" of the conditions facing El Alto's then 650,000 residents. The report expressed enormous concern about El Alto's "irrational" and "chaotic" organization: anarchic and illicit land sales, disarray in the city's sprawling open-air markets, and an expanding population whose growth outpaced the city government's ability to provide basic services including electricity and potable water. Young Alteños faced limited access to education and dismal job prospects. This atmosphere, the report argued, "generates population pressure and a series of tensions and generational conflicts, and a brewing cauldron for confrontation, frustration, and all kinds of anti-democratic and anti-systemic (illegal) actions" (Indaburu 2004: iii). Further, the report held that the city's many trade unions and neighborhood associations acted as uncompromising, militant channels for strategically escalating social conflict. In a context of widespread poverty and disaffection, they accused unscrupulous, "self-interested" *dirigentes* (labor or community leaders) of fomenting discord for personal gain and power (iii).

In my interviews with them, Bolivian and foreign democracy-assistance workers similarly characterized Bolivia as a country plagued by authoritarian "collectivist" practices and antidemocratic sentiments that threatened to undermine the political modernization project begun under the LPP. As the Indaburu evaluation stated: "In this war of El Alto, the official institutionalism of the State and the systems of government are losing battle after battle against a discourse of separation, exclusion and violence, a discourse promoted by a frustrated population that has been put-off and ignored, egged on by the dictatorship of certain neighborhood and labor leaders, which has meant that official institutionalism has become clandestine, or has been subordinated to those leaders" (41).

In this political cosmology, El Alto intensifies wider Bolivian tendencies due to the historical confluence of its indigenous and miner populations.

What troubles critics most about these "collectivist" organizational forms is the way they are understood to impinge on individual freedom and individual rights to self-determination.[23] Rather than supporting a true, "participatory democracy," these associations subject their members to fines and sanctions to enforce members' participation in mass mobilizations, instigating regular blockades, strikes, and marches (Indaburu 2004: 49). In sum, analysts argue that El Alto's social, economic, and infrastructure problems, coupled with collectivist organizing tactics, have poisoned democracy in the city.

Such studies point rightly to residents' discontent with state policies and the failure to deliver basic services like sewage, potable water, health care, and education—as well as other commonplace sources of frustration in the city. They also correctly identify the confluence of political organizing tactics utilized by many trade and neighborhood associations. Yet these characterizations portray El Alto as a carnival of disorder and barely contained rage, a city crippled by its own political culture and the sectarian organizing tactics of trade unions, neighborhood associations, and other social organizations. These portrayals frequently skim the historical context in which those strategies emerged, focusing instead on the tactics themselves, and explicitly link the use of disruptive tactics to violence. In doing so, they define the terms of intervention as a need to counteract a pathological political culture and to liberate individual Bolivians from these strictures. The problem is not a lack of political participation, but rather too much—and the wrong kind. Yet this image of El Alto as a city besieged by conflict is not limited to debates about the legitimacy or abuse of leaders—of dirigentes and their political tactics. Bolivian analysts, donor representatives, and ordinary citizens alike often fret over the "conflictual" tendencies of their Alteño neighbors. I heard comments about "conflictual Alteños" so frequently that I started to keep a file dedicated to the ways people had warned me *"así son los Alteños"* or *"that's just how Alteños are."* In these accounts, blockades, strikes, and laying siege to the capital are an extension of tendencies inherent to "conflictual" Aymara migrants. These characterizations mirror what Andrew Canessa calls the "long tradition of seeing highland indians as telluric embodiments of a harsh and unforgiving Andean environment" (2008: 53).

Let me give some examples.

One afternoon I sat with a government bureaucrat, Daniela, chatting about her work with the Ministry of Justice. Daniela made the trek every morning to El Alto from her home in La Paz. She found her work rather unsatisfying and the commute made her even less enthusiastic. That morning we were catching up on current events. Sugar shortages were causing long lines and angry debate about rising food prices following the Morales administration's botched effort to end gasoline subsidies over the Christmas holiday. The move sparked angry protests, as bus fares and food prices skyrocketed. As the demonstrations escalated, Morales was forced to withdraw the decree and declare himself to be "listening to the people"—positioning himself as the people's president who responds to protest not with gunfire, as Sánchez de Lozada did, but with understanding and reason. Morales nevertheless bitterly decried the protesters as infiltrated by right-wing neoliberals bent on his destruction—rather than angry market vendors, housewives, and day laborers who could not absorb the sudden price hike.

A month had passed since the so-called *gasolinazo*, but food prices were still elevated, sugar supplies were down, and citizens were hotly debating where to place the blame. Her superiors had told Daniela that as a government employee (and a Movement Towards Socialism militant or party member) she could obtain sugar from one of the El Alto supply stations where residents were lining up at dawn to receive their quota. Daniela recounted how she arrived at one such storeroom, government ID in hand, and pushed her way to the front, past the long line of Aymara women waiting their turn. Much to her dismay, Daniela found that the storeroom had run out of the promised sugar. "People picked theirs up earlier in the day, and it seems like they sold off the rest [illicitly]." Daniela grew indignant with what happened next: "And the people [waiting in line] turned on us! They were so enraged. But that's how Alteños are—truly conflictive [*Pero así son los Alteños. Bien conflictivos*]. They want everything by force. They want everything right now. You know how they are."

"Is that really how they are?" I asked Daniela. "The price of sugar is up," I continued. "People are poor and angry with food prices on the rise. Could that be the issue?"

Daniela considered my argument. "Well, maybe it's their educational level," she offered. "They don't have education like we do in La Paz. La Paz is so different. Here [in El Alto] they just want to lynch you."

Much like euphemisms in the United States where "urban" stands in for "black," Daniela's comments about education indexed something else: race, a perceived rural-urban divide, and the widespread sentiment that El Alto residents were somehow inherently conflictive owing to their indigenous roots.[24] But she also invokes vigilante violence: "they just want to lynch you."

El Alto has received a great deal of negative attention due to "lynching" violence, as *vecinos* (neighbors) apprehend suspected criminals and physically assault them, sometimes to the point of killing them.[25] The city is riddled with dummies hung in effigy and explicit graffiti that declares "Thief that is caught will be burned alive," among other threats. Helene Risør (2010) has argued that these warnings reflect some of the more fearsome ways Alteño vecinos try to unmask criminal types and secure themselves against potential dangers in the absence of a reliable state. At the same time, Alteños are often themselves deeply critical—and fearful—of state agents. As one resident put it to me, "You cannot trust the police. Police and thieves share the same bed." For the anthropologist Daniel Goldstein, lynching violence is not an *unintended* consequence of underfunded police departments. Rather, it epitomizes neoliberal logics of "responsibilization" amid chronic insecurity (2005: 391). Bolivian state agencies explicitly espouse a discourse of "citizen security" that, Goldstein argues, encourages private citizens to take justice into their own hands (2004; 2005: 404; 2012). That context, however, was suppressed in Daniela's comments. Instead, by invoking education and lynching in short order, Daniela attributed the anger she witnessed from the women standing in line for sugar to the innate characteristics of a group of people: highland Indian migrants to the city of El Alto who bring with them uneducated, barbaric, uncivil practices like lynching.

Alteños themselves sometimes speak in these terms. Azucena, whose parents grew up speaking Aymara, once quipped that I had been taken hold of by the conflictual tendencies of *lo indio*—of Indianness. I had been infected by proximity. We were discussing language differences one afternoon, and I mentioned that for some reason I felt emboldened to stand up for myself in Spanish in ways I often didn't in English. In Spanish, I said, I was braver, more defiant. I speculated that it was because speaking Spanish was like putting on a mask or being an actor playing a role. Azucena laughed and corrected me. "No, no, it's not the Spanish," she said. "You spend your time hanging out with Alteños. *Te ha agarrado lo indio.*" *You have been grabbed hold of by Indianness.* And Indianness, she went on to explain, meant being more aggressive. It was, she implied, an inherent characteristic of Aymara people—but it was also contagious. I had caught the Aymara bug. Without intending to degrade, Azucena reproduced the widespread racialization of Alteños' biocultural disposition to being conflictive.

I am not suggesting that advocates of the culture of peace paradigm or ADR are consciously seeking to attribute conflictiveness to Alteños' ethnic background. My point is that the global push for promoting ADR and the culture of peace paradigm has *intersected* with widespread notions about the relationship between culture and conflict in Bolivia. "Culture of peace" as an idiom simultaneously creates an opposing category: a culture of conflict.

And in Bolivian debates about conflict, racially marked groups are often singled out as being predisposed to confrontational forms of doing politics.

These characterizations tend to dismiss blockades and street protest as the self-interested maneuvering of *dirigentes interesados*. Blockades don't express valid demands, but rather manipulated ones. Or they are the outgrowth of an essentialized cultural tendency among Andean Indians toward conflict, frequently conflated with violence. As with blaming dirigentes interesados, that cultural lens displaces attention from the larger economic and political dimensions of the demands themselves. Aid platforms thus intersect with the ruins of structural adjustment and existing racial tropes, while frequently disparaging tactics movements have used to confront persistent inequalities. And, as I argued in the previous chapter, following years of institutional reform efforts, many donors further shifted their attention to this "conflictive culture," advocating rehabilitated democratic skills, habits, sensibilities, and values under the banner of promoting a culture of peace. But what, exactly, is a culture of peace?

A Culture of Peace

The Norwegian sociologist Johan Galtung was one of the principal architects of conflict-resolution studies. Galtung popularized the term "structural violence," frequently utilized by anthropologists concerned with social, political, and economic inequality.[26] Galtung has been instrumental in disseminating those concepts through channels like the *Journal of Peace Research* (which he founded), his work with the United Nations, and his appointments at numerous universities worldwide. When I began researching conflict-resolution aid programs in Bolivia in 2008, Bolivians working with them regularly invoked Galtung and the American sociologist John Paul Lederach[27] as they spoke about the theoretical frameworks they utilized for understanding how conflict emerges and operates in the country.

ADR practitioners, conflict researchers, and agencies like the UN invoke the "cultural" dimensions of conflict in a number of different ways. One way "culture" is invoked is through what Galtung termed "cultural violence." What Galtung means by "cultural violence" is something rather akin to Bourdieu's notion of symbolic violence: the sociocultural symbols that justify and normalize both direct physical and structural violence—or entrenched social, political, and economic inequality (Galtung 1990).[28] These are the signs, symbols, institutions, and ideologies that buttress disparities in wealth and power. In contradistinction to such *cultural* violence, the United Nations

Educational, Scientific, and Cultural Organization (UNESCO) defines a "culture of peace" as

> a commitment to peace-building, mediation, conflict prevention and resolution, peace education, human rights education, education for non-violence, tolerance, acceptance, social cohesion, mutual respect, intercultural and interfaith dialogue and reconciliation, together with development considerations. It is a conceptual as well as a normative framework envisaged to instill in everyone a global consciousness and firm disposition to dialogue. The culture of peace is a collective attempt to create paths for harmonious coexistence, and regain the capacity to think about peace and order as dynamic forces of social, economic and political life, which endure through myriads of actions inspired by mutual respect and sincere attachment to non-violence. (UNESCO 2013: 6)[29]

That is, cultures of peace can be contrasted against the culture of war, violence, confrontation, exclusion, and intolerance. These definitions frequently cite education as a tool of cultural transformation *and* socioeconomic and political equality as a critical dimension of ensuring peace. Such definitions insist that peace cannot be achieved without substantive equality—an approach Galtung characterized as "positive" peace.

For many advocates I met, ADR is part of that transformative but nonpartisan toolkit: offering communication skills, conflict analysis frameworks, and opportunities to rehearse dialogue, deliberation, and negotiation. Yet, in practice, many target groups (e.g., Bolivia's "at-risk" youth and political militants) seriously question the concept of peace invoked by these programs, equating them with pacification. These concepts get hitched to local and national discourses about culture *and* violence, leading Bolivian audiences to hear and interpret the implications of these terms quite differently. As the epigraph in the introduction to this book indicates, Galtung is well aware of how attributions of violence and unruliness can be utilized to denigrate the people who are the victims of political-economic inequality, racism, and social exclusion. But Galtung's—or the United Nations'—*original* use of "culture" and its various meanings is not my point. Rather, my aim is to show how and why the globally circulating concept of constructing a *culture of peace* has encountered skeptical audiences in Bolivia.

Bolivian NGOs have been some of the principal channels of projects aimed at deescalating social conflict and promoting negotiation and deliberation as mechanisms to achieve a culture of peace. Prior to 2003, a number of foreign donors and NGOs were already promoting these techniques. For example, the German Technical Cooperation Agency (GTZ) worked in and around northern Potosí with a program called Ayllus en Paz (Ayllus in peace).[30] Following violent clashes in 2000, the program sought to deescalate conflicts between rural communities contesting land limits by reorienting inter-ayllu clashes into participatory budgeting models created under Bolivia's LPP.

On the heels of the 2003 unrest, the European Commission (EC) mobilized funds to support "laboratories of peace" with a rapid-aid program titled Negotiation, Deliberation, and Dialogue. The EC channeled those funds through Bolivia's nascent JUNTOS, an organization that makes appearances throughout this chapter, in order to address the country's "governability crisis." Over the course of the next few years, the culture of peace concept traveled with Bolivian *conflictologos* (conflict-resolution specialists) as they moved between European and U.S.-backed projects, shared conference spaces, attended ADR training workshops, and entered state bureaucracies. With them, concepts like culture of peace gained traction, if not a singular meaning. Those multiple and sometimes conflicting meanings were evident as I spoke with culture of peace advocates like JUNTOS's Santiago Mujica, who sought to distinguish his understanding of "culture of peace" from that of other institutions, including the Bolivian human rights ombudsman, the Defensor del Pueblo. Santiago explained,

> There are people from the Defensor del Pueblo. I respect them; they are good professionals, all of them. But their vision is more in the line of human rights—the need to defend the citizen against the state. Not of seeking a relation of equal to equal. For me a culture of peace means [resolving conflicts] between equals. But the Defensor defends the weak before the state. It's a different mentality. I understood culture of peace as "You and I are equals, we will respect each other. Not just tolerance. Respect." I don't know if I am defining it correctly. . . . Of course we held internal seminars [within JUNTOS] on interculturality, on culture of peace. But two days in a seminar is never enough to homogenize the ideas.

The concept may not have been standardized within organizations like JUNTOS, but it certainly was becoming ubiquitous.

Consider how José Pérez, the director of one of El Alto's integrated justice centers (IJCS), characterized his work: "Conciliation should be a real opportunity . . . for changing people's behavior. It's a chance for people to realize that the path they have chosen is not satisfying . . . and that there is another way, which is that of peace and tranquility. Conciliation, like all other forms of conflict resolution, seeks peace. Which is why our first slogan for the Centers was 'A Culture of Peace,' though many people misunderstand its meaning." For Pérez, conciliation is a tool for critical self-reflection, for changing interpersonal behavior, and for promoting a larger orientation toward peacefulness and tranquility.

Organizations along the political spectrum utilize the concept in their campaigns. However, just what people and organizations mean by promoting a "culture of peace" was and is always up for debate, and it is precisely that polyvalence that enables its spread and adoption within political platforms that are sometimes understood to be critical of each other. As I have noted, it is now enshrined in Bolivia's new constitution, a centerpiece of the Morales administration's *proceso de cambio* (process of change) platform. Further, Bolivia's most recent conciliation law (Ley 708), adopted during Morales's tenth year in office, includes specific references to promoting a culture of peace. Article 3:3 states, "Culture of Peace: The methods of alternative dispute resolution for controversies contribute to *Vivir Bien*" (the good life), effectively linking the "culture of peace" concept and the methods of ADR to a precept derived from highland indigenous communities and frequently invoked by Morales.

The various ways activists, NGOs, state agencies, and donors appeal to building a culture of peace offer transferable insight into emergent modes of governance that transcend the left and right in a divided country. Culture of peace campaigns frequently focus on cultivating the capacities of "ordinary citizens" to make Bolivia *governable* by improving on their temperaments and communicative skills and discouraging recourse to "conflictual" tactics.

This framing of the purposes of promoting a culture of peace stands in tension with some of the principle theories of conflict transformation (CT) advocated by people like Galtung and Lederach, and that have influenced organizations such as JUNTOS. Conflict transformation advocates would likely recoil at the idea that confrontation must be averted (and, they would decouple conflict from violence). Lederach himself has critiqued the emphasis on conflict analysis and negotiation skills at the expense of relationship building and *confronting* inequality (1997: 107).

My point is that as these concepts and methods are incorporated into aid portfolios, those dimensions of CT theories may not travel as readily. That dynamic may be due to ideological differences: certain donors prioritize stability, governability, and individual responsibility. Critics might therefore characterize culture of peace programs that appeal to equanimity in the face of persistent inequality as co-opting the language of conflict transformation. But that erasure may also be due to aid structures that demand quantifiable measures to justify continued funding, demonstrating that an NGO is putting donor money to good use, and using indicators such as attendance as proxies for success. Short-term, mass-produced conversatorios generate the needed numbers (Ellison 2015). So too do inexpensive, antiviolence "vaccine" campaigns like the one I describe further below. The slower work of building relationships and transforming unjust social systems is, quite simply, harder to count. Either way, culture of peace campaigns frequently emphasize the communicative skills of individual participants. And they often do so in forums known as conversatorios—training sessions meant to help foster that culture of peace by allowing people to observe and then rehearse those skills. Despite that apparently widespread appeal, however, some participants find the entreaty to peacemaking dubious.

Conversational Politics

Conversatorios are pervasive in Bolivia and generally refer to forums intended to discuss current events ranging from new antidiscrimination or domestic violence laws to debates over the appropriate use of oil and gas revenues. I could translate "conversatorio" as discussion group, forum, public debate, or model dialogue. Some conversatorio organizers see their work as engaged in a radical critique of Bolivian society where political issues are explicitly discussed and confrontational forms of activism are encouraged. Yet while the notion of holding a public debate places an emphasis on the contentiousness of disagreement and argumentation, the idea of modeling dialogue in culture of peace campaigns places the accent on seeking harmony.

In my experience observing culture of peace campaigns, organizers frequently intend the audiences of the conversatorio to both witness and begin to interiorize the dispositions that make dialogue and deliberation possible, and to reorient themselves toward the negotiation table. These are, organizers insist, skill sets that know no political party, no political allegiance per se. These are qualities that people may learn to cultivate across the political spectrum. In these framings, negotiation skills are nonideological in and of themselves. Instead, they become *methodological vehicles* for tolerant encounter, deliberation, mutual understanding, and, ideally, more effective social transformation.

Conversatorios are thus representative of the shift I described in the previous chapter—a shift from governance strategies focused on improving state institutions (capacity building) to those preoccupied with changing Bolivians themselves (capacitación). That is, governance is not just exercised through government ministries and bureaucrats, but also is enacted by shaping the behavior of individual citizens.

The French historian-philosopher Michel Foucault (1991, 1995 [1979]) coined the term "governmentality" to capture what he characterized as a shift in the aims of governance: from exercising control over territory to managing populations by inculcating within them dispositions that allow them to be more easily governed. Foucault challenged scholars to see governmental rationalities operating not by force, but by seduction: we are enticed to behave in particular ways. Modern power, for Foucault, is capillary; it operates through schools, hospitals, prisons, and psychiatric facilities. As we are subject to various evaluation rubrics and performance indicators, we begin to embrace them and self-regulate (what he called "technologies of the self"). We come to value these measures and our ability to meet them. In turn, we subject others to those rubrics, evaluating their behavior and finding it wanting. Drawing on Foucault, the political philosopher Wendy Brown argues that we must abandon our taken-for-granted notions of "tolerance as a transcendent or universal concept, principle, doctrine, or virtue so that it can be considered instead as a political discourse and practice of governmentality that is historically and geographically variable in purpose, content, agents, and objects" (2008: 4). The same could be said of behavioral changes invited by culture of peace programs.

Anthropologists have turned their attention to the transnational organizations that enable state institutions to further outsource, as it were, governance.[31] Kimberly Coles's (2009) work on transnational election monitoring is illustrative. Coles shows how transnational election monitoring serves a "governance strategy aimed at controlling and transforming the conduct of Bosnia-Herzegovina and Bosnians, as well as Bosnian democracy" (129). Election supervisors enact forms of governance at multiple registers, operating through their "sheer," "mere," and "peer" presence. Though apparently "passive," foreign election monitors *embody* transnational governance interventions, as well as model the ways Bosnians should perform democracy in their own state. Election watchdogs are symbolic, pedagogic, and suppliers of a normalizing gaze—that is, they incite those who are observed to change their behavior.

At conversatorios like the one described in the opening vignette, participants are meant to embody deliberation and dialogue for an audience, while also shoring up within themselves these orientations. Take, for example, the opening words of a conversatorio staged by the neighborhood transformation program Barrios de Verdad (run by the La Paz municipal government). Before a crowd of friends and family who had come to see their loved ones receive certificates of participation, the MC explained that graduating members of the class would be demonstrating the skills they had learned. Conversatorio panelists would take turns commenting on a preordained topic, showing, as one youth participant explained, that "our city . . . can initiate activities of pacification and no longer ones of confrontation."

Just as volunteers in ADR programs were meant to both model and be transformed by their work as community mediators, so too conversatorio participants are both an audience to this self-transformation and an active embodiment of a culture of peace. Such conversatorios relocate the promise of democratic governability and political and economic stability within the self of ordinary citizens equipped with values and skill that enable conflict deescalation and management.[32] Under the rubric of building a culture of peace, schools, NGOs, legal aid centers, faith-based organizations, book fairs, and a variety of other institutions and spaces provide an arena in which people learn to act in accordance with the principals of tolerance, dialogue, and deliberation. Clashing ideas are to be expected—even celebrated—but participants learn (or are *meant* to learn) how to discipline, manage, and transform their expression.

Yet these broadly circulating concepts do not reflect ideological consensus, but rather a vast terrain of struggle over the aims and means of governance in the country. Julieta's critique in the opening vignette is illustrative of these tensions. As I show in the final sections of this chapter, culture of peace advocates regularly encounter audiences that are deeply suspicious of all the talk of peacemaking. It is precisely in those spaces of encounter that target audiences raise doubts about the means and ends of peace, and try to reassert other possible interpretations of conflict.

Inoculating against Violence

Despite their efforts to nuance the concept of peacemaking—for example, insisting on the need to get at the root causes of strife—culture of peace advocates have not been able to shake many people's suspicions about the ulterior motives of their programs. At the public events I attended, facilitators regularly faced objections, especially from activists. UN representatives and NGO workers reported similar dynamics. This distrust owes in part to programs' association with foreign donors, raising questions about the *strategic* interests behind such campaigns and invoking criticisms raised by the Morales administation. But the skepticism also owes to how participants *interpret* the call to peacemaking itself.

Take, for example, a conversation I had with Robert Brockmann, who co-ordinated the United Nations Development Programme (UNDP)'s Convivir–Sembrar Paz (Live Together–Sow Peace) campaign in Bolivia. Although it was a relatively small program within the UNDP, the office had produced a series of beautifully shot, emotionally charged TV spots. Brockmann recounted the origin of UNDP's culture of peace program as stemming from violent confrontations in 2008 in the Media Luna Department of Pando—a stronghold of Morales's opposition.[33] Those clashes left thirteen people dead and escalated already-intense regional divisions. Brockmann proudly showed me the resulting videos, and I remember finding them deeply affecting as I hunched over his computer screen in the UN offices.[34]

The first video evoked the discord surrounding one of Bolivia's many recent referendum votes. In it, a group of youth wearing jerseys that say "Sí" ("Yes," a reference to voting in the referendum) runs into another group wearing T-shirts declaring "No." After some initial, antagonistic exchanges, tensions escalate. The youth grab sticks and rocks, and begin to menace each other. A woman scoops up her child and flees. Two little boys wearing jerseys for Bolivia's national soccer team appear on screen, playing with a soccer ball. One loses control of the ball and it goes bouncing between the two groups facing off at the end of the field. Surprised, one of the young men catches it on his knee, while another heads it back to the children—who thank them. The groups regard each other with dawning, mutual recognition and throw down their weapons. The TV spot then invites viewers to listen to others and to opt for peace. A second video features an elderly veteran of the Chaco war dressed in his full military regalia. The frail man stands facing the camera, quietly weeping and calling for peace in his beloved homeland.

Short on resources, Brockmann told me, Convivir–Sembrar Paz had been forced to focus on smaller activities. In one, an "inoculation" campaign against violence, organizers handed out "vaccines"—M&M candies—and had participants sign a commitment to nonviolence in their homes, schools, and other areas of their lives. Ironically, he told me, the caustic government minister Juan Ramón Quintana had participated in the campaign and even took his own dose of the candy vaccine.

But not all the groups that Sembrar Paz approached wanted to participate. Brockmann explained: "There's a whole generation of youth who have learned that the only way you can reach political goals is through violence. If you propose peace, they accuse you of being with the right." Acknowledging and incorporating the critique of pacification (subjugation) into his account of their activities, Brockmann insisted, "We make it clear that when we say 'peace' we don't mean peace to maintain the status quo, but rather, peace for change. Once the shooting begins, the possibility of maneuvering are zero. Healing wounds takes generations." Brockmann explained that in addition to those who feared participation might raise suspicions about their political allegiances, the campaign also had trouble populating its videos with representatives of all regions and accents of the country. It was, he told me, extremely difficult to find "indigenous [leaders] who had not made public pronunciations supporting violence."

Similarly, the staff at the IJCs reported that their audiences were sometimes suspicious of the culture of peace slogan. As one center director explained to me, "People confuse peace with putting people to sleep. Some think that peace means . . . not having the ability to react, or protest, or confront other ideas. But . . . you can respond reasonably, with other ideas, without the need to turn to violence. Culture of peace means having the capability to resolve conflicts maturely and responsibly."

Both comments highlight the ways in which culture of peace advocates invoke peacemaking as a characterological process but not one predicated on inaction. Brockmann insisted that resorting to violence actually limited the range of possible future action, sometimes for generations to come. And, it's not about being passive, the IJC director insisted. It's about maturity, about responsibility. It's about behaving like a responsible adult. Resorting to violence, to confrontation, is a sign of personal, political, and moral immaturity. Without intending to, however, the director's framing reinscribes some of the ways that critical commentators may infantilize people involved in more disruptive forms of political engagement. Frequently those critiques highlight the illiberal and "backward-looking" agendas of indigenous movements and other expressions of sindicalismo as an indication that Bolivia—or at least particular populations within the country—has not yet reached democratic adulthood.

Peace Lite

Just as Brockmann reported, politically active young people I spoke with were wary of invocations to peacemaking. In June 2004 Canela, for example, got a call from her cousin inviting her to a workshop sponsored by the U.S. Embassy. Canela was doubtful, but after some cajoling, she decided to tag along. The event, she told me, was an homage to Martin Luther King Jr., and the embassy had invited a lot of youth organizations, including, Canela told me, "very political and radical youth organizations" like the explicitly left-ist NGO where she worked. The organizers "talked about how King was this great antiracist leader, like a union leader who fought for justice. It was a workshop on conflict resolution and culture of peace." She told me,

> There was a sociologist who was supposed to be an expert, but he seemed more lost than everyone else. They used very simple language, like "you must not fight. You must negotiate. We in Bolivia transmit a bad image [to the rest of the world], that's why we can't develop [economically]. I can't remember the exact words. Then we watched a video about Martin Luther King who fought against racism. They divided us into groups and told us to create a slogan for world peace and that they were going to record whoever had the prettiest voice to disseminate the recording. I'm sure they got a lot of mileage out of what we did that day. But it seemed really "lite" to me.

Canela concluded that "culture of peace meant that you don't fight, you don't question, you don't criticize—or at least that's how I understood the message." In her recollection, the workshop leader argued that Bolivia's underdevelopment was due to its negative image as an unruly, unstable country; the responsibility for underdevelopment in the country lay at the feet of those who provoked constant unrest.

I asked how the young attendees reacted. "They just listened politely." Not every conversatorio becomes a contestatorio. Canela paused, gathering her thoughts:

> Look, I'm not against a culture of peace. There was another project in the leftist NGO where I was working—about culture of peace. We were working on the issue of voluntary military service [military service in Bolivia is mandatory]. After what happened in February and October of 2003—you know, [the state] used youth [conscripts] for violence [against protesters]. We said, "We cannot turn our guns on our own people." That was [the military's] way of doing culture of peace: pacifying the people with arms, a way for the military to control social movements.

I asked Canela to clarify what she meant.

"This was during that period when the U.S. wanted to set up military bases in Bolivia. We agreed with the idea of a culture of peace, but not the vision of USAID—to control [Bolivia] in order to export. We meant it as anti-*militarism*. But how did USAID use culture of peace? [They said,] "It's antidemocratic to do blockades. It's antidemocratic to fight. Marching is antidemocratic.'"

"But," Canela concluded, "democracy is when we all have rights and obligations—and it's your right to protest."

Canela wanted to reclaim the notion of "culture of peace" from what she perceived as a "lite" version that decried disruptive forms of political engagement as destabilizing, antidemocratic, and antidevelopment. When I asked her about the criticisms of dirigentes (association leaders) pressuring neighborhood residents and union members to engage in protests, marches, and blockades, Canela shrugged: "Look, dirigentes are not saints. But mobilizations come from the people. It is we, the people, who demand democracy. Dirigentes are never lacking in bread. Only the poor are affected [when protests provoke repression or are accompanied by scarcity, as they were in 2003]." By contrast to peace lite, Canela invoked culture of peace to criticize mandatory military service and the American military presence in Bolivia (and the United States' demands to legal exceptionalism for its citizens—namely military personnel—in host countries).[35] Further, Canela's criticism of the workshop reveals the ways the culture of peace concept ultimately serves as a framework for advocates and critics alike.

Through her study of development projects in Indonesia, Tania Li draws our attention to the fissures and contradictions in improvement schemes that produce "prickly subjects" and even countermovements.[36] Similarly, as Postero (2007), Lazar (2008), and Orta (2013) have shown, Aymara, Quechua, and Guarani Bolivians have taken projects like neoliberal multiculturalism and poached it for resources to mount a critical politics that is rooted in but pushes beyond neoliberal agendas and rationalities.[37] Canela is one such "prickly subject," challenging the "lite" version of "culture of peace" she encountered during the workshop, while also drawing on the concept to advocate demilitarization.

Bret Gustafson's (2009) study of bilingual education reform in Bolivia is illustrative. Gustafson calls Western education the "quintessential apparatuses of governmentality" (20). Nevertheless, he argues against reducing bilingual education reform to "an extension of neoliberalism" or a "privatizing and Westernizing conspiracy to rule teachers, Indians or both" (20). Rather than simply extending the reach of the state into indigenous lives and territories (or serving as a neoliberal wolf in bilingual education's clothing), Gustafson shows how Guarani scribes transgress and transform state projects through their engagement with them. While Gustafson warns against un-critically celebrating education reform, he approaches these policies as his Guarani informants did: as "an emergent field of encounter and conflict" (4). Culture of peace campaigns, like democracy-promotion programs broadly, have become one such field of encounter and conflict. These tensions were evident as ADR and culture of peace advocates encountered doubtful, bris-tling audiences.

Multicultural policies created new mechanisms of political recognition and participation. Similarly, with the spread of ADR and culture of peace campaigns, sponsors argue that the best way to substantially change un-equal conditions is to help people become more effective vehicles for their demands—whether with the state, a multinational corporation, or an ag-grieved spouse, friend, or neighbor. Toward those ends, conversatorio or-ganizers frequently present them as a kind of rehearsal space, one in which participants can begin to interiorize an alternative disposition toward politi-cal participation, intersubjective communication, and conflict transforma-tion. Yet as I found, some conversatorio participants refuse those terms of recognition.[38]

A Conversatorio or a Contestatorio? A Dialogue or a Talkback?

It is a Friday evening and the director of Bolivia's Colectivo Akhulli has in-vited me to a conversatorio with Carlos Hugo Laruta.[39] I have recently heard Laruta, a sociologist who worked for the UN's peace taskforce in Central Amer-ica, give a talk on his latest book examining indigenous conflict-resolution methods. That glossy book launch was held in the hip, tree-lined Sopocachi neighborhood and included a coterie of ADR advocates, academics, foreign donors, and the press. But the current venue is very different: a working-class neighborhood and an institution known for its critical voice and political activism. Akhulli, a collective of indigenous activist-intellectuals based in La Paz, was founded on the premise of critiquing Western epistemologies and historiography of highland indigenous communities—and I am particularly keen to hear the exchange at the event. Unlike the kinds of conversatorios I am used to seeing run by other NGOs, I suspect this one might be a little different.

The conversatorio is intended to discuss a hotly debated antiracism law supported by the Morales administration. The new law had sparked strong criticism for its criminalization of any person who expresses—or institution that publishes or promotes—hate speech. I am hoping the conversation will go a little deeper than the limited discussion at Laruta's press-oriented book launch. But I don't anticipate the degree of outrage that the affable Laruta provokes among Colectivo Akhulli's audience over the next two hours. In this conversatorio, Laruta appeals for harmony amid Bolivia's roiling political conflicts; the reaction he receives, however, is anything but harmonious. I soon realize that I am witnessing something better described as a contestatario rather than a conversatorio: a heated speakback rather than an agreeable dialogue.

Laruta quickly launches into an opening story. It's *his* story. Speaking with a pedagogical tone bordering on political stump speech, Laruta recounts how his own parents' marriage crossed regional and racial divides. "I am telling this story to show you why I made the life decision several years ago to work so that Bolivia might live in peace. I do not wager on confrontation because I have decided to opt for life. I prefer to focus on that which unifies us [rather than divides us], and to work in a way that is as harmonious and peaceful as possible." As the son of a highland Aymara father and a mother from Bolivia's lowlands, Laruta describes himself as a child of two worlds: "the world of *chuño* and the world of citrus and yucca."[40] As a result, Laruta explains, he chose to work for reconciliation between the two, "to work for peaceful and harmonious mechanisms to deal with the problems of our country."

Laruta then shares two stories meant to illustrate his point. The first involves a confrontation in the rural province of Ballivian, where Laruta describes witnessing a clash between two musical bands during an *entrada*, or dance parade. One group, Laruta tells us, played *música autóctona*, or indigenous music, on wind instruments. Their group was suddenly interrupted when the group of *comerciantes*, or merchants—a term indexing a wealthier, urbanized group of Bolivians—came around the street corner with a full brass band, their music overpowering the other groups. Their drunken revelry, Laruta tells us, overtook the whole street. The tension almost led to blows. But what would have happened, Laruta asks us, if each group had tried to be more accommodating to the culture of the other? How else might they have better dealt with the conflict?

Laruta's second story proves to be even more provocative. Laruta asks the group to think back to the horrifying events of May 2008 in the city of Sucre. On that day, a group of rural campesinos, who marched in support of Bolivia's first indigenous president, Evo Morales, were rounded up on the main plaza, beaten, forced to strip, and made to renounce their indigenous heritage while onlookers jeered them with racial slurs. Their bloodied faces and stripped bodies had shocked many Bolivians, provoking outrage at the brutal expression of unabashed racism. Others suggested that Morales's support-ers had strategically provoked the confrontation, knowing that the march would produce conflict that the Morales administration could manipulate politically.

The common version of those events, Laruta tells us, was that the event was a racist attack against defenseless campesinos—reflecting the latent and more overt racism troubling the country. The Morales administration used the event to justify the new law against "racism and all forms of discrimina-tion," the very topic of the evening's conversatorio. But Laruta insists to the group that he does not think the 2008 event was driven by racism. Sure, rac-ism was a factor, he acknowledges, but it was secondary. The real root of the conflict, Laruta tells us, was what he terms "political intolerance."

In Sucre, he tells us, "We saw that the faces doing the beating looked al-most identical to the faces being beaten. What happened in Sucre cannot be understood without contextualizing it: a pugnacious circumstance [*cir-cunstancia pugna*] that dated back months to a conflict between [Sucre's] urban population and the surrounding rural population. It was a politicized context characterized by an ideology of confrontation that already existed." This wasn't a racist act, Laruta insists, but a political one—complemented by racist ideas. It occurred because "we haven't constructed a form of citizenship sufficient to address these issues." Sure, he allows, there are people who are directly responsible for the attacks, but if we think about it differently, we are all "co-responsible [complicit] in creating circumstances that promote politi-cal intolerance as a shared feeling."

Laruta's comments provoke sharp disagreement. In response, a young man I'll call Marco, interjects:

> What we have here is the conflict between the noble Indian and the sav-age Indian. When the Indian is bad, it's because he talks back [porque es contestón]. He was a submissive Indian, but when he got into poli-tics, that really hurt. They say Evo is surrounded by white people who control him, but whether you want it or not he's the face [of the govern-ment]. The way I see it, the only way to avoid confrontation is to have the Indian go back to lowering his head. *Cambas*—sorry for the offen-sive term—will never accept us at their level. It will only be a tranquil country if Indians lower their head again.[41]

Of course, Marco is not advocating that Indians should adopt such an approach—that they lower their heads to bring peace to the country. Rather, he is critiquing Laruta's insistence that everyone shared blame for political intolerance in Bolivia. Marco argues that in Laruta's framing, the burden falls on Indians "lowering their heads" so as to put Cambas at ease. If peace is what you want, submissive noble Indians are what you need. Inverting the racist American idiom of "uppity" black women and men who step out of their (subordinate) place, Marco claims being contestón (mouthy) is an unwillingness to bow before oppression. But that refusal, he argues, is perceived as aggression—even violence—by people accustomed to power and privilege. As Beth Povinelli writes, "Liberal cultural recognition shifts the burden and responsibility for maintaining liberalism's exceptionalism from dominant to subaltern and minority members of a society. The subjects of recognition are *called to present difference in a form that feels like difference* but does not permit any real difference to confront a normative world."[42] Marco suggests that Laruta is asking indigenous Bolivians to present cultural difference without discomforting *mestizo* and white Bolivians—the model "permitted Indian," described by the Bolivian sociologist Silvia Rivera Cusicanqui.

Laruta balks at the suggestion that submissiveness was the only way to avoid confrontation. He holds out one hand and then places the other above it. The problem, he insists, is that "we were here—with a lot of discrimination against [indigenous] communities, but instead of leveling things out," he says, flipping the order of his hands and then slapping one down upon the other, "we are here. We have just reversed the discrimination." *Indigenas* are now on top, Laruta explains, "when really, where we should be is here," he says as he intertwines his fingers: "integrated." Laruta repeats these gestures, asserting his point. Bolivia is simply living an inversion of unequal power rather than being truly integrated. I watch the young woman sitting across from me turn crimson as Laruta speaks. She shakes her head vigorously in disgust.

This heated exchange drove home several points to me as I moved back and forth between institutions and activists promoting conflict resolution through conversatorios and as I watched the responses of the audiences for these conversatorios. The exchange highlights just how much incredulity conflict-resolution advocates encounter among the people they are trying to convince of the value of peaceful negotiation and its accompanying sensibilities and practices—though we saw with Canela's workshop, not all audiences react as strongly. The context was a debate over a specific law—just the kind of topic deliberative democrats might identify as an ideal subject of thoughtful dialogue and negotiation. Further, there is a *reasonableness* in Laruta's approach. Who would want to see continued violence? But the response by Laruta's audience was one of profound skepticism about what was being asked of them. More than disagree with Laruta about the *content* of his argument, those gathered disagreed with the entire premise it represented.

Laruta attempted to reframe his point as a call for mutually respectful integration, tolerance, and equality—rather than a simple reversal of power relations between historically subjugated Bolivian Indians and powerful, European-descendant Bolivian elites. He even foregrounded the shared phenotypic markers between aggressors and victims: "the faces looked identical." For Laruta, this constituted "indigenous-on-indigenous" violence, evidence of political rather than racial intolerance. But his audience was not convinced. Marco explicitly interpreted Laruta's call for peaceful dialogue as necessitating indigenous capitulation in expressing dissent. In so doing, he challenged the conflation of phenotype with race, pointing to the more complex racial ideologies operating in Potosí, as in other parts of Bolivia, as well as how particular expressive forms (being contestón) are themselves racialized.

Indeed, this contestatorio revealed not only how conflict-resolution advocates frame their efforts as adopting a certain disposition of tolerance amid widespread political intolerance, but also how these programs implicitly—and sometimes quite explicitly—locate *conflictualness* in particular groups of people, namely indigenous and poor Bolivians' (co)production of political intolerance. Chuño and yucca, in Laruta's words, index cultural difference. Recognition of that difference is predicated on its tolerant expression. The cost of admission for such multicultural recognition, however, is steeper for the "culture" of chuño. As Marco insisted, one must not be contestón because it makes Cambas (a category that is itself racialized—white) uncomfortable.

Laruta's audience interpreted his invitation to dialogue as requiring one side of a larger political struggle to articulate their demands in ways less threatening to mestizo and white Bolivians. The contestatorio thus critiques the underlying expectations about communicative practices guiding the invocation to building a culture of peace in Bolivia. Such expectations about the threshold for participation stood in tension with participants' own analyses of the limits of deliberative ideals and liberal promises of cultural recognition (multiculturalism) amid ongoing political struggles and lived experiences of socioeconomic inequality.

Conclusion

Widespread characterizations of violence and unrest in El Alto frequently reinforce the notion that the *causes* of conflict in Bolivia stem from the inherent character of El Alto's population—reflecting and intensifying broader tendencies in the country. In these accounts, El Alto holds within its ever-expanding city limits a destabilizing combination of rural Aymara immigrants and displaced miners—who brought with them the confrontational tactics of their campesino and labor unions. Further, the city is overrun by dirigentes mafiosos willing to put sectarian and personal interests ahead of the common good. For other analysts, legitimate grievances about persistent inequality have fueled the escalation of violence in the country and the appeal of more confrontational tactics, producing political and economic instability and posing an existential threat to liberal democracy. It was against this "culture of conflict" that many culture of peace programs sought to promote tolerance and deliberative skill sets, deescalating broader social conflict through both interpersonal, therapeutic interventions and new communicative practices.

The conversatorio is one paradigmatic expression of the ways the culture of peace concept is mobilized in Bolivia by people and institutions that are seeking to transform how politics is done in the country. This approach to de-escalating social conflict often recognizes and acknowledges people's frustrations with state failures and inequality. Nevertheless, in locating the solution in individual skill sets and sensibilities, it may place the burden of conflict transformation on the individual's or group's expression of dissatisfaction. Rather than seeing confrontational tactics as a product of structural violence and efforts to challenge it, such campaigns may place the accent on changing conduct rather than on changing conditions.

Indeed, for activists like Julieta, Canela, and Marco, the discourse of promoting a culture of peace remains suspect; it is an attractive patina on a policy program that they believe aims to demobilize powerful social movements—at the expense of asking tough questions about economic and social inequality. To use Julieta's imagery, a culture of peace is akin to pouring water on the flames of justice. Similarly, Canela derides the "lite" version of peacefulness and democracy articulated in the workshop she attended, suggesting that donors are merely seeking to domesticate El Alto's more contentious forms of "doing politics," and in doing so, they cheapen the role of protests in securing civil rights in the United States.

But just as the notion of building a culture of peace is multivalent, so too is the notion that El Alto is conflictual. In the wake of the 2003 uprising, many people celebrated what the residents of El Alto had achieved as a political victory for socially, politically, and economically excluded Bolivians. It was a victory made possible by those same "conflictual" tendencies. Take, for example, the way Raúl—a volunteer at one of the IJCs who went on to be-come a lawyer—explained the situation:

> You've seen those drinks that say "shake before use" on the bottom, right? We Bolivians are like that. "Shake before use" [*agitar antes de usar,* literally, agitate before use]. If we don't insist, insist, insist—agitate—then we never get anything. So we [in the IJCs] had to insist [on our demands for change] too. [Before we insisted on having pro bono lawyers at the centers] people would leave unsatisfied, unhappy. So we said we had to change the integrated justice centers, and we were able to achieve a lot of really important changes. Now the centers are full and enjoy the trust of the people; they come back, they feel well attended, happy.

For Raúl, the positive changes made to the structure of El Alto's IJCs were possible only because some people were willing to agitate for change—to see a situation as unjust and to insist on something different. In Raúl's account, this quality describes Bolivians generally, not just Alteños—and it's ultimately a *positive* characteristic. Much like Julieta, Canela, Marco, and many others anonymously invoked by donors and advocates who have encountered these cautious, critical audiences, Raúl redefined conflictualness as a mode of po-litical refusal.[43] Against accounts of El Alto as pathologically predisposed to conflict, Raúl, Julieta, Canela, and Marco insist that agitation is a political disposition that favors justice: a willingness to be contestón.

A Market for Mediators

Consulting on Conflict

For two months, five nights a week, a group of NGO workers, public servants, police officers, human rights lawyers, and others interested in conflict resolution have been gathering late into the evening for a diploma course on alternative dispute resolution (ADR). The course is being offered by a private Bolivian university in conjunction with a Bolivian NGO and an American law school. With each module, a new set of experts in ADR—from Bolivia and the United States—lead us through key concepts and a variety of exercises and worksheets meant to help us learn the tools of the trade. We spend our evenings working in small groups, practicing negotiation skills and mapping the actors, interests, and possible outcomes of various conflicts, tracing their escalation and denouement. Guest lecturers highlight the conceptual differences between negotiation, conciliation, mediation, and commercial arbitration. Course participants debate the usefulness of methods coming from the Harvard Program on Negotiation, American law schools, and European development consortiums.

It's a lively group of people who, in their professional lives, are often thrust into helping manage the very social conflicts we are now using as case studies in the class. There's a lawyer working for the human rights ombudsman,

Derechos Humanos, and a public servant who periodically misses class sessions in order to help mediate fraught territorial limits between two rural Andean communities. There's a high-ranking official in the Bolivian police force, a former congressman, and staff members from several Bolivian NGOs that are working on issues related to indigenous rights and environmental justice.[1] Many of the people in the room have been doing some form of conflict analysis and intervention for years, whether or not they had formal training in ADR.

Historically the Catholic Church—and more recently Derechos Humanos—played a key role in mediating conflicts between the state and social movements. However, conversations regularly turn to the ways these institutions have lost their credibility. In the absence of trusted, "traditional" mediators, course organizers suggest that Bolivia's recurring political conflicts require trained professionals. Thus aspiring participants have joined the diploma course to bolster their résumés and to get the credentials they will need to join their instructors as experts in the field.

Take, for example, one of the course lecturers, Julian Aguilar. Aguilar is a lawyer specializing in commercial arbitration. Before beginning his lecture, he rattles off his qualifications: a long résumé of international travel (Uppsala, London, Japan, the United States) and formal education in business law. Aguilar periodically inserts anecdotes about conversations with Japanese businessmen regarding the challenges facing Bolivia's economic development, or lessons learned in cross-cultural negotiation with his counterparts in Asia. These are subtle reminders of the cosmopolitan flavor of his work, and Aguilar positions himself as a transnational ADR professional.

Although he was scheduled to lead our module on commercial arbitration, Aguilar proposes that we expand the conversation to the broader topic of negotiation because it is useful in a variety of settings. "The Harvard system of negotiation," he insists, "is the only acceptable approach in the entire world. Others exist, but their doctrinal underpinnings are nonexistent [when compared to Harvard]." Like others who have led conflict-resolution modules in the diploma course, Aguilar reminds his audience that "conflict is natural, it forms part of life in all communities, all countries, all societies, all companies, and government entities, every family, couple or person. It's good that there is conflict—but it must be moderated and well managed." Social scientists would agree with Aguilar's emphasis on the *productive* dimensions of conflict, as would many ADR scholars. One of the *effects* of emphasizing conflict's productivity, however, is that it bolsters the market for expertise in dispute resolution.

Aguilar lists off the many reasons negotiation—as a technique of ADR—is so widely celebrated and sought: "It's an opportunity for both sides to grow, an opportunity to discover novel options, to better know the Other, to define the rules of interaction, to let out hidden feelings, and to analyze our actions in an objective manner, to reach compromise involving all [stakeholders], to improve communication." The list is expansive and resonates with the communicative concerns of culture of peace advocates, and Aguilar introduces several role-playing games to help us practice negotiation in small groups.

The final weeks of the diploma course are dedicated to applying those concepts, analytic tools, and negotiation methods to specific conflicts rocking Bolivia. The instructor, Jaime Martínez, is a jovial ADR professional who has worked with various organizations promoting conflict analysis and resolution. Like Aguilar, he has traveled abroad for specialized study in international relations and peace building. He's worked with the Germans, the Dutch, and the Office of the Vice President, Álvaro García Linera. Martínez also brings a healthy dose of critique to the "utopia" of Harvard's approach to negotiation, which he shares with the class and with me during a subsequent interview. Influenced by the "do no harm" development practitioner literature, Martínez is wary of good intentions. He leads the class in a series of reflections on the unintended consequences of foreign aid and NGO interventions in the wake of natural disasters. Like assessments of development more generally, Martínez has already anticipated and incorporated critique: He addresses concerns of power, and acknowledges that he takes a human rights *universalist* approach to culture—while recognizing that there are many legitimate criticisms of that position.

Martínez distributes a thick set of photocopies—a kind of conflict-analysis workbook known among specialists as a *metodo para la creación de escenarios* (method for the creation of scenarios). It's a systematic methodology for defining the conflict at hand, identifying actors that are both central and peripheral to any given conflict, and mapping possible outcomes—both worst- and best-case scenarios. He explains that while the methodology is time-consuming and complex, and requires a lot of practice, it is now invaluable among people who want to work with NGOs, state agencies, and foreign donors that fund projects under the banner of conflict resolution.

Martínez holds up the packet and waves it jokingly at the group: "I have given you something really important here. This methodology can earn you a lot of money as a consultant," he says with a laugh. Martínez is teasing—but only a little. People chuckle at the openly economistic statement. But his teasing tone does not alter the reality that one appeal of the diploma course

FIGURE 3.1 Participants in an ADR course map out the stakeholders to various conflicts in Bolivia. Photo by author.

is the credentials—and, by extension, the better economic prospects—it offers. Martínez has given us a mechanism for sorting through the many layers of a given conflict, *but also* for marketing ourselves as conflict-resolution professionals, or *conflictologos*. Along with certificates of participation in the course, participants now hold in their hands a technology of conflict analysis that will enable them to insert themselves into the inter/national market for conflict expertise.

Indeed, ADR offers an expansive range of uses for practitioners and potential employers. Along with well digging, infrastructure development, health promotion, gender empowerment workshops, microcredit, and indigenous rights, conflict is an organizing theme for donors and the organizations hoping to *captar* (capture) their funds, leading some development professionals to respecialize in conflict analysis and resolution. Against the backdrop of the widespread NGO-ization of both classic development aid and democracy promotion in Bolivia, local aid brokers have appropriated those terms and positioned themselves as conflict-resolution experts, taking up the mantle of promoting ADR and building a culture of peace against Bolivia's "culture of conflict."[2]

In their study of international business-dispute resolution, Bryant Garth and Yves Dezalay (1996) dub the coterie of jurists who helped to create the global field of commercial arbitration "moral entrepreneurs."[3] Garth and Dezalay are heavily influenced by Bourdieu's analysis of fields—in this case professional legal fields—and social capital. They trace the way jurists transformed the legal apparatuses in their home countries and then positioned themselves within those new legal fields as the virtuous arbiters of private justice.[4] "Rule of law" specialists circulate worldwide, targeting countries that have yet to fully harmonize their legal structures in accordance with international standards, and peddling their expertise in judicial reform and ADR.[5]

Bolivia's conflictologos can be understood as moral entrepreneurs in their own right. After spending two months together practicing conflict analysis, learning negotiation skills, and applying those tools to contemporary conflicts in Bolivia, holding class BBQs and sharing personal stories, the group had forged both a professional network and friendships, myself included. And, indeed, scholars studying policy and policymaking frequently trace the circulation and marketing of expertise along routes such as these.[6]

Yet one of the dangers of focusing exclusively on the ways people work to create and then capitalize on this market for expertise is that it reduces their involvement to instrumental or cynical maneuvering of an elite class of people, without accounting for the *meaning* people derive from their work.[7] Such an approach also makes it difficult to account for the enormous appeal that ADR and the culture of peace concept hold, including for people who are critical of donor assumptions and/or affiliated methods.[8] As I argued in the previous chapter, the culture of peace concept and related ADR programs run the risk of winnowing out questions of substantive equality and justice, and of demonizing direct action.[9] If that's the case, then why do people with political commitments to more radical social change nevertheless invoke these concepts and methods for their own projects?

I have suggested that this continued support is due, in part, to how flexible these concepts and methods are: they mean different things to different people—who mobilize them toward different ends.[10] But that support also is rooted in the personal meaning and satisfaction that ADR advocates derive from their involvement in these projects. ADR offers frameworks through which many practitioners understand themselves as contributing to social justice—while earning a living. Nevertheless, exclusively highlighting the value of ADR for improving access to justice, or emphasizing the personal satisfaction advocates derive from their involvement in it, would miss the ways that donor priorities and funding structure the kind of work that gets done in Bolivia.

This chapter seeks to understand the relationship between markets for expertise and meaning making, as Bolivian conflict-resolution specialists work to expand their professional opportunities and make a living "while doing some good." As I show, ADR is part of how many conflictologos I interviewed imagine themselves and their life's work—their *proyectos de vida*. Yet they often cannot shake other's perceptions—and their own self-doubt—over whether they are serving powerful foreign interests or shoring up ideological projects they might otherwise reject.

The anthropologist William Roseberry's (1994) use of hegemony is instructive for thinking about the ways that ADR and the culture of peace concept have come to shape—and perhaps limit—the terrain of struggle over democratic personhood, legitimate political action, and conflict itself in Bolivia. Roseberry has argued for using Gramsci's concept of hegemony "not to understand consent but to understand struggle" (1994: 361).[11] As Roseberry insists, "What hegemony constructs, then, *is not a shared ideology* but a *common material* and *meaningful framework* for living through, talking about, and acting upon social orders characterized by domination."[12] Bolivia's conflictologos periodically push back against the appealing claims made by global ADR advocates. Nevertheless they do so while invoking ADR as a meaningful framework for tracking their personal and professional paths, and for supporting justice.

These are not disconnected groups of people. Bolivia's nascent army of peacemakers circulates between state agencies and small NGOs, donor organizations and diploma courses, and international conferences and training workshops. They buy each other's books and cite shared conceptual frameworks. As they do so, they narrate their life trajectories, as they have moved—physically and ideologically—across the deep regional-political divides of the country, between confrontational forms of politics and negotiated settlements. The very technologies of development work they utilize, including the needs assessment workshops, applied research projects, and the "method for the creation of scenarios" workbooks distributed by Martínez, exemplify this relationship between markets and meaning making, as nascent ADR brokers seek new professional opportunities through conflict resolution.

Gloria Salazar: Conciliation for All!

A number of jurists were instrumental in helping to expand the field of ADR in Bolivia, first through the promotion of commercial arbitration, and later as a resource for the broader public. Dr. Gloria Salazar, for example, conducted a study on behalf of the United States Agency for International Development (USAID) during the late 1990s that concluded that ADR services should be expanded beyond private commercial interests, and then played a role in helping to craft the statutes that further institutionalized and legitimized both court-annexed and extrajudicial ADR. She described herself as having had an epiphany; she had worked on earlier efforts to introduce commercial arbitration, but she came to see those efforts as devoid of social usefulness. Working alongside an emerging group of Bolivian ADR advocates, Salazar told me, "We left aside arbitration essentially for the National Chamber of Commerce and private businesses. But the question was 'How are we going to conceive of conciliation for all?' We said that it has to be within reach of all citizens so that it is democratized, so it spreads, and so that all citizens have access to justice that is free of charge whenever possible."

For Salazar, the task was obvious, as was the end goal: to create a network of conciliators who could spread the gospel of ADR and, in doing so, transform their own orientation toward the justice system, as well as that of others. As Salazar explained,

> What did we need? We needed to train people to multiply, to replicate others. That was the work of all of 2005. . . . What do you want? To achieve a culture of peace. I don't need a [single] conciliator. I need legions of conciliators. Legions. It's a multiplying effect. I train you as a conciliator. What will you do? You will speak with your brother, your friend, and [in doing so] you are training [others]. And what will he do? He will speak with another person, and another. And another. Like a chain. That was the intent.

Salazar came to see it as her personal mission to promote ADR to a broader audience and to train "legions" of conciliators to carry the mantle. Much like Dezalay and Garth's (1996) "moral entrepreneurs" of commercial arbitration, Salazar became a key player in helping build the legal architecture that would consolidate the work of the integrated justice centers (IJCs) and other settings where ADR could be practiced.

This more expansive understanding of ADR and its transformative capabilities had two important consequences. First, it consolidated the legal and institutional framework for promoting conciliation under the banner of constructing a culture of peace. Second, it contributed to the growing market for expertise in conflict resolution—for commercial, interpersonal, and sociopolitical disputes. These efforts were neither isolated nor spontaneous, as I demonstrated in chapter 1. ADR's expansion in Bolivia reflects both unique historical circumstances (i.e., the 2003 uprising) *and* a global "commonsense" approach to judicial reform. Moral entrepreneurs like Salazar both contributed to this expansion and benefited from it. Those benefits included employment and the social capital of shaping national policies, but it also included feeling like they were contributing toward something important, a social good beyond their personal benefit.

Let me turn, then, to the experience of three aid brokers who helped forge the country's national network of IJCs. Members of the team responsible for creating and helping to implement the IJCs were often at pains to assert that their efforts were not mere copies of traveling development paradigms or performances in the service of foreign political agendas. Instead, they often highlighted their critiques of donor models and insisted that the centers were uniquely "made in Bolivia."

Cecilia: Of Best Practices and Donor Salaries

The October 2003 uprising in El Alto occurred just as USAID was concluding its judicial reform program focused on the criminal procedures code (chapter 1). Cecilia Ibáñez, an Argentine lawyer and legal scholar, was working with that project. When reflecting on the impact of the uprising on USAID's work, Cecilia emphasized the shifting terrain of implementing agencies contracted to carry out those projects, as well as the impact of their institutional differences on the work she and her team were trying to accomplish. Management Sciences for Development, Inc. (MSD)—a for-profit development firm contracted by USAID—was responsible for the judicial reform project that initially employed Cecilia. USAID would later contract the work of the IJCs to another for-profit development firm known as Checchi.

Cecilia was initially impressed by Checchi's work. She explained, "Checchi has a project in Colombia, the houses of justice, which work well. It's fantastic, and I had a chance to visit them. In Guatemala they have what they also call justice centers—although it is more tied to the formal justice system; it has also worked well."[13] However impressive those models were to her, Cecelia was frustrated that Checchi simply wanted to reproduce them in Bolivia. For Cecilia, the difference between implementing agencies was stark, even if the team working on the centers remained largely unchanged. She attributed this shift to an institutional "culture" of technology transfer:

> Checchi works on the issue of conciliation and on the [judicial] reform issue, and in the two issues they had the same logic. [Their logic is] "I have this toolbox I've tested in Colombia or Guatemala, I'll implement it here too and it will be the same!" I don't think they really felt the differences at the level of the centers, which were already opening, but for us [in the implementing team] it was really weird. We had gotten used to a certain freedom in our work [with MSD], and again one sees this imposition from the cooperación. Many times it's not so much . . . an imposition from the head of the cooperación, but rather an internal [imposition] from the [implementing] organizations.

For Cecilia, the implementing agency—not USAID itself—made all the difference in determining the extent to which Bolivian staff could design programs that responded to the Bolivian context.

Cecilia saw her work as simultaneously local and global. She had traveled to visit the USAID-backed programs in Colombia, to learn more about the work of MSD and Checchi in judicial reform and ADR projects throughout the region. The mandate came from a foreign donor. But the team, she told me, was determined to design a project that was reflective of El Alto's specific needs. When Checchi took over MSD's work, Cecilia argued, the *implementing* agency sought to reassert—to impose—its own interests and expertise at the expense of "local" knowledge, pushing existing platforms and "best practices" with little regard for the design team's efforts to map Alteño demands. The tension was a recurring one: "I finally just had to leave [the project]. I mean, it was unbearable working with them, really, because they never took the time to learn about what happened in Bolivia."

Cecilia also had plenty of criticisms for her Bolivian counterparts, particularly people she encountered during her prior work on the criminal procedures code. She was disgusted by how easily donors were able to push through their objectives—a dynamic she attributed to the scramble for foreign funding and its distribution along patronage networks. By contrast, Cecilia argued that the Morales administration had a healthy dose of skepticism about donor agendas; she appreciated their willingness to debate the issues. She told me,

I always thought it was more interesting to work with [Evo's] function-aries, because one can be with or against [his policies], but the [MAS party] people would sit down with you and they *knew* the Constitution, they *knew* how to debate, and they didn't debate the kinds of things you are used to debating with people in a suit and tie, but rather they stated things with more logic, and with more resistance. None of this "Come, impose on me whatever you like," that I had seen during the five previ-ous years I had worked in Bolivia.

Cecilia gave voice to critiques I heard from other donor representa-tives, including a project coordinator with a German aid program that was promoting ADR. Both women argued that their Bolivian counterparts were willing to simply accept—wholesale—donor impositions because they fed clientelistic relations. The instability of Bolivian politics, they argued, exacer-bated this dynamic as people sought to redistribute funds quickly before they were no longer in a position to do so.[14] Cecilia thus gave voice to widespread sentiments among Bolivians and foreign donors about the uses and abuses of development aid funding at the national and municipal levels.

Cecilia continued, "It's kind of an entrepreneurial vision of the public, no? 'Here I am in Congress, and I will get as much out of it as I can, I'll take advantage. And in exchange for it, well, whatever the cooperación [foreign donors] wants is fine.' It's a very individualist vision." In El Alto, similar sen-timents are often expressed in accusations about misspent money intended for *obras*, or public works projects.[15] The idioms of obras and accusations of individualism, or *egoísmo*, are common tropes in Bolivia for asserting social control over *dirigentes* (association leaders) through allegations of misspent project funds.

Moving beyond accusations of corruption, however, Cecilia further pointed to the ways foreign funding has restructured the Bolivian economy and created a class of citizens whose livelihoods are heavily dependent on foreign donations and programmatic platforms.[16] Yet Bolivia's development and NGO professionals experienced their own kind of precariousness, subject to the reputations of particular projects and the politics of particular donors. Independently, both Cecilia and I had spoken with former contractors who lamented that they could no longer find work because their association with USAID tainted them. One woman associated with the early phases of the IJCS described it as a kind of stain on her résumé, one she could not scrub off.[17] Cecilia, however, rejected this explanation, saying that in all her time work-ing post-USAID with the Office of the Vice President (under Álvaro García

Linera) it was never a problem. Instead, she interpreted those complaints as the frustrations of people who had grown accustomed to NGO and consultant salaries and were unwilling to accept a significant dip in income. She explained,

> From my perspective the paradigmatic cases in Latin America are Bolivia and Guatemala, where the cooperación raised the quality of life for a number of people. And when the cooperación began to pull out, or when problems emerged between the cooperación and the government—or when [the government said] we don't have to just open our doors for you to come in here and impose your agenda—many of the functionaries, many of the technicians who worked with the cooperación, began to resist the Proceso [de Cambio, Evo's political platform]. So, it seems to me that [there are] a lot of progressive people with good intentions, but to put it in black and white, they miss the old salaries they had with the cooperación.

When Morales rattled his sword against the undue influence of la cooperación (foreign donors, but especially *American* donors), Cecilia argued, people got resentful about the threat to their livelihoods in the externally funded landscape of donor projects. Of course, Cecilia was in the unique position of being an Argentine jurist: untethered to the Bolivian job market (she later took a job in another country) and perhaps less subject to accusations of colluding with the Morales administration's opposition.

The degree to which the cooperación internacional has profoundly shaped the landscape of Bolivian politics and development work has led some critics, as Rodríguez Carmona (2009) notes, to characterize Bolivia as a "subsidized democracy" or a *proyectorado* (a kind of project protectorate, a colony of development aid). Critics argue that donor institutions have become substitutes for national ones, generating not institutional *capacities* (as promised) but rather *debilities* and dependencies. Cecilia refocused this critique on the so-called NGO class—the people who depend heavily on salaries paid by foreign-funded projects—as well as the ways donor funds are drawn into existing clientelistic practices, redistributed along those patronage networks.

Yet the NGO class that Cecilia critiques is multitiered; within it, few are making the elevated salaries often associated with high-ranking national staff. It includes program directors working with Checchi and Company Consulting, Inc. and Management Sciences for Development Inc. (MSD), The Danish International Development Agency (DANIDA), and the German Organisation for Technical Cooperation (GTZ, now GIZ). But it also includes

Bolivian sociologists on short-term contracts, office secretaries, young "front-line" workshop facilitators, drivers, and security guards who stand in flimsy shacks outside fancy office buildings—all people whose livelihoods are tied to project funds and whose incomes are far more modest. And then there are the foreign consultants, whose salaries are, by comparison to their Bolivian counterparts, astronomical.

What I want to emphasize here are the ways that debates over the purposes, abuses, dependencies, and hierarchies of development aid form the backdrop against which ADR's moral entrepreneurs interpret their labor and that of their peers. Women like Cecelia Ibáñez and Gloria Salazar have helped expand the market for expertise in the field of conflict resolution by creating the legal frameworks enshrining ADR and by brokering new institutional arrangements and donor projects. But the very existence of that market for expertise is the source of much political debate and repositioning. Cecelia's Bolivian colleagues, Paola Chacón and Esteban Piñera, confronted changing donor priorities and increased scrutiny about their previous employers—forcing them to grapple with both the material impact on their incomes as well as how to interpret and represent the significance—the meaning—of their work.

Paola Chacón: ADR "Made in Bolivia"

Back in November 2003, Cecilia Ibáñez approached the university educator Paola Chacón and asked if she would be interested in helping MSD conduct an assessment of Alteño demands. Paola passionately recounted to me the process of conducting the study that would guide the creation of the IJCs: from an initial curiosity over what El Alto residents meant when they cried out for "justice" during the October uprising to a program that would offer alternatives to the formal legal system. "My sense is that [MSD] thought that the people of El Alto were really litigious. That they always wanted to litigate, and that they wanted to learn about the criminal procedures code," Paola told me.[18]

The MSD team was struck by the images of Alteños chanting their demands for justice. "You were here then, right?" she asked me. "Do you remember? When all those people died, you could see the women on television chanting." Paola tensed her shoulders and balled her hands into fists on her desk, shifting her voice to mimic the anger and sorrow people expressed at the time: "They cried out, '¡Queremos justicia! ¡Queremos justicia!' [We want justice!]. They wept. Remember? They cried out on television demanding justice, but we didn't know what they meant. We thought that to want justice was to demand that judges act correctly." MSD contracted Paola as a kind of applied researcher—the sort of position many Bolivians trained in the social sciences obtain with international aid organizations, NGOs, and government ministries. She saw herself and the judicial reform team as trying to solve a puzzle: people in El Alto were demanding justice, but what, exactly, did that mean?

Paola held a series of meetings with neighborhood vigilance groups to identify what residents thought were the most important issues facing their communities. What she found surprised her. Women would pull her aside after meeting with focus groups to say things they did not (dare) articulate during the formal gatherings. They described their struggles with domestic violence and their need for child support from negligent fathers. These, Paola concluded, were the real concerns troubling El Alto residents, particularly women—not the macro-economic policy demands made by the Alto's Federation of Neighborhood Associations (FEJUVE), an organization that played a key role in mobilizing the 2003 protests. El Alto residents now simply refer to "the October agenda" to invoke the list of policy changes that coalesced around nationalizing gas and rejecting neoliberal reforms. By contrast to those systemic critiques, Paola argued that people's demands for justice were far more concrete, including unreliable spouses and routine indignities.

Paola was emphatic that the design of the centers reflected Bolivian *particularities*. In her stories, she focused on the physical labor she performed: conducting surveys and focus groups, traveling around El Alto to interview residents about their demands. Those surveys and focus groups can be understood as a "need technology" utilized by the MSD team to produce knowledge about the population of El Alto in the service of their larger governance project (Hanson 2007). Anthropologists concerned with the techniques and technologies of development work frequently analyze the maps, surveys, project reports, and other tools used by state and nonstate (NGO and supranational) agents alike to make populations knowable—to produce new categories of intervention.[19]

These methodological tools for identifying and defining problems for intervention are ubiquitous in Bolivia, as are workshops to train people in the terminology of NGO work: in performance indicators, mission and vision statements, POAs (*plan operative anual*, or annual operating budgets), and grant writing. My argument here is that their usage offers insights into the ways such "need technologies" enable NGO workers, consultants, and conflictologos to experience their efforts as something rooted fundamentally in the Bolivian experience rather than as a traveling model imported from another context.

Through these need technologies, Paola and her team honed in on several major goals: the centers would transform the lives of not only the *clients* they served, but also the young legal professionals and neighborhood residents who would labor there *as volunteers*. Organized around the powerful trope of *vecinos* (neighbors), volunteers trained *from* the neighborhood would help solve problems *in* their neighborhood. A related goal included shaping future legal professionals by exposing them to the plight of poor clients. Paola explained, "This was an idea that came from Cecilia Ibáñez of Argentina. A new generation of lawyers, who are committed [to the people] and aren't trying to trick them. Here they would go to the school of life. Here they are going to cry with the poor and learn to work in solidarity. So that was the hidden objective, the hidden curriculum. To form a new kind of human resource." Switching into English to drive home her point, Paola concluded, "It was [an idea] that was *made in Bolivia.*"

I was struck by Paola's phrasing, "made in Bolivia." I had heard her colleague, Esteban Piñera, use the same expression a year earlier while I was conducting preliminary fieldwork and interviews in La Paz. And yet, as I have described, volunteerism is an existing component of USAID-backed ADR projects operating globally, and it is rooted in popular justice programs dating back to the community mediation and San Francisco community boards model.[20] Further, each center's emphasis on recruiting neighborhood residents and aspiring legal professionals for voluntary work reflects globally circulating appeals to compassionate labor: replacing—or heavily supplementing—state service provision and *paid* public servants with that of an *unpaid* "laboring public" (Muehlebach 2011).

Paola, however, casts volunteerism as a Bolivia-inspired approach to popular justice *by focusing on the process* of conducting surveys and focus groups. The embodied practices of data collection affect how development brokers understand the outcomes of their labor as project proposals grounded in El Alto. Ferguson and Gupta's classic analysis of the spatial practices of states and NGOs emphasizes how people come to understand and experience the state as a relationship of "vertical encompassment" despite its fragmentary nature (2002: 983). My point here is not how citizens experience the state or "transnational apparatus" of NGOs, but rather how those agents relocalize their efforts through data-gathering practices. Paola casts the centers and their emphasis on volunteers as rooted in Alteño realities—even if it was the dream of an Argentine contractor who had studied the use of volunteers in USAID-funded projects in Colombia and Guatemala; even if those projects had been inspired by popular justice models in the United States; even if both implementing agencies (MSD and Checchi) had long histories of promoting ADR as part of their institutional platform.

The very technologies of the development trade led Paola to *experience* an international donor platform as a project that was uniquely made in Bolivia.[21] Paola's *memories* of conducting these assessments were visceral and rooted in El Alto: they included the mournful appeals of women who gathered around her after the workshop ended and the fear that crept through her as she made her way home late at night, passing through the notoriously assault-prone Ceja.[22] These development artifacts were borne of the exhausting process of facilitating all those workshops in the bitter cold. The sensory, embodied quality of deploying those "need technologies" helped reinforce the *localness* of the proposals she helped co-construct. These visceral qualities also reinforced the meaning these experiences held for Paola in thinking about her personal and professional trajectory. She often reflected with me about how she too was transformed. But Paola's colleague Esteban pushed the argument further, forcefully positioning himself and the design team's work as confronting Bolivia's "culture of copying" and also taking a stand against it.

Esteban Piñera: Against a "Culture of the Copy"

Esteban Piñera directed the project for MSD and then Checchi, working closely with both women. In an interview, he framed his concerns less in terms of employment or the economic interests of Bolivia's "NGO class" and more as a historical tendency that had plagued the country since its independence in 1825. On a blindingly bright day, I sat with Esteban on a park bench not far from USAID's headquarters in La Paz. As we talked about his work coordinating judicial reform projects—first with MSD and later with Checchi—Esteban frequently referred to the books he was reading that inspired further reflection on his professional trajectory and the challenges facing Bolivia in the plurinational era. Esteban lamented what he called Bolivia's "culture of the copy," and insisted that he personally pushed back against his American superiors when they advocated that the team travel to visit other ADR-implementing countries in order to observe their legal aid models.

Esteban spent much of our second interview critiquing aid efforts that sought to impose externally designed prototypes. He argued that American contractors urged his team to reproduce "best practices" from other contexts. He positioned himself as trying to break with this pattern. But he also described what he believed to be a Bolivian propensity to "merely copy" foreign legal systems and models. This was not, he insisted, a new phenomenon specific to USAID. He explained, "The policy of Bolivians since we were liberated [from colonialism] was, 'I like to copy.' Our entire legal system is copied. President Santa Cruz in 1835 or '36 brought copies of the French codes, but he never understood *our* reality. [Bolivian] society is qualitatively different [from French]. These codes, this [legal] institutionality, were never ours; [they were] foreign."

As Esteban put it, simply importing "best practices" would be akin to "putting on an arm that is not your own. It will never work. It isn't coherent. The first thing you have to do is understand your own body." In framing legal imports this way, Esteban broadened the critique beyond contemporary debates about the imposition of aid agendas and the role of USAID in the country to a historical pattern of adopting foreign models.

By contrast to such mimicry, Esteban argued, he and his MSD team hoped to do something different. Esteban recalled, "We had a really outstanding group of people and we started to discuss [the issues] . . . and we said, no, we are not going to go for the technical solution, 'There is conflict here, let's put in a court.' Not at all. Instead, we asked citizens [their views]. First we asked what kinds of conflicts they have and if anyone resolves those conflicts for them—and the answer was 'No.'" For Esteban, the decision to focus on alternative conflict-resolution mechanisms was a rejection of the "culture of the copy" and of a Bolivian disposition toward litigiousness. He highlighted, as Paola did, the techniques of survey and focus groups as emblematic of the ways the IJCs reflected a bottom-up enterprise. As such, Piñera insisted that the centers reflected *Bolivian* reality, Bolivian demands, *and* Bolivian solutions. And, as with his colleague Paola, the appeal to the "made in Bolivia" quality of the centers belies an existing American donor agenda that *included* prior efforts to promote informal dispute-resolution mechanisms throughout Central and South America beginning in the 1990s.

There are a number of possible explanations for why Paola and Esteban cast their work in terms of newness, *Bolivianness*, while Cecilia more openly acknowledges the influence of the donor platform. An obvious explanation would be their differential positioning: Cecelia is an Argentine jurist with experience working with transnational legal organizations; she analyzes the programs from the position of someone who is herself circulating within an *international* network of legal training and expertise. Others might interpret Paola's and Esteban's insistence on the program's Bolivianness as naïve or disingenuous. Such an interpretation might suggest that both are strategically repositioning their work in the midst of a widespread critique of U.S. aid, downplaying the foreign quality of the programs and instead emphasizing the ways they responded to local demands. A third explanation might be that they are so heavily invested in giving meaning to their work or positioning themselves as innovators that they ignore or suppress institutional parallels across country contexts.

I think such characterizations flatten the complex ways people like Paola, Esteban, and Cecilia—including professional development workers, applied social scientists, and researchers—are often entangled in the politics and conflicting aims of programs like the IJCS. As the anthropologist Brett Gustafson has noted regarding his role in conducting focus groups and interviews that were utilized to justify new legislation on bilingual intercultural education, those efforts may be reduced to political tokens despite a development worker or researcher's best intentions (2009: 141). Setting out to revolutionize the Bolivian education system, Gustafson and his colleagues were later forced to ask themselves, "Had we spoken truth to power, or had development made us speak?" (2009: 141). That ambivalence resonates with the adamant—yet sometimes disquieted—ways Bolivian aid brokers characterized their work as uniquely "made in Bolivia." People like Esteban and Paola worry they have been ventriloquized to speak on behalf of donor agendas, and yet they recall their exhausting labor and their commitment to speak back against a "culture of the copy."

Insisting that the IJCS were made in Bolivia, Paola and Esteban invoked the postcolonial discourse that pits Bolivian reality against the imposition of foreign agendas, and reflects people's self-consciousness about the widespread critique that NGOs and foreign donors were furthering neoliberal policies and U.S. strategic interests. Indeed, many governmental websites and billboards promoting Evo Morales's decolonization platform include the logo *Hecho en Bolivia: Consume lo nuestro, emplea a los nuestros* (Made in Bolivia: Consume our products, employ our people). The ragged font mimics an ink stamp cast against the red, yellow, and green of the Bolivian flag. Paola and Esteban invoked the logo—and stamped the IJCS with this ubiquitous postcolonial slogan. Esteban even took it a step further, telling me that like Bolivian quinoa or alpaca wool, the centers might now be ready for export to *other* places that could learn from the Bolivian model; he held this aspiration despite his own refusal to copy model programs imported from elsewhere.

Ironically, both Esteban and Paola code-switched into English to tell me that the IJCS were uniquely made in Bolivia. Not the Spanish *hecho en Bolivia*. That sudden use of English seemed to betray a nagging contradiction: for all their efforts—the focus groups, surveys, and late-night meetings with neighborhood associations—the resulting program nevertheless fit neatly within an existing, contractor-specific intervention strategy, and ultimately served the much simpler purpose of helping USAID get a toe-hold in El Alto, as it had always desired. Had Paola, Esteban, Cecilia, and others working on the project spoken back to USAID by refusing to simply adopt existing model programs and best practices from Guatemala and Colombia? Or had USAID made them speak in the language of ADR?

In discussing Paola's experience, I emphasized the embodied practices that led her to experience the origins of the centers as uniquely "local." In Esteban's case, rather than reduce his framing to misrecognition (or misrepresentation), I want to suggest that this emphasis on the "local" origins of these transnational campaigns in part reflects the ways ADR has captured people's imaginations. ADR, like the broader idiom of building a culture of peace, has become a meaningful framework for the people tasked with its spread. That meaningfulness is evident in the ways they speak about their own experiences of struggling to make sense of and then respond to Alteño demands, or innovatively breaking with a "culture of the copy." The appeal of ADR and the broader culture of peace concept has been enabled—perhaps created—by an expanding market for expertise in the field of peace building. But its resonance, as I show in the following sections, owes much to the ways advocates and practitioners narrate their involvement as part of their proyectos de vida.

The Blockade Is the Invitation

Santiago Mujica's personal and professional trajectory reflects one such proyecto de vida or life project. Santiago did not work with the IJCs. Instead, his life trajectory was entwined with conflict-resolution programs targeting the mining sector. I met Santiago through his work with the Bolivian NGO JUNTOS, and encountered him again in the diploma course that I described at the beginning of this chapter. A former miner and longtime union organizer, Santiago was first introduced to ADR in a workshop sponsored by a Canadian aid agency whose stated objective was to provide Bolivian mining communities with skills that would make them more effective in their negotiations with Canadian and other transnational mining corporations.

As we talked about his experience working with the Canadians, Santiago often mentioned criticisms he had heard about that kind of collaboration—namely, that it was a form of co-optation. He would pause and pose it to me as a question. Of the time he was flown by a Canadian mining company to a conference of indigenous leaders invited to talk about their struggles on behalf of their communities, he asked me, "Do you think that could have been—what do they call it? Co-optation?" Before I could answer, he continued: "I suppose it could have been. I can see that." Nevertheless, Santiago believed the approaches he was learning would be useful for the communities he cared most about: miners and their families. That belief was rooted in his biography.

Over the course of his life, Santiago moved from working as a *militante* (member of the union base) to occupying a position as a *dirigente sindical* (labor leader) in one of Bolivia's most famous mines to administering foreign-funded ADR projects with the mining sector and broader Bolivian society. Eventually, Santiago parlayed his experience training mining organizations in negotiation skills into a job with the newly created JUNTOS. Santiago's work with NGOs and foreign donors was both a source of financial security and part of a moral imaginary in which he understood his efforts to promote ADR as enmeshed in a longer life project *luchando* (struggling) on behalf of Bolivia's mining communities.

Santiago came of age politically during the late 1960s and early 1970s—a period of enormous social and political upheaval, when Bolivian military dictatorships targeted and violently repressed mining unions with the financial and ideological support of the U.S. government. At age sixteen, Santiago went to work in the Catavi mine, replacing his father who had taken ill with silicosis (black lung) and stepping in for an older brother who was away at university. Santiago spent two years working in the mine while attending night school, along with an older group of adults. His older classmates introduced Santiago to class analysis and Marxist thought. "Older people [in the mines] talk a lot about politics," Santiago explained. For Santiago, political engagement was a process of on-the-job training. The year 1967 was particularly important: "The youth began to ask, 'how do we incorporate ourselves into the Guerrilla del Che?' 'What is going on with the Communist Party?' This was the process of formation. You start to learn who are the Trotskyites, who are the Communists, who are the Maoists. How many kinds of Trotskyism there are in the [mining union's] Assembly."

Santiago took time away from the mine to fulfill his requisite military service (*cuartel*), but he continued to debate politics with his peers. While in cuartel, Santiago read the work of Marcelo Quiroga Santa Cruz, a public intellectual and social critic who served as the Minister of Mining and Energy under the Bolivian president Alfredo Ovando. "A group of us would talk about nationalization: What was it? Who was directing it? So we started to read Marcelo Quiroga about the need to recover [natural resources]. This [experience] led me to affiliate a little more to the left." His return to the mines coincided with a series of nearly back-to-back coups and military dictatorships, as well as human rights abuses including the disappearance of social critics (among them Quiroga Santa Cruz).[23] Over the next decade Santiago held various positions with mining unions, mobilized to free political prisoners, and was a political prisoner himself.

Santiago's experiences as both a militante and dirigente shaped his understanding of conflict and how it could be mobilized. He explained, "My understanding of conflict was that it was a necessity, an arm of the struggle for *revindicación* (defense) of the interests of the workers and the impoverished. I understood conflict, like a strike, a blockade, other actions, were a right of the people to make their views known." He looked back at these experiences as a period when he learned to "make conflict" as a political tactic.

When Santiago was introduced to theories of negotiation and conflict resolution, he interpreted the new conceptual apparatus through the lens of an experienced union organizer. He came to ADR later in life, but he also picked up ADR alongside a whole technical toolkit: the planning methodologies of NGO work and donor-reporting processes. Santiago was employed on a project with a Bolivian organization that worked exclusively with the mining sector and that enjoyed financial support from Canadian donors. For Santiago, his experience working with foreign donors and NGOs changed his way of thinking. He learned how to speak in the language of NGO projects, annual operating budgets (POAS), and measurable goals. Over coffee one afternoon after the diploma course ended, he told me:

> There I learned about POAS, but also about results, objectives, *marcos lógicos* [the ubiquitous indicator-oriented planning matrices used by NGOS]. I learned about what it means to work for results, for objectives. But I also learned about . . . the alternative education [model] of Paulo Freire. So there we also were trained in pedagogical methods. There I learned the theory of *capacitación*. I learned that what I had been doing with my life was completely different. I needed to adjust myself to these new theories.

"Why did you feel it was necessary to make the adjustment?" I asked.

Santiago explained, "Because we were accustomed to deliberation and vertical management in the unions. Right? First the debate, one accusing the other." The deliberation Santiago went on to describe was not the kind of deliberation most deliberative democracy programs might envision.

"Accusations?" I asked.

"Of course. Accusations. Your *base* accuses you," Santiago explained, utilizing the term for rank-and-file union members. "But also your political opposition. The Maoist comrades will never agree with a Trotskyite comrade. Or if a Trotskyite spoke, you always had to disagree."

"You always had to disagree? Always? It was just taken as a given?" I asked.

"Of course," Santiago continued. "So it was a debate of *positions*. In which you needed to use coercion, pressure, manipulation to get the vote. Union diplomacy involved organizing your buddies. 'You, go stand in that corner. You, in the other. I will call on you in the right moment.' That was our methodology," he told me, chuckling. Santiago found the educator Paulo Freire's popular education approach compelling. He explained:

> I thought, these were tools we could have used before, but since we didn't know about them, we didn't use them. I thought, "We've got to take them to the unions." That was my view. I thought this methodology, this way of reflecting with groups could help—*should help* the workers to be more reflective. I didn't see it as a rejection of what I was doing before, but rather a different way of doing what I had been, only more productive.

Alongside the work of Freire, Santiago learned new models of conflict resolution through his work with the Canadian cooperación. He came to see the concepts and theories of negotiation as persuasive resources for furthering the interests of workers in the mining sector—and marginalized Bolivians more generally.

Through his work with a major mining NGO and their Canadian funders during the late 1990s, Santiago also began to travel internationally. He flew to conferences in Peru and Canada for capacitación and began to forge his own training methods, combining his experience and sensibilities from working as a dirigente with the new theories he was encountering. Santiago grew critical of the ubiquitous Harvard school of negotiation, arguing that it failed to account for the kinds of inequalities and constraints Bolivian dirigentes usually faced when they left their communities to negotiate with government officials.[24] As he explained, "In my experience they name you as representative in the [union] Assembly at 4 P.M. and by 7 P.M. you are on an overnight bus to the capital. You travel all night by bus, and then you arrive in the morning to have a meeting with the minister. . . . You only have time to prepare in the corridor if the minister or some authority is running late to the meeting."

Santiago, who described his union job as strategically "*making* conflict," said he found ADR to be really just a "systematization" of the work he was already doing. "Culture of peace" and conflict resolution, Santiago told me, gave him a new language and conceptual resources to approach conflict in a methodical and nonviolent way. He now trains others in those tools through his work with JUNTOS.

Sometimes, however, Santiago clashed with donors' interpretations of the kinds of political tactics employed by sindicatos—the strikes, blockades, and forms of political pressure that, we learned in the diploma course, constituted an escalation of conflict and a form of coercion. As Santiago once told me during a tea break during the course, "The blockade isn't the *end* of negotiation. It's the beginning. It's the *invitation* to negotiation." Indeed, the multiple interpretations of conflict become evident when people like Santiago are dismayed to find that the donor institutions that they work with differently interpret the words, symbols, and practices utilized by trade unions and neighborhood associations, among other loci of protest. While his Canadian and later European colleagues understood strikes and blockades to signal an *escalation* of violent conflict, Santiago insisted on recognizing those political tactics as an *invitation* to dialogue. Paralleling some of the debates over the relationship between direct action and negotiation among researchers in the United States, Santiago insisted on not seeing these two approaches to conflict as opposed but rather in dynamic interplay.[25] For Santiago, the blockade was not the final stage of an intensified conflict, but rather the opening of a much longer process, he told me; his European and Canadian colleagues didn't understand the Bolivian logic of mobilization.

Santiago was surprised and a little dismayed by the ways his foreign colleagues reacted when sindicalista strategies did not fit neatly within the ADR conceptual map. "For them, the first blockade, or the first strike, and you were already operating outside the book. First you had to make your demands known," Santiago explained, indicating his colleagues' views on the proper procedure for opening a negotiation. "But [that's not how it works] in Bolivia. So I would sit there and listen silently [during workshop presentations]. Partly because I was paid to be there. But partly because I was already starting to get annoyed."

"What was annoying you?" I asked Santiago. "Was it that their negotiation methods were inadequate for the Bolivian context?"

"Yes, but also because they isolated me. They seemed to see me as competition. Like, 'how are we going to train this guy so he can just take our *pega*,'" Santiago said, using a word that implies a job attained by connections, by patronage—only he was applying it to foreign experts. "To a certain extent, that was my goal. I said to myself, 'They don't know I can win at this game.'"

Santiago admits that they were right to see him as competition: he was studying their methods, learning their concepts, and finding them wanting. He believed he was better positioned to articulate those ideas to audiences like those he used to lead as a young dirigente in the mines. He realized he could market himself as a local expert with specialized knowledge in the tactics of sindicalismo, particularly in the mining sector.

Santiago did win at the game, successfully parlaying his knowledge of sindicalismo and his exposure to the tools of ADR into a late-in-life career as a respected conflictologo. Santiago now interprets his union-organizing experience through the lens of ADR and vice versa. Santiago's involvement with culture of peace programs was not a rejection of those sindicalista tactics— nor a call to demobilize. Instead, Santiago incorporated his understanding of those tactics into an ADR framework that can identify a conflict's "life cycle," something he saw as dynamic, recurring, and culturally specific to Bolivia and its peasant and mining unions. He reconfigured the ADR toolkit accordingly in his presentations to other mining communities and the examples he used during training courses. In so doing, he made himself a more marketable local expert, a "broker" of sindicalista knowledge, an interpreter of ADR for new audiences, both foreign and domestic.

Conclusion: Life Projects, Made in Bolivia

Many studies of policymaking show how development paradigms circulate, are appropriated, and then transformed through intermediaries or local brokers like Santiago.[26] What I have emphasized in this chapter is the ways promoting ADR and working toward building a culture of peace have become a source of both gainful *and meaningful* employment amid the growing market for expertise in conflict resolution.

Paola Chacón, whom we met earlier, talked about her role in helping to design the IJCs as her first exposure to thinking seriously about her own rights and obligations as a Bolivian citizen, and particularly as a woman. Paola narrated her time helping to develop the centers as a process of personal transformation. For Paola, her embodied experience of traversing El Alto's unlit, unpaved neighborhoods—sometimes late at night and with an acute sense of vulnerability—deepened her feeling that she had been involved in something consequential, in something that might truly contribute to Bolivian society and especially the plight of the poor. An educator by training, she felt the experience had educated *her* about her own rights as well as the needs of others, especially women.

One way to interpret Paola's and Santiago's narratives is as those of aid contractors maneuvering within the moral economy of NGOs and donor-funded projects, in which notions of personal and social transformation are at a premium. Such an opportunistic interpretation of their personal and professional narratives reduces them to cynical calculations, but it also obscures the ways certain development platforms become pervasive precisely because they have become meaningful frameworks for both advocates *and* *critics*. Think back, in the previous chapter, to Canela's scathing critique, and then her subsequent appeal to the culture of peace concept.

To revisit Roseberry's assertion, "What hegemony constructs . . . is not a shared ideology but a common material and meaningful framework for living through, talking about, and acting upon social orders characterized by domination" (1994: 361). It is difficult to speak outside of that framework, even if one is criticizing it. This is not a case of people using the master's language to construct something wholly and radically other. It is not a "hidden transcript" in the sense that James Scott (1990) describes some forms of subaltern resistance. Rather, ADR and its accompanying discourse of promoting a culture of peace *is that* meaningful framework through which people like Santiago, Cecilia, Paola, Esteban, and countless others think about what it means to be politically engaged and to do work for justice in El Alto and in Bolivia more generally. Some do so while linking justice to entrepreneurial solutions to poor people's problems, while others reject those same claims.

Many Bolivians who have worked with social organizations like unions or indigenous rights movements also have been participants in NGO projects aiming to provide capacitación in a variety of topics ranging from project management and participatory budgeting to Freirian-style adult education to negotiation skills. Similarly, many Bolivians who received degrees in the social sciences put that training to work on NGO and donor-financed projects. In Bolivia, academic knowledge is often produced in collaboration with NGOs and donor agencies, and on behalf of the state itself. As Gustafson notes, throughout Latin America, social scientists "allied with movements for social change" have been criticized for becoming "agents of a depoliticizing, technocratic approach to development in support of the market" (2009: 137).[27] Yet as he argues, this critique can flatten the dynamic ways social scientists and professional NGO workers have been involved in development programs that straddle the line between pro-market programs, pro-indigenous social movements, and calls for more radical change. Applied research and other

FIGURE 3.2 Flyers around La Paz advertise workshops on working with NGOs and securing donor funding. Photo by author.

forms of academic knowledge production have thus "constituted the battleground in the unsettled war over the future of the market, state and nation" (Gustafson 2009: 138).

Bolivian academics and activists frequently rely on development aid and the NGO sector for their livelihoods *and* as vehicles for meaningful proyectos de vida. The concept of having a proyecto de vida even draws on the language of NGO and donor projects to articulate a sense of purpose. Proyecto de vida conjures that familiar vocabulary, invoking life's vision and mission statements, its objectives and indicators of success, revealing a life course in which one's gainful employment and political commitments are intertwined. For many of the ADR advocates I interviewed, this notion of constructing a proyecto de vida allowed them to articulate a sense of self over time that was deeply inflected by work on social issues, where NGOs and conflict resolution could not be reduced to a paycheck and a bump in class status. For NGO workers and culture of peace promoters, these were deeply meaningful projects, ones that train participants and brokers to speak in the language of operating budgets and indicators that justify continued funding, but also provide a language for social transformation and justice. Attending to the *proyectos de vida* of ADR advocates reveals the interplay between markets and meaning making that is integral to the ways these programs persevere, even amid strident critiques.

ADR and culture of peace advocates like Santiago Mujica have not "autonomously chosen the particular issue over which they will struggle" (Roseberry 1994: 362). In the case of ADR and culture of peace campaigns, foreign donors have largely defined the terms of contestation by *defining the terms of financing*, as well as by determining which kinds of organizations they wish to engage. This network of international actors and institutions is part of the winnowing process; preoccupied with governance through civil society, these actors co-construct the institutional arrangements, lines of funding, calls for projects, and various other mechanisms that further narrow the terms of the debate about conflict and its causes in Bolivia. Indeed, this dynamic is one of the reasons offered by the Morales administration for cracking down on how donor money is disbursed, demanding greater coordination with state development plans as a means of reasserting sovereignty against the influence of foreign aid (a move that critics characterize as silencing civil society).

As I have shown, development technologies such as surveys and focus groups enable brokers to experience and re-frame a global donor platform as a uniquely local project, domesticating it. ADR brokers further insert their own personal and professional histories into those efforts, and they wrestle with shifting political terrain in which they work.[28] The very people interpolated through these projects and discourses nevertheless "encounter inconsistencies that provide grist for critical insights."[29] These are the fissures into which ADR's brokers and intermediaries make meaning, make policies, speak back to donors, strategically utilize donor language to obtain funding for their projects, and generally make their livelihoods in the field of conflict resolution.

Navigating Alto Lima

District 6's residential neighborhoods blanket the foothills of the Andes, blooming like little rows of adobe and brick flowers. Many Aymara residents migrated to El Alto from rural Andean hamlets during the 1980s and 1990s, alongside the droves of miners who were "relocated" during the privatization of state-owned mines like Catavi and Siglo XX. Others have settled in El Alto far more recently. These neighborhoods are home to university students, young bureaucrats, women who work as household maids (*empleadas*) in neighboring La Paz or as *comerciantes* (traders or small businesspeople) in nearby markets, and men who drive the lumbering Micro buses and speedy minibuses that clog El Alto's streets. And like much of El Alto, the residents of District 6 are often on the move; they circulate back and forth to their natal communities in the rural provinces where they continue to plant potatoes and quinoa in family plots, act as patrons for an annual fiesta, or serve a term among their community's rotating leadership positions so they can retain their land claims. Others migrate for stretches of time to Brazil to work in garment factories, or labor in mining cooperatives to the north, returning on weekends to spend time with family. Others, still, participate in the widening trade circuits that take them from the container ships docked in Chilean ports to Chinese electronics factories.[1]

Despite its reputation as a largely poor city, El Alto is not economically homogeneous. Displaced miners helped establish the city's older, middle-class neighborhoods, with cottage homes, full plumbing, gas installations, and decorative gates. El Alto is now also famous for its glaringly bright "chalets"—multistoried structures painted in various shades of neon, sporting gleaming tile exteriors and reflective glass siding. Press outlets from the

BBC to Al Jazeera celebrate these chalets for the uniquely Alteño aesthetic and their testimony to accruing wealth and comfort in a city that is often misrepresented as universally impoverished. But El Alto's neat, settled neighborhoods give way to unfinished homesteads, where adobe bricks temporarily fill empty concrete frames until a family can gather the funds necessary to complete the project. Those rough exteriors mask interior walls plastered smooth, papered with decorative calendars and posters declaring fútbol allegiances. Peripheral neighborhoods are still unevenly connected to sewage systems and paved roads, and many residents complain bitterly about their acute feelings of insecurity, both physical and economic, in these marginal *barrios*.

District 6 comprises many small neighborhoods, including Alto Lima (second section), where the integrated justice center (IJC) is located. But it is most famous for the sprawling 16 de Julio open-air market, which unfurls twice a week—on Thursdays and Sundays. The broad commercial avenue of 16 de Julio is lined with multistory brick and concrete structures with enormous picture windows where shopkeepers display their wares. These permanent storefronts sell the tools of El Alto's many trades: hand-operated and high-powered electric sewing machines, huge warehouses advertising portable metal gas ranges and the pushcarts used by itinerant food peddlers, large plastic tubs that women use to wash clothes, or clean yarn for knitting alpaca shawls.

Fashion-savvy seamstresses display the most striking color combinations of their *polleras,* the heavy, multitiered skirts worn by many Aymara women in El Alto. Other storefronts boast a variety of ornate *Morenada* costumes they rent to neighborhood associations planning their anniversary *entrada* (dance parade). Jewelry shops carefully display the extravagant gold and pearl brooches worn by Aymara women on special occasions—when dancing or serving as patrons for those entradas. The avenue is punctuated with the brightly painted satellite offices of microfinance institutions and the omnipresent concrete rooms rented by *prestamistas* (moneylenders) who help finance Alteños' commercial endeavors.

ON THURSDAYS AND SUNDAYS vendors erect temporary stalls that overtake the streets of 16 de Julio. Shop owners unfold wooden stands where they sell tennis shoes and tracksuits, sweater sets and pollera petticoats, decorative plastic flowers and soccer balls. Like most commercial districts in Bolivia, products and produce are organized thematically. Blocks of electronics and plumbing supplies give way to used cars and used clothing, cleaning sup-

FIGURE RECESS 1 AND FIGURE RECESS 2 Vendors working in the 16 de Julio market in El Alto. Photo by author.

plies, stacked crates of newborn chicks and guinea pigs, and pirated DVDs of Bollywood films, K-pop music videos, and the annual Tinku festival in Macha. Produce vendors hawk mottled pink and yellow sweet potatoes known as *oka*; the hard, shriveled chuño; and spindly chamomile stalks, while butchers display elongated cow's tongue and rippled tripe, among other cuts of meat.

Along the periphery, small metal shacks are home to *Yatiris* (traditional healers) and vendors who prepare *mesas* (offerings to Pachamama) according to the particular yearnings or challenges each customer is facing. They cobble together candies shaped like desired objects (a house, a car, a sign of better health), bright cotton, tinsel, llama fat, and incense, and then wrap the offering in butcher paper until it can be burned.

Taxis laden with wooden wardrobes or mattresses lurch slowly among the throngs of shoppers. Less-established vendors drape blue plastic tarps over dusty stretches of packed earth and unload mounds of lower-quality, used American clothing. Many items still bear the tags from Goodwill and the Salvation Army, where they originated before being shipped in massive containers to ports in Chile, distributed to middlemen on the coast, and then redistributed again to vendors in El Alto. Here on the edge of the market, El Alto drops off precipitously into the gaping bowl of La Paz. The newly installed cable-car system now ferries curious tourists along with La Paz residents eager for a bargain.

The seamstresses, part-time prestamistas, and storefront butchers working in 16 de Julio and surrounding neighborhood markets are the primary clients of District 6's IJC. Nearly all of these comerciantes work in Bolivia's vast "informal" sector, where commerce and kinship are deeply intertwined.[2] They include itinerant vendors selling toilet paper, housewares, and gelatin in plastic cups, and the shop owners who offer rotisserie chicken, two-liter soda bottles, or beauty products out of the storefronts built into many residential compounds. The market stalls and lending agencies that punctuate these streets are central to the lives and livelihoods of the people living in District 6, but they also fuel many of the conflicts that bring residents to the legal aid and conciliation center.

Conciliating Conflict in District 6

District 6's IJC was the first one built in El Alto, forged from a collaboration between the United States Agency for International Development (USAID), the Ministry of Justice, and the Alto Lima neighborhood association and its vigilance committee. The neighborhood association donated a plot of land to the project, and the center now sits just across from the deputy mayor's office. That center, in turn, served as the pilot project for what would become a national program.

As I described in earlier chapters, program designers initially trained local residents as community mediators, believing that they could offer solutions to their neighbors' problems—solutions that state institutions could not. In addition to the resolution of specific complaints, program designers also sought to disseminate information on human rights, including a child's right to an "identity" (a birth certificate) and a woman's right to live a life free from domestic violence. The program distributed pamphlets and recorded radio "spots," while center volunteers and staff supplemented their conciliation services with civic education workshops.

By the time I arrived on the scene, however, that approach had shifted. After assuming control of the centers, the Ministry of Justice phased out community volunteers and replaced them with a small crew of public servants (i.e., a director, conciliator, and pro bono lawyer) and legal aid interns from local universities. When I returned for short visits in 2014, 2016, and 2017, many centers were operating with an even more skeletal staff.

As I conducted research in 2010 and 2011, however, the IJC in District 6 was lively with clients seeking legal advice and conciliation services and young interns gaining experience and university credit. Occasionally the center enjoyed an on-site psychologist (in training)—usually another college-age student getting credit for an internship. First-time clients would hover awkwardly in the doorway, uncertain of how to proceed. On busy days, interns would encourage them to take a seat in one of the rows of plastic chairs lining the center's vast open space and wait their turn. The center's glass-enclosed offices housed the director and the occasional pro bono lawyer, while the conciliator enjoyed a sturdy wooden door and blinds, adding a degree of privacy. Angry voices would sometimes breach those walls, and clients scurried in and out of the conciliator's office, making photocopies across the street or consulting with waiting kin who soothed babies while their mothers negotiated child-support payments with estranged spouses.

During an initial intake, interns would ask for a quick description of the issue at hand and then explain a client's legal and nonlegal options. Cases of domestic violence might require encouraging a client to pursue a criminal case against an abuser, to get a letter of referral to the forensic medical examiner, and take a trip to a psychological service NGO for evaluation in order to compile evidence. For administrative procedures like correcting birth or marriage certificates, interns would list the necessary documentation and steps for making those corrections and send the client off to the appropriate offices in downtown El Alto or La Paz. For most complaints brought to the center, however, staff encouraged clients to try conciliation before considering legal options.

If that person agreed to try conciliation (and most did), interns drafted an invitation letter for the other party. If both parties appeared for the appointment, a trained conciliator would take turns inviting each to offer an interpretation of the events that had produced tension. After mapping out the conflict from the perspective of both parties, the conciliator would then ask both to offer possible solutions. For a conflict over an outstanding loan, the debtor might propose a repayment schedule. Or a wife might propose a sum for monthly child support from her estranged husband. Some conciliators I observed intervened very little into the process of developing proposals, encouraging clients to "really think about what you need," or "consider how much it takes to raise a child," while others offered specific suggestions when both parties wavered. Others, still, openly chided clients who, in their judgment, made stingy or unrealistic proposals (I saw these interventions most often in cases of child support).[3] Should the parties reach an agreement about how to resolve the dispute, the conciliator types up the arrangement into an accord, which includes a description of the conflict and a series of numbered resolutions. She then reads the document aloud to the parties before having them sign it, and then adds her own institutional stamp and signature. Conciliation appointments might take an hour, or stretch for multiple sessions until an agreement could be reached—unless none appeared on the horizon. In those cases, the conciliator would draft a document declaring the "impossibility of an accord" and explain the legal options available if the parties in conflict wanted to pursue the matter further.

As I worked alongside a rotating cast of interns and conciliators, we found ourselves stretching the limited resources available at the centers. Printers broke or ran out of ink. One intern, Olivia, once stitched a printer ribbon back together with a needle and thread, then tried re-inking the cartridge with a marker to get through the day. The institution relied heavily on paper to print pro bono legal briefs, letters of invitation, and conciliation accords, but clients would have to run across the street to a small store to make the necessary photocopies that accompany every bureaucratic process in Bolivia.

Staff and former interns reminisced about what it was like working at the center during the height of USAID's financial support. The equipment was new and the funding for paper and printer cartridges was plentiful. More important to them, they said, were the deep friendships they developed with

each other and with the neighbors who attended alternative dispute resolution (ADR) training sessions, took civic education and domestic violence
workshops, and participated in the center's dance troupe during local entradas. That camaraderie was evident as I spoke with the handful of volunteers
who continued to frequent the center despite the official disbanding of the
volunteer program.

While some center directors and conciliators were lawyers, others were
educators or had degrees in the popular interdisciplinary field of *comuni-
cación social* (social communication). For a number of conciliators and program designers, the purpose of the centers was to create a space that was
wholly distinct from the state legal system and that offered clients an approach to conflict resolution that didn't resort to the intercession of lawyers,
judges, or other legal professionals.[4] Program designers initially balked at
the suggestion of offering pro bono legal advice in addition to conciliation
services precisely because it seemed to muddy the formal/informal boundary they sought to erect in these so-called extrajudicial spaces.[5] As I learned
during the course of my fieldwork, however, District 6 was also a place where
staff and volunteers came to challenge that original vision, and they pushed
the work of the centers back toward the *formal* legal system (see chapter 6).
One of those people was Dr. Paloma Gil.[6]

Paloma began her career at the centers as a volunteer, though she lived in
neighboring La Paz. A lawyer by training, she was new to conciliation and
learned "on the job" as a volunteer before receiving formal training through
the Ministry of Justice and USAID. Despite the program's emphasis on offering alternatives to the state legal system, however, Paloma often found herself
pushing for a more expansive role for *legal* aid. She felt it unfair to promise
residents accessible solutions to their problems, only to shuttle them off to
unreliable bureaucratic offices when their needs exceeded the solutions that
conciliation could offer. The experiences of women facing domestic violence
in particular led Paloma to start providing pro bono legal aid on the sly,
drafting *memoriales* (legal briefs) despite the protests of donor representatives. Eventually, Paloma's efforts to more explicitly incorporate recourse to
the formal legal system would become the norm; the centers incorporated an
abogado (lawyer) alongside volunteers/interns and conciliators.

The buildings themselves were a testament to this interplay between the
formal and the informal; indeed, the two operated in one space. In District 6,
the IJC occupied the vast open area to the left of the entrance, while, to the
right, a small "mixed" courtroom held session, covering family, civil, and
criminal cases. This combination proved confusing to many new clients who

were uncertain of the distinction between the two offices. Interns sometimes grew impatient with their bewilderment, insisting that the line between the two was clearly marked—conceptually, if not within the physical space itself.

That effort to draw (or erase) this in/formal distinction is something we call an *emic* debate in anthropology—that is, it is something that staff wrestled with in their own discussions and practices, and it was not something I am trying to assert as a real boundary that exists (or should exist) between the two. As I discuss in chapter 6, socio-legal scholars insist that state-administered legal systems and informal mechanisms for dispute resolution frequently entail hybrid processes and institutional arrangements (a dynamic Menkel-Meadow 2013 calls "process pluralism"). Nevertheless, this boundary marking (or boundary erasing) was mirrored in ongoing national debates about the relationship between the state (often glossed "Western") legal system and customary law or indigenous justice. In many ways, contemporary Bolivian debates about indigenous autonomy revisit questions raised by an earlier era of research on the relationship between European legal orders and indigenous law in colonial and postcolonial contexts, or what Sally Engle Merry (1988) termed "classic legal pluralism" in her far-reaching overview of the field. To close this *cuarto intermedio* (recess), I want to briefly present Boaventura de Sousa Santos's notion of interlegality as a useful analytic approach to these divisions—or appeals to them—going forward into the chapters that follow.

Interlegality, Authority, and Conciliation

Frequently, after explaining how ADR worked, conciliators would find themselves in the position of having clients ask them to render judgments, despite their insistence that participants needed to assume responsibility for negotiating their own solutions. It was a recurring request, one I witnessed and that conciliators mentioned in our interviews: "People always expect me to render a judgment. I have to tell them, I'm not a judge, I can't decide for you. I cannot make you sign any document," Dr. Sonia Campos told me. One interpretation of this pattern might be that clients simply misunderstand the conciliation process due to a lack of experience with it or an unclear explanation at the outset.[7] Perhaps they mistake the conciliator for a judge, just as many people couldn't quite understand that the nominal distance between the judges' quarters and center was meant to demarcate a space between the formal and informal. Or, it might reflect, as some conciliators insisted, that people want an affirmation for their perspective (and judgment in their favor) despite the fact that conciliation is intended to elicit mutually beneficial solutions. Sally Merry (1990), for example, found that working-class residents of Massachusetts wanted to have their views and positions affirmed, and they wanted to utilize the state to do so.

In the Bolivian context, this constant appeal to the intervention of the conciliator to adjudicate the conflict may also reflect people's experiences with dispute-resolution practices in rural hamlets and marginalized barrios, where local authorities are responsible for managing conflicts by allowing people to air their grievances (often in the presence of extended families), and then determining solutions with appeals to both shared norms and community mechanisms of enforcement and/or reconciliation.

Conciliators and interns frequently tried to make sense of the expectations that clients brought to their sessions, including expectations about the role of the conciliator. Some, like Sonia Campos, narrated it with exasperation: after countless requests that she render judgment, she was baffled by the inability of people to "take responsibility" for their own solutions. Others saw a direct relationship between people's culturally informed expectations and their requests for conciliator judgments—though their proscriptions for handling those tensions differed. Another conciliator, Sebastián Costa, for example, saw it as a cultural norm that demanded an overhaul. For a legal intern, Álvaro, however, it was a cultural expectation worthy of respect and accommodation in plurinational Bolivia.

Consider how Álvaro—a young, Aymara legal intern—reflected on a case that appears in chapter 4. The center director, Dr. Paloma Gil, had called for a cuarto intermedio to allow the different parties to reflect on their positions before trying, once more, to reach a solution. As we waited, Álvaro asked me how Americans think about conciliation. I offered a simple definition: that the conciliator is a third party trained to facilitate communication and help disputing parties arrive at a jointly agreed-upon solution.

Álvaro responded, "Sure, an academic could say that about the role of the conciliator, but you have to remember, a humble citizen isn't going to think that way. He's going to think [of the conciliator] in terms of authority. That's the difference between an academic and the people here. . . . Who are the people who come to the center? What is their birthplace? Their origins? Their reality?"

"Well, I have seen the case files, I know that most were born in the [rural] provinces but now they live in El Alto and return to their home communities periodically—although the younger generation was often born here in El Alto," I offered. "Exactly," Álvaro nodded: "They are from the provinces, so their reality is in the province from which they have migrated. Their cultural roots are in the countryside. Under what logic do they understand how to resolve disputes? Under the logic of an authority—to see authority is to respect it; it is not a synonym with mockery. It is respect. Authority is almost sacramental, but this is why authority exists—you must offer your services [as an authority] as a free social service."

As we spoke, Álvaro built his argument about how to interpret this pattern: people using ADR services at the IJCS are primarily rural Aymara in origin, and consequently, "however long they have been in the city, their expectation is that authorities enact a kind of sacramental leadership, a role that demands respect and reverence, and that the person in the conciliator role should understand that cultural context and carry out their sessions accordingly." I scribbled notes as he spoke. The morning stream of clients slowed to a trickle, and most returned home to prepare lunch for their children.

"You have to take culture into account," Álvaro concluded. "Some say that the law is a normative product. But I think it is always going to be a cultural product." When pressed to offer his version of "culturally appropriate" conciliation, Álvaro called for more formalism, verticalism, and ritual that would mimic people's expectations—expectations, he insisted, that were transposed from their experience with rural authorities. In doing so, Álvaro argued *against* some of the primary aims celebrated by many ADR advocates, including building toward horizontal relations that do not rely on an external imposition by an adjudicator. He also challenged some of the characterizations of *justicia originaria* as hyper "informal" and indigenous governance as especially horizontal in its practice.

By examining both staff and clients' expectations through the lens of "interlegality," we might avoid some of the pitfalls of appeals to legal pluralism in which, to use Boaventura de Sousa Santos's terms, "different legal orders are conceived as separate entities coexisting in the same political space" (1995: 473; Harrington and Merry 1988). One problem with this popular conceptualization of legal pluralism is that it reinforces the idea that there is a clear rural-urban/Indian-*mestizo* divide. That is, such appeals to plural legal and normative orders in plurinational Bolivia can create the image that the "Western" legal system is something wholly distinguishable from "indigenous" modes of conflict resolution. This was a conceptual division I often observed not only in discussions of what constituted legal pluralism in Bolivia, but also workshops that discussed "Western"-styled ADR methods (MARCS) and indigenous (originaria) conflict-resolution methods (MORCS).

Much like characterizations of customary law, ADR, in this framing, becomes something unmoored from history—including the American community mediation movement's linkages to studies of indigenous conflict-resolution practices in other contexts.

This question of what we mean by legal pluralism is particularly charged in Bolivia as indigenous activists, legal scholars, anthropologists, and government officials grapple with how, exactly, to implement the plural juridical orders promised by Bolivia's 2009 Constitution, only the latest in a longer history of efforts to institutionalize "customary" or indigenous jurisdictions (Albó 2012; Postero 2017). During the constitutional assembly, the Unity Pact, an alliance of indigenous and peasant groups, called for confronting the epistemological injustice committed against indigenous peoples, and elevating of a model of citizenship based on "collective subject that transcends the monocultural liberal model based upon the individual citizen" (translated and quoted in Postero 2017: 54).[8]

As I conducted research, the Ministry of Autonomy and Ministry of Justice were still working through the statutes that would make it possible to enact these juridico-political visions concretely, spawning workshops and national conferences, op-ed pieces and scholarly debates about jurisdictional limits (*la ley de deslinde jurisdiccional*). Many people turned their attention to places like Jesús de Machaca (Álvaro's natal municipality), one of the first municipalities to apply for recognition as an indigenous autonomous region with its own constitution, statutes, and mechanisms for resolving conflict. Municipalities like Jesús de Machaca have come to epitomize indigenous demands for autonomous political power and the Morales administration's promise of a transformative, decolonizing political platform (el proceso de cambio/the process of change).

Critics, however, argue that "the government continues to pay lip service to the principles of decolonization and plurinationalism, while simultaneously acting to restrict and undermine the practical implementation of indigenous rights to self-governance" in a variety of ways (Cameron 2013: 184). Yet, the process of constructing indigenous autonomy also has proven to be internally contentious. As John Cameron (2013) has shown, across predominantly indigenous municipalities "indigenous leaders mobilize different understandings of history and seek to construct and project historically based identities in efforts to generate legitimacy for competing visions of how institutions of indigenous self-governance should function" (2013: 180).[9] Debates over this promised state-restructuring project and how it should be enacted were often paralleled in El Alto's IJCs.

Dr. Gil would reminisce about the times when community leaders from rural hamlets (*Mallkus*) burst into the center to contest the jurisdiction and moral authority of conciliators to resolve disputes that they saw as *their* domain, their jurisdiction. Other times, she recalled, community authorities would seek her services on conflicts they had failed to resolve, hoping she might have better luck. Interns were often perplexed with how to direct inquiries for clients whose conflicts spanned both their rural, natal communities and their urban dwellings in Alto Lima; anxious that they would be "observed" or reprimanded by the judge or his staff for overstepping their jurisdiction, interns would redirect those inquiries to the central offices at the Ministry of Justice for clarification.[10]

Coincidentally, Álvaro was involved in efforts to design the statutes of the new *autonomia indigena* (indigenous autonomy) in Jesús de Machaca. Above, he presents *his* vision of history, identity, and indigenous governance in his natal municipality while interpreting the relationship between indigenous justice, authority, the state legal system, and the conciliation center where he works. He links his own nascent legal career to helping plurinational Bolivia resolve what autonomia indigena would mean in practice while positioning himself as a broker of that transformation. Yet that transformation would grind to a halt for Jesús de Machaca just one year after we spoke; internal divisions over how best to construct indigenous self governance could not be resolved, leading the municipality to reject autonomy, at least for the moment (Cameron 2013).

By contrast to the notion that indigenous or "customary" law and European or state legal orders coexist in the same political space, yet remain distinctly separate (and internally homogenous), "interlegality" is "the conception of different legal spaces superimposed, interpenetrated and mixed in our minds, as much as in our actions, either on occasions of qualitative leaps or sweeping crises in our life trajectories, or in the dull routine of eventless everyday life" (Santos 1995: 473; see Merry 1988 on "the new legal pluralism" and Valverde 2015 on "legal assemblages").[11] In District 6, the interpenetration of multiple legal and normative orders was evident in the ways people imagined how disputes should and would be resolved when they came to the IJC, as we see in some of the above dynamics and in the chapters to follow. Alto Limeños regularly appeal to both Mallkus in their natal communities and presidents of the urban neighborhood associations (*dirigentes*) to help adjudicate disputes.[12] They rely on *compadres de matrimonio* (godparents of a marriage) to offer advice and to "correct" the behavior of young couples gone astray. Experiences with itinerant judges and other state officials further informed people's expectations of how a dispute would be resolved.

Santos's notion of interlegality is useful for recognizing how legal consciousness is shaped by the interplay of these legal-normative orders.[13] But it is also useful for understanding how center staff tried to make sense of the expectations their clients brought to their offices—particularly as they vexed staff members' own assumptions about how ADR *should* function. In practice, some conciliators sought to accommodate those expectations. Other times, they sought to redirect or explicitly alter them. What Álvaro identified as a quality meriting respect and accommodation, other conciliators characterized as vertical, authoritarian logic, an impediment to personal responsibility and maturation—and one that required transformation.

And what were the conflicts bringing people to the IJC? Alto Limeños approached the center seeking advice on how to obtain child support from a domestic partner working in Argentina, Brazil, or Spain, as many Alteños do. They lodged complaints against a bricklayer who never completed an adobe wall. They inquired about their options for leaving a husband after years of chronic violence. They sought information about how to obtain a birth certificate for a child, or how to file an inheritance claim. Sisters brought their disabled brother, claiming he was suffering neglect and developing bedsores while other kin cared for him. Urban-dwelling families rallied behind aging parents who still lived in the *campo* (countryside), amid accusations of elder abuse by adult sons. Had I worked in District 8 or District 1, I would likely have seen many more cases of residents seeking to "regularize" their land titles, or accusations of illicit land sales (*loteadores*).

But many residents of District 6 came to the IJC because they were buckling under the weight of multiple debts owed to friends, family, and banking institutions. Indeed, conciliators in several of El Alto's centers reported that conflicts over interpersonal debt were overtaking their usual caseload of "intrafamilial conflict" and child support. Those debts were so inescapable during my time at the center that they are the focus of the final three chapters of this book. It is to those cases—particularly cases at the intersection of debt, violence, and kin obligations—that I now turn.

Between Compadres There Is No Interest

"You are not part of this conflict."

Nine people and a child arrange themselves in a semicircle in the back room of the integrated justice center (IJC). The space, which once hosted alternative dispute resolution (ADR) training sessions and celebratory group meals for volunteers, is now gathering dust, as funding for training and community building has evaporated following the departure of the United States Agency for International Development (USAID). Several ceiling panels have gone missing, exposing the structure behind. Pigeons flutter and scrape between the corrugated plastic roof and foam ceiling. Staff periodically use the space for cases like this one, when a mass of people shows up for a conciliation session. Usually, however, they siphon off all those extra people—explaining that only the two feuding parties may enter, except in cases involving minor children who are party to a dispute.

Parents, *compadres* (coparents to godchildren), siblings, and cousins of disputants regularly sit in clumps in the waiting room. Others pace outside the spiked metal gate surrounding the center. Unsure of what to do while they wait, these relatives buy Coca-Cola at a corner store, whose business also specializes in photocopies, manila folders, *timbres* (judicial stamps), and other items clients must obtain during their sojourn in the center and the adjacent courthouse. Sometimes feuding families engage in a little informal negotiating themselves, quietly trying to repair relationships between their two households while a young couple works through their marital problems separately with the conciliator. Other times, physical altercations erupt. Anxious parents of adult children approach staff, imploring that they be allowed into the session to offer their advice. The response they get is often the same: conciliation is only between the *two* parties directly involved in the conflict. But occasionally—like today, when these nine adults and a child are gathered in that semicircle—Dr. Paloma, the center director, makes an exception.

Dr. Paloma understands Aymara but has asked Álvaro, one of the center's interns, to help translate for the elderly disputant. Paloma and Álvaro stand before those gathered. A small child sidles up and blinks back at the semicircle. An Aymara man in his seventies stands up to introduce himself. He wears a smart gray suit, baby blue button-down shirt, and moss green fedora. He is the godson of the elderly woman at the center of this conciliation session: Doña Petrona.

Doña Petrona sits silently through most of the session, folded in on herself. Creased eyes gazing downward, she quietly gums her coca leaves. Her family has brought along a stout young lawyer who periodically wanders off into the waiting room to talk on his cellphone. Dr. Paloma informs the family that the lawyer can observe but would not play a role in the conciliation session.

Several younger women sit like a Greek chorus behind Petrona, clucking their worry and discontent.

A third, distinct pair sits apart from the semicircle: a husband and wife who have lived with Petrona in her small household compound for the last twelve years.

This complicated mass of people consists of kin and neighbors trying to deal with a disagreement that has arisen between the elderly woman and the middle-aged couple. The compound where the couple has been living with Doña Petrona is one of thousands that fill El Alto: an enclosed patio with high adobe walls subdivided into smaller household units.

The couple, Gregoria and her husband, René, has been paying 10 Bolivianos (Bs) a month in rent (roughly US$1.40). Over the course of their decade-long stay, however, they also paid to install the water and sewage system in the compound, wired the house for electricity, and made other improvements. They are seeking reimbursement for their investments: 4,000 Bs (or about US$571). Petrona and other members of the family reject their request and want Gregoria and René to vacate the premises. Petrona's champions argue that the low rental cost should offset the price of the household improvements and that Petrona has no obligation to reimburse the couple.

As Paloma explains conciliation, a thirty-something woman leaps up in the back, identifying herself as a neighbor. Her voice trembles with anger or nerves and she punctuates her words with "doctora" and "doctorita," showing her deference to Paloma (who is a lawyer and middle-class professional, a bureaucrat) while trying to establish some intimacy and elicit sympathy (the diminutive "doctorita" is familiar). The incensed woman describes Petrona's plight: "She lives in misery. She lives with a dirt floor with just her little rabbit and a cat. No human should live that way."

Paloma has allowed the full group into the conciliation room, but she now interrupts the woman to rein in her participation: "Excuse me, *Señora*, but you, the neighbor, are not part of this conflict."

By allowing Petrona's godson and neighbors into the room, Paloma has in some ways acknowledged the widespread expectation in El Alto that kin and other social relations should be present and involved in resolving the conflict. But she quickly moves to reassert the dyadic nature of the conflict by silencing *terceros* (third parties): this dispute is between two parties, she insists. You, ma'am, are not part of the conflict.

René interjects: "To pay for gas, we worked hard. Water, electricity—I have been generous enough to pay for all of these things [for the household]." The neighbor woman stands indignantly and pets Petrona's shoulder: "She has suffered so much!"

Gregoria adds, "To pay for the installations I had to borrow from the bank! Forgive me, *doctorita*, but I have suffered to pay [for these improvements]."

Petrona's godson, the elderly amauta, appeals to the group. "We are brothers and sisters, are we not [*Somos hermanos, no ve*]?" he asks the room. But before he can get his footing to continue, his appeal to familial solidarity sparks an angry exchange of words.

More arguing ensues as Paloma tries to work the group toward a compromise, offering suggestions that the different sides reject. Finally, she exasperatedly throws her hands in the air to indicate the possibility of defeat: "This is not the court; I cannot do any more [than what I am doing]. Nobody is obligated to sign an accord here. Everyone needs to calm down. If you cannot [resolve this dispute] by conciliation you can do so through the courts. You have your lawyer here, so you will have to rely on him." After months of talking with Paloma about her approach, I have learned that this warning—and the theatrical arm gesture—is a common strategic device she uses. One of her tools for persuading stubborn, warring clients to compromise and opt for conciliation is to invoke their other option: the lengthy, expensive state legal system. Wouldn't compromise be a better option? And, indeed, compromise they often do.

Yet beyond immediate strategies for encouraging conciliation over the courts, the exchange also points to a recurring tension in El Alto's IJCs. It's a tension between efforts to narrow the range of voices present in conciliation sessions to only the directly disputing parties, and efforts to respect people's expectations that conflicts are best resolved through the active involvement of multiple intermediaries. Those expectations are shaped by clients' experiences with rural Andean authorities (*Mallkus*), neighborhood leaders (*dirigentes*), and kin (especially godparents) who frequently act as mediators when conflicts arise. They are also shaped by their experiences with state agents working in rural outposts.

In many ways, these expectations about conciliation and the role of conciliators reveal what the legal scholar Boaventura de Sousa Santos (1995) has called "interlegality." As I explained in the "Brief Recess" chapter, interlegality reflects the complicated ways in which multiple legal and normative orders become "superimposed, interpenetrated and mixed in our minds" and find expression in mundane encounters like those we saw at the centers (1995: 473).[1] But interlegality is not the only explanation for why these tensions emerge. This clash over terceros is also provoked by the complexity of how such disputes actually occur in the everyday lives of Alteños—where social worlds and interpersonal conflicts cannot be reduced to neat dyads.

When ADR scholars and practitioners talk about *dyadic* forms of conflict resolution, they are usually referring to negotiations between two parties without the aid of a third-party mediator. The presence of a neutral, third person makes conciliation itself "triadic." Here, however, I use "dyad" to highlight how conciliators conceptualized conflict and personhood in the centers, and sought to impose order on both. For many conciliators, sloughing off terceros is a matter of penetrating the unspoken needs and interests of individuals, getting below the noise generated by third parties; it allows disputants to resolve those conflicts unfettered from other social constraints (like meddling kinfolk). In the above session, René and Gregoria constitute one party; Petrona, the second; and Dr. Paloma Gil serves as the mediator (with the help of an interpreter). But Petrona, Gregoria, and René did not come alone. And my argument here is that it's worth paying attention to the presence of those so-called terceros.

At the heart of this chapter is a tension between ADR practitioners' dyadic way of conceptualizing and treating conflict and the sociological reality of

El Alto residents.[2] To get at these tensions, I examine the overlay between conflicts we saw in the IJCS and Andean practices related to knitting and reinforcing social ties, creating expansive webs of intimacy and obligation, care and mutual indebtedness.[3] One of the most powerful ways this happens is through *compadrazgo*, or coparenting/godparenting. These debt-laden relationships are vital to social life in El Alto and produce understandings of the self as constituted by these intersubjective relationships. Yet those social relations are also taxed by the very practices that constitute them, including widespread informal lending between kin and other social relations.

The tension provoked by extricating the dyad in conflict from those broader relations—from terceros—is not merely a disjuncture between how ADR professionals would *prefer* to resolve disputes and how, say, rural Mallkus or neighborhood association leaders might do so in the presence of a larger community. Rather, compadrazgo and related forms of social obligation deeply shape the *kinds* of conflicts we saw in the IJCS. In sequestering parties from terceros, conciliators make the unwieldy, tangled social relations that constitute those conflicts manageable. But in so doing, they erase significant patterns of conflict—and how those intimate conflicts are connected to broader political-economic forces. Ultimately, these artificial (though perhaps pragmatically necessary) simplifications have consequences for how conflicts in El Alto are conceptualized and treated—by disputants, state agents, and nongovernmental agencies seeking to intervene into El Alto's (and Bolivia's) so-called hyperconflictiveness.

I begin by discussing compadrazgo and other practices that produce the obligations that shape so much of social life—and understandings of personhood—in El Alto. I then return to the ways conciliators sought to distinguish parties in conflict from terceros, and thus make order out of dense webs of social relations and their ensuing conflicts. A particularly complicated web of debts shared between three pairs of compadres shows why conciliators might want to impose such dyadic structure. And why clients might value it too. But it also offers insight into what is erased by removing terceros: debt burdens produced through both informal social lending and the expansion of microfinance services in Bolivia. I conclude by looking at how microfinance agencies and Alteños themselves increasingly deride the very social practices both rely on as impediments to entrepreneurial forms of citizenship. In doing so, I lay the groundwork for the two chapters that follow, and I hope to demonstrate how good-faith efforts to improve the lives of

FIGURE 4.1 An El Alto residence following a *ch'alla* celebration. Photo by author.

ordinary Alteños may nevertheless fail to offer lasting solutions to the problems they face.

Personhood, Compadres, and Conciliation

Let me return to the story of Doña Petrona and her tenant kin, Gregoria and René. After a lengthy back-and-forth, it appeared the conciliator had found a compromise: Petrona agreed to reimburse the couple for half the requested expenses, and the couple would vacate the premises. Yet just as they were about to sign a conciliation accord outlining that agreement, Gregoria and René interjected a few additional stipulations. "We want to take the corrugated roof tiles," Gregoria added. After some grumbling, Petrona's flank conceded. "And the electrical cables we installed," René exclaimed suddenly. With this last petition, Petrona's entourage exploded in outrage. Gregoria and René were recalling the bits of metal, plastic, and wiring they had invested into the shared home. They were, in effect, deconstructing the house, divesting it of the incremental improvements made over twelve years of close coresidence.

What does it mean for Gregoria and René not only to demand reimbursement for the financial contributions they made to outfitting the house, but also to ask for the very component parts, stripping it bare of plastic roofing and wires? In part, they are striving to recoup their *material* investments. But given the centrality of homebuilding to constituting ties of relatedness in the Andes, this deconstruction suggests a kind of de-kinning at work.[4] Pulling electrical wiring from the walls, scaling wooden ladders to ply corrugated plastic, and unmaking the physical infrastructure of the home are part of the process of dismantling their relationship with Petrona.

This dismantling is particularly poignant in El Alto, a city built principally by highland Aymara migrants like Petrona, familiar with roof raising and other practices of constructing homes, and kinship, through the collaborative labor of friends, neighbors, and family members. As Jessaca Leinaweaver notes, in the Andes, "Key life events are marked in the inhabitants' relationship to the house . . . and the house in turn shapes the social relationships that are carried out within and in reference to it" (2009: 789). Roof-raising activities are but one expression of the many ways Alteños construct relatedness through the *protracted* course of building a home together and then tinkering with and extending the structure as resources become available.

In El Alto, multigenerational households frequently shelter many kin: adult siblings and their spouses, parents, grandchildren, sometimes elderly aunts or others unable to care for themselves, as well as unrelated tenants. Plots of land are divided into smaller units within a single, adobe-walled compound, or families build upward, their skeletal brick structures dotting the horizon. El Alto's household units frequently (though not always) reflect the virilocal practices of rural Andean communities, with women moving to live with their in-laws.[5] In those intimate spaces, kin share the daily activities of washing clothes, caring for children, and tending to a few sheep or small brood of chickens. But they also share troubles and frustrations: a son who stumbles home drunk after a soccer match to fight with his young wife in the wee hours of the morning; a daughter-in-law's moneylender making a scene while neighbors watch through their windows; a brother's estranged common-law wife trying to serve him court papers for child support.

In addition to cohabitation, social relationships in El Alto are frequently knit together through a variety of debts, both moral and material, which are understood to be dynamic, with protracted temporalities. Ethnographers working in the Andes have examined practices such as feeding, labor reciprocity, and child circulation, among other embodied practices that express the moral economies of mutual obligation.[6] These authors show the work that goes into constantly producing and maintaining that relatedness and the sense of *cariño* (affection/care) that accompanies it.

People's invocation of cariño is not the fuzzy stuff of tenderness for another person, but rather a relation that demands material expression and work. Indeed, anthropologists such as Jeanette Edwards and Marilyn Strathern (2000) have written strongly against "sentimentalized" characterizations of kin relations, arguing that we see them, in Michael Lambeck's terms, as both "gift and theft" (2011). Long-term ethnographic research on kinship reveals that making and breaking those ties "entails promises and breaches of promise, acts and violations of intimacy, and acts of forgiveness and revenge" (Lambeck 2011: 4).[7] In El Alto, those often-fraught relations are lived out in the everyday practices of rearing children, loaning money, unloading potatoes to share during an *apthapi* (shared meal), *pijchando* (chewing) coca leaves, and other ordinary moments people share as they go about their lives and affirm or contest their relations with each other.[8] As people relate stories about those relationships, they are often riven with both cariño and coercion.

Compadrazgo is one of the principal practices through which people extend kin networks.[9] Godparents may be named for a child's baptism, *rutucha* (the rite of the first haircut), and high school graduation, among other occasions marking the course of a person's life. Compadrazgo relations can also help resolve disputes. During intake sessions at the center, clients often described seeking the advice and mediation of their *compadres de matrimonio* (godparents of the marriage) during fights over drinking, household expenses, or accusations of infidelity. These were not the imagined neutral third-party mediator of ADR.[10] Rather it was an intimately involved godfather (*padrino*) or godmother (*madrina*) (plural: padrinos), who is part of the larger social network of the couple. Sometimes that intermediary enacts what Laura Nader (1990) describes as a "harmony ideology," at the expense of exposing and ending abuse. Other times, padrinos chasten violent spouses or offer refuge to a godchild who chooses to leave a marriage.

Ideally, godparents continue to play a role in a child's life, though in practice many are far less involved. But the terms compadre or *comadre* (co-father or co-mother) refers to a different relationship. It's the relationship between the parents of those children and the godparent. That is, compadres are co-parents; the relationship that godparenting forges is not merely between the godmother and her godson, but rather between the two forms of parentage. First names fall out of usage; comadre and compadre become an almost singular means of address. Such compadrazgo networks constitute broader social ties in which people are nested, including more vertical relations established with people of a higher economic status (Leinaweaver 2008).[11] This *relational* quality of personhood is important to explicate because conflict-resolution programs I observed envisioned a different kind of disputant.

In the U.S. context, we throw around concepts like "rugged individualism" to capture the sense that a person, however shaped by a family, remains an autonomous being; her life trajectory, both its successes and failures, is of her own making. Political liberalism reflects a similar conceptualization of the person; central to its political project is individual liberty understood as personhood unfettered from social or political binds.[12] By contrast, rather than seeing autonomous individuals as merely connected to others through these ties, anthropologists have insisted that the intersubjective, interdependent relations produced through godparenting and other forms of sociality *constitute* the person herself. An individual is not merely tied to others; rather, she is made up of, or knit together by, those thickly interwoven ties.

Strathern (1988) coined the term "dividuals" to argue that Melanesian personhood *comprises* social relations.[13] That is, a Melanesian's sense of self is relational, mutable, or "fractal." Depending on the context, on the person with whom she is interacting, a different dimension of herself comes to the fore (i.e., her kin allegiances, her identity as a mother or sister).[14] This is not to suggest that people don't "accumulate personal biographies" over a lifetime; rather, in Penny Harvey's words, those individuals are "immersed at the same time in the processes through which those biographies take shape [*se hacen efectivas*] through their interaction with others" (2014: 80–81; my translation). Such an understanding of personhood demands that we pay attention to social relations—the terceros—accumulating in the waiting room and what they reveal.[15]

Meddling Terceros

Conciliators who explicitly forbid the entry of terceros argued that family members worsened conflicts as they brought their own interests and influence to bear on problems. They told stories of interfering in-laws or other nosy family members who exacerbated intimate quarrels. On the cusp of reaching an agreement, they told me, those extended family members could send a conflict spiraling out of control and undermine all the hard work that had been done to bring the two parties to a solution.

Paloma, for example, began her career at the IJCS as an unpaid volunteer before rising to her position as the center's director. When we met, she was widely respected for her ability to coordinate with neighborhood leadership and for her efficacy as a conciliator, pro bono lawyer, and sympathetic listener. On her first day on the job, however, Paloma was asked to conciliate a dispute between a young couple. "I was thrown into the pool like somebody who doesn't know how to swim; I had no idea what conciliation was!" she told me. An experienced neighborhood volunteer helped Paloma guide the couple toward an agreement. She was elated. Then they left her office—and things quickly soured. Paloma explained, "We had conciliated it really well, and then their relatives reignited the conflict; we had to conciliate it all over again."

Those experiences led Paloma to devise a plan where she would meet with the waiting families following conciliation, anticipating their intervention: "I decided to first conciliate the two parties and then call in the family to explain [the decision] so they would understand and support [it], and maybe hug and give kisses and calm down. I bring the family in at the end . . . because I don't want them to think I imposed [the decision]. That's a big problem in the courts—the case ends and everyone goes out and attacks each other. [But] it's important that it's just the two parties." But Paloma's approach to managed inclusion was not the norm.

Sebastián Costa, a conciliator working in peri-urban District 4, reported that disputing parties also arrived at his conciliation sessions with terceros, including padrinos of the marriage, who expected to *tener la palabra* (or "be allowed to speak"—an oft-invoked phrase in Bolivia). This pattern reflected conflict-resolution practices in rural communities, he argued, where disputing parties included the broader community and were resolved through the advice and adjudication of indigenous authorities. He was sympathetic to the impulse. But, he insisted, these expectations were ultimately destructive, not conducive to people taking responsibility for their conflicts and their resolution.[16] "There is a clash," he continued, "of visions between the integrated justice centers with their Western visions that hold that it is the generators of the conflict who should generate the solutions: those individuals." Cultural norms inviting terceros into the equation, he insisted, were unproductive, instead "generating dependency, taking away people's power of decision. If you are interested in generating a culture of peace you have to be willing to question these traditional practices." By contrast, ADR could empower atomistic individuals to direct their own lives. For conciliators like Costa, this was a cultural phenomenon that demanded transformation for the good of the people involved.

Conciliation appointments thus became spaces where clients' expectations of the role terceros would play vexed the staff's dyadic approach to disputing and the underlying expectations it reflected: that discrete individuals should be responsible for resolving their interpersonal conflicts.[17] Conciliation might be, as the educator Cecilia Ibáñez had envisioned, an opportunity to learn self-reliance in the face of an unresponsive or arbitrarily present state. Or, as Costa hoped, it could be an opportunity for clients to turn inward for solutions rather than relying on family members—whose presence complicated, or even escalated, interpersonal conflicts. Or, as Dr. José Pérez, the director of District 1, suggested, it might provide a chance for clients to assume responsibility, and, in the process, learn to embody a culture of peace and mature citizenship.

In all of these framings, the focus of the work being done is first and foremost on one's interior self. [18] That self is a self in process, a self who is subject to change.[19] When that self-in-progress is in conflict with another, similarly self-contained person, she must be isolated from the meddling of terceros in order to make that transformation possible. While a mediator may keep them on track when old angers or unarticulated desires arise and threaten to derail progress, these two must learn to bear the responsibility for negotiating a solution.[20]

I don't mean to suggest that the ideal type of personhood, which Costa frames as "Western," reflects an actually existing and particularly "Western" way of being a person in the world, although the mythology of rugged individualism is widespread—in the United States at least.[21] As Edward LiPuma (1998), Janet Carsten (2004), and Karl Smith (2012) have argued, *ideologies* of individualism do not negate the reality of interdependence that characterize most people's lives in London, Louisville, or Lausanne. Yet this ideal type of personhood frames the conciliation encounter by constructing disputants as people who can and should be unmoored from relations with meddling terceros for the good of those involved. Even if this rugged (or atomistic) individual is a fiction, it is a fiction that has real effects in shaping how Bolivian conciliators practice their trade. Nevertheless, this *ideology* of personhood strains against actually existing social practices in which a person is, indeed, nested.

This tension between the dyadic approach to personal responsibility and the *interdependent* reality is not merely a gap between liberal notions of personhood and, say, anthropological notions of a socially embedded, fluid, "dividual" self.[22] Rather, it is indicative of just how difficult it is to compartmentalize conflicts in El Alto. That difficulty owes to how everyday social practices *produce* the kinds of conflicts we saw at the centers. The tension over terceros reflects real differences between how ADR conceptualizes *conflict* itself as dyadic and how many Alteños experience the conflicts they bring to the centers.

One significant way these tensions surfaced was in conflicts over debt. Gregoria's reference to the debts she incurred from the bank in helping to improve the household compound she shared with her elderly relative, Petrona, invokes a broader economic context for their dispute. It also reflects a recurring pattern of conflicts we saw at the centers: disputes revolving around interpersonal and microfinance loans that mapped onto extensive social networks. And the results were messy.

Examining the ways lending relationships produce *both* kin *and* conflict helps us get away from timeless, romanticized notions of Andean personhood, as well as the recurring binary between Western/non-Western understandings of the self.[23] My aim here is to analyze the practices that go into making social relations tangible, material in people's lives—and also cause strain and discord. As I show in this chapter and those that follow, informal, interpersonal loans between friends and kin fashioned social ties *and* threatened to sever them. Those lending practices were some of the primary reasons people came to the centers pursuing conciliation. Other times those loans hovered in the background of seemingly unrelated disputes. Yet while conciliation seeks to isolate conflicts between disputing parties, debts like the ones described here exemplify the sociological reality of lending and its resulting conflicts: they cannot easily be reduced to neat dyads.

While conciliators tried to simplify and isolate conflicts in order to manage these messy webs of debt and construct "actionable" conciliation accords, these conflicts reveal just how artificial the boundaries between disputants and terceros really are in practice. Further, conciliation sessions over debt expose the ways microfinance programs have both shadowed and helped to produce social networks forged through lending, revealing the limits of ADR for redressing some of the primary sources of conflict in the city. The effort to compartmentalize such disputes—insisting on the dyadic nature of debt conflicts—may contribute to the further depoliticization of lending-related conflicts in El Alto. Let me give an example for one such conciliation session.

"Between Compadres There Is No Interest"

On this bright October morning, the center conciliator calls me into her office. She is swamped with a conciliation appointment that is taking longer than expected. Another tangle of married couples is waiting for their session.

She asks if I can help them start talking through the issues until she can take over with the official conciliation session and finalize an agreement—if they can reach one.

There are two issues, she explains to me, pulling out a sheet of paper. "A debt between two men, and then another woman who has shown up saying she is also owed a debt from the first man." She draws me a diagram:

Person who made loan (1) to → (2) Debtor,
(3) Person who made loan → person (1)

"Be emphatic," she tells me. "You are dealing with one loan, and then the other. Separately."

First up, Hilario and Ignacia owe Severino and Nieves money.

I start by reminding the group about the aims of conciliation, using a variation of the script I learned while working at the center. I invite Severino, who has called for the conciliation appointment, to explain what happened from his perspective. Severino is a badger of a man. He is also quite possibly drunk. I pause to ask the conciliator for guidance; she encourages me to continue prepping them since he insists he's only "a little hungover" from the previous night. "I am," he proclaims, "perfectly able to continue." Compact but muscular, Severino's hair is a thick crown of curls. He is regularly on his feet, shouting, speaking over people, while his wife tries to shush him, slapping at his arm. As I have learned in my training, I repeatedly remind them that if we cannot remain respectful we will have to suspend the conversation until people are in a better frame of mind. This admonition usually brings everyone back to their seats.

Severino explains that his neighbor, Hilario, approached him, asking for a loan. "He came crying to me, 'I owe this bank, that bank, another bank. Please lend me some money.' I gave him a loan for a week. But he never paid. He did give me 150 Bs [US$21.50], but that was just for interest." Both parties still understand the remaining amount to be 500 Bs or roughly US$71.

Hilario points at Severino and says, "He came to my house threatening my children. My son said, 'Why not kick his ass?' But I am not that class of person who goes around hitting people."

Hilario counters by trying to insert the *other* debt into the conversation—the one Severino owes his compadres, who are sitting in the waiting room.

Before I can intervene, Severino invokes the conciliator's words, spoken as she introduced me to the group and they agreed to sit down with me until their formal session, when she explained they would have to deal with the two debts separately. He shoots back at Hilario: "I know the law, the law of God, and those things cannot enter; this is just about us!" Citing God (and the conciliator), he rejects terceros.

Hilario's wife, Ignacia, offers her version of the situation: "I had all these debts and my daughter was also sick, so we couldn't get enough money together to pay them back. So this man," she says, indicating Severino, "went around to all our neighbors telling stories, saying we didn't even have enough food to eat." Ignacia is trembling.

Severino tries to speak over her. His wife slaps at his shoulder. "Listen, listen," she hisses at him.

Ignacia continues, "And then he comes to our house and starts kicking the door and screaming 'Piece of shit! When are you going to pay me?'" Ignacia explains that she and her husband believe they have already paid one quota to Severino and Nieves. She and her husband made a payment to Doña Lourdes—the woman waiting outside for her turn—*on behalf* of Nieves and Severino for a debt *they* owed. It looks like this:

(1) Nieves and Severino owe their compadres → (3) Lourdes and her husband, Miguel.

(2) Hilario and Ignacia → made a payment to (3) Lourdes and Miguel on behalf of (1) Severino and Nieves's debt to their kin.

Hilario and Ignacia want the amount they gave to the couple waiting outside (Lourdes and Miguel) to be considered as if it were a quota already repaid to Severino and Nieves.

Severino is incensed by the proposal—and uses the conciliator's efforts to compartmentalize the debts as fodder to mount his defense. "That's between my compadre and me, you have nothing to say about that. I am a man. I am a man!" I ask Severino to lower his voice and to be respectful. He pushes hard on my shoulder and barks, "No, you listen to me! *Escuchamepues.*" His wife looks at me, alarmed. I try to maintain my composure and calmly reply, "Don Severino, please take a seat."

The group eventually reaches a provisional agreement of two payments of 250 Bs (US$36), and the return of a sound system that Severino and Nieves are holding as collateral. Having arrived at a tentative plan, I prepare to send them to the conciliator.

But as we close, Nieves introduces a new issue. She starts speaking angrily about a funeral they had all attended several months prior. "We put in two cases of beer, but Hilario's brothers only returned one of the cases. His brothers owe us another 160 Bs for that other case of beer," she explains.

Hilario is furious. "That's a problem you have with my brothers, not me," he says, waving his hand dismissively. Nieves has taken off her hat and extends her hand in their direction, imploring: "But how are we supposed to *cobrar* [to recover the debt]?"

"Doña Nieves," I say, mimicking my instructions, "for now we need to focus on this specific debt between your two families. [The conciliator] would need to address the other situation directly with the people involved." I, too, have reasserted the dyadic nature of our efforts, and Nieves nods her acquiescence mournfully.

Eventually the two families settle on a tentative payment system, amounts, dates, and a timetable for returning the collateral. Hilario and Ignacia leave the room to wait for a meeting with the conciliator to finalize the agreement and sign the accord. The waiting couple, Miguel and Lourdes, enters the room.

Miguel says that Severino approached him asking for a loan because he didn't have any capital. Miguel originally loaned Severino 1,000 Bs (approximately US$143), and now he owes him the last 400 Bs (US$57) of the original loan.

Nieves, Severino's wife, challenges this version of the events.

"That's not how it happened," she says. "They approached *me*. They encouraged *me* to take the money—they loaned me 500 Bs [US$71.50]. When I did that, my husband beat me," Nieves remembers, bringing up the kind of "background" violence I examine in chapter 5. "Later they [again] asked me, 'How much do you want?'" Nieves mimics someone pulling out a bundle of money from inside a jacket and pretends to thumb through the cash. She blames her compadres for pressuring her to take more money, to "hold on to it" (*agarrarlo*) for a while. She implies that this was pushy and suspicious on their part, suggesting that they were acting like *prestamistas* (moneylenders) toward her.[24] Nieves then starts tallying her own memory of small repayments she claims are not being acknowledged. "I only owe 300 Bs (US$43)," she concludes.

"We still haven't addressed the interest," Miguel interjects.

Nieves's face falls and she beseeches her kin, "Between compadres one doesn't charge interest! My husband doesn't want to hear anything about the debt. He drags me around. He hits me. But we went into debt as a family," Nieves pleads with her comadre, Lourdes. "You know how much I gave you," she moans in Lourdes's direction.

Lourdes turns her body away from Nieves. She wraps her face ever more tightly in her fleece shawl, pulls her broad-rimmed bonnet down over her eyes, and shakes her head, "No." Lourdes seems to be sinking under the discomfort of confronting Nieves over the debt. She slips open her shawl enough to count on her fingers, tallying the small payments Nieves has made. She insists that she still owes her 400 Bs (approximately US$57).

Yet Lourdes appears to have been moved by her comadre's appeals. She mumbles something under her breath. I ask her to speak up. "I am a mother too," she says. "I understand what it's like to feed children." Lourdes turns to her husband and quietly implores him, "Just accept the 300 Bs." Miguel looks frustrated and shakes his head no, saying, "I also have children and bills to pay." He wavers a moment and then gives in to his wife's intercession. Sighing, he agrees to the 300 Bs. Severino, who has remained silent, suddenly sits up and interjects, "I don't want to swindle anyone; I follow the law of the Lord!" His compadres and wife ignore his outburst and continue to negotiate.

Nieves offers to pay in staggered quotas. Miguel shakes his head. "No, we want it in one lump sum. It's been four years! Look, we don't have a problem with [Nieves]," he directs at me. "But her husband, he's a drunk. You see how he is. He comes to assault the family. He's really aggressive. We don't have a problem with our comadre."

Nieves interjects: "He isn't helping me at all with this. He doesn't want to hear anything about the debt. He beats me. He yells at me. [The debt] is just between me and them," she says emphatically, in effect making Severino a socially defined tercero to the conflict. Nieves and her compadres reach a tentative agreement before heading into the formal conciliation session where they will revisit the source of conflict and proposed solution, finalize the payment plan, and sign an accord.

"His First Word May as Well Have Been 'Debt'"

For months, I watched as center interns extolled the value of ADR for resolving such conflicts; I too conducted intake sessions with clients and set up appointments for precisely these kinds of messy, interlocking debts. As I watched the debt-related appointments accumulate in District 6, I wondered if we were witnessing patterns that were specific to the residents of Alto Lima—a neighborhood populated largely by *comerciantes* (merchants) who made their living working at 16 de Julio, or the smaller neighborhood markets that spring up each week.

Yet conciliators and center directors working in other neighborhoods reported similar patterns.[25] As Costa told me, "In the past family conflicts—especially child support and violence—seemed to dominate, but this year the thing I am seeing more of is debt." Costa opened his appointment calendar and quickly tallied the cases. "For example, this week I am seeing seven sessions on debt. Microcredit is just really generating a lot of conflict." The more I followed cases like the ones above, the more I saw how efforts to promote the "financial inclusion" of residents of El Alto had become entangled with kinship practices ranging from sharing household compounds to informal lending to one's comadre to help her pay off bank quotas or to cover a child's medical bills. Debt was unavoidable, and it was multilayered. Center clients would spontaneously lament their indebtedness while relating other tensions in their homes. My own comadres unloaded stories of loans made and never repaid. Sometimes, they were the lender. Other times, the borrower. More frequently, they were both: at one moment, they were the person to give; at other moments, the one to receive. The linkage to microfinance and other bank loans, however, must be situated in the broader context of mutual aid in El Alto.

In El Alto, as with other places in Bolivia, social obligations frequently involve social and material debts that are understood to be mutually obligating, often expressed in the concept of *ayni*. Ayni frequently refers to labor exchange, like that which goes into roof raising and harvesting. But people also invoked ayni when referring to other debts, whether cases of beer provided during wedding celebrations or cash lent to a comadre needing capital for her small pollera-making business. Ayni has both temporal and material dimensions.[26] That quality was reflected in a phrase many people used to explain the concept to me: "today for you, tomorrow for me." That tomorrow, however, might be years from now. Embedded in the concept is the notion that life is fraught with moments in which we all find ourselves with unmet needs and must rely on others for support—emotional, physical, and economic.

Understood within the broader literature on credit and debt, anthropologists have shown that indebtedness must be understood as socially productive; a debt is not *inherently* positive for the lender or negative for the person in debt.[27] Marcel Mauss's seminal work *The Gift* (1954) has heavily influenced studies of credit and debt through its focus on the ways credit and debt relations both create group solidarity *and* build systems of domination or hierarchy.[28] As Gustav Peebles explains, "The ethnographic task over many years has been to study how the credit/debt nexus is productive of social ties, alliances, enmities, and hostilities, rather than to make normative pronouncements concerning whether credit is liberating or debt is debilitating" (2010: 234). Clara Han similarly qualifies her study of the domestic strains produced by "the double-edged credit economy" in Chile, saying that although credit "has generated perpetual indebtedness, it also offers material and temporal resources for livelihoods affected by labor instability" (2011: 25, 9). For Han, credit, while enormously stressful, also allows debtors to imagine alternative futures, and to care for kin suffering from mental illness and addiction in the wake of neoliberal economic restructuring.

In Bolivia, as in postdictatorship Chile, kin networks play a critical role in mitigating economic precariousness. These domestic relations nevertheless can wear under the "constant and awkward friction among kinship obligations and dependencies, liberal family forms and discourses of self-responsibility," that circulate in El Alto, as with neoliberal Chile (Han 2011: 13). Like Han, I found that my own compadres, friends, and center clients articulated a similar sense of living a "*vida prestada*" (a life on loan). They regularly lamented how those debts shot through nearly all their interactions. As one client told me, her family's life had been so impacted by the tensions of indebtedness that her children's "first word may as well have been 'debt.'"

There are multiple levels at which kinship is created, reasserted, battered, and eroded through these debts and their ripple effects throughout the extended social network. In the example I gave, Nieves tried to assert the moral economy of lending with her kin. There is something qualitatively different, she insisted, between a loan made between comadres and a loan made by a prestamista or the bank. *Entre compadres no hay interés.* Between compadres there is no interest. Despite her protests, I found that even between compadres, lenders were regularly charging interest.

As I spoke with women who openly worked as moneylenders and others who rejected the title, it became clear that many were charging monthly— and sometimes weekly or even daily—interest rates upward of 10 percent and 20 percent, and demanding collateral for those loans. Nico Tassi (2010) argues that market vendors in La Paz's Eloy Salmon district lend according to a "postulate of abundance," charging interest as a way of making that money grow. This understanding resonates with Olivia Harris's (1995) work on credit/debt as a kind of socially reproductive fertilizer.

Center clients, by contrast, rarely invoked such fecund language to characterize their interest rates. Instead, debate over interest—its excessiveness or its mere existence—was one way Alteños evaluated the socially productive or antisocial quality of lending. Many insisted that charging interest was a matter of necessity, a means to coerce delinquent compadres into repayment. They too owed countless debts to other friends, kin, neighbors, and prestamistas—and, as I describe here, and in the chapters to follow, they were often heavily indebted to microfinance institutions. Those debts helped produce

FIGURE 4.2 A sign for one of the integrated justice centers against the backdrop of billboards that advertise nearby banks and microfinance institutions. Photo by author.

and re-produce forms of kinship, care, and obligation. But they were also fraying social ties as neighbors and kin called in loans, demanding abrupt repayment years later—as Lourdes and Miguel demanded of Nieves. Marshall Sahlins (2011) has suggested that "where being is mutual, the experience is more than individual." Yet where *being* is constructed in part by mutual indebtedness, when the bank comes for one, it comes for all. That which thickens kinship ties may also thin and break them.[29]

Ayni in an Era of Microcredit

Anthropologists aren't the only ones to notice how poor people marshal their social networks during times of economic duress. Since the late 1970s, microfinance agencies have targeted the social networks of poor people to expand the reach of finance capital while helping to insure against risk.[30] For example, in her research among craftsmen in Cairo, Egypt, Julia Elyachar shows how the rubric of "social capital" reconceptualized the survival strategies of the poor. Rather than acting as "obstacles to economic development," planners and social scientists now characterized those social practices, networks, and survival strategies—the "social capital" of the poor—as a critical "resource for reproducing global markets, maintaining global stability, and achieving economic growth" (Elyachar 2005: 9). In particular, they have targeted the social networks of poor women to channel capital and encourage entrepreneurship, promoting microfinance as a mechanism of social and economic inclusion for women.[31]

In Bolivia, microfinance institutions have followed this global trend. As I noted in chapter 1, Bolivia's relationship to microfinance dates back to its first wave of neoliberal reforms during the 1980s, when it was attached to structural adjustment programs (Bolivia was the guinea pig). Once celebrated as a success story for its borrowers' repayment rates, the microfinance sector suffered a crisis when a recession rocked the country in 1999.[32] Unable to repay their loans, over-indebted borrowers took to the streets and to hunger strikes. Yet as Elisabeth Rhyne (2004) has shown, after a period of contraction, the microfinance sector rebounded in the early 2000s. Now the IMF and Economist Intelligence Unit characterize Bolivia's microfinance institutions as "some of the best in the world" (Heng 2015).[33]

Clients at the IJCs frequently carried the glossy folders given out by microfinance institutions that targeted women for incorporation into borrowing groups in which women are expected to hold each other accountable for meeting monthly microcredit quotas. As Caroline Schuster (2014) has argued, this is not simply a matter of microfinance institutions piggybacking on existing social networks, but rather a credit extension platform that *produces* those gendered social networks by utilizing women as the "social collateral" for each other's loans (see also Kar 2017).

Anthropologists studying microfinance have illuminated the disjuncture between the ways microfinance institutions market themselves as providing seed capital for small enterprise, and the actual uses of those loans.[34] By contrast to the popular microfinance narrative of supporting small business owners, in practice many borrowers frequently obtain loans to cover basic needs in the face of "eroding and unstable wages and the privatization of public services" (Han 2011: 26)[35] Although many center clients stated they were utilizing loans to help finance a seamstress business or to purchase merchandise to sell as itinerant vendors in the 16 de Julio market, many others were accessing credit to pay school fees or to cover unexpected medical bills. Others, still, reported using loans to meet social obligations, for example, financing their responsibilities as sponsors of fiesta-cargo celebrations in their natal hamlets or making contributions to wedding and baptismal celebrations. Such uses allowed them to invest in social reproduction, generating and strengthening social ties, but were not themselves economically profitable.

Microfinance is not responsible for the advent of informal lending practices in El Alto. Bolivians—including Aymara women—have long been involved in lending and borrowing practices, making a living as moneylenders or simply helping out friends, neighbors, and kin as they face recurring economic hardship. However, microfinance's diffusion in Bolivia over the last thirty years has complicated and compounded existing lending practices by creating bigger and more unwieldy debts. It does so by pulling more family members and friends into debt relationships through microfinance groups and having them sign as guarantors on individual loans, as well as the widespread practice of borrowers procuring new loans to repay the old.[36] As Sohini Kar (2017) notes in her study of Indian MFIs that require women to secure male guarantors, "lending institutions are highly aware of the ways in which credit intersects with domestic life. . . . The reshaping of familial life through financialization is not simply an unintended outcome; rather, MFIs attempt to harness these relations of guarantee in the service of enfolding the poor into financial networks to hedge against the very risks of lending to the poor" (315).

Dyadic Debts and Domesticated Conflict

This is the complex, interwoven nature of many of the debt-fueled conflicts that came to the center. In practice, however, center staff regularly reasserted the dyadic relationship of each conflict as interpersonal. They employed this tactic partly to make conflicts more manageable: it's a logistical problem. Could the disputes between Hilario and his wife, Ignacia; Lourdes and her husband, Miguel; and their compadres, Severino and Nieves, have been resolved in one massive group session? Perhaps not. But the staff also insisted on this compartmentalization of conflicts because of how they conceptualize conflict *and the responsibility to resolve it*. Staff I spoke with envisioned conciliation as a means of instilling people with the skills to personally manage conflict, empowering them to assume responsibility for the lives they lead. Blocking out terceros cultivated personal accountability. An ideal type of personhood necessitated an ideal type of conflict. In practice, however, this insistence on a dyadic approach to conflict resolution in El Alto may serve to domesticate

FIGURE 4.3 Fast cash is available from moneylenders and pawnshops like this one in the 16 de Julio market. Photo by author.

and depoliticize patterns of social conflict that are threatening to unmake social lives and survival strategies among Alteños.

I don't mean to suggest that center staff and other service providers were unaware of these challenges—or unsympathetic to the strains they produced. Conciliators, center directors, and interns were often grappling with *similar* debts and resulting disputes in their own households. When I asked center staff and bureaucrats at the Ministry of Justice about these patterns, many acknowledged *and lamented* the extraordinary caseload built around informal lending—approximately a third to half of his sessions, according to Costa. Nor do I want to suggest that clients wanted all those social relations present; for some, it was truly a relief that they were excluded. Nevertheless, the dyadic vision of ADR narrows the scope of the conflict to an individual debtor-creditor relation, a private little dyad divorced from broader patterns.[37] The room for critique was reduced to deep sighs, painful grimaces, and sympathy for the señoras and their desperation.

As I show in this and the chapters that follow, framing debt conflicts as private matters—as interpersonal disputes—both reflects and sustains an entrepreneurial approach to citizenship. It does so in part by patching together mechanisms for repayment that enable borrowers to meet their microfinance quotas, too. Yet as I conducted fieldwork, lenders and borrowers themselves were starting to decry the social networks they once celebrated.[38] Rather than enabling people to pursue entrepreneurship while offering a solution to risk management, critics disparaged forms of sociality they understood to be antithetical to entrepreneurship—promoting, instead, vice and irresponsible behavior. These discourses conjure up older idioms to talk about the barriers to individual success. In so doing, they place the blame for distressing scenes like those described here at the feet of people who have failed to sufficiently adopt an entrepreneurial subjectivity, who remain encumbered by *burdensome* social relations that threaten—rather than ensure—repayment. Let me conclude this chapter by reflecting a little on this move to blaming debt problems on alcohol consumption, dance, and the forms of sociality they represent. Here, social networks are not a *resource* for poor people to help themselves, but rather an impediment they must escape if they want to succeed as entrepreneurial citizens.

"I Prefer to Stop Eating, Dancing, and Drinking in Order to Pay My Quotas"

Much anthropological and ethnohistorical work in Bolivia examines the centrality of alcohol consumption patterns in Andean sociality.[39] These practices include inviting neighbors to share beer and food and to *pijchar* (chew) coca leaves after offering prayers to recently deceased kin during All Souls Day. Friends, siblings, and compadres may pack themselves into a brother-in-law's minibus to drive out to the rural hamlet where his wife and her sisters grew up—as I once did with my friend Enriqueta and her extended family. On the way there we took swigs of *vino casero* (homemade wine) and munched on roasted peanuts and *pasank'allas* (sugar-coated corn puffs). The bus was heavily loaded with *tant'awawas* (bread babies) and sugarcane stalks used to construct a memorial to Enriqueta's mother. Each of us carried heavy woven bags brimming with oranges and other brightly colored treats that the family distributed to neighbors who offered prayers for her mother in the small community graveyard.

Women sat in one circle while men formed another ring as Enriqueta and her sisters offered overflowing plates to late arrivals: spicy pork poured over rehydrated chuño, boiled potatoes, and roasted bananas. Adult kin hauled cases of beer and dispensed brimming handfuls of coca leaves while parents dispensed sugarcane slices to small children with wind-chapped cheeks. The three sisters periodically retreated to the edges of the field to mumble prayers and bury offerings to the vital force known as Pachamama. In addition to beer and homemade wine, some men passed around a small plastic bottle of what amounts to rubbing alcohol—used to sprinkle *mesas* (offerings) and providing the wince-inducing sips that burn your lips, throat, and stomach lining.[40]

Alcohol is central to many such moments in the day-to-day lives and celebrations of Bolivians living in El Alto and surrounding rural hamlets: inviting new compadres to drink during the ritual first haircut or at the baptism of a child, providing cases of beer at wedding celebrations for a cousin or brother-in-law, or acting as a sponsor of the annual fiesta in your natal community in a rural hamlet near the shores of Lake Titicaca. Neighbors stack cases of beer and pour full, frothy glasses for each other at neighborhood *entradas*—the dance parades that shut down entire blocks of El Alto as residents celebrate patron saints and their neighborhood anniversary.

Andeanist scholars, including Abercrombie (1998), Canessa (2012), Harvey (1991), and Saignes (1989), have examined the ways alcohol is central to creating and re-creating forms of social memory, and to producing that sense of self I described earlier—one that is composed of social relationships. Drinking is almost always done in pairs—or more accurately pairs upon pairs upon pairs, as each person repeatedly invites another in the circle to drink and is in turn invited by others to partake. These are not isolated dyads, but rather dyads that are interwoven into wider webs of relations enacted through invitations to drink, eat, and pijchar coca. Those circulating glasses of beer help reassert the primacy of social relationships with both the living and dead. Alcohol consumption in these celebrations is a form of communion with kin and spirits, ancestors and neighbors.

But alcohol consumption also produces a great deal of anxiety, frustration, anger, and debate about excess and alcohol-fueled violence—both intimate violence and violence that occurs on the street between total strangers.[41] Evangelical Christians (*evangélicos* or *cristianos*) generally eschew alcohol consumption (in word if not always in deed), among other practices that evangélicos reject as idolatrous and morally corrupt. Refusing the invitation to drink at fiestas has proven particularly taxing on relationships between Catholics and their evangelical Protestant kin and neighbors, forcing them to renegotiate the ways that sociality is both embodied and imbibed.[42]

Alteño friends and kin—both evangelical and Catholic—often describe to me their discomfort and the difficulty of refusing alcohol without causing discord and consternation among their friends and relatives. Azucena, for example, told stories of feeling enormous pressure to participate in weekly outings with her colleagues at the bank where she once worked. Unable to refuse drinks, Azucena started skipping the after-work celebrations, only to find herself marginalized within the office. My own attempts to refuse alcohol were met with scorn. I often relied on female friends to intercede with their relatives, begging forgiveness for the gringuita's inability to keep up with the prolonged celebrations.

The harmful dimensions of alcohol consumption and its influence in El Alto are hotly debated—among residents and nonresidents alike. As Helene Risør (2016) has detailed, El Alto neighborhood watch groups and youth organizations have recently attacked brothels and bars, accusing owners and patrons of fomenting deviancy, enabling violent assault, and promoting promiscuity. These moral panics have given way to very real efforts to torch and shutter houses of ill repute. President Evo Morales even declared alcohol consumption to be a national security issue. The Morales administration has moved to develop new regulations on adulterated and homemade alcohol (i.e., vino casero) as a public health concern, and it introduced new legislation and policing efforts aiming to crack down on drunk driving. These platforms are quite similar to movements in the United States where, as Malcolm Gladwell puts it, we "moralize, medicalize, and legalize" the social and personal burdens of alcohol consumption (2010: 71).

But this concern for Andean alcohol consumption patterns is not new. As Spanish colonial authorities sought to make sense of libation rituals and Andean religiosity, they frequently derided Andean Indians for being slothful, drunken, and idolatrous. As Abercrombie (1998) has shown, "Andean libation rituals came to be inscribed as forms of excessive drinking, and memory techniques were taken for drunkenness and amnesia" (140). This "triumvirate" of "drunkenness, idolatry, and avoidance of labor" (222) was particularly disconcerting to colonial rulers who worried about how to discipline Indian labor in order to secure tribute. Abercrombie suggests that industriousness was a euphemism for coercing Indians into a forced wage-labor system where authorities hoped they might learn to "conduct social relations and construct social position and obedience to the laws of god and king through the medium of money" (1998: 225). Alcohol was an impediment to that industriousness. Thus alcohol has long been central to both social life in the Andes and to anxieties over the undisciplined labor of Andean Indians.

The residue of those colonial concerns with alcohol consumption as an impediment to efficient labor continues to bubble up in everyday conversations about life and work in El Alto, now tied to extending financial services to the poor. Take, for example, an ad that appeared in a special pullout promotional section of the popular newspaper *Pagina Siete* (Page Seven). In a special edition of the paper's business section, the microfinance institution Ecofuturo took out a full-page advertorial with one of their model clients, José Silvestre Quisbert. In the advertorial, Silvestre Quisbert, a fifty-seven-year-old carpenter, expresses gratitude for the ways that microfinance repayment timelines have restructured his own spending and saving habits. That new timeline, he suggests, has profoundly transformed his personhood and his relationships with others. Silvestre Quisbert describes being previously involved in microfinance groups where relations among members were mediated through shared loans and heavy drinking:

> I didn't know about credit before, but I learned that there were institutions that gave loans to groups of people. I formed a group and took out credit, *but the group didn't work for me*—because I met my quotas but others failed to make their payments, and everyone was punished. They punished us for three months denying us credit, but afterward they didn't want to loan to us. Since I have a strong personality, I even had fights with my loan officer. . . . I lost my temper. I was left saddened by the experience of working in a group. *The thing is, we as Bolivians have the custom of grabbing the money and spending it in the cantina, but we don't leave after dividing up the money. Instead we start [to drink heavily].*[43]

The word borrachera (heavy drinking or drunken carousing) is inserted into the text parenthetically as if to underscore the scandal of going to the bar. The MFI group members in Silvestre Quisbert's woeful tale aren't drinking away their profits—they are drinking away their capital. But now, he tells the reader, he is able to take out private loans that he alone administers, freed from the tethers and the burden of other participants.

Further down in the interview, Silvestre Quisbert expresses pride in his punctuality and a life now organized around meeting his monthly quotas: "I prefer to stop eating, dancing and drinking for the eighth or ninth of every month in order to have my quota ready," he asserts. The advertorial, however, siphons off a few words for its headline; in bold letters it declares not *moderated* consumption (skipping two days) but rather its complete rejection: "I prefer to stop eating, dancing, and drinking in order to pay my quotas." Silvestre Quisbert is a model microfinance recipient, a model citizen-entrepreneur who places responsibility, seriousness, and sobriety above the siren song of drink and revelry. In doing so, Silvestre Quisbert positions himself (or is positioned by the ad developers) as one willing to give up forms of drunken sociality, replaced by the virtues of sobriety and *individual* responsibility.

In the promotional ad we see how contemporary discourses about the value of entrepreneurship and individual responsibility have supplanted previous efforts to extirpate the idols and sloth associated with Andean libation practices.[44] In his testimony, the entrepreneurial self rejects both the social *obligations* associated with and the social *burdens* produced by alcohol—for the promise of individual prosperity. What's interesting about this advertorial is how it anticipates and redirects emerging critiques of group loans by braiding those criticisms together with local idioms concerning cultural patterns of alcohol consumption. The publicity piece thus acknowledges the critique and distances the institution from increasingly maligned group lending practices, positioning Ecofuturo as aware of these problems and offering a better alternative to its borrowers: individual loans.

Through the "testimony" of José Silvestre Quisbert (the genre itself a play on the sober testimony of newly minted evangélicos), the piece suggests that the failure of loan groups was not due to the lending approach of banking institutions per se. Rather, the problem lay in the ways those lending practices were warped by *borrowers*—misused for partying, drinking, and other self-harming *social* behavior. The blame resides with borrowers who fail to slough off social practices and vices that stand as barriers to successful loan repayment and productive entrepreneurial citizenship. Ecofuturo invites borrowers who are willing, like Don José, to sever those ties. Ironically, as I found at the center, reliance on those social ties are often the only ways borrowers were able to pay off mounting debts—*including* ones incurred through individual loans from microfinance institutions. As they faced the increased difficulty of paying back *those* debts, clients spun ever more complex webs of interpersonal lending through their friends, neighbors, and kin.

Conclusion

Conciliation frequently relies on a "triadic" approach to resolving conflicts: with the aid of a third party, disputants are meant to forge their own solutions to interpersonal problems. Nevertheless, these sessions assume that conflict occurs between two parties: a dyad of disputants. Conciliators frequently attempt to impose a dyadic model of conflict onto the situation to make it more manageable, and also to help instill in people a willingness to take personal responsibility for the solution. Center clients, however, often bring different expectations of who should participate in conflict resolution. They bring along sisters and mothers, cousins and compadres, aunties and neighbors. Much like Doña Petrona, they bring along a lot of kin. They bring along ADR-defined terceros. Those kin are as important to people's lives and livelihoods as the commercial endeavors they undertake in the markets. But they are also central to how people experience conflict and seek its resolution.

ADR practitioners frequently stressed that disputants should be isolated from terceros, presuming or encouraging them to behave as autonomous individuals. By contrast, through kinship practices such as coresidence and compadrazgo, terceros play a key role in constituting the very personhood of the people in that negotiation room. However, taking seriously the role of terceros is also more representative of how conflicts actually unfold over issues such as debt. These are not private, interpersonal disputes between two parties; rather, specific conflicts operated more like nodes in a complex network of relationships that are both knit and frayed by lending practices.

Beyond "cultural" expectations of who should participate in a conciliation session, the dyadic compartmentalization of conflict belies the real complexity of how these conflicts occur in El Alto. The conciliation appointments between Nieves and Severino, Lourdes and Miguel, Hilario and Ignacia, expose how these lending practices both comprise sociality and threaten to tear it apart. Thus while dyadic approaches to conflict management may help resolve some disputes concretely—especially when coupled with Paloma's approach to including terceros postconciliation—the underlying causes of those conflicts remain multistranded and unresolved.

Such terceros constitute the social relations that have been celebrated as the social *capital*—and that have served as the social *collateral*—of the poor. And yet, in conciliation sessions and among microfinance participants, debates emerge over what constitutes fruitful, admissible, or pathological forms of sociality. Andeanist scholars have argued that the trio of drinking, dancing, and eating are central to constructing and reinforcing social ties in Bolivia, and these same practices are explicitly named by José Silvestre Quisbert in his testimony appearing in the advertorial.[45] Ecofuturo ventriloquizes Silvestre Quisbert to cast those social practices as anathema to economic productivity and security, and it invites other participants to eschew such anti-entrepreneurial relationships—and to take advantage of the MFI's individual loan programs.

During conciliation sessions over debt, two platforms of development aid thus become entangled with one another: one advocates poverty alleviation by extending credit and encouraging entrepreneurship; the other promotes conflict deescalation by encouraging the urban poor to resolve disputes through ADR and not the courts or violence. Their shared underpinnings included an expectation that people's needs are better served by empowering them to be entrepreneurs of their own financial and peace-filled futures rather than by relying on state-sponsored entitlements or solutions. These entanglements are evident in discourses and development projects that link small business ownership (built through microfinance) to virtuous citizenship. But those entanglements are also evident in conciliation sessions, as friends and relatives utilize the IJCs to cope with crushing debts and the resulting disputes—securing repayment for MFIs, too.

Aid programs and the Ministry of Justice may miss an opportunity to identify and redress the larger political economic dimensions of these "private," "interpersonal" disputes when they erase those patterns and compartmentalize conflict into neat dyads. But this compartmentalization raises another question. *Is* this merely a missed opportunity, an unintended consequence of a good-faith effort to redress the frustrations many Alteños experience in their everyday lives? Or is ADR operating in the way American critics warned during the 1980s: as a mechanism for "dampening class conflict" by individualizing disputes at the expense of political analysis and collective action?[46] I return to these questions in chapter 6. Regardless of the good-faith efforts of staff, the effect is a jerry-rigged system of debt repayment that may erase all of the scrambling that is occurring below the surface to meet those quotas.[47]

The Conflictual Social Life of an
Industrial Sewing Machine

As microfinance institutions (MFIs) proliferated in El Alto, Doña Pilar seized on the opportunity.[1] Pilar had several income-generating strategies, including selling rotisserie chicken and packaging homemade "chocolate-like" drink mix with her teenage children. But Pilar's other microenterprise was lending. Pilar, like a number of women I met in District 6, took out small loans from MFIs that she then redistributed among friends. She charged her borrowers interest on those interpersonal loans with the aim of generating a profit. She lent to friends and neighbors, but also to strangers, as her social network started telling *their* friends, kin, and acquaintances that Pilar might also lend to them.

Soon, however, Pilar's borrowers began to fail her. Enmeshed in webs of MFI loans and informal debts owed to friends and relatives, she told me, her borrowers simply stopped paying her back. Friends asked her for money, then begged for understanding when they couldn't repay the principal, let alone the added interest she charged.

Burned by several such experiences, Pilar started requiring collateral. Borrowers left electronics, gas canisters, important paperwork, and jewelry, "all kinds of things," she told me. One man even left her the deed to his house. "I still have it here," she said. "The deed and even the document verifying signatures. I have all his documents. He never came back to get them," she shrugged.

One woman left her an electric Mitsubishi "industrial" sewing machine.

I soon came to see that industrial sewing machine as emblematic of a much larger pattern of conflicts affecting Alteños. The story of the industrial sewing machine is a story about the ways that debt and violence are entangled—as entangled as the lives of the women connected to that machine. At first, however, the violence associated with the sewing machine was itself invisible.

I might have never known it was there.

"The señora was supposed to pay me back in fifteen days and I would return it," Pilar told me. But the woman never returned for her machine—or paid Pilar back. When Pilar ran into her in the market several months later, the woman simply told Pilar to keep the machine; she was in no shape to pay the debt. So Pilar was left with a sewing machine she didn't really need or want.

Pilar had a friend, Doña Justa. Justa was involved in a microfinance group with other women in the neighborhood. Justa and another friend, Doña Nicolasa, had started a small storefront shop to sell their *polleras*, the thick, multitiered skirts worn by Aymara and Quechua women. Pilar had loaned money to Justa before, and Justa had always paid her back. Then, four years ago, Pilar approached Justa and suggested she buy the sewing machine. Making polleras is difficult; stitching the thick layers of fabric is tough with a hand-powered crank. "I told her, 'This machine can make it easier.'"

"Ya," said Justa, recounting her version of the events to me later. "I thought why not? It will help me in my business." So Justa bought the sewing machine from Pilar, planning to pay her 2,000 Bolivianos (Bs) in small installments (approximately US$286). Justa paid an installment or two: 100 Bs, 200 Bs. And then the payments stopped. "A few times I found her in the market," Pilar told me, "and she'd say, 'I'm going to pay you back, Doña Pilar! I promise I am going to pay you back.'" But she never did.

Meanwhile, Justa was struggling to make ends meet in her small business venture with Doña Nicolasa. The two women borrowed money to rent a little storefront, located in the nearby 16 de Julio market. They were also borrowing money to purchase materials for the substantial polleras they sewed. Both Justa and Nicolasa were involved in several microfinance groups, including one with Justa's sister, Manuela, and her mother. And both women took out additional loans from other women—people like Pilar—to meet their monthly quotas. Justa later insisted to me that her sales were going okay, but

Nicolasa was unable to cover her side of the partnership as her own sales flagged.

Justa, Manuela, and Pilar all remembered that Nicolasa had started to run into trouble when she tried to make it as a *prestamista* (moneylender) too: Nicolasa took out microfinance loans and then distributed the capital among other women, charging interest and collecting collateral, much as Pilar had done. But Nicolasa's borrowers weren't paying her back, and her polleras weren't selling.

The failing business was affecting both women. Manuela implied that Nicolasa's decision to go into moneylending and make fast cash—money she didn't *earn* but rather borrowed—had tainted her pollera business. Expressing her disapproval, Manuela said Nicolasa was running around in jewels and beautiful shawls bought on credit—and on the backs of other women to whom she gave loans with interest. But Nicolasa's flash was, Manuela suggested, a house of cards that began to collapse as her own debtors failed to pay her back—including her friend and business partner, Justa.

Justa, meanwhile, was scrambling to pay off multiple debts with friends and their microfinance groups. She asked Nicolasa for advice. Nicolasa introduced her to Doña Carmen, another neighborhood woman known as a prestamista. Justa begged Carmen for a loan, but because Carmen didn't know Justa personally, she refused to make a loan to her directly. Instead, Carmen gave the money to Nicolasa to pass along to Justa. Nicolasa was now responsible for repaying the loan she circulated to Justa.

At some point, Carmen demanded collateral for that loan. Though Nicolasa was the "official" loan recipient, Justa offered Carmen a sewing machine (the same one she had bought a few years earlier from Pilar but had yet to pay off).

Once again Justa managed a few quota payments on her debt to Carmen but never returned the full principal. Carmen held on to the industrial sewing machine and an additional pollera skirt as collateral, and hounded Justa in the market when she would catch her there.

And the interest started to mount.

Justa later told me she practically became a shut-in as she tried to avoid her creditors, especially Doña Carmen. She would run into Carmen on the street, where Carmen would publicly berate her over the unpaid debt.

"Pay me back and I won't have any more reason to bother you," Carmen spat at Justa during their conciliation session, admitting to the harassment.

The looks from her neighbors were too much to endure, Justa told me, and her elderly father—with whom she lived—was irate at the shame she had brought to the family. But the debt Justa owed Carmen was just one among many. As more creditors showed up on the family doorstep, Justa's father repeatedly threatened to throw her out, while her siblings intervened on her behalf. Her relationship with her husband grew tense and sometimes turned violent.

A couple of years later, Justa's creditor, Doña Carmen, needed a loan herself. Carmen approached a woman who was known around the neighborhood as a moneylender (much as Carmen was, herself). "I can give you some collateral," Carmen assured the woman. Carmen offered the moneylender an industrial sewing machine—it was electric and in good shape, Carmen promised.

Doña Carmen's moneylender later explained, "I told her I needed to see [the sewing machine] for myself first before I would give her the loan. People give me all kinds of [useless] things." So the moneylender headed over to Carmen's house to evaluate the sewing machine. She was shocked by what she found there.

"That is *my* machine!" the woman yelped at Carmen. "I *sold* that to Justa!" Carmen's moneylender was Doña Pilar.

"Even the table was the original," Pilar later told me, "with the name *Mitsubishi*. The motor, the table, the machine itself—all original." Carmen realized what had happened and acknowledged that the sewing machine must be the same one Pilar had sold Justa several years earlier. Pilar was in a snit over the situation. Justa had never finished repaying her for the machine and here she was offering it as collateral on a loan.

Pilar told Carmen that she would have to resolve the situation. Carmen, for her part, found Justa in the market one afternoon and dragged her to the integrated justice center (ijc), where I met them for the first time. We set up a conciliation appointment for the next day. Carmen told Pilar about the appointment, and all three showed up at the ijc on a Tuesday afternoon, where they agreed to allow me to follow their case as it unfolded.

As I interviewed the women over the next several months, I learned just how deeply entangled that sewing machine was in a knotted web of debt, family conflicts, and physical and structural violence. I began to see that sewing machine as an artifact of the model of entrepreneurial citizenship that has been promoted by foreign donors and Bolivian officials alike—a development model that ultimately benefits from privatizing the very conflicts it produces and obscuring the violence it helps to generate. I began to see the ijcs as both a party to—and a resource to cope with—the forms of misery and violence produced by Bolivia's ongoing embrace of entrepreneurial citizenship.[2] As conciliators try to compartmentalize violence and debt, to treat them as discrete problems, those artificial distinctions erase debt from cases of domestic violence, and erase violence from cases of interpersonal debt.

THIS CHAPTER BUILDS on the story of Doña Justa and a network of friends and kin who are interconnected through the industrial sewing machine. That machine circulated first as a commodity and then as collateral on several debts owed by different women, and has been tied to domestic violence and a death. Anthropologists have long wrestled with how to represent the violence they encounter in their field sites and among their closest conversation partners. This discomfort with the "ugly" side of fieldwork is particularly salient in El Alto, a city whose predominantly Aymara residents are often pathologized as exceptionally conflictual, violent, drunken, and disorderly, racist tropes that have been applied to indigenous peoples in other places as well.[3] This chapter confronts these characterizations and the very real violence El Alto residents deal with (and perpetrate) on a daily basis in their homes, neighborhoods, and social organizations as they pursue conciliation services.

In the United States, when people talk about domestic violence, the terms are often individualized. It's a characterological problem. In popular discourses, it's the individual pathology of an individual perpetrator. Intervention models premised on this understanding of domestic violence tend to criminalize the perpetrator while seeking to understand and intervene upon his (or her) individual psychology (Adelman 2004: 49). By contrast, in Bolivia, popular discourses about domestic violence often characterize it as a cultural pathology. This approach can quickly shift from a critique of patriarchy writ-large to a racialized explanation of violence: it's rural, it's uneducated, and it's indigenous.

Building on Adelman's (2004) call to examine the political economy of domestic violence or the "battering state," I examine the relationship between political economic formations and domestic violence as we encountered them in the IJCS. The critical literature on alternative dispute resolution (ADR) has pointed to the ways mediation "disappears" or "domesticates" violence as it promotes harmony and reconciliation.[4] In Bolivia, however, ADR practitioners regularly insisted to me and to their clients that "you cannot conciliate violence, you must adjudicate." Despite this assertion, I found that Bolivian ADR practitioners regularly mediate around domestic violence as they draw up agreements. Yet they often did so *at the behest of their clients*—who were anxious to obtain conciliation accords that might help them cope with their debts and other sources of insecurity. Conciliation, for many women, was a form of leverage—however weak.

This chapter is divided into two parts. In the first I return to the case of the sewing machine to show the ways that conciliation cases dealing with debt were shot through with references to intimate and structural violence,[5] and highlight the interplay between the two. Much like the conciliation case described in the previous chapter, where the conciliator compartmentalized the two interlocking debt conflicts, so too this case was handled in a series of independent conciliation sessions (between Carmen and Justa, then Pilar and Justa), but my reconstruction of the events attempts to stitch the story back together; to follow the sewing machine as it connects these women, their debts, and experiences of violence; and as that seemingly isolated dyadic conflict radiates outward into the lives of other friends and kin who tell their own stories of debt-related violence. Those narratives about violence rarely made it into the final accord.[6] When violence did come up, the center staff worried over the inappropriateness of conciliation. Usually, however, those violent tales remained peripheral. The second half of the chapter looks more explicitly at the entanglements of intimate partner violence and debt by examining the reasons why women might choose to bypass the courts in favor of conciliation when it comes to dealing with abusive domestic partners.

The violence occurring in Alteño homes, spilling into shared market stalls and on to dusty streets, is intimately tied to and exacerbated by an entrepreneurial model of capitalist development promoted by foreign aid organizations, the Bolivian government, and many nongovernmental organizations alike. ADR then offers a solution—however temporary—to the conflicts those very same development models provoke. By *domesticating* violence (that is, rendering it familial), such conflict can be managed at the dyadic, interpersonal level.[7] Widespread discourses that "culturalize" intimate partner violence further unmoor those forms of violence from the larger socioeconomic context that drives them. Yet even as conciliation programs treat these as isolated problems to be resolved by signing interpersonal conciliation accords or through referrals to other therapeutic services, many clients and staff point to the macro political-economic dimension of their woes.

The Violence of Debt

Doña Nicolasa, Justa's business partner, was dead. Whether by suicide or femicide, her friends were not sure. When Justa had gone to Nicolasa's house upon hearing of her death, Nicolasa's husband claimed suicide, blaming Justa

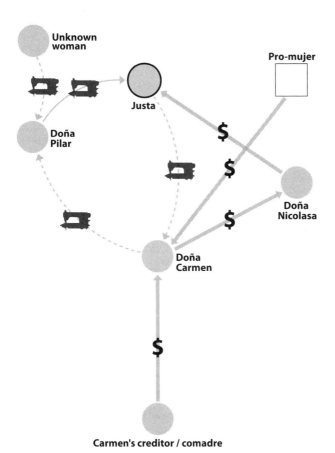

FIGURE 5.1 The circulation of the sewing machine as explained during the conciliation sessions between Doña Justa, her creditor, and a woman who sold her the machine.

for her demise, for driving his wife into the abyss. Terrified by what was unfolding, Justa called her sister, Manuela, and brother-in-law, Germán, who immediately came to her defense. They showed up at Nicolasa's house, looking to support Justa.

The multiple accounts I heard of what happened next described a chaotic and unclear scene: Nicolasa's husband demanded that Justa go procure a death certificate for his wife (without the body) or he would cause legal problems for her; Manuela and Germán called 110 (the Bolivian emergency services number) only to have Nicolasa's husband lock them in the house and refuse to open the door when they heard the police siren pass by.

Was it grief, guilt, or something else that made him act so strangely? Everyone found the circumstances of her "suicide" suspicious, though nobody would say "murder." Instead they told me how Nicolasa had supposedly hung herself using a towel on a shower rod. They shook their heads with disbelieving looks on their face.

"Do you think it was . . . ?" I asked, elliptically. "Yes, we thought it was strange. She was a big woman," Manuela nodded. "That shower rod was so flimsy. How could it have supported her weight? We thought maybe he . . . ," Manuela trailed off.

Fearful, though, of the threats Nicolasa's husband made about causing Justa legal problems, of holding her responsible by association for Nicolasa's death, no one pressed the matter further.[8] I never interviewed Nicolasa's family and was left contending with rumors and suspicions, fears and remorse, accusations and ambiguous recollections. "He had no idea how deeply she was in debt," Manuela said of Nicolasa's husband. "A cousin of ours who worked in the bank had to pull her credit report from the Central de Riesgos [National Credit Bureau; literally, the "Risk Bureau" or risk assessment center] for us to prove how bad it was. Only then did [Nicolasa's family] believe that it wasn't just Justa's fault [that she was in debt]. Doña Nicolasa had something like debts with seven different banks [MFIS]: Pro Mujer, Diakonia, Crecer . . ." Not to mention debts with people like Carmen. Who had loaned money to Nicolasa. Who in turn loaned that money to Justa.

One of the last times Manuela remembered seeing Nicolasa was at a microfinance meeting. Only months earlier, Manuela's cousin had begun working at an MFI and needed to get more clients. He encouraged his cousin Manuela to form her own loan group with women she knew—and he would act as their loan officer. Manuela invited Nicolasa, and for the first round things went fine: everyone paid back their loans and the group completed the cycle. But when the group applied for a second loan, Manuela's cousin pulled her aside. "He told me, 'This woman has a lot of [debt] problems. I'm not going to be able to give her a loan,'" Manuela recalled. When Nicolasa came to the group meeting that day, expecting to get a loan, Manuela tried to explain to her that she couldn't continue with the group.

Nicolasa became frantic. She pleaded for understanding. She insisted that she was only a guarantor on someone else's loan, but that she herself was in good standing. But Manuela's cousin—the loan officer—was insistent. He showed Manuela a printout: Nicolasa had multiple outstanding loans. She had been blacklisted from receiving more credit in the Central de Riesgos. The other women in the group impatiently chided Nicolasa for *perjudicando* (screwing up) the loan process. They hissed and told her to move on so they could finalize their new loan with the officer. Manuela accompanied her out of the meeting space and later chastised the other women for making Nicolasa feel bad.

"Who hasn't been in that position?" she asked them.

The next time Manuela saw Nicolasa, the woman was in the streets looking disheveled. She pleaded with Manuela to help her out. Struggling herself financially, Manuela turned her down. She now looked back guiltily at that moment. Could she have done something to reassure Nicolasa, to prevent her death?

Uncertain of the means of death—hanging or strangulation—all the women connected to the industrial sewing machine were certain of one thing: debt had dealt the final blow to Nicolasa's life. Manuela wavered between lamenting a life lost and a tendency to blame Nicolasa for the choices she had made: Nicolasa had given in to temptation and greed. Manuela reiterated that Nicolasa walked the streets in all kinds of finery. She wore crisp new polleras and gold *adornitos* (little embellishments and jewels) purchased not through the sweat of her labor but rather by her own decision to be a prestamista to other women. By her own hand or that of her husband, Manuela suggested that Nicolasa's death was tied to the seductions, perversions, and abuses of easy money.

Manuela's sister, Justa, was herself deeply scarred—emotionally and physically—from abuses heaped on her by a husband who refused to help his languishing wife pay off her loans. As we sat in the windowless concrete room she called home, piles of unfinished polleras in the corner, Justa pulled down her sweater to reveal a raw-looking mass of flesh, twisted and folded on itself. She grasped at my chest to show me how her husband had clawed at her skin. Although initially superficial, the wound had become infected and healed badly, leaving a hunk of red scar tissue knotted on her light brown skin. I looked up at the Styrofoam swans posted high on the wall bearing Justa's and her husband's names—party decorations from their wedding. "I bet things turned out much differently than you hoped when you got married," I offered sympathetically.

"I just wish he would support me emotionally," Justa lamented. "I wish he were like Manuela's husband. He gives Manuela moral support. But my husband doesn't care. He says, 'The debts are her problem, let her deal with them.'" Justa felt the strain in her other family relations as well. Again and again, her siblings had helped her cover her debts. Her brother Daniel sat down with her one day and systematically mapped them all out, trying to develop a payment scheme. They were many and Daniel was alarmed. Justa's brothers and sisters were growing weary with the stress caused by her money troubles—after all, they too were dealing with their own financial responsibilities. They also made loans to friends and neighbors. And they, too, searched for them in the market, begging repayment.

Tying the Noose

Manuela told many stories of being an ambivalent participant in the brigades of women sent to collect collateral from members of their loan groups—from people like her sister. "Our loan officers would send us off to demand collateral. They never had to get their hands dirty," she told me. Acting like collection agencies, these groups of women—including friends and relatives—would sometimes strip the debtors' homes, taking blankets and televisions, cooking-gas canisters and clothing, all held until the woman could repay her debt.[9] Manuela blamed loan officers (*asesoras*) along with the institution, accusing them of encouraging the women to take out larger loans rather than guiding the women in financial management as MFIS claimed. Like Manuela, other loan-group participants who came to the centers reported the uncomfortable times their presence collecting collateral would awaken the rage of a husband, who, unaware of the extent of his wife's debts, would beat her in front of the group while the women pleaded for his understanding.

Pretty soon, other women learned they could make a business out of providing quick loans to desperate women by sitting just outside the institution's doors. Manuela remembered, "[The prestamistas] opened their eyes, there—because they saw that women who didn't make their payments got locked inside until [they could come up with the money]. So [the prestamistas], they made a business of it! Those women were out there like wolves, waiting." Manuela blamed the institution for pushing the women toward those compounding forms of debt and their inflated interest rates: "[Our loan officer] was always saying 'go get a quick loan outside [from the prestamistas].'"

Repeatedly, Manuela invoked the image of a noose—a noose that was tied by the financial institution. "They put the noose around her neck," she said of Justa's experience with microfinance. "They were putting the noose around our neck," Manuela said of her own experience in a loan group with her mother. "For me it was absurd," she told me yet another time, when describing loan officers who encouraged women to take out large loans. "You were just putting a noose around each person's neck. You were tempting them with money they don't need. They developed vices, became liars. [Microfinance] taught the women to become depraved." In our conversations Manuela often returned to the noose metaphor without, it seemed, any purposeful reference to Nicolasa's death. But the metaphor struck me as an unfortunately apt one.

It was a cycle that, Manuela insisted, led other members of the group to engage in antisocial behavior. Manuela explained: "There are banks that don't understand. They want to see you there destroyed, stripped bare [*pelada*], they want to see you risking your family, your belongings, even the prestamistas live off of this—to make themselves rich, to make themselves bigger, they charge interest upon interest. They have no compassion for bleeding these women dry, they have no compassion for the tears of their children." While banks, Manuela insisted, suffered no remorse in seeing a woman "destroyed, stripped bare,"[10] friends, kin, and neighbors had "learned" to imitate and reproduce that antisocial attitude toward lending. Manuela's use of the word *pelada* is particularly telling. That stripping was figurative, but it was also physical. Much like the practices of housebreaking reported by Lamia Karim (2011) in Bangladesh, loan groups collected collateral in such ways that made women's insolvency very public, producing crippling shame for both the individual debtor and the family members with whom she lived. Philip Mader calls this the "effective repossession of a poor person's social relations" (2016: 102).

While many people in El Alto have long relied on prestamistas for credit, moneylenders have taken on newly significant roles alongside the repayment structure of microfinance: they provide the kind of "payday" loans women like Justa need to meet a looming quota payment. Similarly, Karim (2011) found that in Bangladesh, microfinance did not eradicate moneylending as its proponents suggested it might, but rather it expanded its market. Women like Nicolasa began to see work as prestamistas increasingly appealing for the same reasons: there were so many *opportunities* for lending.

For Manuela it was not the borrowing and lending itself that provoked such strident critique. This was not a rejection of credit itself—something many women wanted. Rather, Manuela articulated a critique of how she saw social lending beginning to mimic institutional lending in ways that stripped people not only of their material objects, but also of the very social ties that make a person human—and humane. Manuela repeatedly compared prestamistas (including friends and kin who acted as prestamistas) to large financial institutions, when they failed to show mercy, or refused to recognize the kinds of social obligations that also laid claim to a family's finances.

It was a theme Manuela returned to when recounting what happened immediately *after* the conciliation session between Justa, Carmen, and Pilar. The conciliator was busy finalizing the accord that Justa and Carmen would sign, as well as a second one between Justa and Pilar. Justa, Manuela, and her brother-in-law had all gone to wait in the sun outside the center, buying a two-liter bottle of Coca-Cola from a neighboring stand and passing around a single plastic cup. Suddenly there was a commotion, and I ventured out to make sure we didn't need to separate the parties. I heard only the final exchange of angry words, as Manuela and Justa rushed toward me. "She's threatening to light candles!" they exclaimed. Baffled by the meaning, I tried to deescalate the tension and invited Carmen and Pilar to step away from Justa and her family. Later I asked Manuela to help me understand her version of the exchange. She explained,

> They were insulting us—when they realized I was [Justa's] sister, [Carmen] started to insult me too. She said, "Oh, you're the sister. You must be a big debtor too, just like your sister!" My husband [Germán] tried to calm me down. He said, "Don't listen. The Lord knows us. Don't pay them any attention. They are trying to provoke you so you lash out and then they can accuse you of harassing them." And they were doing exactly that; these cunning women are good at [stirring up trouble]! That's why Doña Pilar has the skull of her mother. They dug it up from the cemetery and each year they do the mass for her skull. I don't know. I don't believe in these things.

This was the reference to "candles" I initially failed to grasp during the commotion outside the center. Bolivians who own skulls, often called *ñatitas*, preserve them in glass cases, offering drink and cigarettes, adorning them with flowers, and taking them out for special celebrations every November 8. Through their ñatita, celebrants seek protection and intermediation from the deceased (whether or not they knew the owner of the skull in life). In Manuela's account, however, Pilar invokes her mother's spirit, borne in her skull, for vengeance against Justa. It is an act of spiritual violence. Manuela continued, "Carmen said, 'Ah! Now Justa thinks that bringing me here she will solve her problems—now we'll see. Right now I am going to go buy [candles]. I am going to light up the skull.' And so they carried on insulting my sister about everything and about nothing. And she said, 'We are going to buy candles now to ask for her ruin. . . . You say you believe in God—what does God matter to me?' Good thing my husband intervened." Manuela's story of the *calavera* (skull), alongside her tale of Nicolasa's descent into greed as a prestamista, locates these women outside of the social mores of compassionate lending.

Much like anthropological discussions of fast money in postcolonial Africa, where people accuse the inexplicably wealthy of utilizing occult means

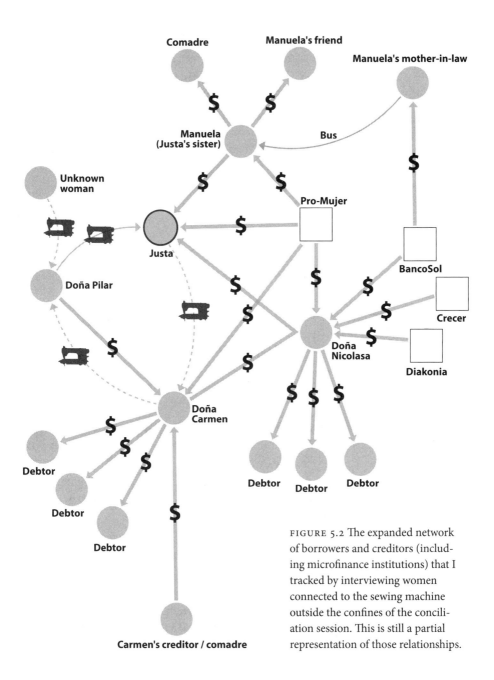

FIGURE 5.2 The expanded network of borrowers and creditors (including microfinance institutions) that I tracked by interviewing women connected to the sewing machine outside the confines of the conciliation session. This is still a partial representation of those relationships.

to gain riches while shirking social obligations, Manuela positions Carmen and Pilar as prestamistas who are without remorse or pity, and are willing to use whatever means necessary to enrich themselves off of the suffering of others.[11] Godless and lacking compassion, they are willing to leave a woman stripped bare, they are themselves engaged in a kind of socially stripped lending that invokes, for Manuela, an evangelical Christian, a darker, occult undertone represented by the ñatita skull. This is not to say that lending and market relations are themselves devilish, but rather divesting those practices of sociality is what makes them sinister.[12] The form of kinship Manuela perceives between Carmen and the calavera of the mother is abused for immoral gain and now utilized to enact a form of spiritual violence against Justa and her family as retribution for the incomplete repayment of her debt.

"Debt Brings Nothing but Enemies"

The drama unfolding over the sewing machine was just one node in a larger web of family relations strained by lending. As Manuela recounted her sister's woes, it prompted her to reflect on her own difficulty paying off a bank loan that she and her husband, Germán, took out to purchase a large Micro bus from Manuela's mother-in-law. "I had this experience with my own mother-in-law," she told me. "This 'pay me every cent' of the cost of the Micro experience, if you can call it that." Manuela had worked as a seamstress while Germán struggled as a taxi driver. In 2000, her mother-in-law convinced the couple that they should purchase the lumbering Blue Bird school bus that the mother-in-law owned with her second husband. These "Micros" originated in the United States in the 1960s, and they ascend the steep inclines between El Alto and La Paz. Drivers can charge lower fees to passengers because of the buses' trudging pace and ample space; micros carry more passengers and can be packed late into the evening when commuters are desperate to find a bus heading to El Alto's unlit peripheries.

Manuela's mother-in-law procured a US$3,500 loan from BancoSol. To do so, she mortgaged Manuela and Germán's home, which she also shared. Manuela's mother-in-law then handed the money over to her son and daughter-in-law. Manuela and Germán then handed the money back to her, theatrically enacting the sale. The couple now bore the responsibility of repaying the bank. What scandalized Manuela was her mother-in-law's refusal to lower the cost of the Micro, a refusal that was made all the more painful by her sense that she was doing everything she could to be a good daughter-in-law. Manuela recounted years of personal sacrifice to help care for her father-in-law as his health declined, and for a brother-in-law who was unemployed: "I always had to be stretching things. And that's how it is with the bank too."

The loan from her mother-in-law ushered in a time that Manuela remembered as extremely taxing, a period of deprivation, unrelenting anxiety, and a continuous need for smaller loans to help cover unexpected and expensive repairs. She told me, "To be honest, Susan, sometimes I took money out [of these microcredit groups] in order to pay off a few quotas with the bank. But we paid it back. Thank God, we always paid it back."

With just a few months left to pay back the loan, Manuela and Germán found themselves in a bind of conflicting obligations. Germán needed to help sponsor his brother's upcoming wedding. The tension between the moral economy of kinship and the bank's repayment schedule stretched Manuela and Germán's finances to a breaking point. Germán asked their loan manager if they could get an extension on their next quota. The answer they got was an emphatic "no." They cobbled together enough money to just barely make the deadline, but as a consequence they were unable to contribute to his brother's wedding expenses. At the party, Manuela's mother-in-law got drunk and unleashed a scathing public attack on the couple, accusing them of not caring enough to make a contribution.[13] "I was sitting in a corner of shame," Manuela told me, "because I was so indebted. I had gone off and gotten into debt all over again [to make the bank payment], and I knew that soon I'd have to pay all those people back."

As Manuela tacked back and forth between her tense relationship with her mother-in-law, kin obligations, and looming bank quotas, Manuela's personal story dovetailed with the 2003 uprising and the widespread anger it expressed. "This was just a little before the fire—before [Alteños] burned [BancoSol's branch office in Rio Seco]. Couldn't they understand? They didn't want to understand!" I wasn't sure if she was directing the accusation toward her loan officer or an entire banking industry symbolized by a burning branch office. I suspect both.

Manuela gestured only briefly to the events of 2003, but as she did, she once again invoked the sense of being denuded, pelada, by banking institutions. She tied interpersonal conflicts to a larger economic system that, she believed, was deforming their lives. The sense of vulnerability and betrayal—by both an unsympathetic mother-in-law *and* the loan officer who wouldn't let her miss a payment—was made all the more bitter when Manuela's brother decided to go into banking. "And now my brother, who is an accountant, is working for the Banco Nacional," She told me. "My own brother!"

Much like the sewing machine, in the IJCs, stories of debt were also stories of violence. It was present in the humiliating words *deudor moroso* (defaulting debtor) that banks and moneylenders would paint in startling white on brown adobe walls, provoking household fights between fathers and daughters. It was present in the screaming fights women had in the open-air market, shouting about long-overdue loans. And it was present in the kinds of domestic violence cases that we handled at the centers, as we drafted letters of referral to the forensic medical examiner so a woman could gather evidence "just in case" she decided to pursue a legal case against her partner. Those expanding circles of conflict radiated outward, as neighbors and kin were drawn into overlapping lender and borrower relationships. And, like a noose, they threatened to asphyxiate friendships and kinships.

Toward a Political Economy of Domestic Violence

Much as I described in earlier chapters on the "culturalization" of conflict in general, popular discourses about violence against women in Bolivia frequently attribute the problem to the patriarchal culture of rural (indigenous) Bolivians and migrants to urban peripheries like El Alto. It's a matter of "education" (which often serves as a euphemism for race and class). In these accounts, domestic violence is a practice that rural Aymara have brought with them to the city as they migrated, packed like coca leaves and alpaca yarn into their heavy *aguayo* bundles. I heard many different people articulate this theory of domestic violence in our conversations, from government bureaucrats to the well-meaning middle-class employers who brought their *empleadas* (domestic servants) to the center in an attempt to help them escape from under the thumb of abusive husbands. I also heard these theories from center clients themselves—who often blamed mothers for reproducing *machista* sons in the city or for being complicit in violence against their daughters-in-law. They also surfaced in discussions of high-profile femicides like the strangulation of a councilwoman, Juana Quispe Apaza, from the rural municipality of Ancoraimes. Quispe Apaza had reportedly experienced ongoing aggression prior to her death, and she was repeatedly barred entrance to participate in political meetings in the rural municipality she represented. Activists interpreted her murder as a politically motivated and culturally inflected femicide or gender-based murder. As an editorial in the Bolivian newspaper *Los Tiempos* argued, "Without a doubt the great number of cases of violence exercised [against women] are with the singular goal of preventing women from being incorporated into public life. . . . This position is supported by the more than 4,000 cases of violence exercised against councilwomen [over a twelve-year period], by men who refuse to admit women's participation in the public sphere *in the name of traditions, ancestral culture, or simply the most primitive form of machismo.*"[14] In drawing attention to her murder, the editorial does not simply critique patriarchy and the violent exclusion of women from political life. Rather, it links violence to an "ancestral culture" threatened by women's leadership.[15] Following her murder, the Evo Morales administration swiftly approved Law 243, "Against Harassment and Political Violence against Women" (on May 28, 2012, though ten years in the making),[16] and later, Law 348, the "Integral Law Guaranteeing Women a Life Free from Violence." Yet Quispe Apaza's case, like so many, has languished in the courts despite the new legislation and movements demanding justice for the victims of femicide.

One of the other major causes people cite for gender-based violence in El Alto is alcohol consumption. Indeed, one of the introductory lessons I learned at the IJC in District 6 was about the ebb and flow of clients—particularly women. On my first day at the center, the director, Dr. Paloma Gil, explained that Mondays and Tuesdays were their busiest days—and thus the days when she most needed extra support. Other staff made similar claims, and I soon came to witness the pattern myself.

But why were Mondays and Tuesdays so busy?

One explanation might be that Wednesdays and Thursdays were market days in this heavily commercial district, and the center emptied as potential clients (especially women) went to work. On Wednesdays, many neighbors living near the center focused their energies on the local street market—unfurling plastic tarps over muddy, unpaved streets where they displayed household wares, used clothing, bags of powdered soap, and thick slabs of recently butchered meat. Others roamed the streets pushing rolling carts from which they sold freshly squeezed orange juice and pork sandwiches. But on Thursdays, the massive 16 de Julio market practically shut down access into and out of District 6; as vendors set up makeshift stalls and throngs of shoppers from El Alto and La Paz choked the streets, the stream of people into the center slowed to a trickle. Some neighbors were working, while others were out shopping.

But that was not the explanation I got. Instead, staff almost universally explained the preponderance of cases on Mondays and Tuesdays in the same way: men get drunk on the weekends and beat their wives, and then on Mondays and Tuesdays the women come to the center to lodge complaints. Weekends were time for parties and soccer games with buddies, baptisms and wedding celebrations, times for partying (*farreando*) with your buddies, or dancing in your neighborhood's anniversary celebration. These were the kinds of social events where people drank, and drank heavily. Men, staff would tell me, would come home drunk and fight with their wives, and those fights would escalate into violence. Occasionally, staff and clients would talk about women's drinking and the resulting fights—with husbands and with in-laws. Stories of drinking and violence were often intertwined. And indeed I spent many weekend nights listening to my own neighbor angrily and then mournfully bang on his compound's thin metal door when his young wife punished his drunkenness by locking him out until he slumped against the adobe wall, defeated.

One such Monday I arrived to find Azucena, one of the center's interns, looking bewildered as she spoke with twelve people who had crowded around her desk. I slipped into her office and faced the bloodied group of middle-aged men and teenage boys with gashed foreheads and split lips, young mothers with bandages wrapped around their heads, and a few unscathed children. "They were here when I arrived at 8:30 this morning," Azucena mumbled quickly to me. Everyone present was related: they were all siblings, parents, and cousins of a single man who had been holding a baptismal celebration the previous day for his infant daughter. The man's wife and her relatives, I came to understand, were in equally bad shape but had taken their battle wounds elsewhere.

Wearing fresh bandages, bruised faces, and confetti still plastered to their skin and hair, the family smelled very distinctly of the alcohol they had consumed the previous day. One young man's hand was heavily bandaged—the result of a pickax wound. The group had been to the neighborhood free health clinic and had already received forensic medical certificates that could be used as evidence of assault in the courts. Azucena looked over their paperwork and shook her head. "These injuries are too severe for us to handle," she explained as she eyed the degree of gravity ascribed to each patient's injuries. "This is a criminal case. I'm going to have to write you a letter of referral to the prosecutor's office." As the group departed sullenly, Azucena opened the windows of the center to try to air out the stench of blood, soiled bodies, and alcohol. I don't know if the man and his relatives pursued criminal charges against his wife and her family, but clearly that festive occasion—and probably the marriage—had been deeply marred, regardless of further legal action. Stories like these troubled me as I started thinking about how to represent intimate, interpersonal violence and its relationship to alcohol in El Alto.

Andeanists studying instances of gender-based violence in Bolivia have produced multifaceted accounts of the role alcohol plays in domestic disputes. Krista Van Vleet (2008), for example, argues that many of the pervasive human rights and women's rights discourses that circulate in Bolivia fail to account for the complex ways people in the rural Andean community of Sullk'ata perceive, justify, or, alternately, denounce certain forms of interpersonal violence.[17] People's interpretation of that violence, Van Vleet argues, depends heavily on whether the perpetrator is sober or drunk: violent acts committed when a person is drunk are "normalized." A drunken person is not in her right mind, and can be forgiven, "but violence between affines is decidedly *not* considered to be custom when people are sober" (168).[18]

Van Vleet further nuances accounts of gender violence in the Andes by examining the interplay between violence, alcohol, and relationships between *women*. Violent episodes between women, Van Vleet argues, often stem from struggles over kinship obligations, as brides work to earn their place among in-laws—and mothers-in-law judge those efforts to be insufficient. She explains,

> Kinship obligations and ambiguities of hierarchy significantly shape the way in which relationships are negotiated. These obligations and ambiguities create the conditions for the emergence of conflict among individuals, especially those related by marriage. Thus violence among women, though not as frequently acknowledged as violence between husbands and wives, is crucial to a more general understanding of domestic violence in the Andes. The violence among women also highlights the ways in which *relatedness is at once intimate and antagonistic*.[19]

Van Vleet challenges worn-out clichés of Andean women being merely (willing) victims of abusive, drunk men. Drunkenness, in Van Vleet's account, is an altered state that allows men *and* women to violently express strained relationships between kin, including between women who occupy vastly different positions of power in a household.[20]

In the centers I observed similar debates about how to make sense of, criticize, or justify violence. Those debates included clients who blamed their mothers-in-law for fomenting discord with their husbands or legitimating his violence if they failed to fulfill certain wifely duties. Clients in District 6 also reported spouses that were decidedly *not* drunk when they hit them. As one woman told me, "My husband is [an evangelical] Christian. He only hits me when he is sober." But clients did not save their criticism of violence for cases when perpetrators were sober, and therefore presumed to be in control of their faculties, as Van Vleet describes. I regularly watched as fathers, mothers, compadres, grown children, and neighbors urged women clients to seek shelter and press charges against violent husbands or adult sons—regardless of their sobriety. Others, however, expressed concern about the shame a woman might bring on the family if she were to denounce her husband—and these were the arguments and justifications that many staff and clients attributed to culture.

Bolivian debates over the relationship between culture and gender-based violence are not new. Some activists I spoke with reconfigured the "Western" feminist critique of patriarchy to incorporate national debates over indigenous notions of gender complementarity, or *chacha-warmi*.[21] The concept of chacha-warmi suggests that a person is a "complete and properly social person" when one forms part of a (heterosexual) couple, a couple whose lives and individual tasks are carried out in complementary ways (Canessa 2012: 229). Andean concepts of chacha-warmi, some activists argue, offer an alternative, egalitarian conceptualization of gender relations that nevertheless presupposes (complementary) differences between the sexes. Yet at events I attended, chacha-warmi advocates frequently provoked skepticism. Critics like those I encountered at a conference analyzing Bolivia's Katarista movement, pointed to forms of violence and social hierarchy that existed within the Inca Empire, challenging the idea of preconquest egalitarianism.[22] They drew on ethnohistorical data as well as composite theories of human nature to challenge the idea that there ever existed a pristine, nonviolent Indian past that was only later "infected" with violence and patriarchy by the colonial encounter.

Aymara women leaders I spoke with sometimes chuckled at the assertion that indigenous communities practice chacha-warmi, telling me, as one did, "it's always the men insisting there was no gender discrimination before the colonial period." But they too would nevertheless appeal to the chacha-warmi concept as an ideal worth pursuing. Indigenous feminists such as Julieta Paredes have urged greater attention to the interplay of indigeneity and class, highlighting the complex class dynamics among urban Aymara residents in cities like El Alto. Paredes has famously sought to rearticulate the Aymara concept of chacha-warmi in such a way that the concept might gain purchase among both urban feminist movements and indigenous rights groups, particularly as these groups have found themselves at odds.

My point is that the debate over how culture perpetuates (or challenges) violence against women may dismiss the implicit critique of chacha-warmi activists: that we need to historicize and interrogate the relationship between colonialism, capitalist governance, and violence. As the anthropologist Sally Engle Merry insists, focusing on culture "blames the havoc wreaked by expansive capitalism and global conflicts on the culture of the 'other.' This absolves the rich countries of responsibility for the suffering caused by these processes and blames local people" (2003: 63–64). By contrast to characterological explanations, Adelman (2004) calls on scholars to examine the political economy of domestic violence.[23] Adelman asks, "How did the current state/economy logic rely on normative ideas about 'the family' to create conditions supportive of flexible capitalist accumulation? How do shifting patterns of employment, when coupled with the contractions of the welfare state map onto pre-existing intra-familial relations? What does the capitalist governance of domestic violence look like?" (2004: 52).

What would such an approach entail in Bolivia? Asking what the capitalist governance of domestic violence looks like in District 6 would require tracing colonial relations of exploitation forward into the contemporary era (see Rivera and Geidel 2010; Calla et al. 2005).[24] How were intrafamilial relations reconfigured under structural adjustment? How have efforts to promote conciliation (perhaps unintentionally) intersected with parallel efforts to produce an entrepreneurial populace? How does conciliation figure within the political economy of microfinance (Mader 2016), especially as it relates to cases of informal debt and its entanglement with interpersonal violence?

As I described in previous chapters, donor institutions began promoting conciliation during the 1990s alongside a broader array of economic and political reforms. Those reforms included the "capitalization" (privatization) of state-owned industries and stringent economic restructuring—a process that helped to produce the city of El Alto. But it also included aid platforms that encouraged citizens to assume greater responsibility for managing their lives, livelihoods, and local resources rather than relying on state services and entitlements. Conciliation paralleled efforts to promote entrepreneurial solutions to poverty and state failure, but in District 6, clients were also using conciliation to *mitigate* the violent outcomes of this entrepreneurial model.

In the centers, economic insecurity, exacerbated by spiraling and compounding debt, was a significant source of intrafamilial tension and violence. Clients' multifaceted experiences of violence, however, challenge more narrow accounts of male-on-female abuse that tend to predominate.[25] Manuela's experience grappling with the debt she and her husband, Germán, owed her mother-in-law exemplifies the ways debt maps onto existing social obligations and familial hierarchies, and often troubles already-strained relationships within families. Manuela's tensions with her mother-in-law complicate the trope of the abusive, alcoholic husband: even as mounting debt and kinship obligations have caused strife within Manuela's family, she provides a strikingly different account of her relationship with her husband. "We were strong enough to confront the situation, and I am proud of my husband—proud of my husband because together we knew how to support each other in the good and the bad times," she told me.

Both Manuela and her sister Justa described Germán as a kind and committed man who stands with *both* women as they face deepening debt crises and violence from other sources. It was the relationship with her her mother-in-law that proved most taxing and that she felt posed a real threat to the family's economic security because of the unforgiving way her mother-in-law made the loan for the Micro and tethered Germán and Manuela to unrelenting bank payments. In their expressions of dismay, both women invoked Germán as an embodiment of virtuous kin relations; they do not reject kin obligations, but rather denounce what they perceive as a distorted version of them.[26]

Nevertheless, the IJC also dealt with many, many cases of violence that *did* fit more neatly into categories of domestic violence perpetrated by men against women. Those cases raised difficult questions about the relationship between violence, debt, and alcohol consumption. But they also raise questions about the role of ADR in a context where debt and physical, gender-based violence are so deeply intertwined—even as staff insist that one must not conciliate violence.

We Do Not Conciliate Violence

Scholars concerned with gender-based or domestic violence have been particularly critical about the ways that harmony ideologies inherent in mediation programs act to "disappear" violence. Sara Cobb (1997) argues that mediation programs lead to the "domestication" of violence by shifting from a rights-based framework to a need-based one. So too Mindie Lazarus-Black argues that women's experiences in Trinidadian courts are deeply shaped by court rites and a culture of reconciliation that contribute to a process of "delegalizing" domestic violence cases. That delegalization process involves "converting a discourse about legal rights into a complaint that is not worthy of legal redress" (2007: 102). That is, domestic violence cases are steadily shed from the justice system.[27]

Women's rights organizations in Bolivia voice similar critiques. Gender justice networks accuse police officers, judges, and lawyers of de-legalizing gender violence through many of these same processes. Critics rightly point to the many impediments that prevent women from pursuing legal redress for domestic violence should they want it, ranging from refusing to respond to distressed emergency calls to encouraging women to reconsider divorce for the good of their children, as well as the many costs associated with pursuing domestic violence cases, from time lost to bribes paid (Calla et al. 2005). In 2004, when I was living and working in La Paz, my neighbors and I called the police on another neighbor—whom we could hear throwing his wife against the wall and breaking furniture while he berated her. The emergency operator answering the phone told me that it was a "private family matter, not police business," and then hung up on me. My neighbors and I resorted to banging on the door until it stopped—for the moment. When I returned to Bolivia in 2016, I heard from multiple lawyers working with gender justice NGOs and the Ministry of Justice that the much-anticipated Law 243 had, in their opinion, lengthened the time to trial and only created more barriers to women pursuing domestic violence charges against their abusers.

Yet by contrast to the de-legalizing processes observed by Merry and Lazarus-Black (where court officials pushed for therapeutic intervention or reconciliation), I found that conciliators and legal aid interns in District 6 regularly *discouraged* women's requests for conciliation appointments with their abusive spouses. Staff asserted that domestic violence was a *delito* (crime) and not appropriate for conciliation, urging instead that women press charges against their abusive spouses court—with the aid of the center's pro bono lawyer. Take, for example, the interaction between Azucena and the mother of a young client.

Eighteen-year-old Berta first came to the center battered and nine months pregnant. Her young husband had kicked her repeatedly in the stomach, nearly causing her to lose the baby. A woman at her evangelical church learned of the incident and brought the young woman to the center. The next time I saw Berta, she cradled her infant daughter in her arms. Her nose still bore a broad scar. Azucena had helped Berta initiate her domestic violence case several weeks prior, but this was the first day her parents attended. Azucena asked Berta's mother why she had not accompanied her daughter before. "What would the neighbors say?" the older woman pleaded anxiously. Berta's father stood silently by her side, gazing down. Azucena furrowed her brow at Berta's mother and shook her head, clucking her tongue disapprovingly:

"And what, ma'am, will the neighbors say if next time he kills her?" Berta's mother fell silent, and Azucena began drawing up the report she would submit to the judge.

Similarly, interns and staff regularly pushed women to reconsider their desire to simply *sentar una denuncia* (to register a complaint) rather than to initiate a full-scale court case against their abusers. Some clients (mistakenly) believed that in making contact with the centers they had formally documented the abuse. Interns struggled to explain that their registry in the computer database was not a formal legal complaint, merely a first step. But many women were reluctant to pursue the cases further. The computer system was filled with numerous domestic violence registries that clients abandoned. Others returned months later to *sentar otra denuncia*, to leave yet another complaint, to get another referral to the forensic medical examiner. Women brought old evaluations from a psychological service NGO, forensic medical certificates, or formal complaints from the special Family Brigade of the police force. They accumulated these documents in legal-sized plastic folders and hid them from partners. They were "just in case" files: just in case a woman decided she'd had enough. But many simply never pursued the charges. I spent hours one week culling abandoned cases from the center's files.

Again and again I heard conciliators, staff, and interns assert that *no se concilia la violencia* (one does not conciliate violence).[28] And although the IJCs encouraged a culture of *conciliation*, or talking things through *por la vía buena* (taking the good road; talking it through rather than using violence or the courts), staff was quick to assert that conciliation was *not* the same as returning to an abusive spouse. In practice, however, the line between conciliating and *not* conciliating violence was a lot less clear. Violence often hovered around the edges of conciliation appointments, mentioned obliquely in quiet filler conversations between parties as conciliators typed up accords, or as clients occupied the silence as staff registered follow-up appointments.

Women who were hammering out debt payments with friends, moneylenders, and comadres would allude to spouses who beat them, as Nieves did in the previous chapter. Here physical violence was peripheral to these particular, dyadic cases meant to resolve disputes between borrowers and lenders. But these stories were not just about violence enacted by male partners. Stories of physical abuse at the hands of mothers-in-law, sisters-in-law, or other family members emerged in the longer narratives women told conciliators about the conflicts that brought them to the center.

Other times, violence was the central reason for why someone approached the IJC. Recall the case of Luz and her estranged husband, Jhonny, whose story opened this book. I had met Luz the day before our stakeout at the yogurt factory when she came to the center seeking advice. Luz was hoping to get Jhonny to use his medical insurance to pay for the removal of several screws that had been placed in her leg after he had shoved her down a ravine, shattering the bone. But her more pressing concern, she explained, was an impending quota payment she needed to make on a loan.

"In February [my husband Jhonny] made me take out a loan—five thousand dollars from BancoSol," she explained as she settled into a seat facing Angelica, one of the center's interns. "The quota is due soon, and now I am the only one paying it off." As she spoke, Luz slid a receipt across the table to me, evidence of the upcoming payment: 1,538 Bs (approximately US$219). Angelica opened a new case file on her computer and asked Luz to detail the history of conflicts with her husband. As she did, Luz wove together accusations of infidelity and violence, detailing an increasingly unhappy marriage, one that fell apart further following the death of their young son.

Around the time that the child died, Luz said that Jhonny was accused of raping a minor. "I had to pay for the girl's medical appointments to make sure she wasn't pregnant while he was being held in jail. We had to pay her family restitution."

Angelica interjected, "Oof! You also *must not* reconcile rape, but they did it anyway!"[29]

"He was always unfaithful," Luz responded, reframing the incident as infidelity rather than sexual assault.

Luz switched back to the violent episode that left her with metal screws in her leg. "He knows what he did!" she exclaimed. "He brings me medicin[al plants] from his community. He says, 'The *curandero* [traditional healer] told me these would fix you.'"

Angelica tried to get Luz to be specific with dates of violence—the beatings, the times he kicked her. "We want you to tell us everything," she explained.

"He grabbed me, he kicked me. He threw me over a stool," Luz said.

"Does he hit you when he's drunk?"

"No, when he's sober. He didn't hit me when I was pregnant, though," Luz clarified. "He was excited about the baby."

Angelica continued to nudge for specificity, the dates and severity of particular incidents Luz has mentioned in a jumble of stories. "How did the fight start in 2008?"

"He was drunk. He kicked me really bad that time, and punched me in the face. I was on the ground," Luz said, lifting hands balled into tight fists and punching downward, imitating Jhonny. As Luz spoke, we were interrupted by loud shouts from the conciliator's office. I stuck my head in the office to make sure the conciliator was okay and didn't need the center's guard to intervene. No longer seated at her desk, she had placed herself between the two men. "Sir, I am the one speaking right now," she told one of them, firmly but quietly. When I returned to my seat I only caught the end of a sentence: Angelica repeating the word "knife."

"And your leg?" Angelica gently prodded.

"It was raining that afternoon and I was on the side of the river planting potatoes. And he pushed me in the ravine! I fainted. I was stuck in the river and I couldn't get out." An elderly man who heard Luz's cries went to fetch help. "The pain was terrible. [My leg] was broken in two places. I was in bed for three months."

Angelica: "Did [Jhonny] take you to get treated?"

"With herbs. He took me to a curandero [traditional healer]. It is on his conscience! But it seemed to be getting better. Three months later they took me to get X-rays."

Susan: "They didn't take you to the doctor for three months?"

"Just curanderos!" Angelica responded incredulously, shaking her head.

"They did the X-ray and the bones were all crossed," Luz explained, holding her fingers up to imitate misaligned bones. "So he took out a loan from his brother [to pay for treatment], but mostly my family had to help [with the bills]." At the hospital, doctors set Luz's leg with metal screws. Years had passed, but they were now causing her discomfort and she wanted to have them removed.

Angelica urged Luz to pursue a case for domestic violence. Luz listened quietly but insisted she wanted to invite her husband to conciliation to deal with the debt owed to BancoSol and to pay for the medical bill. She was resolute. The next morning at 5:30 A.M., Luz and I waited outside the yogurt factory to deliver the invitation letter to Jhonny.

A History of Violence

During her intake with Luz, Angelica elicited a history of violence that she could massage into a legible narrative for multiple audiences.[30] Those audiences included the computer system records, which would provide background information for the conciliator when she saw the couple. Angelica would utilize that computerized case file for her own records—as evidence of her efficacy as a legal aid intern. The center's director and Angelica's internship coordinator at her university would further interpret her self-reporting as they drew up their evaluations of her work so she could get credit. Luz's case would be tallied in reports to the Ministry of Justice just as it was once tallied for reporting functions to USAID to demonstrate the centers' worth and endorse continued funding. Angelica would adapt snippets of that history into a narrative used in referral letters to the forensic medical examiner or psychological services NGOs, among other institutions. And the evidence of abuse contained in that brief, synthesized account would be used to justify the client's need for free services.

The documents produced by those institutions—the certificate from the forensic medical examiner, the detailed history of psychological abuse generated by a local NGO—would in turn provide Luz with an official record of her abuse, which she could submit as evidence in a court hearing (with the aid of the center's pro bono lawyer, in this case, Dr. Paloma). In the event that Luz chose to pursue a legal case against Jhonny, Angelica would coconstruct with Luz a *memorial*, or legal brief, which she would submit to the judge further describing the complaint. Staff would adjust templates to detail the specific instances of violence of this particular couple, while the accused would have to procure his own lawyer to coconstruct a counternarrative before the judge. These are discursive and documentary practices whereby clients make claims for protection and state intervention, and for restitution from abusive parties. And at each step along the way, clients' narratives are elicited, tightened, reframed, repackaged, and simplified.

But beyond insight into this process of coconstructing violence narratives, the process of eliciting an institutionally legible history from Luz reveals deep entanglements among conciliation, debt, and violence. As women like Luz recounted their experiences of violence, many rebuffed the staff's efforts to get them to pursue domestic violence charges against their partners. There are a number of reasons why they might have done so, including fear over how their own family might respond, as well as their own views on what constitutes acceptable or unacceptable levels of violence in a domestic partnership.[31] But one recurring reason they declined staff's efforts to steer them toward criminal charges was that they were seeking immediate relief of more pressing concerns: more pressing than the screws causing her pain, more pressing than legally separating from her violent partner, Luz needed to pay a loan quota to BancoSol.

As I tried to compare the kinds of cases conciliators were encountering in other districts in El Alto, I spoke with Sebastián Costa about what he was seeing in District 4. Costa reported that debt was quickly supplanting child support and other domestic conflicts in conciliation sessions. And he too saw debt and domestic violence issues as interrelated. He told me, "I would say that debt is now the principal cause of family conflict and separation. People start signing documents among themselves to help them pay off debts—these interpersonal debts to pay off microfinance. So you have all these little interpersonal debts generated to pay off the larger microcredit payments. For example, right now I am seeing someone with 15,000 Bs [approximately US$2,143] in debt with various places and people." For Costa, the challenge was figuring out what the center could do to be of assistance in the face of this pattern. He told me, "There's not much we can do for the microcredit debts—that's a separate issue we can't really address. But sometimes the pro bono lawyer can work with a person and the institution—like Banco FIE to help them renegotiate their debt payments. They can help in those ways." These were temporary solutions, he told me, *parches* or patches, Band-Aids on larger problems and larger patterns facing his clientele. But they were also problems with troughs and crests. There were acute moments of conflict that intensified during periods strained by pressing debt payments followed by stretches of relative calm. Costa concluded, "So the principal problems [in District 4] are debt—and what you see is people separate over the debt and then once the debt is paid they go back to living together."

As a consequence, center staff often compartmentalized violent and nonviolent conflicts. Sometimes, as in Luz's case, that compartmentalization was intentional: against Angelica's wishes, Luz insisted on conciliating with her husband so she could deal with her loan payment. More often, that compartmentalization was implicit: violence was less directly linked to the conflict on the conciliator's table, but it was connected nonetheless. In either instance, the effect was the same: staff was left conciliating *around* violence.

I found one of District 6's conciliators, Dr. Sonia Campos, in a reflective mood one late afternoon. The center was nearly empty. People occasionally popped their heads in the door to collect child support payments or to make deposits on outstanding loans. I had spent the last few hours observing several sessions, all of them dealing with debts or domestic conflict. Often parties were contending with both. As we chatted about the last round of sessions, Sonia played with her cellphone and sighed. "You know, there are just a lot of contradictions. Like, we aren't supposed to do conciliation for violence. It says in the law, 'no se concilia violencia.' But we do it all the time. Even the judge is contradictory, conciliating violence cases."

For Sonia, this contradiction was most palpable in cases where women were unwilling to separate from or pursue domestic violence complaints against abusive partners—and instead asked for conciliation accords. "So what do we do?" Sonia asked me rhetorically:

Do we say, "Ma'am, you have to *denunciar* [make a formal legal complaint against an abusive spouse]"? If she says she wants to conciliate, do we say, "I'm sorry, but you must begin a legal case for violence"? [Their husbands] will probably ruin their lives worse, saying "you went off and declared against me." If she says, "I want to give him a second chance," do I say, "No"? What am I supposed to do?

Neither of us had an answer.

Conclusion: Compartmentalizing Violence

I never met the original owner of the sewing machine. Did it start its life as a commodity in the 16 de Julio market, bought by the anonymous woman as she was trying to get a pollera business off the ground? Was it a gift from her husband or borrowed from her comadre? Did she ask Pilar for the loan in order to cover a child's school fees or her husband's medical bills, or to pay a quota with an MFI? Whatever its origin, its entry into this network of prestamistas and debtors, sisters and neighbors, was as collateral on a loan, then a commodity sold to Justa, then twice more as collateral. As it moved between these women it accumulated a biography shot through with violence—violence it helped to produce and to perpetuate, violence that was both physical and structural. In the process, the sewing machine stitched together new relationships as well as hostilities. It is a singular biography that speaks to a broader pattern of both sociality and its unraveling.

In talking about Justa's money struggles, her sister Manuela located those difficulties—and her own—firmly within a broader political-economic context. Amid strident critiques of the ways microfinance has intersected with and expanded social practices of lending and borrowing, Manuela did not disavow women's need for capital for their businesses or cash to cover emergency health costs. Rather, Manuela insisted that the problem lies in the ways interpersonal lending practices come to mimic unyielding financial institutions. This is not to suggest that such interpersonal lending was once free from usury or abusive collecting practices. I do not mean to romanticize the interdependencies enacted through debts owed to friends, neighbors, and kin. Nor do I want to suggest that the interactions between loan officers, branch managers, and other bureaucrats are really as impersonal and exploitative as Manuela suggests. As Sohini Kar (2013) and Caroline Schuster (2015) reveal in their studies of the encounters between loan officers and borrowers, those relations are frequently far more complex—saturated by ethical dilemmas and their own interdependencies.[32] Manuela's assertions about the cruelty of the bank and the avarice of friends-turned-moneylenders may simplify the work of both. Indeed, other clients *lauded* their own moneylenders as being far more understanding, generous, and patient when compared to banks, casting their moneylenders as a saving grace.

But that cruel and impersonal image allows Manuela to contrast her own understanding of socially productive lending from that which she disparages. Manuela uses heavily moralistic language to criticize people like Nicolasa for their pursuit of "fast money," for wealth that is built on exploiting other's urgent needs; she reasserts a moral economy of legitimate lending and borrowing that stands in contrast to antisocial practices exemplified by indifferent institutions and their imitators. And she braids together stories of domestic violence perpetrated by men and women alike with narratives about political uprisings and the burning of BancoSol's branch office by angry Alteños.

In this chapter I showed how indebtedness and economic precariousness intersect with and intensify people's experiences of interpersonal and domestic violence, and how Alto Limeña women like Justa seek to ameliorate that sense of vulnerability through conciliation. As center clients narrated their family histories of violence, or pursued conciliation appointments with their partners, they invoked debt as a central cause of familial tension and marital strife—as well as violence. And as conciliators worked to hammer out accords dealing with loans, they often did so while skirting that violence.

This compartmentalizing of debt and domestic violence did two things. First, it erased the violence entangled in debt complaints. But it also obscured the recurring pattern of debt that was so often present in domestic violence cases. This pattern was not something conciliators and center staff failed to see. Conciliators often commented on the ways these issues were related. It was a troubling dilemma that conciliators like Sebastián Costa and Sonia Campos were unsure of how to resolve. In *trying* to resolve those tensions *at their clients' behest*, however, staff often reproduced the erasure.

This is not a monocausal argument about violence.[33] Nevertheless, a political-economic approach to domestic violence invites us to examine the interplay between factors that shape people's experience of violence, and the ways people navigate those experiences through recourse to the IJCs, among other strategies. As the case of the industrial sewing machine illustrates, the structural violence of economic vulnerability intersected with, exacerbated, and produced forms of interpersonal violence, *including between women*. Further, these sessions reveal how ADR may buttress the very "credit relations permitting the extraction of surplus value from the poor" while obscuring the violence it generates on multiple registers (Mader 2016: 37).

Several times in my conversations with Bolivian USAID contractors, program managers told me that foreign donors had missed earlier opportunities to "really intervene into the family," as one told me. Had they targeted the family earlier, one contractor suggested, la cooperación internacional might have transformed conflict and violence at the level of those intimate social relations and in doing so helped to deescalate social conflict in El Alto. In a sense, the IJCS were operating out of such a model: a model that imagined social conflict to be an expression of interpersonal disputes "scaled up" into broader patterns of confrontation and abuse. By teaching people to manage their conflicts with spouses and mothers-in-law, Alteños would in effect be dismantling the interpersonal foundations of social conflict—perennial conflict that donors feared threatened to destabilize Bolivian democracy. In this explanation of political upheaval, social conflict is *constituted by* the city's many unredressed *interpersonal* disputes or frustrations produced by seeking their resolution from abusive or neglectful state agents.

On one level, this interpretation is correct: large-scale social unrest and interpersonal conflict are entwined. But the idea of a unidirectional relationship between social and interpersonal conflict—where interpersonal disputes and individual grievances "scale up" to produce social conflict—merely locates the roots of that unrest at the level of individual or interpersonal problems that are mismanaged or misdirected. This understanding also locates the *solution* to these conflicts at the level of interpersonal relationships: justice can be offered at the level of the isolated dyad, as I discussed in the previous chapter. Doing so fails to account for the ways that interpersonal disputes and experiences of domestic violence are in fact shaped, exacerbated, and often *fueled by* larger political-economic forces. And, indeed, many of the efforts to produce an entrepreneurial citizenry continue to locate the solution to people's woes at this individual and interpersonal level—while disparaging the "conflictual" forms of social and political mobilization that might draw attention to broader patterns of conflict and their causes.

You Have to Comply with Paper

In the face of overburdened and abusive state bureaucracies, alternative dispute resolution (ADR) programs like those housed in Bolivia's integrated justice centers (IJCS) encourage the poor to circumvent the state legal system and instead pursue voluntary, therapeutic, friendly means of resolving conflicts—through talk.[1] Training programs frequently accentuate the *spoken* dimensions of conciliation rather than the written product; they emphasize improved communication and delving into personal feelings in order to get at the root of interpersonal conflicts. Handbooks developed by donor organizations and adapted by local NGOs teach potential mediators how to peel back the layers of a conflict's "onion," methods for reorienting participants' speech and "active" listening techniques.[2] In Bolivia, advocates often insist on the parallels between ADR and Andean oral traditions, arguing for the cultural appropriateness of such talk-heavy techniques.[3] Orality, in these arguments, is linked to self-determination and flexibility toward more appropriate and culturally meaningful solutions. The *documents* produced by these conflict-resolution sessions, advocates argue, are secondary to the verbal and emotional work of conciliation.

I was surprised, then, to meet people like Virginia, who suggested otherwise.

"You have to comply with paper," Virginia insisted to me, unprompted. I met Virginia as she deposited her monthly quota on a debt she owed to a friend. Virginia had taken out the loan from the woman nearly a decade earlier. "My son was only five. Now he's fourteen. The interest was what got me. It was 10 percent, but what could I do? [The lender] saved me in that moment of need." Two years before we met, however, Virginia's friend grew weary of awaiting repayment. She threatened Virginia with a 20 percent interest rate if she didn't repay her within a year. But Virginia couldn't repay her friend. "I left her some collateral. A heavy blanket. A ring. What can you do? I lost it all," she explained.

Eventually, Virginia's friend presented her with an invitation to a conciliation appointment at the nearby IJC. There, the two women hammered out an accord outlining a schedule of repayment. Because Virginia is illiterate, the conciliator read it back to her before she signed the document. "Now I have been paying her back over two years," Virginia explained as she deposited 80 Bolivianos (Bs) (approximately US$11.40). This was payment number twenty-three. "No matter what, I must make the deposit."

Satisfied with how the arrangement resolved the conflict with her friend, Virginia invited her sister to conciliation. "I sold my sister a room in the house," Virginia explained, "but she hadn't made a paper for me yet. Paper is important. You have to fulfill your papers. Before I didn't have any papers and it really hurt me bad."

I could just as easily translate the word Virginia uses—*papel*—as document. Clients used a variety of terms to refer to conciliation agreements, including *acuerdo* (accord), *documento* (document), and *contrato* (contract). But Virginia consistently used "papel"—paper—in our conversation: "You have to comply with paper." In so doing, she highlights the material object, not merely the words recorded therein. Everything, Virginia insisted, must be done over paper. Even managing arrangements between kin.

Virginia wasn't alone. I found that despite the frequent appeals to informality and orality, clients at the IJCs were anxious to obtain those physical papers. Indeed, clients and staff alike would frequently invoke a phrase I came to view as the unofficial mantra of the IJCs: "Las palabras se llevan el viento," or "Words are carried off by the wind." Oral agreements, they insisted, were fleeting, fragile things as opposed to documents—whose weighty materiality allowed them to be carried, not away, but rather *into* people's homes.

Recent ethnographic work on bureaucracies draws our attention to the materiality and specificity of what the anthropologist Matthew Hull (2008) calls "graphic artifacts," and to the ideologies that surround their production, interpretation, and circulation.[4] Anthropologists have shown how state institutions and bureaucratic agents use documents to make populations "legible" and how these documentary practices make the state tangible in people's everyday lives.[5] Weber's analysis of the role that documents played in the advent of modern bureaucracy and Foucault's genealogy of the multiform "artifacts of bureaucratic knowledge" have inspired work on how documents help produce colonial and modern subjectivities (Riles 1998: 378; 2006). Anthropologists show ethnographically how these subjectivities are coproduced by bureaucrats and applicants, whose bodily suffering or hardship is materialized in patient charts and applications for asylum. That paperwork becomes the basis for making claims on local resources, for pursuing changes in legal status, or for appealing to international donors.[6]

Yet as Veena Das has argued, "Once the state institutes forms of governance through technologies of writing, it simultaneously institutes the possibility of forgery, imitation, and the mimetic performances of its power" (2007: 163; cf. Hansen 2001). Drawing on Das's work, the anthropologist Akhil Gupta analyzes how poor Indians use forgery strategically to overcome bureaucratic domination; forgery not only reveals the way writing functions in a teleological narrative about the relationship between literacy and democracy (e.g., ideals about voting and informed citizenship), but this simulacra also illuminates the mechanisms through which the state achieves its legitimacy, as people strive to "mimic" the state through their use of fake documents (2008: 188). Jeremy Campbell (2014), for example, discovered that Brazilian property speculators "devised an ingenious way to make their forged land titles look and feel authentically aged by using crickets" (244). As my own findings in the centers show, behind such clever mimetic practices is a powerful understanding of what documents do—what they invoke—through their *material* presence and their ambiguously official characteristics.

This chapter examines how residents of El Alto are deploying the documentary services offered by ADR to reorder intimate social relations (Merry 1990) and to formalize them on paper.[7] They do so in ways that are often antithetical to the graphic ideologies of legal aid staff (Hull 2012) and quite surprising, given how antagonistic many Bolivians feel toward the legal bureaucracies they seek to imitate (Goldstein 2012). I argue here that many Alteños pursue conciliation specifically because they are seeking to mimic legal documentary procedures, appropriating the documentary *form* (physical characteristics) of the state legal system in order to materialize returns on investments in social relations that remain outstanding.

That is, residents of El Alto are marshaling the conciliation accords produced by conflict-resolution programs—their size and formatting, the materiality of the document itself—to mimic what Gupta (2012) calls the "authenticating procedures" of the state.[8] Due to the material isomorphism (shared physical traits) between conciliation accords and legal documents, clients appropriate these documents as an easily accessible sign of the state legal system and the coercive apparatus it indexes. Clients rarely came to conciliation because they wanted to talk through their feelings and reestablish some kind of harmonious relationship. Rather, they came to the centers to get that paper. In particular, I explore the appeal that such quasi-legal documents hold for Alteños who are struggling to cope with the prolonged economic insecurity, compounding webs of debt owed to both social relations and banking institutions, and their obligations to kin and others. Papers provide a medium for materializing outstanding moral and material debts, leveraging compliance by invoking the law. As I show, for many clients seeking conciliation appointments, the law is not merely located in the corridors of courthouses or articulated in complaints lodged before a judge. Rather, the law is materialized—made visible, made tangible—in the *documents* produced by legal bureaucracies, *or ones that mimic them.*

Yet Alteños' determined pursuit of papers and their perceived capacity to ensure compliance belie an equally powerful distrust in the ability of the justice system and other state bureaucracies to offer satisfying results.[9] As we have seen, in Bolivia, the law and its accompanying institutional apparatus are widely understood to be *antithetical* to justice. These abuses include the arduous *trámites* (bureaucratic formalities) that impinge on so much of daily life. As Daniel Goldstein argues, despite people's frequent assertion that the state is absent, the law is very much present in the "onerous, confusing, and often fruitless" bureaucratic regulatory regimes through which residents must pass (2012: 6). In such a context, one might expect Alteños to shun the courts and to flee from spaces where the state could meddle in their intimate lives. "People are more likely to just endure their problems," Goldstein argues, "despite the suffering these cause them, rather than deal with the labyrinthine and nightmarish bureaucracy in search of official help" (2012: 23).

Critical studies of the Bolivian justice system highlight people's sharp mistrust of state agents.[10] Amid a pervasive sense of physical insecurity, Bolivians living in marginalized neighborhoods frequently characterize the state as directly complicit in their suffering: from police embroiled with criminal elements to self-serving lawyers who prey on poor clients, and court staff who will expedite—or impede—a case if their palms are greased. The thick compendiums of court documents that law interns stitch together by hand come to symbolize the grindingly slow courts and the many other bureaucratic offices people must visit as they seek redress for their grievances. As this book has shown, ADR was intended to offer an escape from those harms by providing Bolivians with the means to resolve their disputes without resorting to violence or the courts. And yet the law—or something that *looks* like it—still holds appeal.

Sociolegal scholars have argued that state-administered legal systems and informal justice are interpenetrating and situational.[11] My aim here is neither to draw nor to erase such boundaries. Rather, the puzzle I seek to illuminate is how the conciliation accords produced by informal dispute-resolution services invoke the coercive judicial apparatus, and why these material symbols of the law retain such appeal for the very people most vulnerable to its abuses. Many clients like Virginia never take the next step of pursuing a legal case against kin when they renege on the agreements outlined in conciliation accords. Rather, the formality of paper acts as a much-sought-after icon of coercive state power, despite people's profound misgivings toward the state legal apparatus.

The broader social context of lending and borrowing that I described in the previous chapters is an important backdrop to the larger phenomenon I am analyzing here because it shapes the contours of the relations that many ADR clients seek to redraw—and fuels many of the conflicts we saw in the centers. Clients in Bolivia's IJCs are utilizing conciliation to *formalize* informal modes of mutual aid—intertwined moral and material debts—with friends, neighbors, and kin, mobilizing conciliation accords as avatars of coercive state authority within those intimate relationships. In the process, they render the balance of social obligations into a physical ledger backed by the law, wherein one party has fallen behind in their quotas. Despite widespread ambivalence toward the legal apparatus, this is a story about the *appeal* of making social obligations visible and binding through encounters with legal bureaucracies and their documentary procedures.[12]

This chapter unfolds in three parts. I begin by exploring the many ways bureaucratic documentary procedures have shaped interpersonal relationships and citizenship practices since the colonial era. I then return to conciliation accords and their ambiguous isomorphism with legal documents. I contrast the idealized notion that ADR offers therapeutic, talk-based conflict resolution to the urban poor against Alteños' own concern for getting things on paper, and I situate that desire historically. Finally, I consider the intersecting relationship between documents, legal consciousness, and debt to show how documents are a critical mechanism through which Alteños seek to render social obligations visible to the state and, more pressingly, to each other. They frequently do so while challenging the graphic ideologies of ADR professionals who both strive to control what kind of work can be done through paper and engage in their own debates about the (fictitious) boundary between formal and informal justice. It is to the abiding power of paper that I now turn.

"Without Papers You Aren't a Person"

There are a number of ways to interpret clients' emphasis on getting a document, including, as I describe below, documents that contain behavioral and moral stipulations that are not recognized by the courts. Andean ethnohistorians and anthropologists have analyzed the ways Spanish colonial authorities used such documentary procedures as explicit "tools for changing native life-ways" (Abercrombie 1998: 190). The sword and the cross symbolized this civilizing project, but the pen also enabled it: document making became a key tool in a larger effort to remake indigenous subjectivities under the sign of the law.[13] Through *reducciones* and colonial cities populated by scribes and administrators, the church and the new colonial authorities hoped to draw the Indios (a derogatory term) further along the spectrum of civilization, while also incorporating them into new taxation schemes and conscripted labor systems.[14]

Thomas Abercrombie (1998) has argued that memory and meaning are constructed in highland Aymara and Quechua communities through embodied, oral, and ritual practices. Analysts of Bolivian customary law frequently emphasize these same characteristics as cultural markers of indigenous justice.[15] By contrast, colonial and later Republican administrators sought to impose a new order of things through writing, amassing an "archival memory" of land titles, *expedientes* (thick court records bound together by string), lists compiled and signed by notaries, "proofs of merit and service," and other certifications (Abercrombie 1998: 9).[16] These efforts introduced convoluted bureaucratic procedures and amassed enormous compendiums of ritually recorded legal documents. The Catholic Church was one of the primary institutions of recordkeeping, further sacralizing birth, death, and marriage certificates and other accountings of Indian peasants.[17]

Such bureaucratic documents are particularly charged in Latin America given the colonial legacy of arbitrary violence, which was often visited on indigenous people in the absence of *actas de buena conducta*, or acts of good conduct.[18] These acts of good conduct, written by administrative authorities or wealthy landowners, testified to whether indigenous people were complying with colonial efforts to discipline them into new labor regimes, to their good behavior or bad. For example, in the absence of such documents—and sometimes even in their presence—Gastón Gordillo (2006) shows how Toba and Wichi living in the Argentine Chaco faced abrupt execution by colonial armies. Older Toba and Wichi carry these histories around with them, Gordillo argues, in the almost obsessive relationship they developed with state identity documents, which they fastidiously guard.

Yet all this documentation was not simply imposed on a hapless population; rather, the native targets of settler colonial-management schemes were engaged in their own juridical endeavors, producing their own meaning out of legal documents, and appropriating those documents toward their own ends.[19] As Tristan Platt has argued, "Although written documents cannot always be read by their present owners, they can be invoked as literate sources of authority for a legal position articulated orally" (1992: 137).[20] Ethnographers and historians thus draw our attention to the ragged edges and fissures in colonial and contemporary governance strategies.[21] Accounts showing how people relate to and deploy bureaucratic documents (and their counterfeits) provide insight into how the "documented" themselves speak back and work to influence the outcomes of documentation, enumeration, categorization, and surveillance, and mobilize those documents to obtain resources and services, or to entrap the state in its own bureaucratic rationality.[22]

Platt further challenges the oral/documentary distinction in his analysis of colonial Latin America's foundational "myth of the archive." Platt writes that

> shamanic communication with the mountain spirits, for example, is known throughout the Andes, and has often been considered an indigenous source of oral authority which sustains the possibility of an anti-Western discourse capable of fuelling movements of resistance and rebellion. It can be shown, however, that in the region of Potosí at least, the apparent "orality" of the séance is itself permeated with metaphors drawn from Indian experience of the Western archive, indicating that, behind the "orality" of the speech-event, a literate template underpins and frames shamanic speech. (1992: 139)

Speech and writing are thus entangled rather than orality being "engulfed" or supplanted by literacy.[23] Under both colonial and republican regimes, Platt explains that "the act of *dictation* of an order, decision, etc. by a state authority is followed by the act of *writing* by a scribe, notary or secretary; copies are distributed to subsidiary authorities and the person concerned; these copies are *received* with various gestures of respect and obedience; and finally their content is communicated through *reading aloud* to those unable to read" (1992: 139). Much like in the agreement between Virginia and her friend, which was read aloud prior to their signatures, orality and inscription are not unrelated. Workshops and conferences I attended frequently emphasized the *orality* of indigenous conflict-resolution practices *to the exclusion* of the documentary procedures that follow. Yet as Abercrombie (1998), René Orellana Halkyer (2004), and Krista Van Vleet (2008) have shown, rural authorities continue to draw up actas de buena conducta following dispute resolution.

Many clients came to the center with such practices in mind as they circulated between their rural natal communities and their urban El Alto neighborhoods, and as they sought the advice and mediation from rural authorities, godparents, and *dirigentes* (association leaders). This interplay suggests that the distinction between the "Western" legal system and "traditional" or community justice, and the ways this division is spatialized in an urban/rural dichotomy, or characterized by an orality/literacy divide, cannot be sustained. Rather, conciliation programs and their documents are critical sites of judicial interpenetration or interlegality, and such documents are key sites for shaping legal consciousness and strategic engagements with the law.[24]

In contemporary Bolivia, documents occupy a powerful place in people's imagination, with real consequences for how people exercise their rights and assert their social and political belonging. Bolivians compile heavy legal-sized folders packed with birth, death, marriage, baptismal, and other certificates, as well as lengthy legal briefs, military service records, and voting booklets—all with the appropriate bureaucratic seals. Stained with the fading imprints of stamps and signatures, those documents are necessary to apply to jobs, enroll in school, obtain cash transfer resources from the government (i.e., Bono Juancito Pinto), file for child support, and vote in elections. As one intern, Olivia, said as she angrily chastised a client for failing to get proper documentation for her children, "without papers *you are not* a person."[25] You cannot advance a legal claim, register for school, correct typos on a marriage license, or apply for inheritance without your own—and your family members'—certifications. In great chains, documents must vouch for other documents, further crystallizing those kin networks. These graphic artifacts become material proofs of existence, as well as of formal (if not substantive) citizenship.

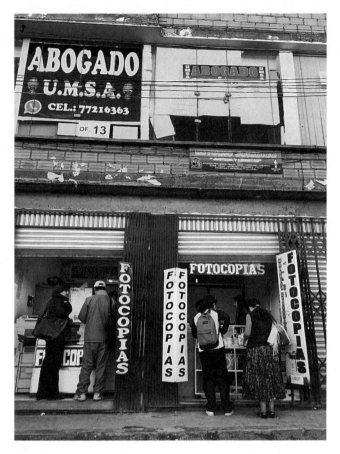

FIGURE 6.1
Alteños make
copious photo-
copies of their
documents outside
the courthouse.
Photo by author.

The colonial preoccupation with obtaining written testaments or "proofs of merit and service" (Abercrombie 1998: 169) seems to live on in the compendiums of certificates that people accumulate in their quest for gainful employment. Unlike the certifications produced by colonial administrators or "acts of good conduct" conferred by wealthy landowners, in contemporary Bolivia, NGOs have become a new force for credentialing. Like many who have worked with NGOs in Bolivia, I have spent many workshop evenings in a corner furiously signing certificates of participation for those who attended a training session, *conversatorio*, or civic education course. This demand for workshop certificates was almost as striking as the abundance of bureaucratic documents each person must accumulate over a lifetime. I watched one day as Alma, a former neighborhood volunteer, visited the center's director to request a letter of recommendation as she applied for a job at another institution. She brought with her a thick manila file folder stuffed with light

FIGURE 6.2 Case files accumulate in a La Paz courtroom. Photo by author.

pink, baby blue, eggshell, and crisp white certificates printed on cardstock. Alma received many of those certificates for attending training sessions at the center, but they also testified to her participation in gender, handicraft, and leadership workshops sponsored by a variety of NGOs scattered across El Alto. She proudly displayed them to me as evidence of her preparation, a tangible proof of her "merit and service."

In addition to providing Alma with material evidence of her preparedness for a potential employer, those certificates indexed the ongoing project of neoliberal responsibilization; they were the physical signs of her "empowerment." They signified ongoing efforts to remake residents of El Alto into democratic participants, capable leaders, and entrepreneurs. And often those roles were understood to be mutually reinforcing. In communicating Alma's "merit and service" and potential to be a good employee, those certificates bridged historical moments, linking colonial bureaucratic practices that evaluated Andean Indians according to their productivity within a new colonial labor management order with contemporary efforts to transform individual people and whole populations into entrepreneurial citizens.

Take, for example, the ways that María—one of the center's clients—talked about her experience working with Pro Mujer (Pro woman), a microcredit institution originally sponsored by the United States Agency for International Development (USAID). As we chatted over tea and pastries, María retreated into another room and, unprompted, returned hugging a heavy folder bursting with certificates. She gently opened the folder and slid it toward me, beaming about her accomplishments and pointing to particularly meaningful certifications. These diplomas exhibited her years of attending workshops—workshops that explicitly aimed to shape her sense of self as well as her behavior. As I leafed through them, I noted that many were tied to the microfinance sector (e.g., entrepreneurship and accounting modules), sponsored by USAID, or run by NGOs advocating women's empowerment and leadership skills via economic independence.[26]

These were proof of María's participation in projects aiming to transform her into an entrepreneurial citizen who knows her rights and obligations within a liberal human rights framework. These experiences meant a lot to her, and she shared her pride with me. But those certificates also made visible many of her disappointments. As she delicately turned over the certificates, her tone turned bittersweet: she remembered friendships forged with foreign aid workers who lost touch; a sense that she had been used to marshal a network of women for an early Pro Mujer pilot project only to feel shut out from meaningful leadership because she lacked the formal education and social status of more elite, *mestiza* women. Her certificates served to verify her capabilities—but only to a point; there was a limit to her expertise. These certificates also made María legible as an entrepreneurial citizen to the expanding network of NGOs operating in El Alto, which could enumerate her participation for their own recordkeeping, reporting functions, and grant applications to funding agencies back in the United States and Europe.

I highlight María's and Alma's preoccupation with collecting certificates as just one expression of the powerful role documents play in shaping how people imagine their own life trajectories not only through the formal documentation of state bureaucracies (birth, death, marriage certificates; voter and military service booklets, etc.), but also through the certification of other agents of governance—namely NGOs. Moreover, NGO certifications carry the extra sense of constructing a *proyecto de vida* by enrolling in alternative education programs or microcredit groups (rather than a state-imposed process of enumeration or certification). Nevertheless, legal documents produced by state bureaucracies remain central to people's lives and livelihoods—and the ways they make claims on the state and on each other.

"Documents Should Mean Something"

The IJCS similarly produced reams and reams of documents, including letters of referral to the forensic medical examiner, to psychological services, and pro bono legal briefs (*memoriales*) for clients pursuing domestic violence cases. But the central and emblematic document produced by the centers was the conciliation accord. The centers were not the only institutions that produce conciliation accords, but as I will discuss, their documentary genre and material dimensions seemed to capture the imagination of center clientele who were desperate to render visible unsettled obligations with intimate social relations.

Alteños seeking conciliation appointments pulled tattered copies of prior, informal agreements out of sturdy plastic folders—money loaned to a nephew as capital to buy a used taxi or to a daughter-in-law to help finance her small shop. The lists might mention jewelry or an alpaca shawl offered as collateral. During intake sessions with staff, clients would verbally add other outstanding debts: cases of beer still owed from a wedding or baptismal celebration; the personal funds spent completing the sewage system, outhouse, or electrical wiring in a property shared by extended family.

Those scraps of paper were like stained maps of old friendships, business partnerships, and kin networks. In addition to adobe bricks, dollars, and promised payments, they tallied disappointments and soured trust. Often, lenders would describe their own complicated webs of debt to explain why they so desperately needed to recover every penny of the many small loans they had made to the people they loved.

Adult children accompanied elderly mothers who were desperate to get a *comadre* (co-mother) or cousin to repay a loan as her own financial situation worsened. Sometimes the recipients of those loans, the borrower, would approach the center first, hoping that conciliation documents would convince irate lenders that they intended to repay, even if only in small quotas extended over long periods of time. Some borrowers would denounce their lenders—usually female friends, family members, neighbors—declaring them to be *prestamistas* or moneylenders (inflected with the connotation of loan sharks) or fraudsters (*estafadoras*). They would accuse them of harassing them in the street, driving them from the market, making scenes in front of neighbors, scaring their children, defrauding their loved ones, or threatening overt violence. Other borrowers would weep with embarrassment, recount downward spirals of debt, and speak of the patience of the person to whom they owed much money and gratitude.

Clients frequently brought the artifacts of previous conciliation attempts at NGOs or the Police Brigade for Family Protection. Many had been disappointed when the other party never appeared for the session or when payments soon tapered off. But again and again, clients insisted on the need to get it down on paper, and they expressed hope that this time the document might appear formidable enough to ensure compliance.

Clients were heartened by the sense that invitations to conciliation carried the symbolic weight of judicial coding. The juridical-sounding name, the inky stamps, seals, and the signatures or for the illiterate—the thumbprints of clients—seemed to inspire hope that this time things might be different. The slippage between the informal and formal, voluntary and compulsory, was evident as people asked for "citations"—the legal term for the court summons that people are served in civil and criminal cases—when making conciliation appointments. Even interns and staff sometimes slipped into judicial speak, forgetting to use the official term, "invitation," to indicate that the letter issued by the center was for a voluntary appointment. Invariably, conciliators would clarify to the disputing parties, "I cannot force you to sign this document; I am not a judge."[27] Yet even the buildings themselves seemed to belie this assertion: each center is housed under the same roof as a "mixed" civil, family, and criminal court, located just down the corridor.

In practice, both ADR advocates and clients often worried about the noncoercive nature of conciliation in a context where, they argued, few people would comply without some threat. As a consequence, and despite all the rhetorical emphasis on volunteerism and mutually beneficial outcomes, staff frequently encouraged strategies aimed at coercing attendance, including delivering invitation letters with the aid of uniformed police. As one intern put it to a client, "How would you react if a police officer showed up at your house? Intimidated! So it's best to go with an officer. It makes people take it more seriously."

Indeed, conciliators and center staff often emphasized that conciliation documents are a *cosa juzgada* (judicial object), equivalent to a judicial sentence that can then be introduced in court for *homologación* (ratification and enforcement) by a judge in the case of a breach (as I will describe here, others downplayed this linkage). But most clients seemed to harbor this expectation *before* the lengthy explanations offered by center staff. This expectation provoked enormous grief and anger when cosignees were tardy with payments following apparently "successful" conciliation appointments. Take, for example, the bitter disappointment expressed by Moises.

Moises was notorious in the center for the sheer quantity of conciliation appointments he kept. On this particular morning, he returned to the center, looking vexed. "I want to make a complaint," he griped. "I had these people sign conciliation documents and they are not fulfilling them."

I explained to a pacing Moises that the conciliator had been called away to the Ministry of Justice. "When the conciliator returns you can discuss the next steps for breach of the accord," I clarified. Moises shifted back and forth, dissatisfied. "No. No! My complaint is bigger. I want to tell the Ministry of Justice that conciliation does not work," he growled. "If they signed a document it means they have to fulfill it. It shouldn't require next steps. Documents should mean something. They must comply with the document. It should fix things." Were conciliation a meaningful act, Moises argued, the document itself would compel people to *acatar*—to obey and meet those obligations. Like taking a police officer.

I argue that this expectation about the work performed by conciliation accords owes much to the accord's ambiguous isomorphism (shared physical traits) with legal documents, and the coercive state apparatus they index. This expectation has been shaped by the ways Bolivians think about themselves and their relationships to state bureaucracies—and to each other—through the production, interpretation, and deployment of both legal and legal-like documents. I say legal-*like* because for both staff and clients, the physical, formal properties of the conciliation document stood as a sign of the *formal* legal system.

Conciliators draft accords after concluding a mediation session, outlining the agreement that parties have reached and the stipulations for how that agreement will be actualized. But I found that the format and purpose of those documents were never fixed—despite efforts to "regularize" their production through periodic workshops and training sessions aimed at staff and interns. These bureaucratic fissures were evident in heated debates I witnessed among center staff about the intended or misguided isomorphism between conciliation accords and legal briefs. Let me offer a vignette to illustrate how these debates unfolded and the larger questions they raised about the work done by paper. This section sets the scene for the final piece of my argument: that cash strapped Alteños are mobilizing the material expression of conciliation and its legal-like properties to render *informal* social obligations and their extended temporalities into binding contracts with fixed timelines, and to make those obligations visible to each other.

Letter- versus Legal-Sized Paper

The staff and interns working in El Alto and La Paz's IJCs have gathered this early Saturday morning for a training session on preparing conciliation accords. We make our way to the Ministry of Justice's lecture hall, complete with university-style rows of seating facing a stage, podium, and dry-erase board. The workshop leader, Ester Abramović, distributes stacks of sample accords produced by the centers among small groups, with names and other identifying information blotted out for privacy. Abramović asks us to identify errors in the documents: errors in *form*, errors in *content*.

After an hour, Abramović calls us back to plenary and begins sorting through the scraps of paper upon which each group has noted its critiques of the conciliation accords they analyzed. She tacks them to the white board, grouping overlapping thoughts, identifying outliers, letting each rectangular slip of paper guide the conversation. It's a question of form or content, she explains: which of these critiques are simple errors of *form*, and which are bigger problems that would ultimately threaten the viability of the conciliation accords themselves?

Suddenly, one group's critique prompts tension among the otherwise relaxed assembly. Their conciliation accord, they explain, was printed on letter-sized paper. Abramović pauses and turns to the group: "Is this a problem in form or content?"

A chorus of competing answers goes up from the crowd. Everyone seems startled. We discover that some centers print their conciliation accords on legal-sized paper. Other centers adhered to letter-sized accords. Participants are shocked to learn that there are varying practices across the eight centers operating in El Alto and La Paz. Grumbling commences. "Our documents need to be consistent with judicial documents," one man argues. "They should be printed on legal-sized paper."

José Pérez, the coordinator for District 1, is seated toward the front of the auditorium. He twists his body to peer at his colleagues, brow furrowed, and raises his hand to comment. Pérez laments the use of legal-sized paper: "We're turning into little courts," he announces sharply. "We have lost sight of the original purpose of the centers." Another voice pipes up: "But what do the regulations say?" And another: "We are now housed in the Ministry of Justice. It should be *legal sized* like all documents that come out of the courts."

Abramović waves her hand dismissively, trying to indicate that this is not a critical point. But Pérez is insistent. Paper size *matters*.

I MET WITH Pérez a few weeks later and asked him to expand on his critique of legal-sized paper. The light entering his office filtered through a layer of women's rights posters and butcher paper hung on the glass partition. Pérez periodically talked me through the diagrams, legal terms, and inspirational quotes about the work of social transformation that he had scribbled across those sheets while training his own crew of interns. "What I was suggesting," he explained, "was a concern I have about this tendency I have seen toward focusing on the conciliation accord as the primary product of conciliation, or the idea that the accord must contain technical elements that are juris- dictional. . . . For example, [the notion] that an accord should necessarily be founded upon [legal] articles and things like that. This implies a regression [in the aims of] conciliation."

For Pérez, the *preference* for legal-sized documents indexed a shift in the meaning and purpose of ADR's "original" goal. The centers, he explained, were intended to distance people from the courts. Increasingly, he lamented, conciliators *also* were drawing up documents that intentionally mirrored legal briefs—not only in form, but also in content: some conciliators, we learned at the meeting, built conciliation accords around specific articles in Bolivia's legal codes. Pérez continued

> For me, conciliation, at least in the way we trained people [under USAID], was another path. . . . It was something that had other charac- teristics [distinct from the formal legal system]. A different tempera- ment. So the concept of conciliation determines a lot. There is a subtle but substantial difference. When a conciliator insists that the accord should contain elements of formal justice, obviously we can correct them [and explain that this] usage of conciliation accords is a misinter- pretation—a perversion—of the initial concept.

The debate at the workshop, he suggested, was part of an ongoing tension between those who wanted to tilt conciliation toward the realm of the formal legal system, to "pervert" and "distort" its original aims, to discard the "alter- native" of "alternative dispute resolution."

Sebastián Costa, a conciliator in District 4, shared Pérez's concerns. Staff members, he suggested, were erroneously encouraging clients to *homologar* (get a judge's signature to legalize a document) conciliation accords immediately

after finalizing the agreement. "What's the point then [of conciliation]," he asked rhetorically, "if all we do is send people back to the courts instead of really resolving their problems?" Costa continued:

> What's the point of the centers if all we do is pile everything on the courts? Conciliation accords should only be homologado in case of going unfulfilled. Otherwise, we aren't empowering civil society— we are just falling back into the same patterns. For what purpose do we exist? Homologaciones can take up to six months. Six months! But if we do a good job resolving the conflict we can avoid all this. And, honestly, we can't rely on the courts. The cases in my [district's] court spent six months paralyzed because the judge had to rotate to another district. There is no consistency. It generated a huge backlog.

Costa blamed this tendency on the legal training of center staff. It was a habit. A rut. They fell back into old patterns of legalism. Costa further blamed the obsession with documentation on the pressure staff faced to generate numbers that would justify their continued funding—from both USAID and the Ministry of Justice. But Costa went further in his critique, arguing that a good conciliation session would so effectively allow clients to get at the root causes of their disputes that no accord would be necessary. Successful conciliation, Costa insisted, shouldn't require a document.

Despite this vocal opposition to legal-sized paper and to the judicial turn it indexed, not everyone agreed. Rather, the workshop debate reflected a recurring tension among bureaucratic staff. Paola Chacón, the educator who conducted the focus groups that formed the basis of the IJCs, explained that the paper-size issue had come up before—when the USAID contracting team was first designing the centers. "We had to systematize the paper size the centers were using," she recalled. For people like Chacón, this material echo between conciliation accords and judicial documents was necessary. She continued: "We have gotten on the wavelength of judges—format, spacing. I don't know if that was how it should have been done. For me, paper is paper. But the format can give it greater formality. And you've got to fulfill [those regulations] if the paper is going to matter, right?"

"Graphic ideologies," Hull notes, "are sets of conceptions about graphic artifacts held by their users, including about what material qualities of an artifact are to count as signs, what sorts of agents are (or should be) involved in them, and what roles of human intentions and material causations are" (2012: 14). Here, we have a dispute over *which* graphic ideology will prevail in shaping the documentary procedures of ADR. But *both* critics *and* advocates of that judicial mimicry agreed on the ultimate *effect* of printing conciliation accords on legal-sized paper and incorporating other judicial elements: if it looks like the law, it must act like the law.

But it is more than that. If it looks like the law, *participants* will *act* differently too. They will be interpellated through the document in different ways. For Pérez, letter-sized paper is meant to call people toward reconciliation through an *alternative*, therapeutic encounter. For advocates of legal-sized paper, it is about the sense of obligation and even fear inspired by legal documents, as well as the view that the paper will stimulate compliance.

And yet these graphic artifacts also harbor widespread distrust and disappointment in state institutions. This tension between desiring legal documents and disbelieving their value ran throughout many of my conversations with clients and staff alike. How, then, can we interpret the recurring turn to these bureaucratic artifacts? If, as I will show, the turn to the judicial realm is driven not only by staff, but also by center clientele, what does this tactic reveal?

I argue that this mimicry of the state legal system and its documentary procedures is not only about utilizing ADR as the first step toward a legally enforceable arrangement. True, the legal-like document produced through ADR becomes a cosa juzgada. But it also does more than that. Papers provide a medium for rendering ethical claims visible and accounting for bruised relations, their imagined audience a social one. This graphic ideology is particularly evident in conflicts tied to debt.

Materializing Debts

Rosa's case is representative of many I saw at the IJC, as Alteños sought to inscribe social lending arrangements into conciliation accords. I met Rosa as she stopped by the center to pick up a quota payment from her nephew. He hadn't made the deposit. Looking deflated, Rosa sighed and shrugged her shoulders. "He's always late." Both Rosa and her nephew are shopkeepers, and Rosa had loaned her nephew capital for his small business. When Rosa asked him to pay her back, "He hid. He ran off to Santa Cruz to escape [the debt]." This put her in a difficult position; she had taken out money from *another* woman to make the loan to her nephew, and now she was left to contend with her own lender—who was demanding repayment. Rosa eventually cajoled her nephew into attending a conciliation appointment and to signing an agreement for monthly payments. He pays his quotas, she explained, but was often tardy. Rosa had responded to her nephew's appeal to her *cariño* (caring) in a moment of need, and they now had a binding accord that she could utilize to pursue a legal claim against him for breach of contract. For the moment, however, she was willing to wait him out, albeit anxiously.

As with Rosa and her nephew, kin-based lending practices are entangled with other forms of lending and borrowing, including loans obtained from moneylenders, neighboring shopkeepers, and friends, as well as banking institutions. As I've shown, many economically strapped Alteños cobble together these bundles to sustain small businesses, supplement irregular incomes, and to cover emergency health expenses, school fees, and unexpected income losses due to strikes, theft, or bad sales. As they do so, however, they also make loans to others in similar circumstances. And, when they speak of their own economic hardship, they frequently relay the difficulties facing *their* borrowers—friends, neighbors, and kin who are enmeshed in their own tangle of debts.

As Alteños make those small loans to each other, they frequently express frustration, resentment, and the sneaking suspicion that friends and relations may be abusing their generosity. At the IJC, clients grimaced as they described feeling obliged to respond to repeated requests. They also told me of feeling ashamed when they denied some of those petitions and the person in question suffered the harmful consequences of being unable to repay *other* loans. But lenders were not exempt from skepticism. Borrowers periodically accused kin of usury and making a business out of their need.

As I described earlier, this complex overlay of debt and social relations has become more pronounced in El Alto as microfinance institutions have proliferated, as they have elsewhere, utilizing poor women's social networks to extend their reach, and *producing* gendered social networks *through* their micro-lending structures.[28] Many Alteños who came to the centers reported that they were only able to repay their numerous bank loans *because* of the vast network of informal credit they drew on through appeals to cariño, *ayni*, and obligation, procuring new loans dispersed across a range of social relations. While debts owed to kin and friends might be postponed, the debts owed to financial institutions have none of the flexibility afforded by appealing to neighborliness or a sister-in-law's compassion. But those people can only be avoided or placated for so long. In-laws, cousins, and even neighborhood moneylenders face their own financial deadlines.

These strains manifested themselves, for example, as kin convinced each other to join credit groups or to sign as guarantors on bank loans, only to find themselves falling irreparably behind on payments. When godparents, siblings, or aunties failed to pay back the principal or the interest, other members of the family would be pulled into the spiral of debt as their names were blacklisted in Bolivia's national credit registry, which one Bolivian bank employee described to me as "the equivalent of having a criminal record." Thus while debt itself is not inherently negative and in fact can be extremely productive of social relationships, Alteños, and especially women, were coming to the centers to document and manage the compounding conflicts those debts could also produce.[29]

My aim here is to highlight the ways the issues I have described in previous chapters coalesce around conciliation accords. As friends and kin increasingly "default" on promised repayments to their informal lenders, those lenders have sought to manage their own precarious repayment schedule through various regimes of documentation. Microfinance thus adds another dimension to the ways the legal consciousness surrounding law-like graphic artifacts operates in the current moment.

These debt-related documentary practices likely have deep roots. In her research into late nineteenth-century legal cases brought by moneylenders to Bolivian courts, the historian Nancy Egan reports that women appear to have been more systematic than their male counterparts in documenting loans made across asymmetrical power relations (personal communication). By contrast, the anthropologist Nico Tassi finds that contemporary Aymara traders in the Eloy Salmón market rely on "extensive and sophisticated kinship networks and informal but solid economic agreements *rarely put on paper or legalized*."[30] Yet in Alto Lima's IJC, clients were eager to get things on paper, and they often came equipped with notations. However, they frequently reported tallying those debts *after the fact* of the loan, insisting that it would have been a sign of bad faith to draw up a document with close relations from the outset.[31] Through ADR, women like Rosa sought the additional formality of law-like documents to reorder those social relations that had become too burdensome, frequently under pressure from the more regimented temporalities of institutional loans. Dionicia's case is emblematic.

"It's Just a Moral Document"

Dionicia came to the center indebted to a number of microfinance institutions targeting women and their social networks, including Pro Mujer and Diakonia, as well as Crecer and Emprender. The day we met, Dionicia's husband, Oscar, accompanied her begrudgingly.

Dionicia and Oscar had previously signed a conciliation agreement wherein he promised to contribute to the payments she was making to several financial institutions. He failed to fulfill those commitments, and now Dionicia wanted to see how she might hold him accountable for breach of contract. Oscar sat listless as Dionicia listed the various debts she owed to banking institutions, and then the many informal loans she had received from friends, neighbors, kin, and moneylenders to help her meet her bank quotas. "I need 800 Bs [approximately US$114] by 2 PM this afternoon [to meet one of my microfinance quotas]," she explained. "But in addition to those debts I owe other people. I owe Julia 500 Bs [$71]. I owe Lidia 600 Bs [$85]. I owe Marta almost 1,700 Bs [$242]. I owe Cecilia 500 Bs [$71]. I am always begging. The person who loaned me 1,000 Bs [$142] did so with interest." She gestured to Oscar, "He thinks I just complain for no reason. He doesn't understand."

A few days later I witnessed a follow-up conversation between Dionicia and the conciliator, Sonia Campos. Looking over Dionicia's accord, Campos shook her head and clarified that the conciliator who had drawn up the previous agreement had done so in error. "He could just make a mockery of this accord," Campos explained, "because between spouses there are no debts. There is no legal basis for it," she continued. "If you want to have your husband sign a document, you must understand it is a *moral* commitment. It has no backing from the law. But if you decide to separate we can do one for child support."

Dionicia paused to consider her options. "I have my little store, my sweater workshop. I have two machines. What happens if we separate?" she asked.

"The law says that all of your belongings will be divided. If you do conciliation you can fix things by talking it out. But if you can't reach an agreement, the judge will make you sell them off and split the money."

At this possibility, Dionicia shook her head, alarmed. "The last time we separated I gave him the [sewing] machine because, why fight? But he used it as collateral on a debt. Where's that machine now? Who knows! But I bought these machines by myself."[32]

"But under the law, it is shared," Campos explained.

Dionicia remained unmoved. She reiterated that she wanted a conciliation accord with her husband, regardless of its "legality."

"Fine," Campos conceded, "but it's just a moral document."

The sighing acquiescence I witnessed from Campos, a lawyer, was familiar. I regularly heard Campos and other staff, particularly conciliators trained in law, bemoan cases they deemed "inappropriate" for conciliation, arguing that they were better suited to the intervention of a psychologist or social worker, or clearly a violation of the law and therefore intended for the courts. Cases like Dionicia's were perplexing for some staff because they unsettled neat distinctions between "actionable" and "nonactionable" accords, and because center clients continued to insist on outcomes that staff believed were inappropriate or unfeasible.[33]

A case similar to Dionicia's sparked debate during the conciliation accord workshop I described earlier. Examining our sample accords, one provoked deeper conversation. In it, a husband agreed to stop drinking and speaking cruelly to his wife. "How could you ever enforce such an agreement?" asked one of the participating interns. "This document is purely moralist." The center director participating in our small group nodded vigorously:

Before, clients would come in saying he hits me, he insults me, he mistreats me psychologically. He drinks. And they signed acts of commitment [*actas de compromiso*] about behaving nice. But there is no judicial entity that can enforce that kind of moral commitment. This accord should have never been signed. It should have been transferred directly to the psychologist and then the judge in a psychological violence court case. There are errors of form and content here. This accord is useless.

The director continued: "You [interns] are from El Alto. You understand. The women demand it anyway. They say, 'It doesn't matter. I want him to sign the document.'"

An enforceable or "legally actionable" accord would be something like an agreed plan of payments between a debtor and nonspousal creditor, with specific dates and quota payments outlined. In the event that the debtor fails to make payments according to that plan, the lender can request a judge's order for immediate payment of the full amount under threat of further sanction. But as Campos explained to Dionicia, this kind of agreement between a creditor and debtor is not legally recognized between spouses. The kind of document Dionicia was requesting would therefore be "purely moralist."

Campos's approach clashed with the position held by conciliators like José Pérez, who believed that ADR clients should be free to incorporate moral commitments without trying to mimic legal documents in form or content. For them, *that was the point* of ADR. Bureaucrats held vastly different views about the kind of enterprise they were engaged in, and the issue of paper size exposed that rift. This lack of unanimity over the purpose and practice of printing conciliation accords reveals how contested the production of bureaucratic documents can be within institutions like the IJCs. Yet rather than blaming their colleagues for being misguided, critics of "purely moralist" accords tended to focus on the *demand* from women like Dionicia. It was the clients, they argued, who doggedly pursued such fatally flawed documents, *despite* staff efforts to persuade them against it. Clients often wanted to include a range of behavioral changes that were not "actionable," and they wanted it in writing.

Much like the "garbage cases" that frustrated court officials in Merry's (1990) study of working-class residents in Massachusetts, ADR practitioners in Bolivia sometimes find themselves battling with clients in an effort to reframe their problems in therapeutic rather than legal terms. Indeed, Merry's claimants wanted to remain within the bounds of the courts and avoid spaces like ADR centers. Yet in El Alto, some staff encouraged their clients to pursue formal legal channels or crafted more legal-like accords. Center clients, however, were perfectly happy to avoid the courts for all the reasons this book has explored; informal spaces held great appeal, *so long as* clients could import the most visible, material, technology of the state: bureaucratic documentation.

As I have shown, the constant appeal to recording moral commitments in conciliation accords may reflect both the powerful influence of bureaucratic legal documents and experiences with similar good conduct agreements utilized by other rural and associational authorities. We also might interpret these maneuvers as ways Alteños are appropriating legal-like documents to strengthen social institutions. Dionicia, for example, wanted to take the marriage contract a step further, to render visible her husband's commitments within the ongoing relationship of the marriage. But something more is happening; we can see how critical it is to Dionicia to get that document, despite her conciliator's protests. The alternatives are too unsatisfying. Her debts cannot wait. Inscribing her husband's moral commitments to her in a legal-like document would have to do.

As Alteños cycle between informal loans owed to intimate social relations—often in the quest to pay off loans from banking institutions—they pursue conciliation accords to manage economic insecurity and limited legal options. Alteños like Dionicia seek to negotiate these dilemmas through their mimicry of the graphic artifacts of the legal system, instantiating those obligations through the materiality of the accord itself. "You have to comply with paper," Virginia told me.

Even as donors hoped that the IJCs would encourage residents of El Alto to avoid the formal legal system and its abuses, this constant turn to documents and their imagined coercive capabilities reflect a broader turn toward the state in both the institutional life of the centers as well as the intimate lives of their clients. Despite deep ambivalences and frustrations with legal bureaucracies, Alteños do so in part because these documentary practices have so deeply inflected their understandings of themselves and have shaped the ways they relate to bureaucracies and to each other. But they also do so because they are pursuing mechanisms to resolve pragmatic and pressing needs, making ethical claims on intimate social relations, and reframing the obligations of social lending in more explicitly contractual terms.

Some center staff did report trying to help the occasional client think about how to renegotiate debt payments with financial institutions, but most remained focused on the resulting interpersonal disputes those loans generated.[34] In neighboring La Paz, the feminist organization Mujeres Creando was plugging along in its own efforts to help desperate women renegotiate their institutional loan payments on an individual-by-individual basis. As Mujeres Creando's Mayra Rojas explained to me, in addition to the organization's previous investigations (Toro Ibáñez 2010) and radio programs aiming to draw a critical eye to the microfinance industry, Mujeres Creando created a program to help individual women renegotiate payment schedules with banks. The organization relied on its considerable public persona to pressure banks to concede; with a winking smile, she told me that branch officers worried that Mujeres Creando would show up with their flashy protest style and acerbic graffiti.

Revealing her own expectations of appropriate kin behavior, Rojas recoiled when I spoke of the ways ADR clients were formalizing informal loans through conciliation accords. She equated such inscription with a "social death." Mujeres Creando, she insisted, was in no position to take on the interpersonal conflicts generated by those loans—nor, she asserted, would the organization want to be complicit in such a troubling practice. And so, without knowing it or coordinating their efforts, these two institutions were laboring to ameliorate the conflicts generated by excessive indebtedness tied to microfinance.

As I described in chapter 4, ADR offers the possibility of intervention into such conflicts at the level of the isolated, interpersonal dispute, but it cannot resolve—and, in fact, may obscure—the political-economic conditions that produced the conflict in the first place. Indeed, conciliation programs may serve as a stopgap measure, but one that enables this precarious arrangement to continue. Yet many clients who come to the center to map out their debts recognize those patterns and complain about them indignantly, acknowledging that the real resolution to their problems would take something more than a conciliation accord. It would take a steady income—for themselves and for the many people with whom they are connected through such loans.

Conclusion

The production of bureaucratic documents has profoundly shaped people's intersubjective lives in Bolivia. For many clients in the centers, the shared physical traits between conciliation accords and formal legal briefs act as an avatar of state law and its coercive capabilities. The isomorphism between conciliation accords and formal legal briefs enables Alteños to marshal the documentary form to bring the "authenticating procedures" of the state home with them as they navigate intimacies and obligations amid prolonged economic insecurity.[35]

These dynamics are particularly evident in the ways clients seek to document social lending practices in order to make those debts legible to each other. Although the document is a cosa juzgada that might be introduced into court, many, like Rosa, eschewed those next steps. They still wanted to avoid the courts for all the reasons described earlier, but they desperately wanted that paper. Alteños' urgent pursuit of conciliation accords exposes the shifting meaning, nature, and temporality of debt as a social relation in Bolivia, and the relationship between sociality and bureaucracies as it is affected by a changing economy and its strict deadlines.

Yet such patterns are not exclusive to debt relations; rather, they are revelatory of the broader appeal of documents that look like the law—however much people distrust the legal apparatus. These practices also suggest that "shadow" bureaucratic documents extend "lawfare," popularized in anthropology by Jean Comaroff and John Comaroff (2006), into intimate relations. And, as those documented in conciliation accords speak back against bureaucrats who would circumscribe their efforts, these practices also reveal how the urban poor marshal ambiguous bureaucratic documentary procedures to give some teeth to moral obligations and to manage social relations they find untenable. This use of conciliation accords—to make social obligations and ethical claims visible—is especially evident in the ways center clients seek to inscribe conciliation accords with what staff critically described as "purely moralist" and "nonactionable" behavior.

With what effects? When it comes to outstanding debts between social relations, these contracts provide borrowers with clear expectations about quota payments and often allow them to stagger those payments according to more manageable sums and timelines. They also offer lenders—who are facing their own tangle of debts—a promise of payment and some relief. Yet these graphic artifacts may have significant consequences for how people relate to the network of friends and kin who make those payments possible. Even as Alteños came to the centers anxious for conciliation papers, many expressed enormous unease and ambivalence about mapping out those debts and inscribing them in the accord. Many shrank physically during the conciliation sessions, turning their bodies away from friends and kin. Recall Lourdes from chapter 4, who sought the protective cover of her fleece shawl, counting out her comadre's debt while hiding her face. But lenders were also borrowers, and they generally recounted their own situations of indebtedness as the justification for why they were pressing so firmly on their kin.

Like Lourdes, many insisted that they needed the money. And they needed it now.

As Alteños cajole—and sometimes threaten—intimate social relations into signing conciliation accords, those expectations and dynamic debts are crystallized into a physical accounting of the relationship and its imbalance of payments. Painfully, many people who come to the centers find themselves shackled by preexisting debt payments to *other* people or institutions, and they are unable to meet the commitments outlined in their accords without seeking additional loans from *other* neighbors and kin—who bellyache about the constant requests for help. And so the cycle continues.

And what happens to the relationship once that balance of payments is paid off? For some, like Virginia, the repayment restores trust and provides relief, both economic and emotional. The relationship survives. But for others, the end of a payment cycle is also the end of the relationship; the contract transforms the moral economy of widespread social lending practices— with its notions of mutuality and extended temporality—into a more explicit debtor-creditor relationship with an expiration date.

Just as I often heard clients and staff invoke the phrase "words are carried off by the wind" when appealing to papers, Alteños regularly lament that "there is no justice" or, more tellingly, that others "make a mockery of justice." When clients do so, they express the pervasive opinion that *both* conciliation and the state legal system regularly fail to ensure compliance or to effectively resolve disputes. Yet rather than wanting legal bureaucracy entirely out of their lives, as ADR advocates might counsel, Alteños' turn to paper reflects a desire for state institutions capable of delivering on their promises—and for friends and kin who will do so too.

Making Do in Late Liberalism

Months after I had followed the industrial sewing machine as it moved from commodity to collateral to commodity and back again, Doña Justa asked if I would be godmother to her son. I agonized over her request for a very long time. Although I was not a conciliator in her sessions with Pilar and Carmen, I had been present to observe them and had conducted interviews with the women connected to that machine—at least the living ones.

Justa had long since paid back those particular debts to Carmen and Pilar, and I had concluded my research at the center. Still feeling deeply ambivalent, I acquiesced to be the *madrina* (godmother) to ten-year-old Abel. Justa was a practicing *evangélica* (evangelical)—but wanted her son baptized in the Catholic cathedral where she married her husband. We went to the information session on baptism and *compadrazgo*, smiling along quietly as the catechist gravely intoned that the godparent must provide spiritual uplift and direction—and keep their godchildren away from the specter of evangelicalism.

On the day of the baptism, Justa arrived at the cathedral in an elegant baby-blue *pollera*, with a magenta shawl fastened neatly by a gold brooch. It was the first time I had seen her this polished, with her thick black braids freshly folded. My new *compadre*, Rubén, drove his Micro bus (similar to the one owned by Manuela's husband) and dressed in a smart green suit jacket. Abel wore the gleaming white sweater I bought for his baptismal garb to symbolize (as we were instructed) his rebirth. He sat earnestly next to me throughout the service, periodically glancing up with nervous enthusiasm.

The biblical texts, which were part of the lectionary, were not specific to this cathedral or Mass. And so I couldn't help but giggle at the first reading—

and the sidelong glances from the gathered parishioners as the lector read Leviticus 19:33–34, instructing those present against mistreating foreigners residing amongst them.

But my smile faded as an elderly man approached the microphone and began reading the second passage in Spanish with an Aymara-inflected clip. My stomach dropped as he spoke. He read: "If you lend money to one of my people among you who is needy, do not treat it like a business deal; charge no interest. If you take your neighbor's cloak as collateral, return it by sunset, because that cloak is the only covering your neighbor has. What else can they sleep in? When they cry out to me, I will hear, for I am compassionate. Exodus 22:26–28." I listened to that passage and immediately thought of the sewing machine Justa bought with high hopes for her pollera business, only to repurpose it as collateral when her debts spiraled. She lost that machine, and she lost her friend and business partner, Nicolasa. I thought of Severino and Nieves. Of Rosa and her nephew. I thought of Luz. These biblical injunctions against usury spoke directly to their experiences. The passage struck me as profoundly fitting for that moment, and, frankly, I was moved.

During one of our first interviews, Justa told me about taking emotional refuge from all of her debts and the stress they were causing her in an evangelical congregation. I perked up, adding that I was struck by how concerns about usury appear regularly in the Hebrew Bible (Old Testament) alongside a serious preoccupation with contracts and their breach. Such readings have fueled many theological-political debates in Latin American Christian base communities, among liberation and political theologians, and fueled fiery sermons against economic exploitation within Bolivia's emergent *teología indígena* (indigenous theology movement). Since the 1960s, Latin American faith communities, particularly Catholic congregations, have been on the frontlines of movements demanding economic justice and human rights, even as more conservative elements coexist with them. I wondered if, like Bolivia's Methodist and Lutheran churches, Justa's nondenominational evangelical congregation ever addressed social justice during their services. Justa nodded along, "ya, ya." But she did not pick up the thread—or seem terribly interested in discussing it further.

I now peered at Justa to see if she registered any response to the text, but she just stared forward at the liturgist. After the service, I made a weak reference to the texts and got a shrugging response. Here, at the baptism, she seemed equally uninterested in the personal or the political-economic connections to the passage, between the biblical references to collateral and her own experience of suffocating debt. Maybe it was awkward—why *would* she want to talk ceaselessly about her own money troubles, especially on such a happy occasion? Maybe it was all far from her mind. Instead, Justa seemed focused on the celebration at hand. As we exited the church, she excitedly positioned us for the congratulatory handshakes and embraces that follow every such occasion, as friends and kin douse the newly baptized, parents, and godparent in thick handfuls of confetti.

Bad Debtors versus Good Citizens

This book has connected national debates over what justice and democracy should look like in plurinational Bolivia to the experiences of people like Justa and her sister Manuela, who are rarely on the front line of massive political actions, yet nonetheless articulate socially embedded framings of responsibility and justice. Manuela traced the circulation of the sewing machine and the abuses it entailed and linked it to her mother-in-law troubles with the Micro bus. She recounted how she sat in a "corner of shame" when she could not contribute to wedding celebrations and resented feeding kin while under economic duress. She decried relatives-turned-moneylenders for mimicking the calculations of banks, echoing Nieves's supplication: "between compadres there is no interest!" Manuela gave voice to the ways families like hers created and sustained their kin through such contributions, but sometimes suffered as a consequence, particularly as they buckled under the heavy economic burdens generated by their ongoing participation in entrepreneurial modes of citizenship.

As I showed throughout the second half of the book, the ordinary acts of tallying that occur in El Alto's integrated justice centers (IJCS) lay bare the strains that political-economic forces place on intimate relations. In so doing, these daily tabulations challenge ideological distinctions between public and private and reveal Bolivians' ongoing moral projects of forging kinship and care amid those chronic burdens. These are routine emergencies that rarely grab headlines like accusations of foreign political meddling, but they are nonetheless connected to continuing efforts to make entrepreneurial and counterinsurgent citizens out of Bolivians by conflating "democracy-as-market-efficiency-and-access" (Appel 2014: 620).

This book has argued that for all the focused and concrete legal relief that alternative dispute resolution (ADR) practitioners hope to offer their clients, ADR programs must be situated within a larger assemblage of aid projects that seek to transform Bolivian democracy, and Bolivians themselves, by fostering entrepreneurship and moderated political participation in the service of democratic governance and economic development (introduction and chapter 1). In such a context, Justa embodies that much-encouraged enterprising spirit as she pursues credit. Conciliators invite Justa to find respite from her pressing economic problems outside the courts and their attendant abuses and also to demonstrate her responsibility as a citizen and a person in the ways she manages disputes that arise from her failed entrepreneurial efforts.

Participation in microfinance remains an exemplary means of embodying virtuous citizenship—and a principal way people cobble together resources (alongside moneylenders and appeals to friends) to cover life's recurring shortages. Yet in the IJCS I watched as Alteños utilized one branch of development aid (ADR) to resolve widespread tensions being produced by another (microfinance). It was only by leaving the conciliation room, tracking the sewing machine, following the interlocking webs of debt, and expanding beyond the dyads of Justa + Carmen and Justa + Pilar, that I was able to situate disputes reckoned in conciliation sessions within a much larger network of debt relations. As center staff works to compartmentalize those conflicts for pragmatic purposes, they isolate two parties in a much larger constellation of relationships. And as Bolivians adopt tools of third-party mediation to privately manage conflicts tied to indebtedness, ADR allows them to repay (some) loans according to schedule, embodying an ideal of the citizen-entrepreneur. As they do so, however, they participate in the ongoing bifurcation of delinquent debtor and good citizen.

This was not a master plan by the U.S. government or Bolivian bureaucrats when they began promoting ADR in poor neighborhoods in El Alto, even though donors saw "good governance" and judicial reform as key components of the neoliberal restructuring initiated during the 1980s and 1990s. And yet the confluence among conflict-resolution programs, debt-repayment cycles, and displaced violence reveals how ADR operates as a tool of informal economic governance, however unanticipated by its designers. That is, commercial arbitration is not the only realm where ADR operates to govern economic relations or to smooth the way for market expansion. Broader conflict-resolution programs also help shore up Alteños as good entrepreneurial citizens who take responsibility for paying off those debts and resolving their conflicts privately. This form of governance occurs precisely at moments when bureaucrats think they are offering clients protection from the vulnerabilities that staff believes are most pressing: intimate partner violence and the neglect of an unresponsive state. Yet, as I have shown, debt conflicts often serve as an acceptable proxy for conciliating violence by helping Alteños deal with unforgiving deadlines and the fallout they generate.

ADR programs thus participate in democracy's domestication by rendering conflicts—and violence—driven by such political and economic forces into manageable domestic disputes.

Domestics, All the Way Down

Throughout this book, I have invited us to approach ADR through the lens of what constitutes *the domestic* and what it means to domesticate. Domestication offers us a way to talk about activist fears over pacification and cooptation. "Domestic" speaks to claims of sovereignty and to ideas about what constitutes the national interest versus foreign agendas. "Domesticate" describes a process of "vernacularization," rendering something homegrown, or contributing to the perception that it was "made in Bolivia" and not in some office in Washington, DC, or Geneva. And "domestic" speaks to the spaces of violence, care, intimacy—and intervention. These registers further invoke ideas about the appropriate relationship between states and their citizens, whether through appeals to the nation as family, or critiques about the ways a state reaches into the lives of its citizens via informal mechanisms, encroaching on their autonomy. Thinking about democracy's domestication—and its relationship to ADR—invites us to consider all of these registers and to look at them together.

Despite the departure of the United States Agency for International Development (USAID), ADR itself continues to undergo a process of *domestication* in Bolivia. One way that happens is through its further incorporation into the country's Constitution, adopted under President Evo Morales, which cites Bolivians' "right to peace" and calls for promoting a "culture of peace" in the country (chapter 2). What does that claim mean when activists like Canela make it versus someone like the sociologist Carlos Hugo Laruta or the *conflictologo* and former miner Santiago Mujica? Indeed, under the Morales administration, ADR has become further entrenched through new legal codes and institutional arrangements. But the ways the Bolivian Ministry of Justice continues to institutionalize ADR also reveal how its expansion reflects struggles over how different Bolivian administrations understand the right relationship between the Bolivian state and its citizens.

When donors or political commentators link particular administrations (like that of Morales) with "collectivist" *sindicatos* and their "instrumental" use of conflict, they often criticize the way these associations reach into "private" spaces like the home as perverse. For example, when neighborhood associations require participation in marches, enforced by fines.[1] But by encouraging citizens to adopt particular orientations toward conflict resolution, namely shedding their "dependence" on state intervention, these same commentators and their affiliated projects also reach into the lives of families. They simply do so with a different conception of the behavior they want to encourage citizens to adopt, and why it serves the good.

In 2011, I asked the then vice minister of justice and fundamental rights, Dr. Nelson Cox Mayorga, about what was different about his work and that of the centers following the departure of USAID. Cox Mayorga pointed to the centrality of the Bolivian state in service provision under Morales: the *state* had assumed exclusive responsibility for ensuring that poor Bolivians had access to court alternatives. He contrasted this commitment strongly with USAID's approach. The recent expansion of court-annexed and prior conciliation (conciliación previa) further reflects the Morales administration's different orientation toward state institutions as a locus of social and political change. Yet when I revisited public servants who had worked with the centers for nearly a decade in 2016—some now working in these conciliación previa offices—they lamented the decline of those *extrajudicial* spaces. They further speculated about the unlikelihood that the newly expanded programs would help decongest the courts and truly satisfy people's demand for justice. Given people's profound mistrust of state agents and the abuses that persist, wasn't this a grave error? Further, lawyers had no incentive to encourage their clients to pursue alternative solutions to their problems—it threatened their income.

Annelise Riles has argued that to position ADR and the formal courts as *antithetical* to each other "is to participate in the very vocabulary that ultimately enshrines ADR as a powerful (that is: effective, efficient, modern, technical, expert, sensitive, flexible, user friendly) *alternative*" (2002: 615; see also Menkel-Meadow 2013 on process pluralism that belies such distinctions between formal and informal). But these Bolivian debates perhaps tell us less about how such institutional configurations actually work than what is at stake in the kind of boundary work their advocates and administrators perform by asserting clear distinctions between formal/informal justice, extrajudicial/court-annexed conciliation, and even state legal systems and customary-indigenous justice. Indeed, Cox Mayorga's tenure at the Ministry of Justice encompassed both the USAID era and the Morales administration, like many whose professional trajectories involved working across shifting government and donor priorities and activist demands. Perhaps a more productive question is what is *done* through appeals to this divide. One effect of asserting that division is that it allows the Morales administration to distance itself from the aid platforms of neoliberal reformers and foreign donors, and to instead assert political sovereignty—or at least to invoke it.[2]

Others use this distinction to draw attention to their aspirations for meaningful decolonization and legal pluralism. During the 2016 National Justice Summit (Cumbre de Justicia), I sat in a large conference room in Sucre and watched as representatives from the Ministry of Justice reaffirmed the role that expanded conciliation programs might play in improving people's access to justice.[3] At the same time, frustrated summit participants agitated instead for reforms to the Ley de Deslinde Jurisdiccional (Law of Jurisdictional Limits). Critics have argued that the law—which determines the competencies of the state legal system and customary law in indigenous communities—*undermines* indigenous sovereignty rather than institutionalizes it.[4] Further, they caution that both court-annexed *and* extrajudicial conciliators may supplant indigenous authorities rather than provide a complementary mechanism to access legal services outside the courts.[5] Activists drew the boundary again in order to assert indigenous sovereignty in contradistinction to the Bolivian state—even as Morales claims to indigenize it.

As of this writing, Morales has renewed his calls for a thorough audit—a *fiscalización*—of NGOs and aid programs operating in the country. Through an accounting of these organizations' finances and political commitments, Morales and his vice president, Álvaro García Linera, argue that they will expose the collusions of foreign donors and political opponents pursuing their agendas via NGO proxies in order to try to undermine his administration. Critics highlight the irony of those accusations, pointing to the ways Morales too benefited from NGO efforts in the country, including donors' support of indigenous movements and human rights campaigns over recent decades.

All this contentious talk of *political* accounting often glosses over the ordinary ways *financial* accounting operates in NGO and donor projects and how those modes of audit have shaped politics in the country. Foreign-funded NGOs must structure their interventions in highly quantifiable ways to satisfy donor agencies.[6] Things as mundane as workshop attendance lists and pamphlet distribution numbers are critical to justify continued support or to question it. Those routine accounting practices foment critiques of inflated salaries paid to foreign consultants, resources that go into overhead rather than programming, and paternalism in donor-recipient relations. But such audits also reflect the ways partisan debates in donor countries spawn reporting functions and platform priorities that affect the kind of work aid recipients may undertake.[7] The U.S. State Department's F process, for example, is reflective of U.S. acts of political accounting—as foreign aid expenditures spark congressional debates over the efficacy and strategic relevance of international development projects (chapter 1). These are *domestics embedded within other domestics.*

Of Conflictiveness and Conflictologos

For nearly a century, Bolivia's *domestic* policies have been ensnared with U.S. strategic interests and donor agendas preoccupied with ensuring a stable and predictable investment environment for foreign capital—as well as staving off more radical political projects that might threaten those interests. As historians of U.S.-Bolivian diplomatic relations have shown, during the Cold War, the United States aimed to stabilize *relatively* friendly governments against the possibility of more antagonistic/pro-communist ones through development aid.[8] In this book, I have argued that U.S. democracy-promotion interventions also have tended to emphasize stability and predictability. Yet this preoccupation was not the sole property of the U.S. mission.

A variety of donor agencies have sought to counterbalance Bolivia's—and especially El Alto's—perceived "culture of conflict" and its overburdened state legal system. ADR in many ways reflects a broader effort to quench the recurring unrest that, donors believe, is symptomatic of state failure and a threat to liberal democracy and economic vitality. Political analysts, both Bolivian and international, characterize "unruly" political tactics, including the routine use of street protest, as antithetical to the common good—alternately decrying these techniques as self-defeating, overly sectorial, or even authoritarian.

Anthropologists and historians too have pointed to Bolivia's "culture of rebellion and political turmoil" (McNeish 2008: 92). But this untamed quality of Bolivian politics does not provoke anxiety alone. Union leaders and activists frequently defend these tactics as necessary to achieve social justice in the context of enduring forms of social and political exclusion, particularly inequalities affecting the country's indigenous majority. John-Andrew McNeish has argued that another way of interpreting recurrent political conflicts in the country is a sign not of state "failure," as analysts fear, but rather of Bolivia's "high-intensity democracy," driven by "the democratic desires of its largely marginalized populations to put an end to exclusion through various forms of insurgency" (92). Or, as Raúl put it in chapter 2, Bolivia is a "shake before use" country. McNeish concludes that "in a sense Bolivia's hyper-active civil society is both a curse and a blessing, making long term political stability untenable, but ensuring that democratic commitment, fervor and innovation continue" (91).

In the previous chapters, I have contrasted this understanding of conflict as a mechanism for achieving meaningful inclusion, substantive rights, and democratic renewal with aid interventions that are concerned with conflict's destabilizing effects—including fears that it erodes faith in democracy. Projects aiming to rehabilitate confrontational dispositions idealize self-reliant citizens who turn toward the negotiation table to settle their conflicts—often while criticizing those who agitate in more belligerent ways. Culture of peace and ADR advocates insist that they are not seeking to *pacify* demands for justice—to cheaply mollify frustrated citizens. Rather, they characterize ADR and related negotiation skills as constructive techniques for building a more inclusive and just Bolivia while avoiding a feared descent into retribution and violence.

Santiago Mujica, whom we encountered in chapter 3, found himself mediating between these two understandings of conflict, drawing on his experience as a mining union *dirigente* and a professional ADR advocate, or conflictologo. Despite their entreaties to peacemaking in the service of justice, conflictologos encounter skeptical audiences who subscribe to Raúl's "shake before use" understanding of conflict—and who critically interrogate the ways specific groups of Bolivians are being asked to moderate their voices. Such *contestatorios* (chapter 2) expose competing political stakes over the "right" relations between citizens and states, as well as how opposition should be expressed. These moments of refusal move beyond simply rejecting that invitation to participate in the dialogue. Intead, activists revalorize the very skills and tactics necessary to be "contestón" and insist that those capacities are crucial for confronting persistent inequalities.

Intimate States

Sian Lazar (2012) has called for attending to the *quality* of citizenship as a means to "radicalize the concept," recognizing citizenship as a "political-ethical project" (334, 340).[9] As Lazar argues, in contrast to liberal framings of citizenship (where legal rights inhere in individual persons), "an alternative ethical project might place more emphasis upon collective solidarity and different expectations of the state, a much more relational and embedded conceptualization of the person" (336). Lazar's argument centers around large-scale movements such as the *indignados* of Greece, Italy, and Spain; all of these movements, Lazar argues, foreground the critical importance of economic justice as a key component of citizenship claims rooted in direct democracy.

But what happens in the interim, in the gaps of these large-scale political movements? Much of this book has focused on those interstices. One of the great values of anthropology is the way that it can move between scales, linking intimate experiences of violence and economic vulnerability to larger-scale political movements, revealing moral claims and daily dilemmas that may never gain the same degree of visibility as the protests snaking their way from El Alto to La Paz. By centering the experiences of women like Justa, Manuela, and others we encountered as they sought redress for their grievances, we see how center clients articulate ethical projects and hold each other to account for bruised relations. As women like Manuela narrate the grinding quality of precarious living, they often refuse to let the Bolivian state, banking institutions, and foreign donors off the hook. Instead, they articulate notions of responsibility and justice—of accountability—rooted in rebalancing asymmetries of power, including how those asymmetries crosscut intimate relations. As Manuela once told me, "Debt brings nothing but enemies." And she was talking about her kin. In this fraught social landscape, foreign donors aren't the only ones suspected of being untrustworthy. The process of staking those claims on friends, neighbors, and kin, however, can often be quite painful.

Alteños, for their part, regularly turn toward the "authenticating procedures" of the state to resolve recurring problems; they rely on legal mimicry to endure amid ever-deepening interpersonal crises. Elizabeth Povinelli calls this the "jerry-rigged" quality of social worlds on the edges of survival (2011: 144). Many conciliation accords reflect this "jerry-rigged" effort to lash together some mechanism for holding intimate partners and kin to account—instilling a sense of obligation now backed by the law (or something that looks like it). As I argued in chapter 6, the materiality of paper invokes an ideal, abstract state capable of ensuring compliance, or what Thomas Blom Hansen (2001) has called the "sublime" state. In the face of dubious judicial prospects, clients deploy law-like documents to add some coercive heft to widespread oral arrangements, interpellating friends, neighbors, and kin through law-like documents as those social relations buckle under the weight of prolonged economic vulnerability. As they do, they invoke an imagined state-citizen relationship that they do not generally experience in their day-to-day lives, although the long-term consequences of those maneuvers are ambiguous.

It remains to be seen whether these forms of endurance—the maneuvers people employ to "make do" in the meantime—ultimately eclipse more collective forms of political engagement, as ADR's earliest critics warned. Alternatively, it may allow people to survive until such a time that they can rally once more to demand the substantive redress of their shared problems. To paraphrase Timothy Mitchell (2011), ADR programs raise questions about whether issues like debt, violence, and domestic economies are regarded as matters of public concern—or ones to be managed through alternative mechanisms.

These questions do not only confront Bolivians. I opened this book by reflecting on the ways ADR concepts have ingrained themselves into many aspects of our lives, whether we live in La Paz, Bolivia, or Lima, Ohio. Globally, ADR has become a pervasive framework for talking about how best to resolve interpersonal tensions and manage political disagreements—be they territorial disputes, divorce proceedings, or contract negotiations. Bolivia's skeptical audiences, however, invite us to reconsider what these appealing concepts and methods can sometimes obscure, namely, the ways they frame the relationships between states and citizens, and render shared struggles for economic justice into quietly managed solutions.

But ADR further exemplifies ongoing struggles over the constraints some would place on how people express opposition. Street protest, burning blockades, third-party mediation, *conversatorios*, court cases, and rural *cabildos* (indigenous community councils where major decisions are taken), are battlegrounds as Bolivians grapple with how to meaningfully enact social justice—as well as to articulate competing claims over both *how* and *where* people should demand it. ADR and affiliated culture of peace campaigns reflect ongoing debates over what expressive forms constitute acceptable ways to demand justice and convey dissent—and who gets to decide those parameters—with implications for El Alto, as well as for Ferguson, Missouri, and Washington, DC.

AFTER ABEL'S BAPTISM and requisite dousing in confetti, our crew of siblings and cousins, aunties and grandmothers, and now compadres, piled into Rubén's Micro bus and went bumping across El Alto to the compound shared by Justa and her parents and other kin. We chowed down on neon-orange cheese puffs and Sprite, and heaping piles of spicy pork served with flaky, white, freeze-dried *tunta* potatoes. Justa's brother Daniel and I discussed the recent judicial elections that had sparked heated political debates for months on end. In the national press, political analysts argued over whether Morales was manipulating or decolonizing the justice sector. Critics accused Evo of stacking the courts with judges favorable to his own political agenda (namely his expressed desire to run for a third term) and of persecuting his political enemies through the law. Daniel rejected these criticisms. "Look," he told me, "in the past all of these political elites made fortunes off of their positions in leadership. The only thing Evo is doing is finally cracking down on all that corruption. Sure, they may be his enemies, but MAS has also gone after its own people. They are really just cracking down, against opposition and *MASistas* alike. It's about time." Our political conversation faded into the background, as Abel opened his presents and his uncles and aunts offered words of advice.

Justa's father, the one who had nearly thrown out his middle-aged daughter because of the shame her debts brought to the family (chapter 5), sat laughing with us. He told stories about the decades he spent working for a rail company before it went out of business. The walls of the small living room were covered in pennants from company soccer matches sponsored by the transportation union (sindicato) that he later joined, and he laced his stories with his own take on the national economy.

Justa's mother howled in exasperation as she recounted how her adult children had surprised the couple on their fiftieth wedding anniversary, arranging a special Mass in their honor and a professional photographer to take a commemorative portrait, which now hung on the wall. "I wasn't even dressed up! I was a disaster! Nobody even gave me a chance to pull myself together," she reproached her children, who chuckled at her consternation. Manuela and her husband showed up carrying a brand-new desk for Abel— and firm words about the importance of being studious.

In other words, life carried on.

I never got to ask Justa about those scriptural passages or what she thought of them—I was leaving for the United States the following week. When I returned a few years later, our conversations had moved on. Instead, Justa got busy celebrating our newly forged kinship. She was still dealing with debts and would quietly vocalize her desire to get more credit, to try to make another go of the failed pollera business. Justa was stitching new kinship bonds— this time with me—expanding a social world that was frayed and torn by mounting debts and soured trust.

There was no promise that the same might not happen to us.

But Justa stitched me into the story of the sewing machine, alongside a group of women whose ties were forged through informal loans and microfinance quotas, cases of beer bought for wedding celebrations and the business transaction between a mother-in-law and her son, crisply wrapped baptismal gifts and freshly anointed godparents plastered in confetti. These were also *proyectos de vida,* life projects and forms of sociality that are at once intimate and political. These intimate moments are entwined with foreign aid and judicial reform, spectacular protests and the quasi-events of impassioned conciliation sessions—where tangled webs of kin and the struggles they endure are always, already, inflected by national political projects and international aid platforms.

Introduction

1. Luz and Jhonny had only one child, who died as a baby. Jhonny is implying that Luz lied in order to humiliate him at his workplace.

2. Interns regularly suggest that clients take neighborhood police along to deliver invitations to conciliation to intimidate the other party, to convince them that conciliation was serious business and not to be mocked (see chapter 6). On several occasions, center clients asked whether I could accompany them to deliver invitations and explain the process to the other party. I informed the center director, who told me I was welcome to do so as long as I felt comfortable. I only did so once, with Luz.

3. Bolivians use the term "doctor/a" to address lawyers. Even when I explained I was not myself a lawyer, that I was an anthropologist, they often reverted to the term to show deference (to acknowledge my "professional" status), as they did with other interns and staff.

4. Erbe 2006.

5. Fisher, Ury, and Patton (2011) coined the BATNA concept in their book, *Getting to Yes: Negotiating Agreement without Giving In* (originally published in 1981), and developed it through their work with the Harvard Program on Negotiation (PON).

6. Bercovitch et al. 2008; Deutsch et al. 2011; Finnegan and Hackley 2008; Menkel-Meadow 2013, 2015; Sharp 2002; Wanis-St. John and Rosen 2017, to name just a few.

7. As Muhlberger (2011) has shown, there are a number of affinities (and rivalries) between theories of ADR and deliberative democracy. However, the distinctive philosophical genealogies of these fields were not neatly drawn in practice, as donor representatives and NGO staff spoke broadly about promoting methods that would enable cooperation toward "mutually acceptable" solutions to disputes and facilitate conflict transformation—and indeed social transformation—in the country. See, for example, Fundación UNIR (2005).

8. Under the Morales administration, the Ministry of Justice has expanded conciliation services and commercial arbitration under new legal codes.

9. See the recently published "BoliviaLeaks: La injerencia política de Estados Unidos contra el proceso de cambio (2006–2010)." Juan Ramón Quintana Taborga

coordinated the publication, which was published by the Bolivian Ministerio de la Presidencia in 2016.

10. Since James Ferguson's *Anti-Politics Machine* (1990), it has become common sense in anthropology to speak of development projects as "depoliticizing," and indeed I examine processes of depoliticization here. And yet donor platforms—especially funding tied to the United States—have become a hot-button political issue. Understanding how and with what effects requires distinguishing between the hyper-politicization of aid programs at the level of national political debates, local struggles over *obras* (public works), and the micropolitical dimensions of NGO work from the ways that these programs strip the issues facing residents of El Alto of their political-economic content, reframing them as either issues requiring technical intervention or as interpersonal problems in need of private resolution.

11. Nader and Metzger 1963; Collier 1979; Greenhouse 1985.

12. Nader 2005.

13. Comaroff and Roberts 1981; Nader and Metzger 1963. For a critical appraisal of ADR export to African countries, see Nader and Grande 2002, and Milner 2002 for a rejoinder.

14. Abel 1982; Harrington and Merry 1988; Merry and Milner 1995.

15. Dezalay and Garth 1996.

16. Calla et al. 2005; Huanca Quispe 2015; Goldstein 2012, 2016; Risør 2010; Wanderley 2009.

17. "El peor trámite de mi vida" was jointly sponsored by the Bolivian Ministry of Institutional Transparency and Fight against Corruption, and the Inter-American Development Bank.

18. On legal pluralism: Merry 1988; in Bolivia, Rivera Cusicanqui 1990 and Stephenson 2002.

19. The Katarista movement was named after the eighteenth-century indigenous rebellion leader Túpac Katari.

20. Kohl 2003; Medeiros 2001.

21. Postero 2007; Van Cott 2000.

22. Customary law is codified in the Bolivian constitution as Jurisdicción Indígena Originaria Campesina. *Campesino/a* is a complex category in Bolivia, as indigenous Bolivians were reframed as peasants during the 1950s. The term often glosses rural, small-scale agriculture and indexes rural unionization schemes associated with Bolivia's 1952 agrarian reform.

23. Albro 2010; Rivera Cusicanqui 2012.

24. Examples of Western-style ADR practices are commercial arbitration, extrajudicial mediation, and court-annexed conciliation.

25. Santos 1995.

26. Wall et al. 2001; Bercovitch et al. 1991; Bush et al. 1994.

27. Some of these earlier debates can be found in Abel 1982. See Hensler 2003 and Harrington and Merry 1988 for overviews.

28. Nader 1990, 2005. See also Pavlich 1996; Cobb and Rifkin 1991; Hofrichter 1982; Silbey 1993.

29. See Sternlight 2006 for a summary of the ways ADR has been characterized as either antithetical to "the rule of law" (in the U.S. context) or supportive of it (i.e., when exported abroad by USAID and the American Bar Association).

30. Quoted in Paley 2002: 476.

31. In Bolivia, see Albó 2008; Albro 2010; Ellison 2015; Gill 1997; Goodale 2008; Aguilar 2014; Lazar 2008; Postero 2007; Medeiros 2001; Rivera Cusicanqui 1990.

32. Brown 2006; Coles 2004; Paley 2009; Sampson 2002.

33. Gills 2000; Cox et al. 2000; Carothers 2007.

34. Carothers 2007.

35. Hoben 1989; Carothers 1999.

36. Finkel et al. 2006. See also work on the causal relationship—or lack thereof— between democracy and economic development: Ikenberry 2000; Lipset 1959; Oxhorn and Starr 1999.

37. Quintana Taborga 2016. See also Zunes 2001, which argued that the U.S. strategy of substituting development aid for military operations in Bolivia immediately following its 1952 revolution was not an "enlightened" policy alternative to military intervention (as was enacted elsewhere in the Americas), but rather represented "interventionism by other means" (34), seeking to moderate or "tame" the 1952 revolution.

38. Ellison 2015; Pacino 2016.

39. Gill 1997; Rodríguez Carmona 2009.

40. Cruikshank 1999.

41. Conflicts over a Brazil-backed road project through lowland indigenous territory (TIPNIS) makes this clear.

42. "Translated": Merry 2006. "Vernacularized": Goodale 2008; Postero 2007. "Hybridized": Shakow 2011. "Refracted": Ellison 2015.

43. Coles 2007; Brown 2006.

44. See also Schuller 2012 for an extended look at the relationship between U.S. aid to Haiti and power struggles between Republicans and Democrats.

45. Feminist scholars and activists have critiqued categorical public/private divides in liberal conceptualizations of politics and citizenship. See McKinnon and Cannell 2013 for an overview of anthropology's engagement with these issues. See also Cattelino 2008 on the home economics movement and the politics of Seminole chickees (houses), and Stoler 1995 on the sexual politics and regulations of intimacy in empire.

46. See Auyero's (2012) "tempography" of political domination, or, "the ways in which waiting, behavior, and submission are connected" in Argentina (5).

47. See "differentiated citizenship" (Holston 2009); "sexual citizenship" (Castle 2008), "proxy citizenship" (Tate 2015), and "cultural citizenship" (Rosaldo 1994; Albro 2010), among many others.

48. Lazar and Nuijeten 2013: 4. Among Bolivianists, see Albro 2010; Canessa 2014; Ellison 2015; Aguilar 2014; Lazar 2004b, 2008; Postero 2007; Shakow 2014.

49. Of course, effort to produce "new citizens" is not peculiar to American- or European-backed democracy-assistance programming. See Dunn 2004; Sharma 2008.

50. Peck and Tickell 2002.

51. Elyachar 2005; Goodale and Postero 2013; Greenhouse 2009; Ong 2006; Schild 2000.

52. Following Mader 2016, I use the encompassing term "microfinance" instead of "microcredit," although my focus here is on microlending projects and not other kinds of services (i.e., insurance or savings).

53. In recent decades, a wide array of organizations has relied on the language of "empowerment" to characterize their efforts. See Sharma 2008.

54. Lazar 2004.

55. See Kar 2013; Karim 2011; Lazar 2004a.

56. See Duvendack et al. 2011; Karim 2011.

57. Biehl and Eskerod 2007; Dunn 2004; Rose 2006; Shore 2010; Shore and Wright 1999; Vannier 2010.

58. Rivera Cusicanqui 2012.

59. See Fabricant 2009; Guss 2006; Gustafson 2006, on the relationship between race, space, and struggles over political belonging in Bolivia, including the transgressive use of dance parades to puncture white space, and the use of physical violence to shore it up.

60. See Ellison 2015 on *multas*, or fines.

61. Dunn 2004; Shore 2010; Vannier 2010.

62. See Wedel 2005 on "studying through," or "tracking policy discourses, prescriptions and programs and then linking them to those affected by the policies" (37).

63. In addition to three months of exploratory research, as well as return trips during the summers of 2014, 2016, and 2017 to follow up with people who appear in this book.

64. The centers have since been renamed *centros de servicios integrados de justicia plurinacional* (centers for integrated plurinational justice). However, I retain their original name from my fieldwork period throughout.

65. "Translators": Merry 2006; see also Brown 2006. For "brokers," see Lewis and Mosse 2006.

66. On several occasions, at the behest of the organizations where I was researching, I wrote internal reports about my observations. Those documents focused on more immediate issues facing the people who worked in these different institutional spaces. They were distinct genres of writing, written internally for audiences with different purposes and needs. I do not reproduce any of that material here.

67. See Appel 2014.

68. Appel 2014.

Uprising

1. Kohl and Farthing 2006; Lazar 2008.

2. Including along the single major highway in and out of La Paz, and in the bustling *ceja* (brow), a commercial district in El Alto that derives its name—like the brow of a hill or cliff—from its location along the edges of the steep descent into La Paz. Until very recently, La Paz was accessible only by sharp switchback roads decending from El Alto. The installation of a new cable car system is reconfiguring transporta-

tion between the two cities—and challenging the efficacy of blockades aiming to stymie urban movement.

3. Ellison 2015.

4. Our network decided *against* applying (as a network) for any funding associated with USAID or related agencies.

5. See for example key studies that link spectacle to politics and protest in Bolivia by Bjork-James 2013; Fabricant 2009; Goldstein 2004; Guss 2006; Gustafson 2006.

6. Rivera Cusicanqui 1984; Ticona Alejo 2000; Ticona Alejo, Rojas, and Albó 1995. See Himpele 2008 on indigenous representations at different historical junctures.

Chapter 1. Fix the State or Fix the People?

1. Calla et al. 2005; Goldstein 2012, 2016; Risør 2010.

2. Eade 2007; Ellison 2017a; Kenny and Clarke 2010; West 2016.

3. See Kohl 2003 and Mader 2016 for similar conclusions regarding state restructuring and neoliberalism.

4. Critical anthropological approaches to policy offer valuable insights into these dynamics. See Greenhalgh 2008: 11; Lewis and Mosse 2005; Li 2005; Wedel et. al. 2005. On the concept of "assemblage" see Latour 1999, 2007; Ong and Collier 2004.

5. Warren and Leheny 2010; Paley 2009; Li 2005.

6. Warren 2010.

7. Siekmeier 2011; Young 2013.

8. Healy 2001: 22; Geidel 2010.

9. Field 2014; Siekmeier 2011; Healy 2001.

10. See also Pacino 2016 on "*servicio* diplomacy"; Young 2013; Zunes 2001.

11. Siekmeier 2011: 10; Rabe 2012.

12. Field 2014; Siekmeier 2011; Young 2013.

13. Kohl 2002.

14. Kohl and Farthing 2006.

15. Kohl and Farthing 2006: 71.

16. The "consensus" continued a pattern that had begun with Bolivia's 1956 stabilization plan devised by George Jackson Eder on behalf of the U.S. government, as the historian Kevin Young shows. Young's analysis offers an in-depth discussion of the plan and the insights it offers into the relationship between individual policymakers and the broader "structural and institutional context in which those policymakers operate," arguing that, "personal morality tends to play only a very minor role in policy making" processes (Young 2013: 533). See also Kohl 2002.

17. Gustafson 2006; Medeiros 2001.

18. Rowat, Malik, and Dakolias 1995; Domingo and Sieder 2001.

19. Dezalay and Garth 2002.

20. Trubek 2001 offers a succinct overview of the Law and Development Movement and its resurgence in the 1990s. See also Dezalay and Garth 2002; McAuslan 1997; Salas 2001: 18.

21. Domingo and Sieder 2001; McAuslan 1997; Salas 2001; Wanis-St. John 2000.

22. Burki 1995; Dezalay and Garth 2002; Garth 1995; Malik 1995; Shihata 1995; Trubek 2001; Weder 1995.

23. Carothers 2001.

24. See also Domingo and Sieder 2001; Humphreys 2010; Malik 1995; Oxhorn and Starr 1999; Salas 2001; Wanis-St. John 2000.

25. Ministerio de Asuntos Exteriores 2002: 3.

26. Ministerio de Asuntos Exteriores 2002: 3. Emphasis and translation mine.

27. Brown, Cervenak, and Fairman 1997; Wanis-St. John 2000.

28. USAID, Bolivia Administration of Justice Program (BAOJ), phase III, final report, August 2001 to December 2003; USAID, Bolivia Strategic Objective Close-Out Report So 551-001, http://pdf.usaid.gov/pdf_docs/pdacd699.pdf, accessed July 17, 2017.

29. The distinction between "adversarial" and "inquisitorial" refers to different methods in presenting evidence. In an adversarial model, legal representatives present evidence while the court referees the process. Inquisitorial courts are actively involved in gathering and presenting evidence. USAID, Bolivia Strategic Objective Close-Out Report So 551-001.

30. USAID, Bolivia Strategic Objective Close-Out Report So 551-01.

31. Wanis-St. John 2000; USAID, Bolivia Strategic Objective Close-Out Report So 551-001.

32. Brown, Cervenak, and Fairman 1997.

33. Ministerio de Asuntos Exteriores 2002; "Evaluación del Proyecto de Reforma Judicial en la República de Bolivia," Oficina de Planificación y Evaluación, SEINTEX (2002), www.oecd.org/countries/bolivia/46777655.pdf, accessed July 17, 2017.

34. Ministerio de Asuntos Exteriores 2002: 23.

35. Domingo and Sieder 2001.

36. USAID, Bolivia Strategic Objective Close-Out Report, So 511-001, "Increased Citizen Support for the Bolivian Democratic System," FY 1998–2003, http://pdf.usaid.gov/pdf_docs/pdacd699.pdf.

37. Staff names are pseudonyms.

38. These analyses seem to mirror the strain and relative deprivation theories of social mobilization that were popular in the 1950s and 1970s, though they have since been widely critiqued. For an overview, see Buechler 2013.

39. USAID, Bolivia Strategic Objective Close-Out Report So 551-001.

40. See Lazar 2008 on the importance of securing *obras* to neighborhood *dirigentes* (association leaders).

41. Gustafson 2006.

42. Fabricant 2009.

43. He was elected to the Supreme Court on March 19, 1999. He served until he became interim president of the republic on June 9, 2005.

44. "USAID Supports Alternative Dispute Resolution in Latin America and the Caribbean," http://pdf.usaid.gov/pdf_docs/Pdaca631.pdf, emphasis mine.

45. O'Donnell 1993.

46. Emphasis mine. Quotes derived from a 2005 Bolivia "Fact Sheet," U.S. Agency for International Development, Washington, DC, July 13, 2005, https://2001-2009.state .gov/p/inl/rls/fs/49024.htm.

47. USAID, Bolivia Strategic Objective Close-Out Report So 551-001.

48. Brown, Cervenak, and Fairman 1997; Shook and Milner 1993.

49. See Merry 1990 on parallel accusations of American "litigiousness" motivating ADR. See also Trubek 2001 on parallels in the transformative aims of the Law and Development Movement as those objectives were resurrected during the 1990s.

50. See Carr 2011 on parallels in U.S. addiction treatment.

51. W. Brown 2005; Cruikshank 1999; Lazar 2004a; Rose 2006.

52. Gill 1997; Hale 2002; Muehlebach 2011; Paley 2001.

Chapter 2. Cultures of Peace, Cultures of Conflict

1. JUNTOS is a pseudonym. Because the NGOs described here are well known in Bolivia, they are likely recognizable to a Bolivian audience, and the events described were public. Nevertheless, I have provided pseudonyms to obscure their appearance on search engines.

2. Names changed throughout, except for public intellectuals like Paredes and Laruta, speaking at public events.

3. For critical appraisals, see Indaburu 2004; for a take on U.S. media representations of Bolivian politics, particularly under Morales, see Gustafson 2008; and, for anthropological research on disruptive political tactics, see Bjork-James 2013; Ellison 2015; Gustafson 2006; McNeish 2008. Wanderley 2009 contrasts everyday strategies of submission, supplication, and corruption (i.e., via *coima* payments) in the face of bureaucratic abuses to those of contestation expressed through mass mobilizations.

4. On patronage and politics in Bolivia, see Lazar 2008, 2004b; Shakow 2014.

5. By contrast, Wanis-St. John and Rosen call for the rapprochement of direct action and negotiation communities in order to develop more effective strategies for justice and social transformation (see also Finnegan and Hackley 2008). And, indeed, many Bolivian proponents of both disruptive political tactics and negotiation are engaged in their own strategizing toward those ends (see Santiago Mujica's story in chapter 3).

6. The "local" category is internal to Bolivian NGOs and public debates.

7. See the emerging literature on refusal, i.e., McGranahan 2016 and Simpson 2014.

8. Coulthard 2014; Hale 2002, 2005; Postero 2007; Povinelli 2002.

9. See also Kay Warren 1998 on Pan-Maya movements in Guatemala, the "fallacies of Indianness," political essentialism, and the ways Maya intellectuals confront their critics.

10. Though frequently translated as "Mother Earth," Pachamama is characterized by Penelope Harvey (1991) as "general force or power rather than a personified deity" (5). Pachamama "is associated with the fertility of the soil and the fecundity of animals and yet is also seen as the cause of illness, sterility, and even death" (5).

11. Fabricant 2013; McNeish 2013; Postero 2017.

12. See Merry 2003 on the "demonization of culture" in human rights debates; cf. Hickel 2015 on the "cultural logic of the anti-democracy stance" in postapartheid

South Africa. In Bolivia, see Barragán 2006 on representations of class and ethnicity in La Paz; Postero 2017 on representations and appeals to indigeneity as a form of statecraft under the Morales administration.

13. W. Brown 2008; Englund 2006; Hickel 2015.

14. Arbona and Kohl 2004: 256; Arbona 2008; Canessa 2004; Postero 2007.

15. De Acosta and Mangan 2002; Orta 2013; Pagden 1986; Rivera Cusicanqui 1990; VanValkenburgh 2017.

16. Healy 2001.

17. See also Canessa 2004.

18. Arbona 2008.

19. Field 2014.

20. Kohl 2003: 161.

21. Kohl 2003; Lazar 2008, 2004b; Medeiros 2001; Postero 2007; Shakow 2014.

22. Ellison 2015.

23. Hickel 2015; Lazar 2008; Ellison 2015.

24. See Canessa 2004 on notions of civilization and the reproduction of hegemonic assimilationist and racist discourses in rural communities.

25. Goldstein 2004, 2005; Risør 2010.

26. Farmer 2004; Gupta 2012.

27. See Lederach's influential work in the field, including his efforts to tease apart the relationship between "culture" and conflict (1996).

28. Feminist peace studies scholars have critiqued Galtung for failing to incorporate gender more carefully into his theories of violence. See, for example, Confortini 2006.

29. This particular definition is featured prominently on the UNESCO website and can be found in the 2013 document "Culture of Peace and Non-Violence: A Vision in Action," http://unesdoc.unesco.org/images/0021/002177/217786e.pdf.

30. Ayllus are, in Andrew Orta's words, a "remarkably elastic" social unit prevalent in the Andes, whose size shifts according to context. As Orta writes, "In some areas, ayllu might be roughly translated as 'close family,' in others it refers to social units comparable to 'communities' or larger, more dispersed groups comprising thousands of individuals" (2004: 31). Ayllus in peace was part of El Programa de Apoyo a la Gestión Pública Descentralizada y Lucha contra la Pobreza (PADEP).

31. K. Brown 2006, 2009; Ferguson and Gupta 2002; Paley 2009.

32. We might compare these approaches to the mechanisms of participatory budgeting (PB) enabled by the LPP and advanced globally by advocates ranging from the World Social Forum to the World Bank. PB emphasizes the allocation of economic resources according to deliberation in community councils, and has proven itself to be easily adaptable to a variety of political projects. ADR and appeals to constructing a culture of peace, however, emphasize the component skill sets that *comprise* that negotiation process. On PB, see Baiocchi 2005; Baiocchi and Ganuza 2014; Hetland 2014. On deliberative democracy: Habermas 1984, 1996.

33. Media Luna translates as "half-moon"; the media luna refers to the eastern lowland region of the country but often stands in euphemistically for European-descendant and landed elites as well as opposition to the Morales administration.

34. The videos were directed by the noted Bolivian filmmaker Marcos Loayza.

35. The 2004 treaty signed between the United States and Bolivia granted immunity to U.S. citizens and military personnel from prosecution in the International Criminal Court.

36. Li 2007: 22. Thinking with Foucault, Li reminds us that "powers that are multiple cannot be totalizing and seamless" (25).

37. Kohl 2003.

38. For additional critiques of recognition politics, see Coulthard 2014; Hale 2002, 2005; Postero 2007; Povinelli 2002, 2011; Rivera Cusicanqui 1990; Simpson 2014.

39. Colectivo Akhulli, a pseudonym, refers to the ceremonial act of sharing coca.

40. A chuño is a blackened freeze-dried potato consumed in the Andes. Here it symbolically stands for highland Indians versus the lowland Cambas, symbolized by citrus fruits and yucca.

41. *Cambas* is a term used for lowland Bolivians in the Santa Cruz region. It is generally used to suggest whiteness and upper-middle-class status.

42. Povinelli 2011: 31, emphasis mine.

43. McGranahan 2016; Simpson 2014, 2016.

Chapter 3. A Market for Mediators

1. One such recent issue was the cross-country march of Bolivians from the lowland indigenous territory known as TIPNIS, which was at that moment demanding the right to the *consulta previa* (prior consultation) on a massive road project.

2. On NGOization in Bolivia, see Gill 1997; Rodríguez Carmona 2009. Anthropologists have analyzed such intermediaries as development "brokers" (Lewis and Mosse 2006), "transactors" (K. Brown 2006), and "translators" (Merry 2006), seeking to understand their positioning in facilitating the dissemination of aid money, rights discourses, and development paradigms, as well as the effects of their intermediation. See Eyben 2011; Lewis 2011; Vannier 2010.

3. Or what Arvidson 2008 calls "professional altruists."

4. See Mattei and Nader 2008: 31.

5. Rather than seeing ADR's proliferation as the simple transfer of best practices or model policies, or as the blanket imposition of a donor agenda, it can be more useful to trace the ways particular institutions and people help to circulate incomplete, inchoate, and hybrid ideas as they bring particular aid platforms to places like El Alto (Peck and Theodore 2010: 169). See Greenhalgh 2008: 16; Dezalay and Garth 1996; Sampson 2005; K. Brown 2006; Gagnon 2006; Merritt 2006; Warren and Leheny 2010. See also Mattei and Nader 2008: 19; ; Dezalay and Garth 2002; Hornberger 2004.

6. Latour 2007; Li 2007; Mosse 2005; Riles 2002.

7. See the edited volume by Bernal and Grewal 2014 for an account both of the early critiques of the "NGOization" of feminist movements and the authors' subsequent analyses of the ways those criticisms may miss crucial insights (in particular, see Hodžić 2014).

8. Arvidson 2008.

9. See also Glen Coulthard's (2014) critique of arguments against direct action as regressive or disruptive.

10. See Mosse 2005 on the ways "participation" proves ambiguous enough to encompass many different positions.

11. While Roseberry was particularly interested in the ways hegemony operates with regard to the state, his insights are also useful for considering the ways it operates through a transnational network of foreign donors, international NGOs, and multilateral organizations.

12. Roseberry 1994: 361, emphasis mine. Gramsci (1971) never presented hegemony as necessarily the proprietary achievement of any one social class. Rather, it is broadly a practice of exercising power and establishing a particular order through *both* consent building and force by taking into account the interests—including economic interests—"of the groups over which hegemony is to be exercised" (161).

13. Conciliation associated with the formal justice system may include judges acting as arbiters or may be required before a court case can proceed (*conciliacion previa*).

14. In the intervening years since I conducted these interviews, the Morales administration has been subject to its own accusations of diverted funding and clientalistic practices, and both women might adjust their assessments. See, for example, accusations about the mishandling and expropriation of the Fondo Indígena (Fondioc) by government functionaries.

15. Lazar 2008; Shakow 2014.

16. Rodríguez Carmona 2009.

17. She bitterly shared a rumor she had heard about a program director for one of USAID's democracy-assistance programs working with the Ministry of Justice under Morales, and she pondered how he had managed to worm his way back into the government's good graces, despite his previous close work with USAID.

18. Merry 1990 analyzes similar arguments about American litigiousness.

19. Davis, Kingsbury, and Merry 2012; Ferguson 1990; Ferguson and Gupta 2002; Li 2011; Merry 2016; Mitchell 2002.

20. See, for example, USAID's Access to Justice program in Colombia, contract No. DFD-I-00-04-00175-00. USAID reported a similar reliance on volunteer labor in its projects in Sri Lanka, Chile, and Ukraine. All are cited in USAID's "Alternative Dispute Resolution Practitioner's Guide," www.usaid.gov/sites/default/files/documents/1868/200sbe.pdf. On ADR and volunteerism, see Merry and Milner 1993; Harrington 1995. For more on the powerful idiom of *vecinos* in El Alto, see Risør 2010 and Lazar 2008.

21. See Li 2011 on how World Bank "community-driven development" projects enroll people in expert designs through participatory mechanisms.

22. The Ceja is a major commercial intersection in El Alto known for crime.

23. Dunkerley 1984; Field 2014; Siekmeier 2011.

24. To situate Santiago's critiques in a larger debate between negotiation and direct action advocates, see Finnegan and Hackley 2008 on how both theorize power in their approaches. Wanis-St. John and Rosen provide a brief and accessible overview of the role of leverage in theories of negotiation (2017: 10 11). See also Fisher, Ury, and Pat-

ton on their concept of BATNA and its relationship to leverage in situations of power inequality between parties in conflict (2011 [1981]: 106).

25. See similar arguments by Finnegan and Hackley 2008; Wanis-St. John and Rosen 2017.

26. K. Brown 2006; Coles 2007; Lewis and Mosse 2006; Merry 2006.

27. See Gill 1997 on "neoliberal" NGOs in El Alto.

28. Lewis and Mosse 2006; Merry 2006.

29. Li 2007: 26. See also Tsing 2011.

A Brief Recess

1. Tassi 2016.

2. The International Labour Organization (Department of Statistics, 2012) estimates that 75 percent of Bolivians labor informally (http://laborsta.ilo.org/applv8/data /INFORMAL_ECONOMY/2012-06-Statistical%20 update%20-%20v2.pdf, accessed June 1, 2017). See Goldstein 2016; Tassi 2016. See also Millar 2018 on moving beyond the informal/formal divide.

3. See Rubinson 2016 for a summary of debates over mediation styles (in the lexicon of U.S. mediation debates, whether they should be engaged in "evaluative," "facilitative," or "transformative" mediation), and a critique of their guiding assumptions.

4. Practitioners I interviewed in Bolivia further debated the ideal type of both mediator training (i.e., the merits of legally trained or nonlegal mediators, such as social workers, educators, or people trained in the field of "social communication"). In the Bolivian context, the specificity of these ongoing scholar-practitioner debates was often quite distant from the daily work of conciliators who operated with their own theories of conciliation, often reflecting which institutions had been responsible for their initial training. USAID's design team included international legal scholars shaped by conciliation models out of Argentina and the American community mediation movement; those trained by a national NGO specialized in conflict resolution and collaborating with American law schools and European donors; and the Ministry of Justice turned toward court-annexed models of conciliation and *conciliación previa,* where plaintiffs are redirected to conciliation when they file a legal complaint.

5. See Coutin 2000; Merry 1990.

6. Legal professionals are referred to as "doctor/a."

7. See Nader 1990 on different patterns of authority and conflict resolution in the Zapotec village where she worked.

8. Santos 2014.

9. See also Tockman and Cameron 2014.

10. Azucena argued that such "observations" were in fact pretexts; judges would encourage their staff to "observe" legal briefs in order to get cases off their desks, effectively utilizing administrative errors as a mechanism for relieving themselves of an excessive workload, whether that excess was perceived by lazy judges, as Azucena cast the pattern, or a reflection of overburdened courts. In the process, such observations further slowed and soured people's experiences with the courts. Compare this with

the ways court-annexed mediation has been analyzed as a means of "docket control" (Rubinson 2016).

11. Santos's initial framing of interlegality relied on spatial metaphors—maps—to examine this pluralistic dynamic. Mariana Valverde has pushed Santos's original insights to introduce the concept of chronotopes, integrating spatial and temporal dimensions of interlegality to capture the "various, always embodied, never rational-istic, 'styles of law' that coexist not only in the same territory but even in the same institution or even the same person" (2016: 180). In so doing, Valverde reclaims Santos's attention to "the (non-spatial) narrative, symbolic, and affective dimensions of different legal mechanisms or legal styles" (2015: 51). Much like the approach to donor "assemblages" I discussed in chapter 1, Valverde and others have suggested we think about legal "assemblages" as "internally pluralistic, with legal actors finding it easy to import and export particular rules, norms, styles of adjudication, or narrative modes, in a constant, moving target process of 'interlegality'" (51).

12. Abercrombie 1998: 87; Goldstein 2012: 144; Van Vleet 2008.

13. Coutin 2000; Merry 1988.

Chapter 4. Between Compadres There Is No Interest

1. Merry 1988; Goldstein 2012 on "legal bricolage" (172).

2. While the practitioner literature describes a plurality of approaches (Fritz 2014), in El Alto I observed conciliators consistently pushing to narrow the scope of who constituted "parties to the conflict." I anticipate that the expansion of court-annexed conciliation will further winnow participation, as the flexibility of extrajudicial spaces is limited by pressure to produce results (cf. Rubinson 2016).

3. Albro 2000; Guaygua 2009; Leinaweaver 2008; Lazar 2004a; Van Vleet 2008.

4. Colloredo-Mansfeld 1999; Leinaweaver 2009.

5. Arnold 2014; Spedding 2014.

6. Albro 2000; Canessa 2012; Colloredo-Mansfeld 1999; Leinaweaver 2008; Paulson 2006; Van Vleet 2008.

7. Carsten 2013; McKinnon and Cannell 2013.

8. Allen 2002; P. Harvey 2014; Saignes 1989; Spedding 2014.

9. Allen 2002; Spedding 2014; Van Vleet 2008.

10. See Riskin's (1996) influential, original "grid" of mediator approaches/styles; see also Waldman 1998 for a discussion of the ongoing practitioner debates over "evalua-tive" versus "facilitative" ideal mediator roles, and Rubinson 2016 on the "disconnect" between mediation's scholarly ideal types and practical realities.

11. See also Spedding 2014; Lazar 2004a.

12. Hickel 2015; Lazar 2004b.

13. Sahlins 2011; Hess 2006.

14. Hess 2006; K. Smith 2012.

15. See the parallels in Rosen's (1984) work on Moroccan personhood and its connections to the Moroccan legal system (1989). Ferguson 2013 has also examined

notions of dependence and social personhood as they intersect with colonialism and capitalism in South Africa.

16. See Harrington and Merry 1988 for an analysis of community mediation ideologies. For example, Bush et al. advocate a transformative approach to mediation cast in terms of "empowerment and recognition" (1994: 23).

17. For underlying expectations, see Rubinson 2016.

18. See K. Smith 2012 for a review.

19. K. Smith 2012.

20. Cf. Merry 1990 on efforts to disqualify and redirect cases toward therapeutic rather than legal solutions.

21. In some ways Costa's theories of personhood and those of his colleagues reflected recurring scholarly debates about what it means to be a person in the West versus the *rest* of the world, in this case, Andean Bolivia. See Carsten 2004; Trouillot 2003.

22. LiPuma 1998: 75; P. Harvey 2014; Rivera Cusicanqui 1990; K. Smith 2012; Strathern 1988.

23. For Andean personhood, see Goldstein 2012. For the binary of Western/non-Western understandings, see Carsten 2004; LiPuma 1998; K. Smith 2012; Sökefeld 1999.

24. Cf. Harris 1995, who suggests that "the usurer and miser, key figures in the European mythology of money, whose characteristics derive from its exchange function, seem strikingly absent in Andean folklore" (305). Further, money is not understood in Laymi, where Harris works, as antithetical to the sacred world, but rather central to it and to social reproduction—even as it may, under certain circumstances, become a destructive force. This productive-destructive duality is reflected, Harris argues, in ritual offerings (316). Here, however, Nieves asserts the antisocial dimensions of the debt/credit relation.

25. Conciliators in Districts 1 and 8 reported a large number of conflicts related to land titles—but noted that debt conflicts were a significant percentage of their caseload. Exact numbers, however, were hard to come by, and as I show in this and subsequent chapters, debts were often a major source of tension for conciliation sessions dealing with other kinds of disputes.

26. Albro 2000; Allen 1981: 165–166, 2002; Hippert 2011; Van Vleet 2002, 2008.

27. See Peebles 2010 for an overview of credit and debt literature. See Graeber 2011 for a *longue durée* view.

28. See Roitman 2003.

29. Carsten 2013.

30. Kar 2013, 2017; Karim 2011; Schuster 2015.

31. Brett 2006; Maclean 2010; Lazar 2004a; Toro Ibáñez 2010.

32. Rhyne 2001, 2004.

33. A working paper by the IMF (Heng 2015) suggests that under Bolivia's 2013 Financial Services Law, the size of microfinance loans is increasing while the number of new loan recipients is on the decline, and suggests that this is likely due to institutional efforts to accommodate new interest rate caps and remain profitable. As Heng

footnotes, BancoSol, for example, had an annual interest rate of 65 percent for its 4,500 borrowers when it began in 1992. As of 2015, that interest rate was 20 percent. See www.imf.org/external/pubs/ft/wp/2015/wp15267.pdf.

34. James 2014; Guérin 2014; Karim 2011.

35. Han 2011: 26; Schild 2007.

36. Brett 2006; Lazar 2004a; Maclean 2010; Toro Ibáñez 2010.

37. See Weston for a critique of the ways that ADR as private justice "restricts public transparency and precedent development" (2014: 302).

38. See Schuster 2015 on the expectations and administrative practices in men's versus women's committees—and what they reveal about the gendered production of social collateral. See Kar 2017 on the dichotomy in loan sizes for men and women in Indian microfinance, and the use of male guarantors that reinforces gender hierarchies contrary to the claims of women's empowerment.

39. Abercrombie 1998; Canessa 2000; P. Harvey 1991; Heath 1958; Orta 2004; Van Vleet 2011.

40. Heath 1958.

41. See P. Harvey 1991 on social versus antisocial drinking.

42. Canessa 2000; Harris 1995; Orta 2004; Van Vleet 2011.

43. Emphasis mine.

44. See Harris 1995 on libations and differential meanings of money.

45. Abercrombie 1998; Lazar 2008; P. Harvey 1991.

46. Hofrichter 1982: 240.

47. See Povinelli 2011 on the "jerry-rigged" quality of life in late liberalism.

Chapter 5. The Social Life of a Sewing Machine

1. The title of this chapter and my discussion of the sewing machine and its biography as both a commodity and collateral draw on Appadurai's introduction to *The Social Life of Things*, as well as Kopytoff's contribution in the same volume (1986).

2. Calla et al. 2005; P. Harvey 2014.

3. See for example Cowlinshaw 2003 on "disappointing indigenous people" in Australia.

4. Cobb 1997; Lazarus-Black 2007.

5. Farmer 2004. See also chapter 2 on cultural and structural violence.

6. Though, as we will see in the following chapter, they did periodically bubble up.

7. See Cobb 1997 for a critique of violence's domestication. Here, however, I am seeking to explain why victims of violence might actually pursue this domestication process owing to other pressing concerns.

8. I reported my suspicions to a supervisor at the IJC, who suggested that at this point, years later, nothing could be done.

9. Brett 2006; Karim 2011; Lazar 2004a. See also Karim 2011 on the institutionalization of rural housebreaking and shaming practices in Bangladesh through microfinance loan-recovery techniques, and Schuster 2014 and 2015 on the gendered production of social collateral as a mechanism of loan recovery.

10. Sohini Kar (2013) and Caroline Schuster (2015) offer crucial insights into the perspectives, practices, and worries of microfinance institutions and loan officers not captured in Manuela's deeply negative characterization of their work. The ethical dilemmas and intimate encounters between borrowers and loan officers that they so carefully explore, however, are beyond the scope of this book.

11. For representative African studies, see D. Smith 2001; Comaroff and Comaroff 1999; Jensen and Buur 2004.

12. See Harris 1995 on the multiple "signifying functions of money" (304); Tassi 2010; Van Vleet 2011.

13. See P. Harvey 1991 on drunken speech and status hierarchies.

14. Emphasis mine. Editorial in *Los Tiempos* published online on May 30, 2012.

15. See www.la-razon.com/ciudades/seguridad_ciudadana/Tribunal-Mujeres -retardacion-Juana-Quispe_0_2390760994.html.

16. See Hodžić 2009 on the selective invocation of culture in gender violence debates and the challenges it poses to anthropologists.

17. See also P. Harvey 1991.

18. See also Canessa 2014; Harris 2000.

19. Van Vleet 2008: 181, emphasis mine.

20. Another way that Andeanist scholars have tried to complicate our understanding of the relationship between violence and alcohol is through studies of the Tinku celebrations in northern Potosí (see in particular Olivia Harris's important 2000 review of studies examining Tinku, gender, and bloodshed). Participants, Tinku scholars argue, believe that blood must be spilled during these annual ritual battles in order to ensure their land's fertility. In this cosmology, spilling blood is a source of strength and social reproduction; rather than an expression of antisocial violence, Tinku is a kind of socially productive violence (Harris 2000).

21. Burman 2011; Canessa 2012; Choque Quispe and Mendizabal Rodriguez 2010; Maclean 2014.

22. Named after Tupac Katari, the leader of a significant indigenous rebellion, Katarismo is a political movement that took shape in the 1970s. The movement sought to articulate class analysis with an analysis of the economic exploitation and exclusion of indigenous people from political power.

23. See also Calla et al. 2005: 14.

24. Silvia Rivera Cusicanqui (2010), for example, has analyzed ways Andean bilateral inheritance regimes and ceremonial rights were challenged by colonial and later liberal legislation. This includes the 1874 "Law of Expropriation (Ley de Exvinculación), which held that the only citizen 'right' vested in adult Indian men was the right to sell their families' access to communal lands" (Rivera Cusicanqui 2010: 33). She then traces these efforts to manage indigenous populations—and how they intersect with gender—forward into the neoliberal era.

25. As we have seen above, Van Vleet (2011) offers a textured discussion of domestic violence beyond male-female binaries, while Pamela Calla and colleagues (2005) situate sexual violence within relations of capitalist production and state legal bureaucracies.

26. Compare their accounts to what Julia Kowalski (2016) found in her work on antiviolence counseling programs in northern India. Kowalski shows how women's rights organizations work *within* kinship ideologies of kin-based interdependency and care rather than conflate them with patriarchal violence. In so doing, Kowalski argues, counselors challenge the idea that one must break with these kinship systems in order to be modern, autonomous subjects, while opening the possibility of respecting "vernacular aspirations to social relationality" (72). Kowalski is quoting James Ferguson (2013: 236).

27. Similarly, Merry found that U.S. court officials in New England frequently "redefine litigants' troubles as moral or therapeutic problems, requiring counseling or mediation but not legal remedy" (1990: ix).

28. Extrajudicial conciliation did not allow for mediating cases involving domestic violence because they could not handle criminal cases. The conciliation law and also the Law 348, the "Integral Law Guaranteeing Women a Life Free from Violence" (Article 46 on the "prohibition of conciliation"), however, do allow for conciliation *in the first instance of violence, when requested by the victim*. Most staff and conciliators I spoke with considered this to be a terrible provision. A high-ranking official in the Ministry of Justice suggested that this provision gave legal backing to existing "cultural" practices of conciliating rape and domestic violence, and she expressed her dismay in the strongest of terms. Indeed, in June 2016, a police officer, Mirko Armando SG, was accused of beating a minor until she suffered a brain hemorrhage that left her in a coma. The assault occurred after a previous incident in which Armando was accused of raping the girl—and had settled with her family via conciliation. "Un policía golpea a una menor y la deja con derrame cerebral," *Pagina Siete*, June 17, 2016.

29. See Goldstein on the private negotiations between the family of Wilmer Vargas and the taxi-trufi guild for the indemnification of his death and burial costs (2012: 83).

30. Anthropological work in addiction clinics, in legal aid centers for asylum seekers, and in talk therapy programs draws our attention to the coconstruction of narratives between staff and clientele (i.e., Ticktin 2006; Carr 2011). Through ethnographic-linguistic attention to the way these narratives are assembled, anthropologists warn us not to read such encounters as flatly referential.

31. Van Vleet 2008; Kowalski 2016.

32. Both Kar and Schuster contribute to a larger anthropological concern for revealing the often-intimate dimensions of these and other bureaucratic encounters (i.e., D. Smith 2007).

33. I do not mean to suggest that gender norms and cultural practices play no role in how certain forms of violence against women are normalized and justified. As we have seen, they clearly do. Nor that wealthy Bolivians do not experience or engage in forms of intimate partner violence. The limited statistics available suggest that domestic violence in Bolivia cuts across class and race backgrounds.

1. See Carr 2011 on the "talking cure" of American addiction treatment. See also Bush et al. 1994; Waldman 1998; Wexler 1999, 2014 on this dimension of ADR.

2. "Modulo II: Capacitacion a la comunidad. Medios alternativos de resolucion de conflictos," Programa Nacional de Acceso a la Justicia, 2nd edition, September 2008 (USAID/Bolivia, Checchi and Company Consulting, Inc.).

3. Albó 2012; Barié 2003; Hammond 2011; Nicolas et al. 2007.

4. Gordillo 2006; Gupta 2012; Hetherington 2011; Riles 2011; Wogan 2004.

5. Hull 2012; Mathur 2015.

6. Flores 2016; Coutin 2000; Ticktin 2006.

7. The legal anthropologist Sally Engle Merry (1990) found that working-class residents of Massachusetts pursue legal resolutions for everyday conflicts with the people in their lives, despite the efforts of court officials who would rather redefine their complaints in therapeutic terms. Merry determines that these "quarrels are fundamentally struggles over the definition and shape of social relationships" (1990: 13). For Merry, legal consciousness is bound up with efforts to transform or escape unfavorable social hierarchies and the strictures of intimate relations through recourse to the law, with consequences for how the state reaches into the intimate lives of its citizens.

8. See Comaroff and Comaroff 2006 on state mimicry.

9. Despite their frustrating court encounters, Merry found that in the United States plaintiffs retain a rather positive view of the law (1990: 178). This conviction stands in stark contrast with the views of many Bolivians.

10. Calla et al. 2005; Goldstein 2012; Risør 2010.

11. Menkel-Meadow 2015, 2013.

12. See Greenhouse et al. 1994 on "use of the court and talk about law as ways local people have of making claims about the legitimacy of a particular way of life" (10).

13. Abercrombie 1998; Gordillo 2006; Rappaport and Cummins 2011.

14. Reducciones were Jesuit missions meant to concentrate and enable the evangelization of indigenous populations. See Saignes 1995.

15. See Hammond 2011.

16. See also Platt 1992; Goodale 2002, Rappaport and Cummins 2011 in Latin America, and Stoler 2009 on the production of colonial archives and the lives contained within.

17. Rama 1996.

18. Gordillo 2006; Wogan 2004.

19. Canessa 2012; Platt 1992; Rivera Cusicanqui 2010; Wogan 2004.

20. See also Orellana Halkyer 2004.

21. Rappaport and Cummins 2011 push for a more expansive consideration of Andean knowledge production, recordkeeping, and communication beyond the alphabetic writing of colonial administrators.

22. Coutin 2000; Hetherington 2011; Hoag 2010; Navaro-Yashin 2007.

23. Platt 1992: 142–143.

24. Santos 1995; Goldstein 2012; Van Vleet 2008; Coutin 2000.

25. In the contemporary era, this liberal conception of law has found expression in human rights discourses, for example, Olivia's criticism that a center client was denying her child his basic human right to an identity mediated by a birth certificate. See Goodale 2008 on liberal conceptions of law, human rights, and subjectivity in Bolivia.

26. Sian Lazar (2004a) has analyzed similar kinds of gendered entrepreneurial citizenship projects operationalized through microcredit NGOs in El Alto. See also Muehlebach 2011.

27. Compare with Rubinson's (2016) analysis of the ways that court-annexed mediation produces similar effects; court-mandated mediation programs generally operate as a mechanism to alleviate overburdened dockets (898) and therefore turn "evaluative," pressing litigants to settle quickly, undercutting all the happy talk of voluntariness, leisurely pace, and therapeutic outcomes associated with "transformative" and "facilitative" mediation.

28. See Brett 2006; Elyachar 2005; Kar 2013; Karim 2011; Lazar 2004a; Maclean 2010; Mader 2016; Schuster 2014; Toro Ibáñez 2010.

29. Han 2011; Peebles 2010.

30. Tassi 2016: 6, emphasis mine.

31. Staff from across various centers confirmed seeing this pattern too.

32. This is not to be confused with Justa's sewing machine. This is an unrelated case.

33. In Bolivia, this tension often centered around what kind of training staff would require in order to become successful conciliators. Could social workers, psychologists, and neighborhood housewives provide effective conciliation, or did conciliators necessarily require training in the law? Only conciliators trained in the law, some argued, were in a position to adequately draft "actionable" agreements. Others felt that conciliators who were not trained in the law were better positioned to do the work of helping people dig deep into the reasons for their interpersonal disputes. While these disagreements parallel de/professionalization debates in the U.S. context, I am more interested in how and why, in the Bolivian context, they coalesced around the conciliation *document* itself—and with what effects.

34. Those who tried to help in this way included both the director of District 8 and a conciliator in District 4.

35. Gupta 2012.

Conclusion

1. Ellison 2015.

2. See also Postero 2010 on the ways the Morales administration has "vernacularized" neoliberalism rather than usher in a postneoliberalist democratic order.

3. And, as we have seen, "access to justice" is a persistent yet nebulous phrase itself open to interpretation.

4. See Albó and Romero 2009; interview with Xavier Albó, "Si el Gobierno aprende a ser más pluralista, en buena hora la derrota," *Pagina Siete*, April 12, 2015, www .paginasiete.bo/nacional/2015/4/12/gobierno-aprende-pluralista-buena-hora-derrota -53147.htm.

5. See Elise Gadea's op-ed piece, "La muerte de la Justicia Indígena Originaria Campesina," *La Razon*, May 22, 2015, www.la-razon.com/la_gaceta_juridica/muerte -Justicia-Indigena-Originaria-Campesina-gaceta_0_2274972601.html.

6. Davis et al. 2012; Li 2011; Merry and Conley 2011; Vannier 2010.

7. Tate 2015; Schuller 2012.

8. Pacino 2016; Siekmeier 2011; Young 2013; Zunes 2001.

9. In my reading of Lazar, citizenship *quality* is not reducible to legal status, and it extends beyond the mere right to *difference* assured by neoliberal multiculturalism.

Abel, Richard. 1982. *The Politics of Informal Justice: The American Experience*. New York: Academic Press.

Abercrombie, Thomas. 1998. *Pathways of Memory and Power: Ethnography and History among an Andean People*. Madison: University of Wisconsin Press.

Adelman, Madelaine. 2004. "The Battering State: Towards a Political Economy of Domestic Violence." *Journal of Poverty* 8(3): 45–64.

Aguilar, Raquel Gutiérrez. 2014. *Rhythms of the Pachakuti: Indigenous Uprising and State Power in Bolivia*. Durham, NC: Duke University Press.

Aiyer, Sri-Ram. 1995. "Foreword." In *Judicial Reform in Latin America and the Caribbean*, edited by Malcolm Rowat, Waleed Haider Malik, and Maria Dakolias. World Bank Technical Paper No. 280.

Albó, Xavier. 2008. *Movimientos y poder indígena en Bolivia, Ecuador y Perú*. La Paz: PNUD/Cipca 71.

———. 2012. "Justicia indígena en la Bolivia plurinacional." In *Justicia indígena, plurinacionalidad e interculturalidad en Bolívia*, edited by Boaventura de Sousa Santos and José Luis Exeni Rodríguez. Quito: Fundación Rosa Luxemburg/Abya-Yala.

Albó, Xavier, and Carlos Romero. 2009. *Autonomías indígenas en la realidad boliviana y su nueva Constitución*. La Paz: Vicepresidencia del Estado Plurinacional de Bolivia/PADEP.

Albro, Robert. 2000. "Fictive Feasting: Mixing and Parsing Bolivian Popular Sentiment." *Anthropology and Humanism* 25(2): 142–157.

———. 2010. "Confounding Cultural Citizenship and Constitutional Reform in Bolivia." *Latin American Perspectives* 37(3): 71–90.

Allen, Catherine J. 1981. "To Be Quechua: The Symbolism of Coca Chewing in Highland Peru." *American Ethnologist* 8(1): 157–171.

———. 2002. *The Hold Life Has: Coca and Cultural Identity in an Andean Community*. Washington, DC: Smithsonian Institution.

Alvarez, Gladys Stella. 1995. "Alternative Dispute Resolution Mechanisms: Lessons of the Argentine Experience." In *Judicial Reform in Latin America and the Caribbean*, edited by Malcolm Rowat, Waleed Haider Malik, and Maria Dakolias. World Bank Technical Paper No. 280.

Appadurai, Arjun. 1986. "Introduction." In *The Social Life of Things: Commodities in Cultural Perspective.* Cambridge: Cambridge University Press.

Appel, Hannah. 2014. "Occupy Wall Street and the Economic Imagination." *Cultural Anthropology* 29(4): 602–625.

Arbona, Juan. 2008. "Sangre de Minero, Semilla de Guerrillero." *Bulletin of Latin American Research* 27(1): 24–42.

Arbona, Juan, and Benjamin Kohl. 2004. "City Profile: La Paz-El Alto." *Cities* 21(3): 255–265.

Arnold, Denise Y., ed. 2014. *Gente de carne y hueso: Las tramas de parentesco en los Andes.* 2nd ed. La Paz: CLASE/ILCA.

Arvidson, Malin. 2008. "Contradictions and Confusions in Development Work Exploring the Realities of Bangladeshi NGOs." *Journal of South Asian Development* 3(1): 109–134.

Auyero, Javier. 2012. *Patients of the State: The Politics of Waiting in Argentina.* Durham, NC: Duke University Press.

Baiocchi, Gianpaolo. 2005. *Militants and Citizens: The Politics of Participatory Democracy in Porto Alegre.* Stanford, CA: Stanford University Press.

Baiocchi, Gianpaolo, and Ernesto Ganuza. 2014. "Participatory Budgeting as If Emancipation Mattered." *Politics and Society* 42(1): 29–50.

Barié, Cletus Gregor. 2003. *Pueblos indígenas y derechos constitucionales en América Latina: Un panorama.* Quito: Editorial Abya Yala.

Barragán, Rossana. 2006. "Más allá de lo mestizo, más allá de lo Aymara: Organización y representaciones de clase y etnicidad en La Paz." *América Latina Hoy* 43: 107–130.

Bercovitch, Jacob, J. Theodore Anagnoson, and Donnette Wille. 1991. "Some Conceptual Issues and Empirical Trends in the Study of Successful Mediation in International Relations." *Journal of Peace Research* 28(1): 7–17.

Bercovitch, Jacob, Victor Kremenyuk, and I. William Zartman, eds. 2008. *The SAGE Handbook of Conflict Resolution.* Thousand Oaks, CA: Sage.

Bernal, Victoria, and Inderpal Grewal, eds. 2014. *Theorizing NGOs: States, Feminisms, and Neoliberalism.* Durham, NC: Duke University Press.

Biehl, João, and Torben Eskerod. 2007. *Will to Live: AIDS Therapies and the Politics of Survival.* Princeton, NJ: Princeton University Press.

Bjork-James, C. 2013. "Claiming Space, Redefining Politics: Urban Protest and Grassroots Power in Bolivia." PhD diss., City University of New York.

Brett, John. 2006. "'We Sacrifice and Eat Less': The Structural Complexities of Microfinance Participation." *Human Organization* 65(1): 8–19.

Brown, Keith. 2006. "The New Ugly Americans? Making Sense of Democracy Promotion in the Former Yugoslavia." In *Transacting Transition: The Micropolitics of Democracy Assistance in the Former Yugoslavia,* edited by Keith Brown. Bloomfield, CT: Kumarian.

———. 2009. "Evaluating US Democracy Promotion in the Balkans: Ironies, Inconsistencies, and Unexamined Influences." National Council for Eurasian and East European Research.

Brown, Scott, Christine Cervenak, and David Fairman. 1997. "Alternative Dispute Resolution: A Guide of USAID." www.usaid.gov/sites/default/files/documents/1868/200sbe.pdf.

Brown, Wendy. 2005. *Edgework: Critical Essays on Knowledge and Politics*. Princeton, NJ: Princeton University Press.

———. 2008. *Regulating Aversion: Tolerance in the Age of Identity and Empire*. Princeton, NJ: Princeton University Press.

Buechler, Steven M. 2013. "Strain and Breakdown Theories." In *The Wiley-Blackwell Encyclopedia of Social and Political Movements*. Malden, MA: Blackwell.

Burki, Shahid Javed. 1995. "Economic Development and Judicial Reform." In *Judicial Reform in Latin America and the Caribbean*, edited by Malcolm Rowat, Waleed Haider Malik, and Maria Dakolias. World Bank Technical Paper No. 280.

Burman, Anders. 2011. "Chachawarmi: Silence and Rival Voices on Decolonisation and Gender Politics in Andean Bolivia." *Journal of Latin American Studies* 43(1): 65–91.

Bush, Robert, A. Baruch, and Joseph P. Folger. 1994. *The Promise of Mediation: Responding to Conflict through Empowerment and Recognition*. San Francisco: Jossey-Bass.

Calla, Pamela, et al. 2005. *Rompiendo silencios: Una aproximación a la violencia sexual y al maltrato infantil en Bolivia*. La Paz: Coordinadora de la Mujer y Defensor del Pueblo, República de Bolivia.

Cameron, John. 2013. "Bolivia's Contentious Politics of 'Normas y Procedimientos Propios.'" *Latin American and Caribbean Ethnic Studies* 8(2): 179–201.

Campbell, Jeremy. 2014. "Speculative Accumulation: Property-Making in the Brazilian Amazon." *Journal of Latin American and Caribbean Anthropology* 19(2): 237–259.

Canessa, Andrew. 2000. "Contesting Hybridity: Evangelistas and Kataristas in Highland Bolivia." *Journal of Latin American Studies* 32(1): 55–84.

———. 2004. "Reproducing Racism: Schooling and Race in Highland Bolivia." *Journal of Race and Education* 7(2): 185–204.

———. 2008. "Sex and the Citizen: Barbies and Beauty Queens in the Age of Evo." *Journal of Latin American Cultural Studies* 17(1): 41–64.

———. 2012. *Intimate Indigeneities: Race, Sex, and History in the Small Spaces of Andean Life*. Durham, NC: Duke University Press.

———. 2014. "Conflict, Claim and Contradiction in the New 'Indigenous' State of Bolivia." *Critique of Anthropology* 34(2): 153–173.

Carothers, Thomas. 1999. *Aiding Democracy Abroad: The Learning Curve*. Washington, DC: Carnegie Endowment for International Peace.

———. 2001. "The Many Agendas of Rule-of-Law Reform in Latin America." In *Rule of Law in Latin America: The International Promotion of Judicial Reform*, edited by Pilar Domingo and Rachel Sieder. London: Institute of Latin American Studies.

———. 2007. "U.S. Democracy Promotion during and after Bush." Washington, DC: Carnegie Endowment for International Peace.

Carr, E. Summerson. 2011. *Scripting Addiction: The Politics of Therapeutic Talk and American Sobriety*. Princeton, NJ: Princeton University Press.

Carsten, Janet. 2004. *After Kinship*. Cambridge: Cambridge University Press.

———. 2013. "What Kinship Does—and How." *HAU: Journal of Ethnographic Theory* 3(2): 245–251.

Castle, Tomi. 2008. "Sexual Citizenship: Articulating Citizenship, Identity, and the Pursuit of the Good Life in Urban Brazil." *PoLAR: Political and Legal Anthropology Review* 31(1): 118–133.

Cattelino, Jessica. 2008. *High Stakes: Florida Seminole Gaming and Sovereignty*. Durham, NC: Duke University Press.

Choque Quispe, María Eugenia, and Mónica Mendizabal Rodriguez. 2010. "Descolonizando el género a través de la profundización de la condición sullka y mayt'ata." *Tinkazos* 13(28): 81–97.

Cobb, Sara. 1997. "The Domestication of Violence in Mediation." *Law and Society Review* 31(3): 397–440.

Cobb, Sara, and Janet Rifkin. 1991. "Practice and Paradox: Deconstructing Neutrality in Mediation." *Law and Social Inquiry* 16(1): 35–62.

Cohen, Amy. 2006. "Debating the Globalization of U.S. Mediation: Politics, Power, and Practice in Nepal." *Harvard Negotiation Law Review* 11: 295–353.

Coles, Kimberly. 2004. "Election Day: The Construction of Democracy through Technique." *Cultural Anthropology* 19(4): 551–580.

———. 2007. *Democratic Designs: International Intervention and Electoral Practices in Postwar Bosnia-Herzegovina*. Ann Arbor: University of Michigan Press.

———. 2009. "International Presence: The Passive Work of Democracy Promotion." In *Democracy: Anthropological Approaches*, edited by Julia Paley. Santa Fe, NM: School for Advanced Research Press.

Collier, Jane F. 1979. "Stratification and Dispute Handling in Two Highland Chiapas Communities." *American Ethnologist* 6(2): 305–328.

Colloredo-Mansfeld, Rudi. 1999. *The Native Leisure Class: Consumption and Cultural Creativity in the Andes*. Chicago: University of Chicago Press.

Comaroff, Jean, and John Comaroff. 1999. "Occult Economies and the Violence of Abstraction: Notes from the South African Postcolony." *American Ethnologist* 2b(2): 279–303.

———. 2006. "Figuring Crime: Quantifacts and the Production of the (Un)Real." *Public Culture* 18(1): 209–246.

Comaroff, John, and Simon Roberts. 1981. *Rules and Processes: The Cultural Context of Dispute in an African Context*. Chicago: University of Chicago Press.

Confortini, Catia. 2006. "Galtung, Violence, and Gender: The Case for a Peace Studies/Feminism Alliance." *Peace and Change* 31(3): 333–367.

Coulthard, Glen Sean. 2014. *Red Skin, White Masks*. Minneapolis: University of Minnesota Press.

Coutin, Susan Bibler. 2000. *Legalizing Moves: Salvadoran Immigrants' Struggle for US Residency*. Ann Arbor: University of Michigan Press.

Cowlishaw, Gillian. 2003. "Disappointing Indigenous People: Violence and the Refusal of Help." *Public Culture* 15(1): 103–125.

Cox, Michael, G. John Ikenberry, and Takashi Inoguchi, eds. 2000. *American Democracy Promotion: Impulses, Strategies, and Impacts*. Oxford: Oxford University Press.

Cruikshank, Barbara. 1999. *The Will to Empower: Democratic Citizens and Other Subjects*. Ithaca, NY: Cornell University Press.

Das, Veena. 2007. *Life and Words: Violence and the Descent into the Ordinary*. Berkeley: University of California Press.

Davis, Kevin E., Benedict Kingsbury, and Sally Engle Merry. 2012. "Indicators as a Technology of Global Governance." *Law and Society Review* 46(1): 71–104.

de Acosta, José, and Jane E. Mangan, eds. 2002. *The Natural and Moral History of the Indies*. Durham, NC: Duke University Press.

Deutsch, Morton, Peter T. Coleman, and Eric C. Marcus, eds. 2011. *The Handbook of Conflict Resolution: Theory and Practice*. Malden, MA: John Wiley and Sons.

Dezalay, Yves, and Bryant Garth. 1996. *Dealing in Virtue: International Commercial Arbitration and the Construction of a Transnational Legal Order*. Chicago: University of Chicago Press.

———. 2002. *The Internationalization of Palace Wars: Lawyers, Economists, and the Contest to Transform Latin American States*. Chicago: University of Chicago Press.

Domingo, Pilar, and Rachel Sieder, eds. 2001. *Rule of Law in Latin America: The International Promotion of Judicial Reform*. London: Institute of Latin American Studies.

Dunkerley, James. 1984. *Rebellion in the Veins: Political Struggle in Bolivia, 1952–1982*. London: Verso.

Dunn, Elizabeth C. 2004. *Privatizing Poland: Baby Food, Big Business, and the Remaking of Labor*. Ithaca, NY: Cornell University Press.

Duvendack, Maren, Richard Palmer-Jones, James G. Copestake, Lee Hooper, Yoon Loke, and Nity Rao. 2011. "What Is the Evidence of the Impact of Microfinance on the Well-being of Poor People?" London: EPPI-Centre, Social Science Research Unit, Institute of Education, University of London.

Eade, Deborah. 2007. "Capacity Building: Who Builds Whose Capacity?" *Development in Practice* 17(4–5): 630–639.

Edwards, Jeanette, and Marilyn Strathern. 2000. "Including Our Own." In *Cultures of Relatedness: New Approaches to the Study of Kinship*, edited by Janet Carsten. Cambridge: Cambridge University Press.

Ellison, Susan. 2015. "Replicate, Facilitate, Disseminate: The Micropolitics of American Democracy Promotion in Bolivia." *Political and Legal Anthropology Review* 28(2): 318–337.

———. 2017a. "Corrective Capacities: From Unruly Politics to Democratic Capacitación." *Cambridge Journal of Anthropology* 35(1): 67–83.

———. 2017b. "'You Have to Comply with Paper': Debt, Documents, and Legal Consciousness in Bolivia." *Journal of the Royal Anthropological Institute* 23(3): 523–542.

Elyachar, Julia. 2005. *Markets of Dispossession: NGOs, Economic Development and the State in Cairo*. Durham, NC: Duke University Press.

Englund, Harri. 2006. *Prisoners of Freedom: Human Rights and Africa's Poor*. Berkeley: University of California Press.

Erbe, Nancy D. 2006. "Appreciating Mediation's Global Role in Promoting Good Governance." *Harvard Negotiation Law Review* 11: 355–388.

Eyben, Rosalind. 2011. "The Sociality of International Aid and Policy Convergence." In *Adventures in Aidland: The Anthropology of Professionals International Development*, edited by David Mosse. New York: Berghahn.

Fabricant, Nicole. 2009. "Performative Politics: The Camba Countermovement in Eastern Bolivia." *American Ethnologist* 36(4): 768–783.

———. 2013. "Good Living for Whom? Bolivia's Climate Justice Movement and the Limitations of Indigenous Cosmovisions." *Latin American and Caribbean Ethnic Studies* 8(2): 159–178.

Farmer, Paul. 2004. "An Anthropology of Structural Violence." *Current Anthropology* 45(3): 305–325.

Ferguson, James. 1990. *The Anti-Politics Machine: Development, Depoliticization, and Bureaucratic Power in Lesotho.* Cambridge: Cambridge University Press.

———. 2013. "Declarations of Dependence: Labour, Personhood, and Welfare in Southern Africa." *Journal of the Royal Anthropological Institute* 19(2): 223–242.

Ferguson, James, and Akhil Gupta. 2002. "Spatializing States: Toward an Ethnography of Neoliberal Governmentality." *American Ethnologist* 29(4): 981–1002.

Field, Thomas C., Jr. 2014. *From Development to Dictatorship: Bolivia and the Alliance for Progress in the Kennedy Era.* Ithaca, NY: Cornell University Press.

Finkel, Steven, Aníbal Pérez-Linán, Mitchell A. Seligson, and Dinorah Azpuru. 2006. "Effects of U.S. Foreign Assistance on Democracy Building: Results of a Cross-National Quantitative Study." USAID, Vanderbilt University and University of Pittsburgh, Version #34.

Finnegan, Amy, and Susan G. Hackley. 2008. "Negotiation and Nonviolent Action: Interacting in the World of Conflict." *Negotiation Journal* 24(1): 7–24.

Fisher, Roger, William L. Ury, and Bruce Patton. 2011 (1981). *Getting to Yes: Negotiating Agreement without Giving In.* New York: Penguin.

Flores, Andrea. 2016. "Forms of Exclusion: Undocumented Students Navigating Financial Aid and Inclusion in the United States." *American Ethnologist* 43(3): 540–554.

Foucault, Michel. 1991. "Governmentality." In *The Foucault Effect: Studies in Governmentality*, edited by Graham Burchell, Colin Gordon, and Peter Miller. Chicago: University of Chicago Press.

———. 1995 (1979). *Discipline and Punish: The Birth of the Prison.* New York: Vintage.

Fritz, Jan Marie, ed. 2014. *Moving toward a Just Peace: The Mediation Continuum.* London: Springer Science & Business Media.

Fundación UNIR. 2005. *Las piezas del conflicto.* La Paz: Fundación UNIR Bolivia/Plural editores.

Gagnon, Chip. 2006. "Catholic Relief Services, USAID, and Authentic Partnership in Serbia." In *Transacting Transition: The Micropolitics of Democracy Assistance in the Former Yugoslavia*, edited by Keith Brown. Champaign, IL: Kumarian.

Galtung, Johan. 1990. "Cultural Violence." *Journal of Peace Research* 27(3): 291–305.

———. 1996. *Peace by Peaceful Means: Peace and Conflict, Development and Civilization.* London: Sage.

Garth, Bryant G. 1995. "Access to Justice." In *Judicial Reform in Latin America and the Caribbean*, edited by Malcolm Rowat, Waleed Haider Malik, and Maria Dakolias. World Bank Technical Paper No. 280.

Geidel, Molly. 2010. "'Sowing Death in Our Women's Wombs': Modernization and In-digenous Nationalism in the 1960s Peace Corps and Jorge Sanjinés' Yawar Mallku." *American Quarterly* 62(3): 763–786.

Gill, Lesley. 1997. "Power Lines: The Political Context of Nongovernmental Organization (NGO) Activity in El Alto, Bolivia." *Journal of Latin American Anthropology* 2(2): 144–169.

Gills, Barry K. 2000. "American Power, Neo-liberal Economic Globalization, and Low-intensity Democracy: An Unstable Trinity." In *American Democracy Promotion. Impulses, Strategies, and Impacts*, edited by Michael Cox, John Ikenberry, and Takashi Inoguchi. Oxford: Oxford University Press.

Gladwell, Malcolm. 2010. "Drinking Games." *New Yorker*, February 15 and 22.

Goldstein, Daniel. 2004. *The Spectacular City: Violence and Performance in Urban Bolivia*. Durham, NC: Duke University Press.

———. 2005. "Flexible Justice: Neoliberal Violence and 'Self-Help' Security in Bolivia." *Critique of Anthropology* 25(4): 389–411.

———. 2012. *Outlawed: Between Security and Rights in a Bolivian City*. Durham, NC: Duke University Press.

———. 2016. *Owners of the Sidewalk: Security and Survival in the Informal City*. Durham, NC: Duke University Press.

Goodale, Mark. 2002. "Legal Ethnohistory in Rural Bolivia: Documentary Culture and Social History in the Norte de Potosí." *Ethnohistory* 49(3): 583–609.

———. 2008. *Dilemmas of Modernity: Bolivian Encounters with Law and Liberalism*. Stanford, CA: Stanford University Press.

Goodale, Mark, and Nancy Postero. 2013. *Neoliberalism, Interrupted: Social Change and Contested Governance in Contemporary Latin America*. Stanford, CA: Stanford University Press.

Gordillo, Gastón. 2006. "The Crucible of Citizenship: ID-Paper Fetishism in the Argentinean Chaco." *American Ethnologist* 33(2): 162–176.

Graeber, David. 2011. *Debt: The First 5,000 Years*. Brooklyn, NY: Melville House.

Gramsci, Antonio. 1971. *Prison Notebooks*. New York: International Publishers.

Greenhalgh, Susan. 2008. *Just One Child: Science and Policy in Deng's China*. Berkeley: University of California Press.

Greenhouse, Carol. 1985. "Mediation: A Comparative Approach." *Man* 20(1): 90–114.

———. 2009. "Introduction." In *Ethnographies of Neoliberalism*, edited by Carol Greenhouse. Philadelphia: University of Pennsylvania Press.

Greenhouse, Carol J., Barbara Yngvesson, and David M. Engel. 1994. *Law and Community in Three American Towns*. Ithaca, NY: Cornell University Press.

Guaygua, Germán. 2009. "Parentesco andino en la constitución de trayectorias y redes migratórias hacia España." *Tinkazos* 12: 147–162.

Guérin, Isabelle. 2014. "Juggling with Debt, Social Ties, and Values: The Everyday Use of Microcredit in Rural South India." *Current Anthropology* 55(S9): S40–S50.

Gupta, Akhil. 2008. "Literacy, Bureaucratic Domination, and Democracy." In *Democracy: Anthropological Approaches*, edited by Julia Paley. Santa Fe, NM: School for Advanced Research.

————. 2012. *Red Tape: Bureaucracy, Structural Violence, and Poverty in India*. Durham, NC: Duke University Press.

Guss, David. 2006. "The Gran Poder and the Reconquest of La Paz." *Journal of Latin American Anthropology* 11(2): 294–328.

Gustafson, Bret. 2006. "Spectacles of Autonomy and Crisis: Or, What Bulls and Beauty Queens Have to Do with Regionalism in Eastern Bolivia." *Journal of Latin American Anthropology* 11(2): 351–379.

————. 2008. "Reading Bolivia in the US Press." NACLA *Report on the Americas* 41(4): 49–52.

————. 2009. *New Languages of the State: Indigenous Resurgence and the Politics of Knowledge in Bolivia*. Durham, NC: Duke University Press.

Habermas, Jürgen. 1984. *The Theory of Communicative Action: Reason and the Rationalization of Society*. Boston: Beacon.

————. 1996. *Selections from "Between Facts and Norms: Contributions to a Discourse Theory of Law and Democracy."* Cambridge, MA: MIT Press.

Hale, Charles. 2002. "Does Multiculturalism Menace? Governance, Cultural Rights and the Politics of Identity in Guatemala." *Journal of Latin American Studies* 34: 485–524.

————. 2005. "Neoliberal Multiculturalism: The Remaking of Cultural Rights and Racial Dominance in Central America." *Political and Legal Anthropology Review* 28(1): 10–28.

Hammond, John L. 2011. "Indigenous Community Justice in the Bolivian Constitution of 2009." *Human Rights Quarterly* 33(3): 649–681.

Han, Clara. 2011. "Symptoms of Another Life: Time, Possibility, and Domestic Relations in Chile's Credit Economy." *Cultural Anthropology* 26: 7–32.

Hansen, Thomas Blom. 2001. "Governance and State Mythologies in Mumbai." In *States of Imagination. Ethnographic Explorations of the Postcolonial State*, edited by Thomas Blom Hansen and Finn Stepputat. Durham, NC: Duke University Press.

Hanson, Paul. 2007. "Governmentality, Language Ideology, and the Production of Needs in Malagasy Conservation and Development." *Cultural Anthropology* 22(2): 244–284C.

Harrington, Christine. 1982. "Delegalization Reform Movements: A Historical Analysis." In *The Politics of Informal Justice: The American Experience*, edited by Richard Abel. New York: Academic Press.

————. 1995. "Community Organizing through Conflict Resolution." In *The Possibility of Popular Justice: A Case Study of Community Mediation in the United States*, edited by Sally Engle Merry and Neal Milner. Ann Arbor: University of Michigan Press.

Harringon, Christine, and Sally Merry. 1988. "Ideological Production: The Making of Community Mediation." *Law and Society Review* 22(4): 709–735.

Harris, Olivia. 1995. "The Sources and Meanings of Money: Beyond the Market Paradigm in an Ayllu of Northern Potosí." In *Ethnicity, Markets, and Migration in the Andes: At the Crossroads of History and Anthropology*, edited by Brooke Larson and Olivia Harris. Durham, NC: Duke University Press.

———. 2000. *To Make the Earth Bear Fruit: Ethnographic Essays on Fertility, Work and Gender in Highland Bolivia.* London: University of London Press.

Harvey, David. 2005. *A Brief History of Neoliberalism.* Oxford: Oxford University Press.

Harvey, Penelope M. 1991. "Drunken Speech and the Construction of Meaning: Bilingual Competence in the Southern Peruvian Andes." *Language in Society* 20(1): 1–36.

———. 2014. "Los 'hechos naturales' de parentesco y género en un contexto andino." In *Gente de carne y hueso: Las tramas de parentesco en los Andes*, 2nd ed., edited by Denise Arnold. La Paz: CLASE/ILCA.

Healy, Kevin. 2001. *Llamas, Weavings, and Organic Chocolate: Multicultural Grassroots Development in the Andes and Amazon of Bolivia.* Notre Dame, IN: University of Notre Dame Press.

Heath, Dwight B. 1958. "Drinking Patterns of the Bolivian Camba." *Quarterly Journal of Alcohol Studies* 19(3): 491–508.

Heng, Dyna. 2015. "Impact of the New Financial Services Law in Bolivia on Financial Stability and Inclusion." International Monetary Fund. WP/15/267.

Hensler, D. R. 2003. "Our Courts, Ourselves: How the Alternative Dispute Resolution Movement Is Re-shaping Our Legal System." *Penn State Law Review* 108: 165–197.

Hess, Sabine. 2006. "Strathern's Melanesian 'Dividual' and the Christian 'Individual': A Perspective from Vanua Lava, Vanuatu." *Oceania* 76(3): 285–296.

Hetherington, Kregg. 2011. *Guerrilla Auditors: The Politics of Transparency in Neoliberal Paraguay.* Durham, NC: Duke University Press.

Hetland, Gabriel. 2014. "The Crooked Line: From Populist Mobilization to Participatory Democracy in Chávez-era Venezuela." *Qualitative Sociology* 37(4): 373–401.

Hickel, Jason. 2015. *Democracy as Death: The Moral Order of Anti-liberal Politics in South Africa.* Berkeley: University of California Press.

Himpele, Jeffrey D. 2008. *Circuits of Culture: Media, Politics, and Indigenous Identity in the Andes.* Minneapolis: University of Minnesota Press.

Hindman, Anne-Meike, and Heather Fechter. 2011. "Introduction." In *Inside the Everyday Lives of Development Workers: The Challenges and Futures of Aidland.* Sterling, VA: Kumerian.

Hippert, Christine. 2011. "The Politics and Practices of Constructing Development Identities in Rural Bolivia." *Journal of Latin American and Caribbean Anthropology.* 16(1): 90–113.

Hoag, Colin. 2010. "The Magic of the Populace: An Ethnography of Illegibility in the South African Immigration Bureaucracy." *Political and Legal Anthropology Review* 33(1): 6–25.

Hoben, Allan. 1989. "USAID: Organizational and Institutional Issues and Effectiveness." In *Cooperation for International Development: The United States and the Third World in the 1990s*, edited by Robert J. Berg and David F. Gordon. London: Lynne Rienner.

Hodžić, Saida. 2009. "Unsettling Power: Domestic Violence, Gender Politics, and Struggles over Sovereignty in Ghana." *Ethnos* 74(3): 331–360.

———. 2014. "Feminist Bastards: Toward a Posthumanist Critique of NGOization." In *Theorizing NGOs: States, Feminisms, and Neoliberalism*, edited by Victoria Bernal and Inderpal Grewal. Durham, NC: Duke University Press.

Hofrichter, Richard. 1982. "Neighborhood Justice and the Social Control Problems of American Capitalism: A Perspective." In *The Politics of Informal Justice*, vol. 1, *The American Experience*, edited by Richard Abel. New York: Academic Press.

Holston, James. 2009. "Insurgent Citizenship in an Era of Global Urban Peripheries." *City and Society* 21(2): 245–267.

Hornberger, Julia. 2004. " 'My Police—Your Police': The Informal Privatisation of the Police in the Inner City of Johannesburg." *African Studies* 63(2): 213–230.

Huanca Quispe, Rosario. 2015. *La conciliación como medio alternative de solución de conflictos*. El Alto, Bolivia: Self-published.

Hull, Matthew. 2008. "Ruled by Records: The Expropriation of Land and the Misappropriation of Lists in Islamabad." *American Ethnologist* 35: 501–518.

———. 2012. *Government of Paper: The Materiality of Bureaucracy in Urban Pakistan*. Berkeley: University of California Press.

Humphreys, Stephen. 2010. *Theatre of the Rule of Law: Transnational Legal Intervention in Theory and Practice*. Vol. 73. Cambridge: Cambridge University Press.

Ikenberry, G. John. 2000. "America's Liberal Grand Strategy: Democracy and National Security in the Post-war Era." In *American Democracy Promotion: Impulses, Strategies, and Impacts*, edited by Michael Conon, John Ikenberry, and Takashi Inoguchi. Oxford: Oxford University Press.

Indaburu Quintana, Rafael. 2004. "Evaluación de la ciudad de el alto." Contract 511-O -00-04-00047-00, USAID. http://pdf.usaid.gov/pdf_docs/Pnadg073.pdf.

James, Deborah. 2014. " 'Deeper into a Hole?': Borrowing and Lending in South Africa." *Current Anthropology* 55(S9): S17–S29.

Jensen, Steffen, and Lars Buur. 2004. "Everyday Policing and the Occult: Notions of Witchcraft, Crime and 'the People.' " *African Studies* 63(2): 193–211.

Kar, Sohini. 2013. "Recovering Debts: Microfinance Loan Officers and the Work of 'Proxy-creditors' in India." *American Ethnologist* 40(3): 480–493.

———. 2017. "Relative Indemnity: Risk, Insurance, and Kinship in Indian Microfinance." *Journal of the Royal Anthropological Institute* 23(2): 302–319.

Karim, Lamia. 2011. *Microfinance and Its Discontents: Women in Debt in Bangladesh*. Minneapolis: University of Minnesota Press.

Kenny, Susan, and Matthew Clarke. 2010. *Challenging Capacity Building: Comparative Perspectives*. New York: Palgrave Macmillan.

Kohl, Benjamin. 2002. "Stabilizing Neoliberalism in Bolivia: Popular Participation and Privatization." *Political Geography* 21(4): 449–472.

———. 2003. "Democratizing Decentralization in Bolivia: The Law of Popular Participation." *Journal of Planning Education and Research* 23(2): 153–164.

Kohl, Benjamin H., and Linda Farthing. 2006. *Impasse in Bolivia: Neoliberal Hegemony and Popular Resistance*. New York: Zed.

Kopytoff, Igor. 1988. "The Cultural Biography of Things: Commoditization as Process." In *The Social Life of Things: Commodities in Cultural Perspective*. Cambridge: Cambridge University Press.

Kosek, Jake. 2006. *Understories: The Political Life of Forests in Northern New Mexico*. Durham, NC: Duke University Press.

Kowalski, Julia. 2016. "Ordering Dependence: Care, Disorder, and Kinship Ideology in North Indian Antiviolence Counseling." *American Ethnologist* 43(1): 63–75.

Lambek, Michael. 2011. "Kinship as Gift and Theft: Acts of Succession in Mayotte and Israel." *American Ethnologist* 38(1): 2–16.

Latour, Bruno. 1999. *Pandora's Hope*. Cambridge, MA: Harvard University Press.

———. 2007. *Reassembling the Social: An Introduction to Actor-Network-Theory*. Oxford: Clarendon.

Lazar, Sian. 2004a. "Education for Credit: Development as Citizenship Project in Bolivia." *Critique of Anthropology* 24(3): 301–319.

———. 2004b. "Personalist Politics, Clientelism and Citizenship: Local Elections in El Alto, Bolivia." *Bulletin of Latin American Research* 23(2): 228–243.

———. 2008. *El Alto, Rebel City: Self and Citizenship in Andean Bolivia*. Durham, NC: Duke University Press.

———. 2012. "Citizenship Quality: A New Agenda for Development?" *Journal of Civil Society* 8(4): 333–350.

Lazar, Sian, and Monique Nuijten. 2013. "Citizenship, the Self, and Political Agency." *Critique of Anthropology* 33(1): 3–7.

Lazarus-Black, Mindie. 2007. *Everyday Harm: Domestic Violence, Court Rites, and Cultures of Reconciliation*. Urbana: University of Illinois Press.

Lederach, John Paul. 1996. *Preparing for Peace: Conflict Transformation across Cultures*. Syracuse, NY: Syracuse University Press.

Leinaweaver, Jessaca B. 2008. *The Circulation of Children: Kinship, Adoption, and Morality in Andean Peru*. Latin America Otherwise. Durham, NC: Duke University Press.

———. 2009. "Raising the Roof in the Transnational Andes: Building Houses, Forging Kinship." *Journal of the Royal Anthropological Institute* 15(4): 777–796.

Lewis, David. 2011. "Tidy Concepts, Messy Lives." In *Adventures in Aidland: The Anthropology of Professionals International Development*, edited by David Mosse. New York: Berghahn.

Lewis, David, and David Mosse. 2006. "Theoretical Approaches to Brokerage and Translation in Development." In *Development Brokers and Translators: The Ethnography of Aid and Agencies*, edited by David Lewis and David Mosse. Bloomfield, CT: Kumarian.

Li, Tania. 2005. "Beyond 'the State' and Failed Schemes." *American Anthropologist* 107(3): 383–394.

———. 2007. *The Will to Improve: Governmentality, Development, and the Practice of Politics*. Durham, NC: Duke University Press.

———. 2011. "Rendering Society Technical: Government through Community and the Ethnographic Turn at the World Bank in Indonesia." In *Adventures in Aidland: The Anthropology of Professionals International Development*, edited by David Mosse. New York: Berghahn.

Lipset, Seymour Martin. 1959. "Some Social Requisites of Democracy: Economic Development and Political Legitimacy." *American Political Science Review* 53(1): 69–105.

LiPuma, Edward. 1998. "Modernity and Forms of Personhood in Melanesia." In *Bodies and Persons: Comparative Perspectives from Africa and Melanesia*, edited by Michael Lambek and Andrew Strathern. Cambridge: Cambridge University Press.

Maclean, Kate. 2010. "Capitalizing on Women's Social Capital? Women-Targeted Microfinance in Bolivia." *Development and Change* 41(3): 495–515.

———. 2014. "Chachawarmi: Rhetorics and Lived Realities." *Bulletin of Latin American Research* 33(1): 76–90.

Mader, Philip. 2016. *The Political Economy of Microfinance: Financializing Poverty*. New York: Springer.

Malik, Waleed H. 1995. "Overview." In *Judicial Reform in Latin America and the Caribbean*, edited by Malcolm Rowat, Waleed Haider Malik, and Maria Dakolias. World Bank Technical Paper No. 280.

Malkki, Liisa H. 2015. *The Need to Help: The Domestic Arts of International Humanitarianism*. Durham, NC: Duke University Press.

Mamdani, Mahmood. 2005. *Good Muslim, Bad Muslim: America, the Cold War, and the Roots of Terror*. New York: Three Leaves Press.

Mathur, Nayanika. 2015. *Paper Tiger*. Cambridge: Cambridge University Press.

Mattei, Ugo, and Laura Nader. 2008. *Plunder: When the Rule of Law Is Illegal*. Malden, MA: Blackwell.

Mauss, Marcel. 1990 (1954). *The Gift: The Form and Reason for Exchange in Archaic Societies*. London: Routledge.

McAuslan, Patrick. 1997. "Law, Governance, and the Development of the Market: Practical Problems and Possible Solutions." In *Good Governance and Law: Legal and Institutional Reform in Developing Countries*, edited by Julio Faundez. New York: St. Martin's.

McGranahan, Carole. 2016. "Theorizing Refusal: An Introduction." *Cultural Anthropology* 31(3): 319–325.

McKinnon, Susan, and Fenella Cannell. 2013. "The Difference Kinship Makes." In *Vital Relations: Modernity and the Persistent Life of Kinship*, edited by Susan McKinnon and Fenella Cannell. Santa Fe, NM: School of American Research Press.

McNeish, John-Andrew. 2008. "Constitutionalism in an Insurgent State: Rethinking Legal Empowerment of the Poor in a Divided Bolivia." In *Rights and Legal Empowerment in Eradicating Poverty*, edited by Dan Banik. London: Ashgate.

———. 2013. "Extraction, Protest and Indigeneity in Bolivia: The TIPNIS Effect." *Latin American and Caribbean Ethnic Studies* 8(2): 221–242.

Medeiros, Carmen. 2001. "Civilizing the Popular? The Law of Popular Participation and the Design of a New Civil Society in 1990s Bolivia." *Critique of Anthropology* 21(4): 401–425.

Menkel-Meadow, C. 2013. "Regulation of Dispute Resolution in the United States of America: From the Formal to the Informal to the 'Semi-Formal.'" In *Regulating Dispute Resolution: ADR and Access to Justice at the Crossroads*, edited by Felix Steffek, Hannes Unberath, Hazel Genn, Reinhard Greger, and Carrie Menkel-Meadow. Oxford: Hart.

————. 2015. "Alternative and Appropriate Dispute Resolution in Context: Formal, Informal, and Semiformal Legal Processes." In *The Handbook of Conflict Resolution: Theory and Practice*, edited by Morton Deutsch, Peter T. Coleman, and Eric C. Marcus, 1–28. Oxford: Wiley.

Merritt, Jeff. 2006. "Quick Impact, Slow Recovery? Funders' Priorities and the Local Realities of Transition Programming." In *Transacting Transition: The Micropolitics of Democracy Assistance in the Former Yugoslavia*, edited by Keith Brown. Champaign, IL: Kumarian.

Merry, Sally Engle. 1988. "Legal Pluralism." *Law and Society Review* 22(5): 869–896.

————. 1990. *Getting Justice and Getting Even: Legal Consciousness among Working-Class Americans*. Chicago: University of Chicago Press.

————. 2003. "Human Rights Law and the Demonization of Culture (and Anthropology along the Way)." *Political and Legal Anthropology Review* 26(1): 55–76.

————. 2006. "Transnational Human Rights and Local Activism: Mapping the Middle." *American Anthropologist* 108(1): 38–51.

————. 2016. *The Seductions of Quantification: Measuring Human Rights, Gender Violence, and Sex Trafficking*. Chicago: University of Chicago Press.

Merry, Sally Engle, and John M. Conley. 2011. "Measuring the World: Indicators, Human Rights, and Global Governance." *Current Anthropology* 52(S3): S83–S95.

Merry, Sally Engle, and Neal Milner, eds. 1995. *The Possibility of Popular Justice: A Case Study of Community Mediation in the United States*. Ann Arbor: University of Michigan Press.

Millar, Kathleen. 2018. *Reclaiming the Discarded: Life and Labor on Rio's Garbage Dump*. Durham, NC: Duke University Press.

Milner, Neal. 2002. "Illusions and Delusions about Conflict Management—In Africa and Elsewhere." *Law and Social Inquiry* 27: 621–629.

Ministerio de Asuntos Exteriores, Oficina de Planificacion y Evaluacion. 2002. "Evaluación del Proyecto de Reforma Judicial en la República de Bolivia." Seintex. www.oecd.org/countries/bolivia/46777655.pdf.

Mitchell, Timothy. 2002. *Rule of Experts: Egypt, Techno-politics, Modernity*. Berkeley: University of California Press.

————. 2011. *Carbon Democracy: Political Power in the Age of Oil*. New York: Verso.

Mosse, David. 2005. "Introduction: The Ethnography of Donors and Neoliberal Policy." In *The Aid Effect: Giving and Governing in International Development*, edited by David Mosse and David Lewis. London: Pluto.

————. 2011. "Introduction: The Anthropology of Expertise and Professionals in International Development." In *Adventures in Aidland: The Anthropology of Professionals International Development*, edited by David Mosse. New York: Berghahn.

Mosse, David, and David Lewis. 2005. *The Aid Effect: Giving and Governing in International Development*. London: Pluto.

Muehlebach, Andrea. 2011. "On Affective Labor in Post-Fordist Italy." *Cultural Anthropology* 26(1): 59–82.

Muhlberger, Peter. 2011. "A Deliberative Look at Alternative Dispute Resolution and the Rule of Law." *Journal of Dispute Resolution* 145.

Nader, Laura. 1990. *Harmony Ideology: Justice and Control in a Zapotec Mountain Village*. Stanford, CA: Stanford University Press.

———. 2005 (1995). "Civilization and Its Negotiations." In *Law and Anthropology: A Reader*, edited by Sally Falk Moore. Malden, MA: Blackwell.

Nader, Laura, and Elisabetta Grande. 2002. "Current Illusions and Delusions about Conflict Management—in Africa and Elsewhere." *Law and Social Inquiry* 27(3): 573–591.

Nader, Laura, and Duane Metzger. 1963. "Conflict Resolution in Two Mexican Communities." *American Anthropologist* 65: 584–592.

Navaro-Yashin, Yael. 2007. "Make-Believe Papers, Legal Forms and the Counterfeit: Affective Interactions between Documents and People in Britain and Cyprus." *Anthropological Theory* 7(1): 79–98.

Nicolas, V., M. Fernández, and E. Flores. 2007. *Modos originarios de resolución de conflictos en pueblos indígenas de Bolivia*. La Paz: Fundación PIEB, Fundación UNIR.

O'Donnell, Guillermo. 1993. "On the State, Democratization, and Some Conceptual Problems: A Latin American View with Some Glances at Some Post-Community Countries." *World Development* 21(8): 1355–1371.

Ong, Aihwa. 2006. *Neoliberalism as Exception: Mutations in Citizenship and Sovereignty*. Durham, NC: Duke University Press.

Ong, Aihwa, and Stephen Collier, eds. 2004. *Global Assemblages: Technology, Politics and Ethics as Anthropological Problems*. Malden, MA: Blackwell.

Orellana Halkyer, René. 2004. "Interlegalidad y campos jurídicos: Discurso y derecho en la configuración de órdenes semiautónomos en comunidades quechuas de Bolivia." PhD diss., Faculteit der Rechtsgeleerdheid, University of Amsterdam.

Orta, Andrew. 2004. *Catechizing Culture: Missionaries, Aymara, and the "New Evangelization."* New York: Columbia University Press.

———. 2013. "Forged Communities and Vulgar Citizens: Autonomy and Its Límites in Semineoliberal Bolivia." *Journal of Latin American and Caribbean Anthropology* 18(1): 108–133.

Owusu, Maxwell. 1997. "Domesticating Democracy: Culture, Civil Society, and Constitutionalism in Africa." *Comparative Studies in Society and History* 39(1): 120–152.

Oxhorn, Philip, and Pamela Starr, eds. 1999. *Markets and Democracy in Latin America: Conflict or Convergence?* Boulder, CO: Lynne Rienner.

Pacino, Nicole. 2016. "Stimulating a Cooperative Spirit? Public Health and US-Bolivia Relations in the 1950s." *Diplomatic History* 41(2): 305–335.

Pagden, Anthony. 1986. *The Fall of Natural Man: The American Indian and the Origins of Comparative Ethnology*. Cambridge: Cambridge University Press.

Paley, Julia. 2001. *Marketing Democracy: Power and Social Movements in Post-dictatorship Chile*. Berkeley: University of California Press.

———. 2002. "Toward an Anthropology of Democracy." *Annual Review of Anthropology* 31: 469–496.

———. 2009. "Introduction." In *Democracy: Anthropological Approaches*, edited by Julia Paley. Santa Fe, NM: School for Advanced Research Press.

Paulson, Susan. 2006. "Body, Nation, and Consubstantiation in Bolivian Ritual Meals." *American Ethnologist* 33(4): 650–664.

Pavlich, George. 1996. "The Power of Community Mediation: Government and the Formation of Self Identity." *Law and Society Review* 30(4): 707–733.

Peck, Jamie, and Nik Theodore. 2010. "Mobilizing Policy: Models, Methods, and Mutations." *Geoforum* 41(2): 169–174.

Peck, Jamie, and Adam Tickell. 2002. "Neoliberalizing Space." In *Spaces of Neoliberalism: Urban Restructuring in North America and Western Europe*, edited by Neil Brenner and Nik Theodore. Malden, MA: Blackwell.

Peebles, Gustav. 2010. "The Anthropology of Credit and Debt." *Annual Review of Anthropology* 39: 225–240.

Platt, Tristan. 1992. "Writing, Shamanism and Identity, or Voices from Abya-Yala." *History Workshop Journal* 34(1).

Postero, Nancy Grey. 2007. *Now We Are Citizens: Indigenous Politics in Postmulticultural Bolivia*. Stanford, CA: Stanford University Press.

———. 2010. "The Struggle to Create a Radical Democracy in Bolivia." *Latin American Research Review* 45(4): 59–78.

———. 2017. *The Indigenous State: Race, Politics, and Performance in Plurinational Bolivia*. Berkeley: University of California Press.

Povinelli, Elizabeth. 2002. *The Cunning of Recognition: Indigenous Alterities and the Making of Australian Multiculturalism*. Durham, NC: Duke University Press.

———. 2011. *Economies of Abandonment: Social Belonging in Late Liberalism*. Durham, NC: Duke University Press.

Quintana Taborga, Juan Ramón, ed. 2016. *BoliviaLeaks: La Injerencia Política de Estados Unidos Contra El Proceso de Cambio (2006–2010)*. Ministerio de la Presidencia, Estadio Plurinacional de Bolivia.

Rabe, Stephen G. 2012. *The Killing Zone: The United States Wages Cold War in Latin America*. New York: Oxford University Press.

Rama, Angel. 1996. *The Lettered City*. Translated by John Charles Chasteen. Durham, NC: Duke University Press.

Rappaport, Joanne, and Tom Cummins. 2011. *Beyond the Lettered City: Indigenous Literacies in the Andes*. Durham, NC: Duke University Press.

Rhyne, Elisabeth. 2001. *Mainstreaming Microfinance: How Lending to the Poor Began, Grew, and Came of Age in Bolivia*. Bloomfield, CT: Kumarian.

———. 2004. "Surviving the Crisis: Microfinance in Bolivia, 1999–2002." In *The Development of the Financial Sector in Southeast Europe*. Berlin: Springer.

Riles, Annelise. 1998. "Infinity within the Brackets." *American Ethnologist* 25(3): 378–398.

———. 2002. "User Friendly: Informality and Expertise." *Law and Social Inquiry* 27(3): 613–619.

———. 2006. "Introduction." In *Documents: Artifacts of Modern Knowledge*, edited by Annelise Riles. Ann Arbor: University of Michigan Press.

———. 2011. *Collateral Knowledge: Legal Reasoning in the Global Financial Markets*. Chicago: University of Chicago Press.

Riskin, Leonard. 1996 "Understanding Mediators' Orientations, Strategies, and Techniques: A Grid for the Perplexed." *Harvard Negotiation Law Review* 7: 7–51.

Risør, Helene. 2010. "Twenty Hanging Dolls and a Lynching: Defacing Dangerousness and Enacting Citizenship in El Alto, Bolivia." *Public Culture* 22(3): 465–485.

———. 2016. "Closing Down Bars in the Inner City Centre: Informal Urban Planning, Civil Insecurity and Subjectivity in Bolivia." *Singapore Journal of Tropical Geography* 37(3): 330–342.

Rivera Cusicanqui, Silvia. 1984. "Oprimidos pero no vencidos: Luchas del campesinado aymara y quechua de Bolivia, 1900–1980." La Paz: HISBOL-CSUTCB.

———. 1990. "Liberal Democracy and Ayllu Democracy in Bolivia: The Case of Northern Potosí." *Journal of Development Studies* 26(4): 97–121.

———. 2010. "The Notion of 'Rights' and the Paradoxes of Postcolonial Modernity: Indigenous Peoples and Women in Bolivia." Translated by Molly Geidel. *Qui Parle: Critical Humanities and Social Sciences* 18(2): 29–54.

———. 2012. "Ch'ixinakax utxiwa: A Reflection on the Practices and Discourses of Decolonization." *South Atlantic Quarterly* 111(1): 95–109.

Rodríguez Carmona, Antonio. 2009. *El proyectorado: Bolivia tras 20 años de ayuda externa*. 2nd ed. Vol. 16. La Paz: Plural Editores.

Roitman, Janet L. 2003. "Unsanctioned Wealth; or, The Productivity of Debt in Northern Cameroon." *Public Culture* 15(2): 211–237.

Rosaldo, Renato. 1994. "Cultural Citizenship and Educational Democracy." *Cultural Anthropology* 9(3): 402–411.

Rose, Nikolas. 2006. "Governing 'Advanced' Liberal Democracies." In *The Anthropology of the State: A Reader*, edited by Aradhana Sharma and Akhil Gupta. Malden, MA: Blackwell.

Roseberry, William. 1994. "Hegemony and the Language of Contention." In *Everyday Forms of State Formation: Revolution and the Negotiation of Rule in Modern Mexico*, edited by Gilbert Joseph and Daniel Nugent. Durham, NC: Duke University Press.

Rosen, Lawrence. 1984. *Bargaining for Reality: The Construction of Social Relations in a Muslim Community*. Chicago: University of Chicago Press.

———. 1989. *The Anthropology of Justice: Law as Culture in Islamic Society*. Cambridge: Cambridge University Press.

Rowat, Malcolm, Waleed Haider Malik, and Maria Dakolias, eds. 1995. *Judicial Reform in Latin America and the Caribbean*. World Bank Technical Paper No. 280.

Rubinson, Robert. 2016. "Mediator Models and Comparative Dispute Resolution: Of Grids and Gatekeepers: The Socioeconomics of Mediation." *Cardozo Journal of Conflict Resolution* 17: 873–1071.

Sahlins, Marshall. 2011. "What Kinship Is (Part One)." *Journal of the Royal Anthropological Institute* 17(1): 2–19.

Saignes, Thierry. 1989. *Borracheras andinas ¿Por qué los indios ebrios hablan en español?* Cuzco, Peru: Centro de Estudios Rurales Andinos "Bartolomé de las Casas."

———. 1995. "Indian Migration and Social Change in Seventeenth-Century Charcas." In *Ethnicity, Markets, and Migration in the Andes: At the Crossroads of History and Anthropology*, edited by Brooke Larson and Olivia Harris. Durham, NC: Duke University Press.

Salas, Luis. 2001. "From Law and Development to Rule of Law: New and Old Issues in Justice Reform in Latin America." In *Rule of Law in Latin America: The International Promotion of Judicial Reform*, edited by Pilar Domingo and Rachel Sieder. London: Institute of Latin American Studies.

Sampson, Steven. 2002. "Weak States, Uncivil Societies and Thousands of NGOs: Benevolent Colonialism in the Balkans." In *Cultural Boundaries of the Balkans*, edited by Sanimir Resic and Barbara Törnquist-Plewa. Lund, Sweden: Lund University Press.

———. 2005. "Integrity Warriors: Global Morality and the Anti-Corruption Movement in the Balkans." In *Corruption: Anthropological Perspectives*, edited by Dieter Haller and Cris Shore. London: Pluto.

Santos, Boaventura de Sousa. 1995. *Toward a New Common Sense: Law, Science, and Politics in the Paradigmatic Transition*. New York: Routledge.

———. 2014. *Epistemologies of the South: Justice against Epistemicide*. New York: Routledge.

Schild, Veronica. 2000. "Neo-Liberalism's New Gendered Market Citizens: The 'Civilizing' Dimensions of Market Programmes in Chile." *Citizenship Studies* 4(3): 275–305.

———. 2007. "Empowering Consumer-Citizensor Governing Poor Female Subjects? The Institutionalization of Self-development in the Chilean Social Policy Field." *Journal of Consumer Culture* 7(2): 179–203.

Schuller, Mark. 2012. *Killing with Kindness: Haiti, International Aid, and NGOs*. New Brunswick, NJ: Rutgers University Press.

Schuster, Caroline E. 2014. "The Social Unit of Debt: Gender and Creditworthiness in Paraguayan Microfinance." *American Ethnologist* 41(3): 563–578.

———. 2015. *Social Collateral: Women and Microfinance in Paraguay's Smuggling Economy*. Berkeley: University of California Press.

Scott, James. 1990. *Domination and the Arts of Resistance: Hidden Transcripts*. New Haven, CT: Yale University Press.

Shakow, Miriam. 2011. "The Peril and Promise of Noodles and Beer: Condemnation of Patronage and Hybrid Political Frameworks in 'Post-neoliberal' Cochabamba, Bolivia." *PoLAR: Political and Legal Anthropology Review* 34(2): 315–336.

———. 2014. *Along the Bolivian Highway: Social Mobility and Political Culture in a New Middle Class*. Philadelphia: University of Pennsylvania Press.

Sharma, Aradhana. 2008. *Logics of Empowerment: Development, Gender, and Governance in Neoliberal India*. Minneapolis: University of Minnesota Press.

Sharp, Gene. 2002. *From Dictatorship to Democracy: A Conceptual Framework for Liberation*. 3rd ed. Boston: Albert Einstein Institution.

Shihata, Ibrahim. 1995. "Legal Framework for Development: The World Bank's Role in Legal and Judicial Reform." In *Judicial Reform in Latin America and the Caribbean*, edited by Malcolm Rowat, Waleed Haider Malik, and Maria Dakolias. World Bank Technical Paper No. 280.

Shook, Vicki, and Neal Milner. 1993. "What Mediation Training Says—or Doesn't Say—about the Ideology and Culture of North American Community-Justice Programs." In *The Possibility of Popular Justice: A Case Study of Community Mediation in the United States*, edited by Sally Engle Merry and Neal Milner. Ann Arbor: University of Michigan Press.

Shore, Cris. 2010. "Beyond the Multiversity: Neoliberalism and the Rise of the Schizophrenic University." *Social Anthropology* 18(1): 15–29.

Shore, Cris, and Susan Wright. 1999. "Audit Culture and Anthropology: Neo-liberalism in British Higher Education." *Journal of the Royal Anthropological Institute* 5(4): 557–575.

Siekmeier, James. 2011. *The Bolivian Revolution and the United States, 1945–Present*. University Park: Penn State University Press.

Silbey, Susan S. 1993. "Mediation Mythology." *Negotiation Journal* 9(4): 349–353.

Simpson, Audra. 2014. *Mohawk Interruptus: Political Life across the Borders of Settler States*. Durham, NC: Duke University Press.

———. 2016. "Consent's Revenge." *Cultural Anthropology* 31(3): 326–333.

Smith, Daniel Jordan. 2001. "Ritual Killing, 419, and Fast Wealth: Inequality and the Popular Imagination in Southeastern Nigeria." *American Ethnologist* 28(4): 803–828.

———. 2007. *A Culture of Corruption: Everyday Deception and Popular Discontent in Nigeria*. Princeton, NJ: Princeton University Press.

Smith, Karl. 2012. "From Dividual and Individual Selves to Porous Subjects." *Australian Journal of Anthropology* 23(1): 50–64.

Sökefeld, Martin. 1999. "Debating Self, Identity and Culture in Anthropology." *Current Anthropology* 40: 417–447.

Spedding, Alison. 2014. "Contra-afinidad: Algunos comentarios sobre el compadrazgo andino." In *Gente de Carne y Hueso. Las Tramas de Parentesco en los Andes*, 2nd ed., edited by Denise Arnold. La Paz: CLASE/ILCA.

Stephenson, Marcia. 2002. "Forging an Indigenous Counterpublic Sphere: The Taller de Historia Oral Andina in Bolivia." *Latin American Research Review* 37(2): 99–118.

Sternlight, Jean R. 2006. "Is Alternative Dispute Resolution Consistent with the Rule of Law?" *DePaul Law Review* 56: 569–592.

Stoler, Ann Laura. 1995. *Race and the Education of Desire: Foucault's "History of Sexuality" and the Colonial Order of Things*. Durham, NC: Duke University Press.

———. 2009. *Along the Archival Grain: Epistemic Anxieties and Colonial Common Sense*. Princeton, NJ: Princeton University Press.

Strathern, Marilyn. 1988. *The Gender of the Gift: Problems with Women and Problems with Society in Melanesia*. Berkeley: University of California Press.

Tassi, Nico. 2010. "The Postulate of Abundance: Cholo Market and Religion in La Paz Bolivia." *Social Anthropology/Anthropologie Sociale* 18(2): 191–209.

———. 2016. *The Native World-System: An Ethnography of Bolivian Aymara Traders in the Global Economy*. Oxford: Oxford University Press.

Tate, Winifred. 2015. *Drugs, Thugs, and Diplomats: US Policymaking in Colombia*. Stanford, CA: Stanford University Press.

Tendler, Judith. 1975. *Inside Foreign Aid*. Baltimore: Johns Hopkins University Press.

Ticktin, Miriam. 2006. "Where Ethics and Politics Meet." *American Ethnologist* 33(1): 33–49.

Ticona Alejo, Esteban. 2000. "Organización y liderazgo aymara: La experiencia indígena en la política boliviana 1979–1996." La Paz: Universidad de la Cordillera.

Ticona Alejo, Esteban, G. Rojas, and Xavier Albó. 1995. "Votos y wiphalas: Campesinos y pueblos originarios en democracia." *Cuadernos de investigación* 43. La Paz: CIPCA.

Tockman, Jason, and John Cameron. 2014. "Indigenous Autonomy and the Contradictions of Plurinationalism in Bolivia." *Latin American Politics and Society* 56 (3): 46–69.

Toro Ibáñez, Graciela. 2010. *La pobreza un gran negocio: Un análisis critico sobre oeneges, microfinancieras, y banca.* La Paz: Oficina Contra la Usura Bancaria, Mujeres Creando.

Trnka, Susanna, and Catherine Trundle. 2014. "Competing Responsibilities: Moving beyond Neoliberal Responsibilisation." *Anthropological Forum* 24(2): 136–153.

Trouillot, Michel-Rolph. 2003. *Global Transformations: Anthropology and the Modern World.* New York: Palgrave Macmillan.

Trubek, David. M. 2001. "Law and Development." In *The International Encyclopedia of the Social and Behavioral Sciences*, vol. 11, edited by Neil J. Smelser and Paul B. Baltes. Amsterdam: Elsevier.

Tsing, Anna Lowenhaupt. 2011. *Friction: An Ethnography of Global Connection.* Princeton, NJ: Princeton University Press.

UNESCO. 2013. "Programme of Action Culture of Peace and Non-Violence: A Vision in Action." Intersectoral Platform for a Culture of Peace and Non-Violence, Bureau for Strategic Planning. http://unesdoc.unesco.org/images/0021/002177/217786e.pdf.

Valverde, Mariana. 2015. *Chronotopes of Law: Jurisdiction, Scale and Governance.* New York: Routledge.

———. 2016. "What Counts as Theory, Today? A Post-Philosophical Framework for Socio-legal Empirical Research." *Revista de Estudos Empíricos em Direito* 3(1): 172–181.

Van Cott, Donna Lee. 2000. *The Friendly Liquidation of the Past: The Politics of Diversity in Latin America.* Pittsburgh: University of Pittsburgh Press.

Vannier, Christian N. 2010. "Audit Culture and Grassroots Participation in Rural Haitian Development." *PoLAR: Political and Legal Anthropology Review* 33(2): 282–305.

VanValkenburgh, Parker. 2017. "Unsettling Time: Persistence and Memory in Spanish Colonial Peru." *Journal of Archaeological Method and Theory* 24(1): 117–148.

Van Vleet, Krista. 2002. "The Intimacies of Power: Rethinking Violence and Affinity in the Bolivian Andes." *American Ethnologist* 29(3): 567–601.

———. 2008. *Performing Kinship: Narrative, Gender, and the Intimacies of Power in the Andes.* Austin: University of Texas Press.

———. 2011. "On Devils and the Dissolution of Sociality: Andean Catholics Voicing Ambivalence in Neoliberal Bolivia." *Anthropological Quarterly* 84(4): 835–864.

Waldman, Ellen A. 1998. "The Evaluative-Facilitative Debate in Mediation: Applying the Lens of Therapeutic Jurisprudence." *Marquette Law Review* 82: 155–170.

Wall, James, John Stark, and Rhetta Standifer. 2001. "Mediation: A Current Review and Theory Development." *Journal of Conflict Resolution* 45(3): 370–391.

Wanderley, Fernanda. 2009. "Prácticas estatales y el ejercicio de la ciudadanía: Encuentros de la población con la burocracia en Bolivia." *Íconos: Revista de Ciencias Sociales/FLACSO* 34: 67–79.

Wanis-St. John, Anthony. 2000. "Implementing Alternative Dispute Resolution (ADR) in Transitioning States: Lessons Learned from Practice." *Harvard Negotiation Law Review* 5: 339–381.

Wanis-St. John, Anthony, and Noah Rosen. 2017. "Negotiating Civil Resistance." *Peaceworks* No. 129. Washington, DC: United States Institute of Peace.

Warren, Kay B. 1998. *Indigenous Movements and Their Critics: Pan-Maya Activism in Guatemala*. Princeton, NJ: Princeton University Press.

———. 2010. "Trafficking in Persons: A Multisited View of International Norms and Local Responses." In *Inescapable Solutions: Japanese Aid and the Construction of Global Development*, edited by Kay B. Warren and David Leheny. London: Routledge.

Warren, Kay B., and David Leheny. 2010. *Inescapable Solutions: Japanese Aid and the Construction of Global Development*. London: Routledge.

Wedel, Janine R. 2005. "U.S. Foreign Aid and Foreign Policy: Building Strong Relationships by Doing It Right!" *International Studies Perspectives* 6: 35–50.

Wedel, Janine, Cris Shore, Gregory Feldman, and Stacy Lathrop. 2005. "Toward an Anthropology of Public Policy." *Annals of the American Academy of Political and Social Science* 600: 30–51.

Weder, Beatrice. 1995. "Legal Systems and Economic Performance: The Empirical Evidence." In *Judicial Reform in Latin America and the Caribbean*, edited by Malcolm Rowat, Waleed Haider Malik, and Maria Dakolias. World Bank Technical Paper No. 280.

West, Paige. 2016. *Dispossession and the Environment: Rhetoric and Inequality in Papua New Guinea*. New York: Columbia University Press.

Weston, Maureen A. 2014. "Retired to Greener Pastures: The Public Costs of Private Judging." In *Justice, Conflict and Wellbeing: Multidisciplinary Perspectives*, edited by Brian H. Bornstein and Richard L. Wiener. New York: Springer.

Wexler, David B. 1999. "Therapeutic Jurisprudence and the Culture of Critique." *Journal of Contemporary Legal Issues* 10: 263.

———. 2014. "New Wine in New Bottles: The Need to Sketch a Therapeutic Jurisprudence 'Code' of Proposed Criminal Processes and Practices." *Arizona Summit Law Review* 463. Arizona Legal Studies Discussion Paper No. 12–16.

Wogan, Peter. 2004. *Magical Writing in Salasaca: Literacy and Power in Highland Ecuador*. Boulder, CO: Westview.

Yamada, Shoko. 2014. "Domesticating Democracy? Civic and Ethical Education Textbooks in Secondary Schools in the Democratizing of Ethiopia." In *(Re) Constructing Memory: School Textbooks and the Imagination of the Nation*, edited by James H. Williams. Boston: Sense.

Young, Kevin. 2013. "Purging the Forces of Darkness: The United States, Monetary Stabilization, and the Containment of the Bolivian Revolution." *Diplomatic History* 37(3): 509–537.

Zunes, Stephen. 2001. "The United States and Bolivia: The Taming of a Revolution, 1952–1957." *Latin American Perspectives* 28(5): 33–49.

capitalism. *See* microfinance; neoliberal restructuring

Carmona, Rodríguez, 105

Carsten, Janet, 144

CCP, 47–48, 53

Central de Notificaciones, 39

chacha-warmi, 182

Chávez, Hugo, 16

Checchi and Company Consulting, 102–5

citizenship: counterinsurgent, 18–25, 29, 223; differentiated, 22; documentation and, 199–205; entrepreneurial, 18–25, 29, 60–61, 156, 160–78, 204, 223–24; rights and, 46–60, 131, 229–30

civil society, 14, 41–43, 56–62, 71, 120, 228. *See also* democracy; indigenous justice processes; interlegality; legal pluralism

class: culturalization of conflict and, 62–94, 178; foreign aid and, 95–120; gender and, 182–83; organizations based on, 11, 113–17; rights and, 9, 22. *See also* culturalization of conflict; gender; race

Clinton, Bill, 55

Cobb, Sara, 184

Code of Criminal Procedures (CCP), 47–48, 53

Cohen, Amy, 11

Cold War, 43–44, 228

Colectivo Akhulli, 88–89

Coles, Kimberly, 82

colonialism, 7, 14–15, 67–68, 128, 158–59, 183, 196–205, 249n24. *See also* neoliberal restructuring

Comaroff, Jean, 219

Comaroff, John, 219

Community Boards of San Francisco, 8, 59, 108

community mediation. *See* alternative dispute resolution (ADR)

compadrazgo, 138–62

conciliación previa. *See* court-annexed conciliation

conciliation. *See* alternative dispute resolution (ADR); court-annexed conciliation

conflictologos, 95–120, 225, 229. *See also* expertise

conflict-resolution. *See* alternative dispute resolution (ADR)

conflict-resolution studies, 77

conflict transformation (CT), 80–81

Constitution of Bolivia, 10, 66, 80, 131, 225, 236n22

conversatorios, 64–68, 81–93, 231

Convivir-Sembrar Paz campaign, 84–85

Coulthard, Glen, 67–68

counterinsurgency campaigns, 44, 55

counterinsurgent citizenship, 18–25, 29, 223

counternarcotics laws, 41, 48, 52–55

court-annexed conciliation, 5, 226–27, 236n24, 244n13, 245n4, 252n27

Cox Mayorga, Nelson, 226

Crecer, 214

criminal tribunals, 37–40

CT, 80–81

cultural hegemony, 100, 118, 244n12

culturalization of conflict, 28, 62–94, 99, 163–93, 228

cultural violence, 77

culture of copying, 109–12

culture of peace, 62, 64–94, 99–102, 112, 116–17, 225, 229–31, 242n32

Cumbre de Justicia, 26, 227

DANIDA, 105

Danish International Development Agency (DANIDA), 105

Das, Veena, 196

debt: documentation of, 212–20; kinship and, 24, 133–62, 224, 230, 247n24; violence and, 163–93

decolonization, 9–10, 111, 131, 227

Decree No. 28586, 53

delegalization of domestic violence, 184–88

deliberative democracy, 6, 91–93, 114, 235n7

democracy: assistance programs for, 6–8, 12–20, 23, 35–36, 40–63, 228; deliberative, 6, 91–93, 114, 235n7; domestication of, 12–18, 93, 225–28; struggles over, 31–36, 71–73, 87–88, 93–94, 228–29

democracy-assistance programs, 6–8, 12–20, 23, 35–36, 40–63, 228. *See also* judicial reform

Derechos Humanos, 96

development technologies, 107–9, 120. *See also* technocratic aid

Dezalay, Yves, 99, 101

Diakonia, 214

differentiated citizenship, 22
documentation of conflict resolution, 194–220, 230, 252n33
domestication of democracy, 12–18, 93, 225–28
domestication of violence, 167–68, 184
domestic violence, 1–4, 26, 57, 107, 125, 148–49, 163–93, 224–25, 250n28, 250n33
drug war, 48, 53–55
Dunn, Elizabeth, 20
dyadic conflict resolution, 137–62, 168, 186, 193. *See also* triadic conflict resolution

Ecofuturo, 159–62
Economic Intelligence Unit, 153
Eder, George Jackson, 239n16
Edwards, Jeannette, 141
Egan, Nancy, 214
Elyachar, Julia, 152
empowerment: ADR as a form of, 12, 18, 58–61; through microfinance, 21–22, 153, 204. *See also* alternative dispute resolution (ADR); gender
Emprender, 214
entrepreneurial citizenship, 18–25, 29, 60–61, 156, 160–78, 204, 223–24. *See also* microfinance
European Commission (EC), 62, 79
expertise, 6–7, 26, 66, 95–120, 204, 226

femicide, 163–93. *See also* gender-based violence
Ferguson, James, 108, 236n10
Ferguson protests, 231
Financial Services Law, 247n33
foreign aid: democracy-assistance programs and, 6–8, 12–20, 23, 35–36, 40–63, 228; judicial reform and, 4–7, 36–66, 102–6, 223–24; limitations of, 227–28; strategic interests of, 12–20, 83–84, 100, 111, 120, 168, 227–28, 236n10, 237n37. *See also specific organizations*
Foucault, Michel, 22, 82, 196
F process, 227
Freire, Paulo, 115

Galtung, Johan, 77–78
García Linera, Álvaro, 97, 227

Garth, Bryan, 46, 99, 101
gas war. *See* uprising, October 2003
gender: microfinance and, 21, 213–14; rights and, 5, 22, 117, 182, 250n26; violence and, 163–93, 250n28, 250n33. *See also* class; domestic violence; race
gender-based violence, 163–93, 250n28, 250n33. *See also* domestic violence
gender complementarity, 182
German Technical Cooperation Agency (German Organisation for Technical Cooperation), 47–48, 79, 105
The Gift (Mauss), 150
Gladwell, Malcolm, 158
Goldstein, Daniel, 8, 60, 76, 197
good governance programs, 41, 45–46, 71, 224
Gordillo, Gastón, 200
governmentality, 22, 82, 87. *See also* entrepreneurial citizenship; neoliberal governmentality; neoliberal multiculturalism; neoliberal responsibilization
Gramsci, Antonio, 100, 244n12
graphic artifacts, 195–96, 211–12
grassroots territorial organizations (GTOS), 71
Greenhalgh, Susan, 42
Greenhouse, Carol, 42
GTOS, 71
GTZ (GIZ), 47–48, 79, 105
Gupta, Akhil, 108, 196–97
Gustafson, Bret, 87–88, 111, 118
Gutmann, Matthew, 13

Hale, Charles, 67
Halker, René Orellana, 201
Han, Clara, 150–51
Hansen, Thomas Blom, 230
harmony ideologies, 11, 141, 184
Harrington, Christine, 11, 59
Harris, Olivia, 151, 247n24
Harvard Negotiation Program, 26, 40, 95–96, 115
Harvey, David, 20
Harvey, Penelope, 142, 157, 241n10
hegemony, cultural, 100, 118, 244n12
Heng, Dyna, 247n33
highland migration, 52–53, 70–71, 93, 121
Hofrichter, Richard, 11

third-party meditation. *See* alternative dispute resolution (ADR)
Tiempos, Los (Bolivia), 178
TIPNIS, 243n1
triadic conflict resolution, 137–62, 168. *See also* dyadic conflict resolution

UNDP, 84
UNESCO, 77–78
United Nations Development Programme (UNDP), 84
United Nations Educational, Scientific, and Cultural Organization (UNESCO), 77–78
United States Agency for International Development (USAID): culture of conflict rhetoric and, 73, 87; culture of copying and, 101–4, 108–12; departure from Bolivia by, 134, 225–26; involvement in alternative dispute resolution by, 5–6, 14, 28, 59, 62, 124–27, 193, 211, 245n4; involvement in microfinance by, 204; strategic interests of, 35–36, 46–56

Unity Pact, 131
uprising, October 2003, 6, 22, 31–36, 50–51, 57, 62, 93, 102, 106
USAID. *See* United States Agency for International Development (USAID)
U.S. Mission, 35
U.S. State Department, 40

Valverde, Mariana, 246n11
Van Vleet, Krista, 181–82, 201

Wanis-St. John, Anthony, 67, 241n5
Warren, Kay, 12, 241n9
Washington Consensus, 45
Weber, Max, 196
World Bank, 32, 40, 45–49, 58, 242n32
World Social Forum, 242n32

Yamada, Shoko, 17
Young, Kevin, 239n16